THE PERGAMON ENGLISH LIBRARY

EDITORIAL DIRECTORS: GEORGE ALLEN AND BORIS FORD

EXECUTIVE EDITOR: ESMOR JONES

The Masks of Hate

D1176051

The Masks of Hate

*The Problem of False Solutions
in the Culture of an
Acquisitive Society*

DAVID HOLBROOK, M.A.

Sometime Fellow of King's College,
Cambridge

PERGAMON PRESS

OXFORD · NEW YORK · TORONTO
SYDNEY · BRAUNSCHWEIG

PERGAMON PRESS

OXFORD   NEW YORK

TORONTO SYDNEY BRAUNSCHWEIG

Printed in Great Britain by A. Wheaton & Co., Exeter

08 015799 8

To the memory of my mother

Then every thing includes itself in power,
Power into will, will into appetite,
And appetite (an universal wolf,
So doubly seconded with will, and power)
Must make perforce an universal prey,
And last, eat up himself . . .

(WILLIAM SHAKESPEARE, *Troilus and Cressida.*)

ουτοι συνεχθειν αλλα συμφιλειν εφυν.

(SOPHOCLES, *Antigone.*)

CONTENTS

PART III

CONCLUSIONS: THE NEED TO BE HUMAN

Acknowledgements

For permission to use copyright material acknowledgement is made to the following:

Associated Book Publishers (International) Ltd. and Grove Press Inc. for extracts from *The Basement* by Harold Pinter, from *The Tea Party and Other Plays* (Methuen and Co. Ltd.), published in the U.S.A. as *The Lover, Tea Party and The Basement*; for extracts, with Random House Inc., from *Culture Against Man* by Jules Henry (Tavistock Publications Ltd.); and, with International Universities Press Inc., for extracts from *Personality Structure and Human Interaction* and *Schizoid Phenomena, Object Relations and the Self* by Harry Guntrip; to Jonathan Cape Ltd. and McGraw-Hill Book Company for extracts from *Life of Robert Fleming* by John Pearson; Jonathan Cape Ltd. (Gildrose Publications Ltd.) and the Macmillan Company Inc., New York, for extracts from *Goldfinger* by Ian Fleming; Chatto and Windus, with the Viking Press, New York, for quotations from *The Flight from the Enchanter* by Iris Murdoch; Routledge and Kegan Paul Ltd., and Basic Books Inc., for quotations from *Psychoanalytical Studies of the Personality* by W. R. D. Fairbairn, published in the U.S.A. as *An Object-Relations Theory of the Personality*; Charles C. Thomas and Professor Ralph Slovenko for extracts from *The Function of Intimacy and Acting Out in Perversions* (M. R. Kahn) from *Sexual Behaviour and the Law*; and United Press International for the Peanuts cartoon (© United Feature Syndicate).

Every effort has been made to trace owners of copyright material, but in some cases this has not proved possible. The publishers would be glad to hear from further owners of copyright material reproduced in *The Masks of Hate*.

CHAPTER 1

Introduction

I SHOULD like to begin by invoking the work of a psychotherapist who survived Auschwitz, Viktor E. Frankl. After the studies I made of psychoanalytical theories of human nature which resulted in my survey *Human Hope and the Death Instinct*, I discovered Frankl's book *From Death Camp to Existentialism*, which expressed the essential implications of recent psychoanalytical thought with great economy. Frankl's economy seems itself a product of suffering; of the intense need forced upon the inmate of a concentration camp to solve urgent existential problems. Frankl was forced to ask himself what it was that enabled him to survive. In the day-to-day circumstances of the death camp he found it was 'the little unnamed acts of kindness and of love': 'I remember how one day a foreman secretly gave me a piece of bread which I knew he must have saved from his breakfast ration. It was far more than the small piece of bread which moved me to tears at that time. It was the human "something" which this man also gave to me – the word and look which accompanied the gift.' (Frankl [67]*, p. 86.)

Essentially, Frankl's conclusion is that what enabled an individual to survive the concentration camp was the preservation of a sense of humanness. This involved the capacity to discriminate, to see that there was good and evil, love and hate: but also to recognise that there was a mixture of these in every human being. The capacity to survive he links with the capacity to bear to be human, weak, mixed, and imperfect.

> From all this we may learn that there are two races of men in this world, but only these two – the 'race' of the decent man and the 'race' of the indecent man. Both are found everywhere; they penetrate into all groups of society. No group consists entirely of decent or indecent people. In this sense, no group is of 'pure race' – and therefore one occasionally found a decent fellow among the camp guards.
> Life in a concentration camp tore open the human soul and exposed its depths. Is it surprising that in those depths we again found only human qualities which in their very nature were a mixture of good and evil? The rift dividing good from evil, which goes through all human beings, reaches into the lower depths and becomes apparent even on the bottom of the abyss which is laid open by the concentration camp. (Frankl [67], pp. 86–87.)

The present work is an attempt to disturb a certain complacency, numbness, or demoralisation in our intellectual ethos today over certain related problems in the sphere of culture. In this sphere 'indecent man' – the phrase seems particularly apt – is not only in the ascendancy. He has, by a certain cunning energy of persuasion, come to persuade us that there is no such division in human nature as that between decent and indecent, good and evil. He has even, perhaps, persuaded us that we need not be human, with this mixture within us, and with all our conflicts and weaknesses.

* Figures in square brackets refer to the Bibliography on p. 263.

1

Those who experienced life in Europe in the war, like Frankl, know differently. Theirs is realism. The vacuous 'permissive' attitude to cultural and social problems which has become prevalent today, is in truth, as I shall try to show, far from realistic. Indeed, in its hypomanic way it seeks to deny those problems of human ambivalence to which Frankl draws our attention: above all, it denies the problem of hate, while those who need to base their approach to life on hate are extremely clever at masking it. In consequence our attention to cultural and social problems is suffering vitiation.

I discussed in *Human Hope and the Death Instinct* the objections we may find in psycho-analytical thought to the nihilism of homunculist theories of human make-up. Frankl sees homunculism as a tendency in our thought to be contested. He sees its nihilism as a product of our age:

> Homunculism ignores in man precisely man himself, the genuinely human, the *Homo humanus*. Either it focusses exclusively on the *Homo faber* – man as a technician or on the Homo sapiens – man idolizing science. But often it simply considers man as a kind of higher mammal, whose ability to stand erect has gone to his head. But modern man needs to consider himself as more than a mere psychophysical being. He is more than a mere organism, he is a person. His noetic existence must not be neglected any longer. In his noetic existence lies an unconditional meaning – his personality *owns* an unconditional dignity – and psychotherapy needs an unconditional belief in this meaning and dignity. (Frankl [67], p. 110.)

So, too, I believe, does culture require an 'unconditional belief in this meaning and dignity'. Whatever offends human dignity and debases meaning is destructive – and contributes to the spreading of hate abroad.

Frankl insists that such a concern with dignity and meaning is by no means sentimental idealism:

> This is neither idealism nor materialism – it is simply realism. I am the sort of realist that Goethe was when he said: 'When we take man as he is, we make him worse; but when we take man as if he were already what he should be, we promote him to what he can be.' . . . Psychotherapy should stick to the words of the Talmud which proclaim, 'Whoever destroys even a single soul should be considered the same as a man who destroyed a whole world. And whoever saves even one single soul is to be considered the same as a man who has saved a whole world.' The possibility of destroying a whole world was never so imminent as today, nor has a boundless respect for the individual person ever been so needed and necessary. (Frankl [67], p. 110.)

My complaint here is that in the cultural sphere we often seem further than ever from such 'boundless respect', while there is much which we do not see that moves rather towards the destruction of souls. Hesitation, that one might possibly destroy one soul, for instance, might be expected to inhibit those who are fascinated by the possibilities of hallucinogenic drugs. Yet in fact some commercial 'pop' stars, psychiatrists, scientists, writers, and philosophers seem to be united today in England by their recklessness over such a complex problem, while in the sexual sphere 'progressive' tendencies seem to be devoted to what a distinguished American existentialist psychiatrist has called 'the degradation of sex that has resulted from its . . . bondage to the human will' (Farber [19], p. 53).

The theoretical fallacies which underlie fashionable prevalent attitudes to human nature I have tried to expose in my previous work. Frankl puts them succinctly when he rejects Freudian and Adlerian theory, and insists that the primary human need is for a sense of meaning in life.

> Apparently, man must have an aim towards which he can constantly direct his life. He must accomplish concrete, personal tasks and fulfil concrete, personal demands; he must realize that unique meaning which each of us has to fulfil. Therefore I consider it misleading to speak of 'self-fulfilment'

and 'self-realization'. For what is demanded of man is not primarily fulfilment and realization of *himself*, but, the actualization of specific tasks in his world – and only to the degree to which he accomplishes this actualization will he also fulfil himself. (Frankl [67], p. 100.)

The false trends in our culture which I intend to examine below are based on the assumption, erroneous as such writers believe it to be, that man's primary drive is to pleasure, power, or self-assertion. Frankl draws our attention to the need for us to devote ourselves to something beyond the self – to giving, and to what Melanie Klein would call 'reparation'. Unless we can find meaning thus, in meetings between the individual and his civilisation, we shall fly into false solutions. The falsity of these solutions manifests what Frankl calls 'existential frustration':

Man is afraid of his inner voice, or his existential vacuum, and runs away to work or to pleasure. The place of his frustrated will-to meaning is taken either by the will-to-pleasure or the will-to-power, even though it be the most primitive form of the will-to-power, the will-to-money. Often, existential frustration leads to sexual compensation. Sexual libido most often becomes rampant in an existential vacuum. (Frankl [67], p. 100.)

The last phrase makes an excellent starting point for the present work. The much-acclaimed sexual 'freedom' in our culture and the behaviour that is said to match this in some quarters seems, in the light of psychoanalytical realism, merely a form of compensation for existential frustration. So, too, does the preoccupation with violence, its exploitation in the mass media, and the parallel increase of violence in the street and campus. In the cultural work most thoroughly examined here, Ian Fleming's novel *Goldfinger*, we find the epitome of the symbolism of compensation for existential vacancy – moving towards the will-to-power and the will-to-money, both of which, together with the will-to-pleasure in depersonalised sex, are implicitly vindicated by Fleming's novels as solutions to the problem of life. As other examples here show, these false solutions are also prevalent in the minority culture in our time, if not predominant.

The expression of the symbolism of compensation, and the way in which it involves others in false solutions, means that such culture has the same kind of effect as homunculism in the field of ideas about man – it is nihilistic, destructive, and negative. It is the expression of hate, of the hatred of being human. This is the problem to which the present work intends to draw attention. In psychoanalytical language it is an attempt to apply the 'schizoid diagnosis' to this sphere. Frankl's is in fact a 'schizoid diagnosis', though he does not use the term, because he places the emphasis on problems of identity and meaning, discarding the Freudian model based on the 'will-to-pleasure', and using rather one based on the quest for identity. The term 'schizoid diagnosis' itself comes from Dr. Harry Guntrip, whose explorations of schizoid problems were discussed in *Human Hope and the Death Instinct*. As Guntrip points out, once Freud's model of human nature is rejected, and once we see human psychic problems as being essentially concerned with ways of overcoming ego-weakness and the '*horror vacui*' of existential emptiness, then our attitudes to social and ethical problems need to be completely reconsidered – and the same is no less true of our attitudes to culture.

Turning to English culture today at large from a study of psychoanalytical theory, with all its realism and gravity, I came to see, as I believe, that we were, by superficial theories of man and society, rendering ourselves helpless in the face of a mounting attack on our humanness. This attack was often disguised as a new 'enlightenment'. This seemed to me the most sinister aspect of the situation – that hate could be so successfully masked and made to seem not only acceptable but good. Yet hate, 'doubly seconded with will and power', seems still the human force likely to destroy civilisation itself, with its roots, in some way, as Shakespeare also saw, in appetite, that 'universal wolf'. Yet things are so inverted that even the Nobel Prize in our time can go to one who has said 'irrepressible violence . . . is man recreating himself' (Sartre).

In order to introduce the reader to the problem of the 'masks of hate' as we experience them day by day, let me turn to my morning's paper. At the time of writing, it is virtually the beginning of a New Year. We have just watched (Christmas, 1968) the breathtaking exploits of three astronauts who have taken a trip round the moon – the first men to enter the unknown regions beyond the earth's gravitational pull. We are full of admiration for the achievements of technology and the fruits of that kind of science which explores outer space.

But now we turn to 'inner space' on the 'cultural pages'. On Monday morning, 30th December 1968, our *The Times* arrived, and on the Woman's Page were featured two individuals who are described as 'clinical psychologists'. They pronounce that 'England is at least fifty years behind the times. It's the most backward country in Europe.' Here cultural progress is discussed in the same terms as economic, technological, and scientific progress. We are invited to feel alarmed at being 'backward'. Phyllis and Eberhard Kronhausen are 'expert commentators on several aspects of sexual manifestation, particularly pornography and erotic art'. They imply that to be 'progressive' and to belong to the world of space exploration, science, and enlightenment, it is important to 'free' our attitudes to sex. Failure to do so is even related to Nazism:

> 'Women' says Eberhard, an Americanized German with a taut, sensitive face, 'have borne the brunt of the whole cultural hang-up on sex. In Anglo-Saxon countries especially it wasn't long ago that they were expected to have no sexual feelings. This very repression has become eroticised and woman has identified with the male aggressor and his distortions of her, just as some Jews did with the Nazis in the concentration camps.'
> . . . The Kronhausens argue in their books that over-repressive attitudes lead to behaviour far more disruptive of social order than the original instincts. (*The Times*).

These individuals had just mounted an exhibition on Erotic Art in Denmark, which was attended by 125,000 people – many of whom apparently took their children. To the readers of *The Times* and followers of 'notable free thinkers' such as Kenneth Tynan, who is mentioned in the article, such 'psychologists' represent a rational and progressive approach which offers to free us from 'inhibition'. They seek to promote a 'sexual revolution' whose consequences will be a reduction of anti-social manifestations. Here 'science' comes to our aid, in 'inner space' as successfully as it has done in 'outer space': or so it is implicitly claimed.

From my point of view the good consequences promised as a result of 'sexual emancipation', however, seem unlikely to follow to anyone who follows Frankl or Guntrip. For one thing, it seems doubtful from their point of view whether our essential problem is the relief of 'freeing' of 'anti-social' *'instincts'* such as the sexual instinct at all. Nor do our problems arise from 'repression', but rather from a failure to find meaning in relationship. It is, of course, true, that there have been attitudes to matters such as women's enjoyment of sex which seem to be inimical to individual fulfilment, in some societies, at various times. But, in the light of object-relations theory, these problems, too, would be seen as problems of *identity* and *relationship*. Where we find woman's sexual needs denied, we should begin to look for hatred of woman and hatred of the 'feminine element' in both men and women. This we may find associated with a fear and hatred of the emotional and creative life and the 'taboo on weakness'.

Where such individuals as the Kronhausens may do good is by resisting the expression of this fear of being human, as in very authoritarian manifestations of censorship. But, on the other hand, their impulse to proselytise so exclusively on behalf of sex and sexual depiction seems itself to be limited because it tends to separate the sexual from the whole being. Why an exhibition of *erotic* art – separated from all other art? Why are these individuals so especially preoccupied with pornography and its 'liberation'? Surely one finds a preoccupation with pornography in patients in case histories often bound up with dissociation and anguish which these individuals have come to the therapist to overcome – along with their preoccupation with pornography? Why are they so especially pleased that people took their children to the Danish exhibition – when, from Melanie Klein's work we have gained insight into the deep fears children have associated with the 'Primal Scene' – fears which are by no means alleviated, but possibly deepened, by witnessing sexual acts or their depiction?

There may, perhaps, be as much that is anti-human in the work of 'sexologists' as in restrictive traditions. Possibly such 'experts' themselves are expressing symbolically by their 'clinical' approach to sex *a fear and hatred of being human*. The reasons why I believe this to be likely will become clearer later. They have to do with the problem, which becomes clear in the terms used by the philosopher Martin Buber, that in separating an objective approach to such functions as sex from 'whole being', we pay the price of reducing that which belongs to the realm of I–Thou to that of I–It. That is, we dehumanise it, and in a sense take the life out of it. Sex becomes a dead impersonal 'object' rather than a living inwardness, subjectively and uniquely experienced. Another element here is that de-emotionalisation which seeks to deny the feminine susceptibility in both men and women – that vulnerable life of sensitive feeling which makes us human.

Such 'enlightenment' compulsively devoted to 'freeing' us in the way of the Kronhausens often established its own successfulness in the world of course, because of its compensatory elements. Yet it involves the destruction of values, incidentally. As *The Times* says of the Kronhausens: 'They are determinedly unworried about the largely disapproving and in some cases sensationalizing reactions to their proselytising zeal; even Hugh Heffner's enthusiastic patronage in the pages of *Playboy*, they say, is better than being ignored, "What if it is sensationally handled? It still means you are getting the message across".'

If their message were the freeing of humanity from the bondage of sexual dehumanisation it would surely hardly be helped by being handled sensationally by journals whose appeal depends upon the depersonalisation of sex and the exploitation of anxieties by titillation for commercial purposes. The truth is that there *is* a deeper, a sinister and hidden 'message' in such 'sexual emancipation' – which is the message of hate. And this is served exactly by the use made of such work as that of the Kronhausens by *Playboy*, since both 'expert' and titillator exploit the same fear and hatred of being human that belongs to compulsive 'bad thinking' about sex as a false way of satisfying existential need. The symbolic purpose is a manic one: to enable us to feel alive, by exploiting what the psychoanalyst calls 'part-object' sex, that is, sex belonging, as it were, to a 'breast' rather than a person. But this kind of sex, detached from meaningful relationship, can never allay the existential frustration for which it seeks to compensate, while at the same time it depreciates human individuality.

My interpretation of such an approach to sex thus sees it as the reverse of the view of itself it presents to the world. It claims to be a work of love: I see it as a work of hate. It presents itself as 'science': in the light of the work of Guntrip and Frankl it appears as homunculism and poor philosophical anthropology, only masquerading as rational under its 'scientific' guise. It presents itself as 'freedom': but I see it rather as a form of ineffective compensation which has destructive effects by dehumanising our attitudes and concepts. In the light of object-relation psychoanalysis it appears as a form of 'false male doing' that threatens potentialities by attacking the realm of 'being' in which we discover and realise the True Self.

If I am correct in my diagnosis – which the reader must judge from what follows – unravelling the spells which such individuals cast over us is a complex matter, and is much more difficult than taking refuge in a hostile or disgusted reaction. Moreover, the application of the 'schizoid diagnosis' enables one to see such work as that of such individuals in a positive light, compassionately – even while rejecting it. The sexologists need to proselytise for 'sexual freedom' in their way because they cannot personally feel real unless they do. For them this is, to take a phrase from R. D. Laing, a 'strategy of survival'. But even so, we must reject their influence since their approach involves living at the expense of others. Their schizoid need for 'reduction of the quality of the relationship desired' (see below, p. 47f.) with all its impulses to fly from being truly human, tends to thrust hate into others.

If this is so, then the success of the Exhibition of Erotic Art in Denmark (which some hope to bring to the I.C.A. in London) is disturbing. It implies that false (or 'hate') solutions have an appeal which can bring them far more acclaim than more realistic and more human approaches to man and his need for a sense of meaning. A new imprisonment of the spirit and a new existential sterility are being purveyed in the name of 'freedom' and 'revolution'.

Homunculism in many forms – from 'naked apery' to sexology – is tending widely nowadays to spread a comfortable cynicism and pessimism about the human condition. This problem I have discussed in my previous work. Here we may, I believe, go further to consider links between the ethos of our acquisitive society and those attitudes to man which become popular and prevalent in it. In our society, as Tawney pointed out long ago, identity has tended to become increasingly attached to ingestion, to taking into oneself. This acquisitive basis for identity not only suits the hedonistic tendencies of industrial–commercial culture, from advertising to entertainment: it also tends to vindicate the underlying pragmatic utilitarianism and *laissez-faire* which dominates the approach of our society to its human problems for historical and economic reasons. So, today, some find congenial those theories which make deductions exclusively and crudely from the study of animal behaviour and seek from these to erect a model of human nature by which 'in the same light as the other animals' we are 'inescapably hostile and competitive'. These theories have been dealt with in a previous work. Here it is only necessary to indicate that there would seem to be elements in our economic system, and especially in the economic structure of the communications industry, which tend to foster nihilistic homunculism so that it spreads into school and university and pervades the whole intellectual ethos.

Pseudo-scientific and 'homunculist' theories have obviously been a gift to the commercial–industrial world, not least commercial entertainment, and those who depend upon its ethos. The advertiser, for instance, feels justified in abusing symbolism and exploiting emotion if he is (after all) only one animal naturally exploiting another: 'Animal reproduction is based on mutual physical attraction of the sexes, and, since the dawn of mankind, *human animals* have used artificial devices to (they hope) heighten their attractiveness . . . ' (advertising executive in a letter to *The Guardian*, 17 August 1968; my italics).

While the quality of public debate on ethical problems declines in consequence of such influences on higher education, genuine science itself loses popularity because it is taken (wrongly) to endorse the picture of man implicit in a society dominated by an acquisitive economy, as a creature whose primary needs are ingestion in various forms, or the 'release' of primary 'instincts' of sex or aggression, according to an ineradicable 'death instinct', or 'pleasure principle'. Meanwhile, in the sphere of the humanities, many intellectuals, as G. H. Bantock says, 'often succumb surprisingly to the trivialities of the mass media'. Bantock quotes H. L. Wilenski from an article in *New Society*, 14 May 1964: 'Intellectuals are increasingly tempted to play to mass audiences and expose themselves to mass culture, and this has the effect of reducing their versatility of taste and opinion, their subtlety of expression and feeling' (Bantock [2]). This has led to a form of *trahison des clercs* in our time, so that even the subjective disciplines threaten to become swamped by homunculist nihilism, 'distraction from confrontation with the problem of existence', and the empty compensations of manic entertainment.

As Frankl says:

> No-one should be surprised today that young people so often behave as if they did not know anything about responsibility, option, choice, sacrifice, self-devotion, dedication to a higher goal in life, and the like. Parents, teachers, scientists and philosophers have taught them all too long a time that man is 'nothing but' the resultant of a parallelogram of inner drives and outer forces. . . .

One's experience of young people, actually, confounds Frankl: most seem by no means to have lost their idealism. But they have to exert it in a world in which many opportunities to find a sense of existential meaning are blocked or hidden behind the prestige of compensatory distractions. And now even creative education itself sometimes comes in for blame – that kind of education which carries the rare spark of a true concern with developing human potentialities.

Yet such problems are often simply not seen by the 'social scientist'. As Suzanne Langer says:

> If the rank and file of youth grows up in emotional cowardice and confusion, sociologists look to economic conditions or family relationships for the cause of this deplorable 'human weakness', but not to the ubiquitous influence of corrupt art, which steeps the average mind in a shallow sentimentalism that ruins what germs of true feeling might have developed in it. (Langer [41]).

This kind of insistence, that where symbolism is corrupted, so is our capacity to live, seems to follow inevitably from the disciplines of 'philosophical anthropology'. It would seem to come naturally from those whose disciplines concern themselves with the Kantian pursuit of the question, What is Man? Neo-Kantian philosophers such as Ernst Cassirer and Suzanne Langer have concerned themselves with man as a 'symbolising and mythologising animal' – a conception which fits into the Kantian epistemology; 'for man carries on his symbolizing activity – and, by an extension of the same process, his mythologising activity – not by accident or effort, but as a pre-conscious expression of the apperceptive imagination in positing and interpreting the most basic features of the world' (Wheelwright, in Buber [5], p. 74).

Cassirer's preoccupation is with 'man's grasp of his world' in terms of *sign* and *meaning*.

This links inevitably with the 'philosophical anthropology' of Buber, whose central categories are *betweenness, thouhood*, or *relationship* according to the context in which he approaches the question. These links between the I–Thou, perception and meaning are endorsed by psychoanalytical thought.

Without going too deeply into Buber's philosophy we may take Wheelwright's account of it in the above-quoted work as a useful summary of a point of view which is emerging from many areas of concern with the nature of human existence: 'By nature each person is a single being, finding himself in company with other single beings: to be single is not to be isolated, however, and by vocation each one is to find and realise his proper focus by entering into relationship with others' (Buber [8], p. 75).

There are other phrases from Wheelwright's account which are also relevant here: 'A being who stands in genuine relationship with others is not self-enclosed, although neither does he cease to be a single self': 'true intercourse and participation with fellow-beings require refreshment and fecundation by means of the strength that only an inner acceptance of monastic loneliness, in some sense, can give' – though this must be a 'monasticism' that 'must never wish to tear us away from our fellow-beings, must never refuse to give us over to them'. And, finally, 'one cannot stand in a relationship to something that is not perceived as contrasted and existing in itself' – 'that is to say, there can only be an entering into a relationship if there is already an independent other, towards which-or-whom one can take up such a relationship. . . . "To know the world as the world", says Buber, "means the outlines of relationship".' (Buber [8], p. 75).

In these statements we may, I believe, see that since our discovery and realisation of ourselves is in complex with our recognition of others and our relationship with them, then that kind of knowing which belongs to *sign* and *meaning* is the essential vehicle of our existence. To know the world requires that we experience relationship: yet only in so far as we know ourselves can we know the world. Thus the energies of intuition and insight, and of personal culture by which we become aware of these, with love in the background, are what primarily make us human and able to deal with the world as human beings. To be able to fulfil ourselves in relationship we must not only be outward-turning towards others, but must also be in touch with our innermost selves: this we can only be through personal culture and those signs and meanings by which we can be in touch with ourselves. Where signs and meanings are corrupted, all these processes by which we are human and know ourselves to be human are corrupted also.

In the light of such insights we can see that our prevalent intellectual fashions are disabled by failing to take into account these subtle regions of relationship with oneself, and with others, in the realm of sign and meaning – upon which our very humanness and our sense of our potentialities, our 'intentionality', depend.

It is perhaps necessary to make clear, perhaps, at the onset, since this is an age of labels and coteries, that when Buber begins to talk about man's relationship with God the present author is obliged to part company, regretfully: his point of view is not a Christian one, and his view is not one that clings to established traditions at all costs. Nor does the author endorse all the various movements concerned, in the England of the seventies, to 'clean up' our culture by authoritarian measures yet we need more discrimination. The problem we are concerned with lies too deep for easy cures, since it involves the whole question of how man thinks of himself and what he conceives to be the point of life. What is necessary is no less than a radical reassessment of every assumption behind our approaches to problems of culture, education, morality, and modes of approach to the question What is life all about? – and how we explore and establish meaning. His attempt at such a reassessment has taken the writer a long time, and it has often been tedious and distasteful. But it seemed pointless to go on with further studies in education and literary criticism, or in creative writing, without facing the questions involved, making a close study of the corruptness of so much in our present culture, and trying to decide where one stood.

I am reminded of Yeats in his introduction to *Gitanjali* by Rabindranath Tagore:

> We have to do so much propagandist writing . . . criticism that our minds gradually cease to be creative, and yet we cannot help it. If our life was not a continual warfare, we would not have taste, we would not know what is good, we would not find hearers and readers. Four-fifths of our energy is spent in the quarrel with bad taste, whether in our own minds or in the minds of others. (Yeats [63], p. xii.)

The situation is even worse when 'bad taste' becomes a widespread acceptance of the anti-human which not only implicitly rejects the values of our civilisation but threatens to destroy all those meanings and dignities by which we can attain a 'boundless respect' for our humanity.

PART I

Culture and the Point of Life

Fig. 1

CHAPTER 2

The Foundations of Identity

IF WHAT corrupts our symbolism is hate, where does this hate come from?

If we reject Freudian 'instinct' theory and other theories which explain man's hate in terms of an impersonal 'id' or 'death instinct', brutish 'reality' under the surface, or some other ineradicable force for which we need not feel responsible, then we have to find some other way of accounting for the origins of hate. In so far as we do, our findings will have implications for culture and ethics and for our responsibilities in these realms. As I have already explained at length in my earlier work on the theories of object-relations psychology, I believe an adequate and convincing account of the origins of major problems such as that of hate can be given in terms of the dimensions of identity and the inward dynamics of 'psychic reality' – that is, in terms of the growth and development of the human person.

Hate may be seen as an inversion or diversion of the primary urge to survive, physically and psychically, as a human being. This interpretation of hate as an existence problem is emerging in psychoanalytical theory from those grave confrontations in which a patient cannot go on living unless he can discover, through his relationship with his therapist, *what it is to be human*. As D. W. Winnicott says; 'Psychotic patients are all the time hovering between living and not living force us to look at this problem, one which really belongs *not to psycho-neurotics but to all human beings*' (Winnicott [60], p. 368).

The existence of the psychotic patient who needs to ask this question and has no secure sense established within him of what the answers might be, also forces us to recognise that there is a kind of individual who has never found himself as a human being. What goes on in the struggle may throw out information which will help us answer the same question in the realm of culture and criticism. In its turn this obliges us to recognise that there are processes which more or less complete themselves in most of us by which we find ourselves as individuals. These processes evidently belong to the realm of I–Thou experience, *to relation*, with which Buber is preoccupied.

As Guntrip says: 'The feeling "I am" leads to the question, "What am I?", i.e. the experience of "being" leads to growth of self-consciousness, self-knowledge, and self-realization' (Guntrip [27], p. 267).

Hate is seen here as a false solution to the question What am I? – or a false way of asking it.

This book is thus written from an unfamiliar point of view, and there are great difficulties here for the author in deciding whether or not the reader can be assumed to have acquaintance with the terms and concepts of inter-personal psychology of any kind. It will make it easier for both the reader and myself if, before I embark on this survey, I

13

briefly state the point of view from which this whole book is written. The view adopted here is roughly that set forth in Guntrip's recent work, *Schizoid Phenomena, Object-relations and the Self* [27], especially the chapter 'Psyche, Ego and the Experience of Being'. Guntrip's approach takes into account an important unpublished paper by Winnicott on Male and Female Elements in the Personality.

Winnicott's account of the origins of identity seems to me the most penetrating insight yet to emerge from psychological theory. The essence of his view is that our foundations of identity are in the experience of *being*, a female element, with the mother. He takes the view that human nature is 'constitutionally bisexual', and tried to ascertain what this means by trying to isolate the 'pure male element' and the 'pure female element' in our make-up.

Winnicott suggests that the nature of the male element in human nature is expressed in 'doing' and the nature of the female element in 'being'. The male element of 'doing' comes later in growth. The nature of the female element is transmitted first at the level of unspoken 'being' by the mother, and it is characteristic of Winnicott's whole approach that, as Guntrip puts it:

> A good enough relationship with a stable mother is the basis of the possibility, through primary identification, of the first nascent experiences of security, selfhood, identity, the definitive start of the ego, making possible in turn a growth in object-relationships, as the differentiation of subject and object proceeds and the baby acquires a 'not-me' world and feels to be a 'me' over against it. Before that, the ego is there as a potentiality, latent in the psyche since the infant starts off as a 'whole human being'. (Guntrip [27], p. 249.)

As Guntrip says, this is akin to W. R. D. Fairbairn's belief in a 'pristine unitary ego'. And it makes for an attitude to human nature which completely reverses the popular Freudian view in which civilised human behaviour is but an unwilling mode of 'adaptation' imperfectly imposed on an animal or 'real id-instincts' beneath the surface.

Guntrip seeks to restate Fairbairn's phrase as 'pristine unitary psyche' with 'latent ego-quality' for 'as development proceeds Ego and Psyche may not be identical' – though they should be in a theoretically perfect development. But every aspect of the psyche that finds expression has ego-quality, though the primary wholeness of the psyche is 'obscured and lost beneath the fragments of a split ego'.

The picture of splitting in the ego given by Fairbairn is most complex: it shows how the self can be divided against itself in a great many ways as we shall see (and itself derives from Freud). But it is important to emphasise, Guntrip believes, that:

> The ego is always a latent possibility in, and indeed belongs to the essential nature of, the *human* psyche. The human psyche is an incipient ego and if were not, it would not be human. . . . All human experience, however unintegrated or disintegrated, must have some degree of ego-quality as the experience of a 'subject'. There has to be a subject to *have* the experience even of depersonalisation and derealization. (Guntrip [27], p. 249.)

Experience of human beings through clinical encounters led Winnicott and Guntrip to believe that where there are problems of human personality they are not problems of conflict with the 'animal' or 'instinctual' – with impersonal, blind, forces in us – but problems of weakness and failure of ego-development. The basis of ego-strength is in 'ego-support' from the mother in the earliest stages of life: identity problems spring from failures between the 'facilitating environment' and the 'maturational processes' in these earliest moments.

The terms used by these psychologists are similar to those used by existentialists – as by those who are seeking to base a philosophical anthropology on the work of Buber and on explorations of problems of identity and existence. Buber's own imaginative exploration of the 'inside' of human experience led him to the same impulse to penetrate to the 'very start of the human identity'. Guntrip quotes Buber on the primal formative relationship that creates human being:

> The ante-natal life of the child is one of purely natural combination, bodily interaction and flowing from the one to the other. . . . [There is] a mythical saying of the Jews, 'in the mother's body man knows the universe, in birth he forgets it'. . . . It remains indeed in man as a secret image of desire . . . the yearning is for the cosmic connexion. Every child that is coming into being rests, like all life that is coming into being, in the womb of the great mother, the undivided primal world that precedes form. From her, too, we are separated, and enter into personal life, slipping free only in the dark hours to be close to her again; night by night this happens to the healthy man. But this separation does not occur catastrophically like the separation from the bodily mother; time is granted to the child to exchange a spiritual connexion, that is, relation, for the natural connexion with the world that he gradually loses. (Buber [7], quoted in Guntrip [27], p. 221.)

As Guntrip comments: 'Buber is here describing the way in which unconscious antenatal symbiosis has to develop into conscious post-natal personal relationship': 'It is impossible for a human being to exist as a human being in isolation. Unless the mother starts the infant off in the process of becoming "an ego in relation" he cannot become a true human person . . . so fundamental is ego-relatedness as a quality of our whole experience . . .' (Guntrip [27], p. 222).

Thinking in 'object-relations' ways thus requires us to reconsider many of our habitual concepts. These have to do with identity, existence, perception, and our relationship with reality. One concept is the concept of 'separation anxiety' arising from birth – a concept which seems to lie behind Buber's remarks above about separation from the mother at birth.

The truth would seem to be that the infant at birth has no clear sense that he is a separate individual, so thus to him separation could have no meaning. This insight emerged from Winnicott's capacity to reach the conclusion that, in a sense, there is 'no such thing as a baby'. We see a baby and it looks like an individual. But from the 'inside', if we can imagine the experience of the baby, he has not yet learned that he is one whole person, in his own body, or that he is separate from the *not-me* at all. To all intents and purposes from his point of view he is not to be distinguished from the mother.

Looked at in a positive way, this allows us to see that to become a human person we have to go through a number of profound experiences, towards integration, personalisation, and the discovery of time and space beginning from primary identification. It is the mother who enables us to create these capacities in ourselves, and the means by which these developments are achieved are *culture*.

Winnicott postulates a particular state in the mother which enables her to do this:

> We notice in the expectant mother an increasing identification with the infant: . . . a willingness as well as an ability on the part of the mother to drain interest from her own self into the baby. I have referred to this as 'primary maternal preoccupation'. In my view, this is what gives the mother her special ability to do the right thing. She knows what her baby could be feeling like. No one else knows. (Winnicott [56], quoted by Guntrip [27], p. 223.)

This 'preoccupation' is not pathological, though it 'shows up as an illness if the baby dies' – so that it seems to be a kind of schizoid state of extension of the personality in some uncanny way. But when it takes its normal course, it is a way for the baby to experience the mother first as 'subjective object' – that is, someone with whom he is fully identified – later to become, by her assistance, his 'objective object': 'It is part of the normal process that the mother recovers her self-interest, and does so at the rate at which her infant can allow her to do so. . . . The normal mother's recovery from her pre-occupation with her infant provides a kind of weaning.' (Winnicott [56], quoted by Guntrip [27], p. 223.)

This 'psychic weaning' is the basis of our discovery of the reality of ourselves and the world – and it takes places through an I–Thou relationship. If this relationship does not go right, then the individual cannot feel the I AM sense, and cannot live in touch with a True Self. Winnicott says:

> Only if there is a good-enough mother does the infant start on a process of development that is personal and real. If the mothering is not good enough, then the infant becomes a collection of reactions to impingement, and the true self of the infant fails to form or becomes hidden behind a false self which complies with and generally wards off the world's knocks. . . . All depends upon the capacity of the mother to give ego-support . . . it is well-cared-for babies who quickly establish themselves as persons. . . . (Winnicott [56], quoted by Guntrip [27], p. 224.)

There are a number of important aspects of human make-up which follow from this insight and have considerable bearing on the cultural problems which we are to explore in this book. The individual who has been adequately loved in infancy is capable of being *alone*. He does not, that is, need to take urgent steps to avoid loneliness, isolation and unreality, and a terror of loss of self. Severe needs for distracting activity are, however, felt by the 'seriously unmothered' infant who suffers from fundamental ego-unrelatedness. The *capacity to be alone* depends upon the individual having a personal culture by which he feels that his union with the mother is symbolised – while this in its turn establishes for him the capacity to be self-reliant and to be alone sustained by his inward possession of the mother and that culture which relates him to all other human beings.

Those who cannot feel this inner security may need to resort to extreme measures, but their use of culture is different. They need to employ culture to express their extreme over-dependence on others – to find that others are 'there' and to establish contact by desperate methods such as using cultural symbolism to alienate others, to exploit them, to try to force them to be 'good', or, in despair of this, to thrust harm into them. One of their problems is that such individuals cannot believe in a benign environment and must needs attempt to feel real by conflict with an environment they cannot help believing to be malignant. Their culture tends to be paranoic. As Winnicott says: 'Maturity and the capacity to be alone implies that the individual has had the chance through good-enough mothering to build up a belief in a benign environment' (Winnicott [56], quoted by Guntrip [27], p. 226).

This belief in a benign environment is at one with a feeling that one has possession of the mother within one: thus a whole subject can feel that the object is also whole and good:

> Gradually the ego-supportive environment is introjected and built into the individual's capacity, so that there comes about a capacity to be actually alone. Even so, theoretically, there is always someone present, someone who is equated ultimately and unconsciously with the mother, the person who in the early days and weeks, was temporarily identified with the infant, and for the time being was interested in nothing else but the care of her own infant. (Winnicott [56], quoted by Guntrip [27], p. 226.)

This conviction of the reality and reliability of good objects in his outer world belongs, of course, to the infant's feelings, and is only to be gained by 'sufficient experience'.

What is it that the infant experiences that establishes this capacity to enjoyably re-member his earliest relation and to feel full of substantiality – psychically speaking?

This, perhaps, we can take further by looking once more at Winnicott's paper on the male and female elements in human nature, and what he says there about the 'basic emotional capacities' belonging to the male and female elements in both men and women. Guntrip distinguished between these 'elements' in health thus:

> The female receives what the male gives in the sexual act, and when she becomes pregnant her part at first is not so much to 'do' as to 'be' for the child. There is nothing she can 'do' but if she ceases to 'be' the child will cease to be. Here being and the baby's being are linked inseparably as a physical fact, and this 'oneness' is carried over into the beginnings of the infant's psychic life. Only gradually can he stand separation on the basis of undisturbed oneness. . . . (Guntrip [27], p. 257.)

So totally dependent is the infant at first, says Guntrip, that the very possibility of the start of his ego-development rests entirely on the mother's capacity to 'be' an adequate source of security. Winnicott is quoted again: 'However complex the sense of self and the establishment of an identity eventually becomes as the baby grows, no sense of self emerges except on the basis of this relating in the sense of BEING.'

We have here a most significant truth which we find embodied in the psychic tissue of every human being. There is a 'true' way of experiencing existence which is through being and 'being for'. Here we may find that silent core of the being where we need to feel security, with which we need to be in touch, and which we need to retreat from the world, in Buber's 'monastic way', to find – yet without seeking to impose upon it by forms of 'male element doing'. Here we may find within ourselves an ontological security from which we can truly 'confront the problem of existence', so that it is possible to feel that life is meaningful.

The female element is the area of 'feeling' – as Guntrip puts it, a 'state of being, of being in touch, of knowing by identification'. There is thus a *female way of knowing and experiencing* – very much belonging to Buber's realm of I–Thou experience. By contrast, as Guntrip points out, 'thinking' is the male element, intellectual activity. Of course, both men and women are capable of both thinking and feeling. But there is a whole range of human capacity, too much ignored by our kind of society, which does not belong to the cognitive, analytical, and abstract. The female element is in a sense incommunicable, but also an area only experienced as the 'still centre' or 'silent core' of being alive. Winnicott speaks of a 'non-communicating central self, for ever immune from the reality principle, and for ever silent. Here communication is non-verbal . . . absolutely personal. It belongs to being alive. . . .'

Communication may 'arise' out of this sphere. But, Guntrip believes, it 'enters into personal relationships in the female way' as it does when the mother 'is' for her baby.

As communication arises, so develops the capacity to exist as a separate, self-possessed, human identity. This development is made, and worked on, by symbolism – and so culture is integral with the realisation of our essential human identity. Here I would like to refer briefly to another important paper by Winnicott in which he discusses the Location of Culture (Winnicott [60], p. 368). In this paper Winnicott finds the origin of culture in the 'transitional object' – the infant's toy or cuddly rag from which, in his earliest years, he will not be parted (and must not be). This transitional object is the first artefact, the first use of a symbol:

> When we witness an infant's employment of a transitional object, we are witnessing both the child's first use of a symbol, and also the first experience of play . . . the object is a symbol of the union of the baby and the mother (or part of the mother). . . . The use of an object symbolises the union of two now separate things, baby and mother, at the point of the initiation of their state of separateness. (Winnicott [60], p. 369.)

We may say that the transitional object both symbolises the union of the baby with the mother, but also his internalisation of the mother, or his at-one-ness with the mother, that make it possible for him to be alone – that is, that makes it possible for him to be truly separate as a human being.

From this first cultural symbol, the child's culture grows as a manifestation of the 'interplay between separateness and union'. As Winnicott says: 'It is these cultural experiences that provide the continuity in the human race which transcends personal existence . . .', and it is this inner possession of a point of meeting between the self and all other human beings that makes us man: 'When one speaks of a man one speaks of him along with the summation of his cultural experiences.'

Winnicott speaks from the position of one who has been asked by psychotic patients, What is life about? And he finds that the answer is not to be given in terms of instinctual satisfactions but in such developments of self-hood as bring a baby 'begin to be' – 'to feel that life is real, to find life worth living'.

PEANUTS

Fig. 2. The transitional object in a strip cartoon.

Where this development of a personal culture goes well, where the mother can 'be' for her baby,

> for the baby . . . every detail of the baby's life is an example of creative living. Every object is a 'found' object. Given the chance, the baby begins to live creatively, and to use actual objects to be creative into. If the baby is not given this chance then there is no area in which the baby may have play, or may have cultural experience; then there is no link with cultural inheritance, and there will be no contribution to the cultural pool. (Winnicott [60], p. 371.)

The essence of being human and of finding a sense of 'what life is all about' is here linked with the development of a creative culture and the ability to make use of what we 'find' and 'make' in experience. This emphasis puts the question of culture at the heart of the whole question of human identity and existential security – and of perception and the effective 'doing' based on it.

Yet it is perfectly clear from Winnicott's paper that he believes that culture can be abused. For instance, he insists that, since culture originates in the mother–child relationship of total dependence, culture implies *trust*. He quotes Plaut, a Jungian analyst: 'The capacity to form images and to use these constructively by recombination into new pattern is – unlike dreams or phantasies – dependent upon the individual's capacity to trust' (Winnicott [60], p. 372). This trust should be regarded as 'sacred', because it is easy to use it to 'clutter' a patient up with 'persecutory elements'.

This book is concerned to demonstrate that it is this very area of 'trust' and of the 'sacred' realm of the use of symbolism for 'creative living' that is exploited in some areas of our culture. While we accept this exploitation, and even ridicule suggestions that it has consequences, inevitably our attitudes to ourselves and the world we live in become 'cluttered up with persecutory elements'. Our attitudes to ourselves and to other men become corrupted at the unconscious level with inevitable consequences in the way in which man behaves towards man. Much of our culture is not only deficient in sources of creative living, but actually reduces living power. We have to divert energy to cope with the hate thrust into us by those who need to exploit this area of trust for their own purposes. Meanwhile, at large, our whole society is given to a 'bustling' False Self activity which seems to justify itself as an aim in life but has no meaning. As Buber saw, it merely prevents us from distraction from 'experiencing the depth of the human problematic as the ennobling centre of [our] life', while more desperate false solutions are thrust upon us.

CHAPTER 3

Dividing Against Oneself

THE effect of an adequate early environment is to enable us to 'be alone without being isolated and becoming a "lost soul" '. Those qualities which Buber requires – that we exist both in relationship but yet are capable of refreshment by seeking touch with the innermost core of the self – are both created by this earliest experience of 'being-at-one-with'. As Winnicott says: 'The capacity of the individual to be alone . . . is one of the most important signs of maturity in emotional development.'

This capacity to be alone in one's security, as Winnicott makes clear, is *established around the signs and meanings of culture*: it cannot exist without symbolism as an aspect of the inner world, and our capacity to work there towards ego-maintenance. But here there is yet another complexity, as we shall see – which is that those individuals who have not been given an adequate sense of being human are also in need of using cultural artefacts for their own desperate ends to feel real – and can use these in 'false' ways, in desperate 'strategies of survival'. There thus arises the problem of hate in culture and the possibility of the abuse of cultural trust.

Culture would seem to spring from the creative female element in us. Guntrip says: 'The female element may be defined as the need to be emotionally susceptible, the capacity for sensitiveness to what others are feeling. . . . The male element (may be seen as) the need to be able to take practical action in an often difficult and dangerous world.' (Guntrip [27], p. 263.)

But here arises a complication, which is most important for the argument of this book – which is that the female element is the 'emotionally sensitive self that can be more easily hurt, and can then be felt as a weakness to be resisted, resented, and hidden behind a tough exterior' (Guntrip [27], p. 263).

We can therefore hate *being* and so come to abuse culture, out of fear of it, as a manifestation of the emotionally sensitive self.

This flight from and abuse of the creative, intuitive 'feeling' area of one's female element is most likely to be taken by an individual who has especial cause to fear this side of himself. And, of course, he will fear it insofar as his mother, when he was totally dependent upon her, at a time when life depended upon this relationship, failed sufficiently to 'be' for him. Here we have to consider what happens when such primal formative processes go wrong or remain incomplete.

Guntrip says that it is always the 'female element' in an individual which is dissociated. For such individuals the mother has not been able to 'be' for her infant, and in desperation has tried, perhaps, to make up for 'being' by 'doing'. This is felt by the infant as 'impingement', so that instead of a firm core of 'being' to his identity he can only become

20

as Winnicott says, 'a collection of reactions to impingement'; all the infant can do is to patch together a sense of self out of his experience of an activity which feels predatory. As Guntrip says:

> . . . bad mothering [forces] the infant to become aware of the pressure of an external and interfering reality at times when he is not feeling needs, and not reaching out actively to his needed object of his own accord. Active adaptation is response to the baby's own initiative in 'seeking', a time when he is capable of accepting and dealing with the movement of the mother towards himself. This allows his internal psychic development to go on undisturbed, according to his own inner nature and laws of growth. Impingement and intrusion on the infant at times when he is not reaching out, and the result is that he withdraws from an unwanted impact. This 'disturbs the continuity and going-on-being of the new individual'. [Winnicott] He is forced to act prematurely to an outer reality which he begins to experience as a threat. Here are the origins of persecutory anxiety. (Guntrip [26], p. 400.)

Here are the origins of the *schizoid* problem of weakness of identity and of the (paranoid) problems of *hate* arising from false solutions to such weakness involving splitting and other problems which we must now look at.

Where the primary experience with the mother was not-good-enough, there is a feeling of a 'lack of a proper centre and no coherent ground'. Guntrip says that from experience the psychotherapist finds such a person trying to become a person by 'doing'. At worst: 'Where there should be a feeling of "ego" there is only the experience of uncertainty, of "not counting", of being "nobody in particular".'

The feeling of I AM, of being real in a real world, is closely bound up with the initial experience of the mother's handling, and it is in the experience of this handling that he creates his sense of being a whole continuous subject, in his body, in relation to a whole and continuous object, in a secure world. But in this handling we need to take into account delicate processes of intuitive communication which belong to 'being for'. In these the mother's breast is central – 'breast' here meaning all those experiences of being fed, of *being given to* at the right moment, of play and symbolic intercourse of all kinds between the mother who feeds and the child who incorporates her both physically and psychically. In this experience it is the satisfactory experience of the 'female element breast' which establishes the sense of *being* prior to *doing* and lays the ground for creativity.

Where things go wrong, as Guntrip says: 'The not very maternal, bustling, organising dominating mother, who is determined that the baby shall "get on with his feed" at the rate her timetable dictates, will present him with a 'pseudo-male-element-breast' which seeks to 'do things' to him' (Guntrip [27], p. 250).

By contrast the more maternal mother can let the infant be quiet with her and let him feed and enjoy at his own pace. There is much more yet to be defined and explored here, but what seems crucial is whether the infant can make use of the female element of his mother, in a true way, to establish being, or whether he takes in from the 'pseudo male breast' a false way of holding together, defending, and preserving an identity, by *doing and being done to*. This false doing includes thinking. And it may also, in later life, include the necessity of 'thinking bad thoughts' to maintain a sense of being alive. In this, I believe, we can see the origins of some manifestations of hate and their cultural significance.

From the therapist's point of view, where there is a failure of these earliest processes of maturation and environment, 'the patient has lost touch with his own potentialities' and the therapist has to help him find himself.

Where 'being' exists, 'doing' naturally follows. But if 'being' is not there but dissociated, then a forced kind of 'doing' will do duty for both 'being' and 'doing'.

> The experience of 'being' would be stultified if it did not lead on to the practical expression of 'doing'. The experience of 'doing' in the absence of a secure sense of 'being' degenerates into a meaningless succession of mere activities . . . not performed for their own proper purpose, but as a futile attempt to 'keep oneself in being'. . . . The experience of 'being' is more than the mere awareness of 'existence'. It involves the sense of reliable security in existence, realised both in knowing oneself as a real person and as able to make good relationships. (Guntrip [27], p. 254.)

While the two elements in human nature may be summed up in Winnicott's phrase 'The male element *does*, while the female element [in males and females] *is*', there is also a kind of doing which is not rooted in being, and so becomes 'mere' activity, futile and meaningless – or even destructive and nihilistic. Sound 'doing' must arise from secure 'being':

> The conscious ego is the ego of separation, of 'doing' of acting and being acted on, and in that sense is the location of the male element in personality. It must derive its strength from the deepest unconscious core of the self that has never lost the feeling of 'being at one with' the maternal source of its life. (Guntrip [27], p. 266.)

If male doing cannot derive strength from this core it can become a false and even destructive activity, while in all of us 'individuality and separate ego-identity', however strongly achieved, are 'always precariously held against threats from the external world'. In these two human facts lie the sources of cultural problems. As Guntrip points out:

> A practical exploitation of this . . . is seen in third degree interrogation . . . (and other systems such as brain washing) intended to break down the resistance of those who dare to be real individuals, by breaking down their entire personality. When people have a nervous breakdown and feel they are 'going to bits' under the pressures of life, this is only a common version of the same thing. (Guntrip [27], pp. 267–8.)

Relationship, contributing in to society, and culture are among the means by which we sustain our individuality and separate ego-identity. In this work we shall see some of the fundamental problems which every human being has to be continually engaged with – from the conflicts between love and hate, ego-strength and ego-weakness, reparation and guilt, to problems of existentialist despair and mortality which no one can escape. A full cultural and imaginative life is a most valuable asset in this continual effort to sustain and develop our individuality and to seek the meaning of life. Yet culture can be abused.

In order to discover ways of discriminating against cultural abuse, we need to see how a personal culture can be in touch with the True Self. This requires that we accept Winnicott's distinction between True Self and False Self, and the implication that there can be false solutions in culture which belong to False Self 'doing', emerging from a failure of 'female element being'. The False Self can take a number of forms and modes. In his essay True and False Self ([57], p. 142) Winnicott discusses among other aspects the False Self as a 'caretaker' self which can exist and have a defensive function – that of dealing with the world until such time as the True Self can be brought into existence. Winnicott classifies False Self organisations in their various forms. There is even a False Self in health: 'the whole organisation of the polite and mannered social attitude, a "not wearing the heart on the sleeve" as might be said.' At the other extreme, 'the False Self sets up as real and it is this that observers think is the real person.' 'In living relationships, work relationships, and friendships, however, the False Self begins to fail. In situations in which what is expected is a whole person the False Self has some essential lacking. At this extreme the True Self is hidden' (Winnicott [57], p. 142.)

In less extreme situations the False Self defends the True Self, and the True Self is 'acknowledged as a potential'. Clinical illness is seen here by Winnicott as having a positive aim, which is the 'preservation of the individual in spite of abnormal environmental conditions'. In other yet less severe cases 'the False Self has as its main concern a search for conditions which will make it possible for the True Self to come into its own' (Winnicott [57], p. 143).

Sometimes, if there is doubt that this can ever come about, the result is suicide, but Winnicott even sees this in positive terms:

> Suicide in this context is the destruction of the total self in avoidance of annihilation of the True Self. When suicide is the only defence left against the betrayal of the True Self, then it becomes the lot of the False Self to organise the suicide. This, of course, involves its own destruction, but at the same time eliminates the need for its continued existence, since its function is the protection of the True Self from insult. (Winnicott [57], p. 143.)

As Guntrip points out, 'false male doing' may include thinking as a form of doing. So it is possible for the False Self to be associated with an intellectual structure:

> A particular danger arises out of the not infrequent tie-up between the intellectual approach and the False Self. When a False Self becomes organised in an individual who has a high intellectual potential there is a very strong tendency for the mind to become the location of the False Self, and in this case there develops a dissociation between intellectual activity and psychosomatic existence. (Winnicott [57], p. 144.)

This kind of dissociation is a prevalent mark of our culture, as will be suggested. And since culture is integral to ego-maintenance, it is also possible for culture to be, like brainwashing, destructive of ego-maintenance: if this is so, then it is the weak who suffer from a culture which excessively exploits hate.

The False Self is created out of the infant's experience of that 'false male doing' which, in the mother, was her bustling substitute for being able truly to 'be' for the child. In that it is created so, it is an attempt to find a 'strategy of survival' and a defence against profound weakness at the heart of identity on the basis of hate.

It tends thus to take the form of a defensive shell, or of activity designed to alienate others, so as to establish a sense of being real through assertion and aggression directed at them. When we come to schizoid problems we shall see how this links up with the substitution of hate for love and the need to feel real by violence. A characteristic figure in the modern world of culture here is, of course, Sartre's hero and martyr Genet, the foundling whose purity of aestheticism as a writer is matched by his reversal of all values in his behaviour. The latter's criminality may be seen as pseudo-male activity based on hate, a strategy of feeling real, and an attempt to convince others and himself of his reality despite an essential vacancy at the core where a True Self should be.

Guntrip illustrates False Male Doing by quoting from the case of a bachelor patient who said:

> 'I used to rush about doing things as a "man about town", copying my mother's social role, my façade for not feeling sure of anything, not being sure what sort of a person I was. . . . As a little boy I was a sissy, I didn't play rough games like boys, I cried easily if hurt. I feel now that my physique is weak and girlish, but I felt I was becoming masculine when I got a motor-bike. Now I have a car but I still phantasy myself as a ton-up youth taking a shadowy girl on the pillion. She never has any real personality but is only there to admire me. When I feel anxious I put on my leather jacket and tight belt round my waist and look at myself in the glass and feel tough and masculine.' (Guntrip [27], p. 256.)

This syndrome is a recognisable way of compensating for ego-weakness in our present-day culture by pseudo-male doing, of which 'James Bond' is the epitome. As Guntrip

T.M.H.—B

says, this may be linked with Adler's 'masculine protest' – an early identification of this pseudo-male, pathological sex-role which appears in both men and women. It receives endorsement as an acceptable and even admirable mode of behaviour, however ironically presented, in many modern works of literature. As Guntrip says:

> It often develops into sadism and destructiveness, and carries the complementary idea of the woman as the weaker sex, an idea which, except in the crude muscular sense, has no counterpart in reality, but which has great importance in psychopathology. When male is equated with sadism, then female is equated with masochism. (Guntrip [27], p. 256.)

Guntrip discussed a number of cases in which sexual symbolism relates to problems of male and female elements in the personality.

Guntrip concludes his exposition of this view of human make-up thus:

> . . . 'being and doing' feeling and acting, are not intrinsically male and female except by biological accident, but have acquired that broad significance as the two elementary constituents of personality. They transcend sexual differences and are simply what belongs to a whole person. . . . There cannot be a whole human being without an integration of feeling with thinking and acting. . . . (Guntrip [27], p. 271.)

From this point of view it is easy to see that our whole capacity to perceive and to interact with the world depends upon what we take in from the male and female elements in our parents and what we can develop of these elements in touch with the True Self.

In considering culture it is important to note that Guntrip makes special reference to one special aspect of this 'schizoid reaction' to impingement:

> . . . overstrain produces an overreaction, and can lead to *hypertrophy of the intellect.* The child grows up to live by *thinking* rather than feeling, and develops a *'false mental self'*. It has to withdraw into itself to deal with its problems with the environment.
>
> Certain kinds of failure on the part of the mother especially erratic behaviour, produce over-activity of the mental functioning . . . there can develop an opposition between the mind and the psyche-soma, since the reaction to this abnormal environmental state the thinking of the individual begins to take over and organize the caring for the psyche-soma, whereas in health it is the function of the environment to do this . . . we find . . . *mental functioning becoming a thing in itself.* . . . (Guntrip [27], p. 401; *my italics*).

This psychology of Winnicott's explains why, as Fairbairn indicates and Guntrip confirms, the intellectual life of any community contains more than a normal proportion of schizoid individuals. Intellectual powers for some can themselves be a 'strategy of survival'. There are individuals who have only been able to survive by substituting intense thought processes for 'being' – mental functioning for them becoming a 'thing in itself' – necessary to make up for the mother's inadequacies and to stand for the 'good mother' itself. This explains how it is that an individual can have intense libidinal attachment to an intellectual system, and explains the intense attachment of groups of people to theoretical political systems as in Marxism and other revolutionary schemata. There is thus a natural link established by psychoanalytical theory between ego-weakness and schizoid problems, intense intellectual activity, the problem of hate, and the feeling that the outer world is threatening, or certainly not benign. There is such a thing as intellectual hate, often paranoid.

The present work is essentially an attempt to demonstrate that many cultural forms have their origins in these areas of early environmental failure and the 'bad thinking' which arises from them. I shall also try to show that our acquisitive society tends, because of its very nature, to foster these 'false solutions' or 'hate solutions' to the problem of identity by attaching identity to doing and getting, sustained by paranoia and the impulse to ingest.

First, however, we have to explore further some complex mental processes such as splitting. We have to imagine how the world feels to an infant who fails to feel the primal contact of 'being' with his mother. Implicit in everything I have summarised above from psychoanalytical theory is the principle, which Fairbairn pronounced for object-relations psychology, that man cannot exist without an object: the goal of libidinal need for him is not pleasure (as Freud thought) but the object which confirms the subject. To be without an object is so terrible to a human being that where the object is unavailable or inadequate, objects have to be 'invented' to which to relate. We now have to imagine an infant threatened with a world in which he cannot find this essential confirmation. Guntrip speaks of this predicament thus:

> Severe schizoid states disclose a total fear of the entire outer world, and deprivation and impinge-ment combine. The world is a frightening emptiness when it does not respond and meet the infant's needs, and a frightening persecutor when it actively and hurtfully impinges. The infant cannot develop a secure and strong ego-sense either in a vacuum or under intolerable pressure and he seeks to return to a vaguely remembered earlier safe place, even though in fact he can only withdraw into isolation within himself. (Guntrip [27], p. 68.)

But this impulse to withdraw, and the frustration of the libidinal urge to exist, provoke further complications. The frustration of libidinal need for good object-relations arouses *aggression*, and since the 'child's ego is a mouth ego' and the libidinal urge to live is closely associated with intense oral feelings, this aggression is experienced like a voracious mouth within one. *This 'mouth' becomes the dominant symbol in all hate* ('and appetite, an universal wolf . . .').

The consequence of this intensification of existence hunger, together with the intensifi-cation of the libidinal need itself, seems to the individual to threaten potential objects themselves – the love-needs become so strong that they seem destructive towards all objects. Since love has been rejected, or it feels so to the infant, he is thus filled with an intense fear that love is harmful, while his voracious love-needs seem to threaten to eat his whole world. Here we have the schizoid problem, which is of an identity so weak that in consequence the needs to exist themselves, and love, threaten the most terrible harm. There is therefore an impulse to substitute hate for love – the consequences of which we shall explore later.

The first schizoid reaction, however, is simple withdrawal, 'away from the dangers of devouring and therefore losing love-objects'. Losing the love-object would be to en-counter total loss of relationship, and so extinction. But at this stage, as Guntrip points out, there is no *concern*. The fear of the schizoid individual is exerted on behalf of the ego and the consequences to it of losing the object. There is often no concern for the object in its own right – and so there is the possibility of a horrifying callousness on the part of a schizoid individual who exists in a pre-moral state of existence. Morality only grows in an individual who has become aware of the distinction between the *me* and the *not-me*, and who has felt concern for the effect of his phantasies on his object – and so is impelled to 'make good' the object, and others, and the rest of the world, in order to stay in existence, confirmed by these.

The first and most primitive expressions of hate may therefore be ruthless and pre-moral. Or, expressions of hate in those who have never achieved a 'healthy moral sense' may be pre-moral – and horrifyingly callous. As Winnicott says; 'Here we find the most ugly crimes. We see the criminal engaged in a desperate attempt to feel guilty' (Winnicott [57], p. 27).

It is this primitive callous (pre-moral) hate that we often encounter nowadays in contemporary culture, as we shall see, together with attempts to vindicate its 'freedom'.

It is interesting and important to note that in such a comment Winnicott is trying to see ruthless and destructive hate as having a *meaning*: a meaning which is related to a 'strategy of survival'. This concern to discover the meaning of violence indicates a most valuable method of approach in the cultural sphere also. There we can see the invocation o violence, in consequence, not in terms of 'valuable release' or a 'safety valve' – but as a f: lse way of feeling real – asserting vitality but by desperate strategies which may, like ruthless and callous murder, be directed at the ultimate and unfeeling exploitation of others, albeit in their vulnerable feelings rather than in their physical flesh.

Here, however, we must pursue for the moment the consequences of withdrawal. We are still in the sphere of schizoid problems – that is, of the first problems of forming an identity at all, for the term schizoid does not mean 'split' in the language we are using, but 'belonging to the earliest existential moments of the human being'. It is from this 'very start of the human identity' that schizoid conditions in patients emerge. If we speak, as Melanie Klein did, of a 'schizoid position', we mean the layer or area in the psychic structure of an individual in the here and now whose ontogenesis is in these earliest moments of living. 'Schizoid' is therefore both an aetiological and diagnostic term.

At this stage, however, we also have to begin to talk of 'splitting' and examine theories of the origins of the ways in which a human being can become divided against himself. This is a human fact we know very well from our own experience and from the experience of others. But how can we explain the way in which man can become turned, even in joy, against himself, even to destruction?

Here I propose to follow the account given by Guntrip of Fairbairn's extremely complicated theories (a more extended account appears in *Human Hope and the Death Instinct*).

We begin with the impulse to withdraw from the outer world into an inner world where the outer world has become too terrible because of 'impingement' and a failure of object-relations – as by encountering an indifferent mother or a mother who cannot 'be' for her child, reciprocate his love, or 'reflect' him. However, as he tries to withdraw, he fears loss of all objects, and if this happened, as Guntrip says, 'presumably the infant would die'. From the beginning, according to Fairbairn, there is a 'pristine unitary ego', but as it discovers this predicament it 'splits' in two. Part of the human self in embryo is directed at dealing with the outer world and part withdraws into the inner mental world.

This seems easily acceptable as a picture of divided energy. But, here again, things become complicated by the fact that a human being cannot exist without objects. The split-off 'part' of the self left to deal with the outer world does not involve the real self. It is merely a 'screen of front-line troops', to use an analogy from Guntrip, and it is con- formist: it simply responds in a reactive way to the meaningless bustling activity of 'impingement'. It is Freud's 'reality-ego', Fairbairn's 'central ego' and Winnicott's 'False Self' – a kind of 'caretaker', often concerned simply to keep things going until the self can be more fundamentally realised. It can never realise the True Self or integrate the whole individual.

But this leaves the True Self, which is in touch with the area of 'being' within, however unfostered, without an 'object' – and this is intolerable. As Guntrip says;

'Psychic reality', instead of registering the active function of dealing with the outer world, becomes a 'place' to live in. As Melanie Klein has shown, the infant internalises his objects and builds up an inner world of object-relations.' Fairbairn regards the infant as internalising his unsatisfying objects in an effort to master them in inner reality because he cannot master them in the outer world. In the result, however, they are felt to be as powerful and terrifying in inner reality as in outer. . . . (Guntrip [27], p. 71.)

These internalisations feel as if they are part of the very structure of the self. The infant can only become himself by taking others into himself and building up a structure based on remembering and experiencing. Now he finds that he must take aspects of others into himself in order to construct a self capable of living. His split-off inward self must have an 'object': yet this object consists of all he can take into himself from the outer world – bad experiences. As Guntrip says, 'a serious predicament has arisen'.

No further retreat seems possible. So a fresh series of manoeuvres are made with the purpose of staying in existence as a person in the face of impossible odds. The mother (or object) has proved unsatisfying, so, according to Fairbairn, she is divided into three aspects within: libidinally exciting, libidinally rejecting, and emotionally neutral – good and undisturbing. This last internalised aspect is, of course, magic in the sense that it represents all that the object is desired to be. It is thus 'projected' back over the actual mother.

This concept of *projection* is also very important for our consideration of culture. It implies that often what we 'see' in someone to whom we are attached is not the actual person at all but a phantasy which we throw over them. Of course, this raises questions of how we 'see' the nature of another person at all. Inevitably, when we 'see' people we are not simply responding to sense-data coming from their appearance. Our interpretations here are immensely conditioned by our inward 'psychic tissue' and by subjective needs to *see what we want to see there*, or by what we are capable of seeing there – for it is our imaginative interpretation of what our eyes receive which we project back over the world. We may not be able to 'see' the actual individual in himself or herself at all. So, as we know from experience, for instance, if we treat a wife as if she were the mother, we may be actually confusing individuals to a disastrous extent. Or we may treat a wife as if she were part of the mother, or even a (female) aspect of ourselves (which perhaps we hate or fear). Such problems indicate that our capacity to see anything at all, in a human way, depends entirely upon how our own mother has 'reflected' us and has been able to creatively reflect us so that we in turn have been able to see the world creatively, and thus, by imagining what accords closely to what is actually there, to perceive out of our capacity for apperception.

Out of its predicament faced with inadequate outer objects and internalised bad objects, the subject, the ego of the infant faced with not-good-enough mothering, divides into a number of split-off elements, one of which is Fairbairn's 'central ego' or 'conformist false self'. This False Self establishes relationship with the external object – not with the object recognised as real, however, but with a 'screen' over whom the infant has projected the image of *an object he desires to be there in the outer world*. This relationship with a projection may not really be a relationship with another at all, but rather something like a closed circuit. As Guntrip says:

The . . . Ideal object is projected back into the real object and what has all the appearance of an external object-relationship is maintained with it by the central ego, the ordinary ego of everyday living. Nevertheless, it is not properly objective relation, for the object is not fully realistically perceived but only experienced in the light of a partial image projected from inner reality. Thus, once some

measure of schizoid withdrawal has been set up, such contact with the outer world as is maintained is
defective. . . . (Guntrip [27], p. 71.)

Meanwhile the internalised elements of the ego are seeking to relate to those aspects of
the object which have themselves been internalised.

The *exciting object* arouses libidinal needs, and to this element of the object becomes
attached the *libidinal ego*. This is the split-off part of the self which seeks to live vitally and
to fulfil itself. It is, as Guntrip says, 'characterised by ever-active and unsatisfied desires
which come to be felt in *angry and sadistic ways*'. This libidinal ego is felt to be like a *great
hungry mouth* capable of swallowing everyone and everything – and we find this libidinal
ego symbolised in many nursery rhymes and folktales as a wolf or dragon. It feels like a
sadistic mouth directed at an exciting *breast* – that is, part of the object, split-off from
the whole object or person. The 'wolf' who whistles at a woman in the street may be said
to be feeling real by directing a phantasy hunger at a breast or partial object: the wolf-
whistle is thus an expression of the needs of the libidinal ego. The cultural importance of
this will become obvious later.

The other element of the internalised object, however, in Fairbairn's model, was a
rejecting object. The infant, we must realise, has at this stage learnt nothing, and has to
learn to be from the object entirely – despite its own primary needs to fulfil itself. When its
love is rejected it concludes that love is harmful, and that it is in itself 'bad'. It then seems
that in order to live it must become involved in rejection. The infant therefore identifies
with the rejecting elements of the bad mother, and turns these cruel and hostile elements
– the hate he believes to be in her – on himself. There is thus a link between the paranoia
of this 'paranoid–schizoid position' as Melanie Klein called it, and the cruel self-denying
forces within individuals which Freud called the Super-ego, sadistically turned upon the
self. Self-hate is also seen as a desperate strategy of survival. Where the infant cannot find
a benign world, the malignancy he experiences in this world is taken into the self, and he
feels that his life is bound up with directing this very malignancy against his own hunger
to be. As Guntrip says:

> . . . attachment to the rejecting object results in an *anti-libidinal ego* based on identification which
> reproduces the hostility of the rejecting object to libidinal needs. Inevitably the libidinal ego is hated
> and persecuted by the anti-libidinal ego as well as by the rejecting object, so that the infant has now
> become divided against himself. This is easy to recognise in *the contempt and scorn shewn by many patients
> of their own needs to depend for help on other people*. . . . (Guntrip [27], p. 72; my italics.)

Much of this conflict between elements of the self takes place in the inner world: and
this has much cultural relevance. As Guntrip says:

> So long as a continuing phantasy life can be kept going by the libidinal and anti-libidinal egos, the
> ego is kept in being, though cut off from outer reality. At one time the libidinal ego is sadistically
> phantasying the incorporation of its exciting object in inner reality: at another the anti-libidinal ego
> has possessed itself of the sadism and along with the rejecting object phantasies, object phantasies
> crushing or slave-driving the masochistically suffering libidinal ego. According to Fairbairn, internal
> objects are psychic structures just as much as partial egos are. The total psychic self 'impersonates'
> objects to itself in the inner world so as to retain ego-identity in phantasied relations. Though this kind
> of inner life results in states of acute 'persecutory anxiety', the ego is still in being; it has not succumbed
> to depersonalisation after breaking off emotional rapport with objects in real life. This is indeed the
> rationale of the creation and maintenance of the Kleinian internal objects world: it is a defence against
> ego-loss, which shows why it is hard for the patient to give it up. . . . (Guntrip [27], p. 72.)

There is thus a kind of symbolic dramatisation of our inner conflicts which we need to
cling to, and to take part in, in order to feel alive. Yet in this drama the major elements
may be self-defeating, self-hating, anti-human, and false. Yet in our world, as I hope to
show, it is these which are at a premium in our culture at large.

CHAPTER 4

The Lure of False Solutions

How do we apply these insights into our intrapsychic life to cultural criticism?

First it is important to note that, from this point of view 'the problem of life', is not seen as a conflict between 'emotion' and 'reason', or 'instinct' and 'civilisation', but a question of what may or may not have been fostered by an adequate environment between what can be found and fostered of the True Self and what can be grown, integrated, and realised by an individual rooted in his True Self. In these processes, since they have to do with the question What is it to be human?, culture is primary and is inevitably related to 'living ethics', or the search to discover 'what it is one really wants' – a quest one cannot make alone, however.

Here, I believe, we shall come to see the importance of Winnicott's way of putting things: 'we take for granted a great deal that had a beginning and a condition out of which it developed.' Where things go wrong with human beings, it is because remarkable and subtle processes have failed to complete themselves. If we look at behaviour in terms of 'reason' controlling 'instinct' we are thinking too mechanically about behaviour as if it were a quantitative opposition between conflicting 'pressures'. What we are failing to see is that our choices and actions are a meaningful activity which manifest the whole quality of the patterns in what Bowlby calls our 'psychic tissue'. That is, we behave morally, for instance, because we have created civilisation within ourselves in our life-experience. Of course, our attitudes and behaviour are modified by laws, moral codes, and intelligence. But, primarily, morality is bound up with psychic health. And when we discuss psychic health from the point of view of someone like Winnicott, we find that he says that the 'wicked' are 'ill', while if we look carefully at wickedness we shall see that there can be 'hope' locked up in it. That is, we can see in wickedness too the symbolism of 'strategies of survival' – ways of feeling real, in those who cannot feel real by any other way, or with any confidence by positive ways. And, as we shall see, we shall find ourselves talking about 'True' and 'False' Self, and strength and weakness of identity rather than 'instinct' and 'intellect' or 'reason'.

The problem of life now appears not as one of 'controlling the self', but of developing the capacity to *be* and to *do* from the centre of the True Self in a continual wrestle with experience. The 'control' which some seem to consider so desirable, by this point of view, would rather seem to reveal absence of maturity. Where 'control' is necessary it might perhaps mark some false relationship between inner and outer experience, impelled by some manifestation of the False Self. 'Control' might mark the attempt to subdue or sustain by artificial activity some aspect of the identity which had remained immature, undeveloped, or ungrown, where a healthy moral sense was absent. In social terms mere 'control' may only induce mere conformity by coercion, with consequent forfeiture of potentialities.

As the reader will by now have recognised, there is implicit, in the point of view I am adopting, a 'prior value judgement' concerning 'the sort of people we admire' – an ideal personality, which is in touch with the True Self. But certainly this view suggests a more hopeful attitude to human potentialities, for obviously if what makes us human and 'good' is being in touch with our True Selves, then we can begin to explore possible ways of enabling individuals to establish this kind of touch.

Such a hopeful view does not, of course, deny that energies of an intensely destructive kind come from human beings: no one in our century could deny the reality of human hate. But, as we shall see, the approach to the problem of human nature based on identity, from the 'schizoid diagnosis', enables us to see hate as a form of False Self solution to the need to feel real. In the individual who feels disastrously empty, hollow, or unreal, the strategy of survival may take the form of intense and ungovernable violence. Thus although there is no death instinct there *is* a pathological death impulse. A patient of Guntrip's said: 'If I was man enough to do it, I'd kill myself.' Guntrip comments: 'as if self-destruction at least would prove that you did have a self to destroy and a self strong enough to do it.'*

Here there are many social and political implications, for in disturbed times, violent individuals tend to predominate over moderates because violence deludes people at large into a feeling of strength. But such strength, like that of the Nazis or the Ku Klux Klan, is seen in the light of the 'schizoid diagnosis' as a manifestation of profound psychic weakness of a collective kind. As Guntrip has said: 'Only the strong can love. It is the weak who hate.'

Turning from theories of human nature to cultural problems, I believe we can see how we can apply these insights. Professor G. H. Bantock has said of the *avant garde* writers in America: 'they prefer passion and the exploitation of crude behaviour to the examination of moral sensibility.' If we follow the advocacy of a Susan Sontag, we may 'prefer passion' to what Bantock calls 'moral sensibility', and this may seem like a liberating revolution. But from the point of view of psychoanalytical insights into ego-weakness and the sources of ego-strength, a more valid objection to the 'violent' writer is that his work represents a form of 'pseudo-male-doing' or False Self activity, i.e. hate. The analogy is with schizoid patients who need to think bad thoughts continually to feel that they still exist. The objection is not to 'passion', which implies deep feeling, but to a hollow posture of falsified False Self assertion, out of touch with True Self feeling (and passion) altogether, and a preference for the anti-human to the human.

An *avant garde* writer who tells us man is 'really an animal' may be a schizoid individual who needs to rely upon 'thinking bad thoughts' as a 'strategy of survival' or upon exerting with all his energy an attitude to man which is impelled by negative and destructive hate. He may also need to attack his audience – in order to feel real himself – at their expense. In this he may proclaim himself a 'martyr to truth', whereas in fact he is really denying his own humanity while seeking to assault the humanity of his audience. Here we need to trace very carefully the origins of our capacities to deal with others from the point of view I have outlined, which sees hate as arising from certain essential failures of relationship and of intra-psychic processes of maturation.

Looking at the problem of culture as a historical and social problem, I believe we can

* From a private communication.

say that at certain times severe existential frustration can prompt an increase in the symbolism of false solutions to such an extent that cycles of hate are set off which may overwhelm true creative solutions and reduce humanness at large.

I believe we can say that the violence, sadism, depersonalisation of sex, and other extreme elements in the various spheres of our culture today are to be seen as manifestations of extreme ontological insecurity – defences against fear of ego-loss, through failure of human contact. Lacking I–Thou experience, and confirmation of identity in a truly confirming human community, we turn to a culture which draws its phantasy material from primitive internal conflict. Or, to put it another way, it has been found by commercial organisations that they can successfully exploit this kind of 'bad' phantasy in a world in which there is a deficiency of creative sources of meaning, belonging to the realm of being and relationship. They purvey 'bad thinking' as a manic source of feeling alive and real. The problem is neatly symbolised for me by a film poster reproduced on the title-page of this part (Fig. 1, p. 11).

The woman as '[partial] object to be consumed' is shown gnawing her fingers in a childish way, as if seeking satisfaction – so, the picture implies, she wants to eat and be eaten. The finger in the mouth is perhaps also a sexual symbol of a penis in the vagina. We want to take her, as an object for our consumption: 'sexual libido becomes rampant'. Yet the implication of the fact that her body is a column of atomic smoke is that possession of her would mean utter annihilation (destruction of the object – and with the object, the whole world). What is symbolised is a 'final release'. The bomb-column is the destructive penis. The ultimate way to feel real is by cataclysmic 'taking' and thrusting badness into the world, consuming by ultimate hate. Of course, our response to the poster belongs to 'mentality': the effect of the poster is that we may feel 'strong' by 'bad thinking'. But there are deep effects on our unconscious phantasy.

This poster is a characteristic hate image: its incidental implications, about sexual relationship and about atomic explosion (to which we are here to be jokingly callous), are profoundly immoral and belong to the schizoid inversions – 'Evil be thou my good' and 'may as well give ourselves up to the joys of hating' (see below, p. 52). But yet the image fascinates us because such a pictogram makes us feel Big and Bad – and so, real – alive, at least. The incidental contribution made to the 'taboo on weakness' is a small but subtle influence which encourages us to reduce our humanity just a little, in the pretence that 'If we are bad at least we are Someone'. And, by implication, to feel really real we need to be less human:* the way to deal with a dangerous world is to be an aggressive thruster and taker. This escape from our own weakness is, of course, endorsed by Sartre, and other modern 'revolutionaries'.

The ethical crux of this problem has been analysed thus by R. D. Money-Kyrle:

> . . . deep in the unconscious, the ultimate source of anxiety is our own aggression, especially aggressive greed, which, however, may seem to threaten us, either from within or without, like a foreign force . . . as a defence against the resulting unconscious intensification of the fear of death, the aggressive component in the ego's will to live may be increased to such a degree that every external object tends to be *unconsciously consumed or as a threat to be destroyed.* (Money-Kyrle [44], p. 110.)

---

* Robert Lowell sees this anti-human element in our symbolism in *For The Union Dead*:
   The ditch is nearer.
   There are no statues for the last war here;
   on Boylston Street, a commercial photograph
   shows Hiroshima boiling
   over a Mosler Safe, the 'Rock of Ages'
   that survived the blast.

These elements are symbolised in the pictogram. Our recognition that the schizoid problems underlying such symbolism are universal, however, must not be accepted as a vindication of an amoral or demoralised position: as if it were true that *tout comprendre c'est tout pardonner*. Insights into the schizoid problem rather lead us to a deeper and more complex – one hopes, a more subtle – ethic. The essential question now becomes: To what degree can we afford to allow any one to live at the expense of others, however great his own need to feel real by hate?

The social and personal dangers are evident from the account given by Guntrip above. Where this kind of conflicting and violent inner phantasy life is found in individuals, it is a defence measure against ego-loss because such individuals have withdrawn into themselves and are out of touch with the world. But their violent phantasy life does nothing to help them to find their way back to the world nor to discover their own potentialities, their True Self, or essential meaning. It is rather a *huis clos*. The strategy of survival, though it is only a defensive manoeuvre, becomes *difficult to give up*, and in so far as it has any effect on their relationship with the outer world, this takes the form of 'persecutory anxiety'. The effect of the exploitation of violence in culture, therefore, may well be to increase persecutory anxiety, fortify defensive manoeuvres, deepen isolation, and to make it more difficult for individuals to discover their human reality and that of those with whom they come into contact. (What real woman can compete with a phantasy amalgam of Brigitte Bardot and a hydrogen bomb?)

We have seen how in infancy compulsive mental activity can become a way to survive when impingement and the failure of mothering leaves an infant without inner security. This intellectual activity can obviously be related to need discussed above to preserve an inward world of 'bad' phantasy and bad objects. Guntrip gives accounts of patients for whom 'bad thinking' was a guarantee against 'emptiness'. Guntrip speaks of 'obsessional thinking':

> It is a defence against the feelings of ego-loss. This patient said, 'I have to have my mind full of problems to worry about so as not to feel empty. It's not really the problems, it's the "feeling empty" that is the trouble.' Thinking of bad things can, in the emergency of a panic and in a short-term sense, be an even more powerful method of retaining the feeling of reality and being in touch, than thinking of good things. (Guntrip [27], p. 227.)

In our culture, I believe, we can see the 'thinking of bad things' prevalent in our periodicals, 'extremist' writing, television violence, sex in film, novel and advertising, the 'frank' talk of 'enlightened' individuals, homunculist theories such as 'naked apery', and the proselytising cant of pseudo-sexual 'revolutionaries', as belonging to a massive manifestation of a prevalent fear of ego-loss and meaninglessness in existence. All these forms of 'bustling' hide us from the stillness in which we can be in touch with being. This activity of 'thinking bad thoughts' prevents us from being 'confronted with the problem of existence.' Where we find such forms of 'bad thinking' prevalent in culture and the intellectual world, we can perhaps diagnose a state in which individuals, though they claim to be more 'realistic 'or 'free', are in fact showing that they dare not confront essential human needs. Instead, they have taken to false solutions to existential insecurity. Their symbolism which emanates from self-hate and a larger-than-life 'badness' is thus not a manifestation of strength or 'martyrdom to truth' but of a fear and hatred of being human, belonging to flight from the realities of our being to 'distraction from distraction by distraction'.

This hate syndrome in our culture may be associated with Guntrip's observation that there is in our society a 'taboo on weakness'. As we have seen, the essential problem in each of us is the dissociation of our female element – that area of the deepest inward self of 'being' where our capacity to feel I AM was established by the mother's 'primary maternal preoccupation'. Since no mother was perfect, everyone has, in this area, a residue of existential hunger – which is the source of all spiritual yearning, the True Self yearning to become fulfilled. This area of being is that of Fairbairn's libidinal ego, the hungry life-seeking self. Yet, also inevitably, by the processes of splitting and division which he explores, everyone's libidinal ego remains hungry and in conflict with other aspects of the self in consequence.

This unfulfilled infant hunger in us, the vulnerable 'female element' of 'being', though it is the source of all our potentialities, is yet hated, because it is felt to be so vulnerable, and it is hated with all the force of the anti-libidinal ego. This energy within us, together with all our structure of 'bad objects' and ego-structures within, would prefer that we substitute this essential anti-human conflict for the discovery of the True Self. That is, in so far as we devise a False Self, to deal with the world on the basis of hate, part of us has a tremendous attachment to an internal structure, every element of which strives to deny that we are human with weak human needs.

As Guntrip says:

> Cultural attitudes drive [us] to feel ashamed of weakness and to simulate strength. Ian Suttie, many years ago now, spoke of the 'taboo on tenderness' in our culture. But the matter goes deeper. The reason why there is a taboo on tenderness is that tenderness is regarded as weakness in all but the most private relations of life, many people regard it as weakness even there and introduce patterns of domination into love-life itself. The real taboo is on weakness; the one great crime is to be weak: the thing to which none dare confess is feeling weak, however much the real weakness was brought into being when they were so young that they know nothing of the import of what was happening to them. You cannot afford to be weak in a competitive world which you feel is mostly hostile to you, and if anyone is so unfortunate as to discover that his infancy has left him with too great a measure of arrested emotional development and a failure of ego-growth in the important early stages, then he soon learns to bend all his energies to hiding or mastering the infant within. (Guntrip [27], p. 178.)

Below we shall see why the 'James Bond' cult is, or was for a time, the myth of our acquisitive society and a source of false strength for millions by which they could phantasy a strength in themselves based on this anti-libidinal denial of weakness.

We have discussed some of the aspects of the *schizoid* problems of the primary development of an identity. To these we need to add some of the complications which arise at what Melanie Klein called 'the depressive position' – and what Winnicott called the 'stage of concern'. Melanie Klein's term refers to the internalised structure of the individual's make-up – and by this term she implies that from this particular stage in growth arise depressive illnesses.

Winnicott's term 'stage of concern' is, however, a more positive one, and it draws attention to the fact that only after a certain stage does the individual become capable of feeling concern for others. He can only feel this once he becomes capable of saying 'I AM' and recognising the difference between the *me* and the *not-me*. At first there is no clear sense of the difference between phantasy and reality, and between the self and others: at this stage the severest existence problems originate. Once the schizoid problems have been solved, however, there emerge the depressive ones which are associated with the growth of a sense of separateness. Schizoid anxiety centres round the fear that one's love may be likely to hurt others. Depressive anxiety has to do with the problem of the effect one's hate is likely to have on others.

In Melanie Klein's view this arises out of the intense need of the child to become a self through incorporation. The hunger of the libidinal ego seems likely to incorporate the object: as the child becomes increasingly aware of the continuing existence of itself and the mother, it develops a constructive urge to 'fill in' and restore the potential damage its phantasies of incorporation may have caused to the object. This is the source of 'creative reparation' – of the satisfactions found in creative symbolism and the source of a healthy moral sense. As Guntrip says:

> The stage of concern . . . may not be reached at all by the infantile ego that is too profoundly disturbed and remains stuck in a paranoid-schizoid state, a state of sheer fear of the outside world and drastic withdrawal from it. A return to object-relations can then *only* be made in the form of a paranoid fear and suspicion of all objects. But lesser degrees of disturbance permit a weakened ego to move on to a capacity to feel 'concern' for objects and to experience anxiety and depression at the possibility of harming or losing or destroying them. But the 'concern' for others felt by a weakened ego is not a fully healthy objective concern arising out of the worth and the interests of the object. . . . It takes a strongly developed ego to love disinterestedly and care for another person basically for that person's sake. (Guntrip [27], p. 170.)

This indicates that our discovery of the 'other' is inevitably painful – and involves recognising all the fears of dangers inherent in our love and hate. To learn to care basically for another person, for that person's sake, involves us in a recognition of our own ambivalence, the mixture of love and hate in us, our own weakness and potential destructiveness.

Out of these problems arise the most perplexing human problems of all. For if we take the normal paths of developing as a human being, through the give-and-take of love, there is inevitable pain, the pain of concern, depressive pain, arising from fear and anxiety about the consequences of our own hate: also at the same time our fear of our 'female' vulnerability threatens our survival. Although our deepest satisfactions and our potentialities for maturity lie the other side of such pain, because in our earliest years it has been associated with the deepest schizoid fears of loss of identity, we will often take any false path rather than experience this pain again, and the recognition of those weaknesses which belong to the primary processes of identity. Yet the pains of 'concern', in our recognition of the existence of others and our concern for the effects of our hate on them, are the very basis of all civilised human life. On the other hand, the desperate satisfactions of 'false doing', 'bad thinking', and hate are also defence mechanisms against the deeper pain of fear of going out of existence altogether. Our choice is to 'be redeemed from fire by fire': our predicament is to be 'consumed by either fire or fire'. But hate only *seems* to be a way out of this dilemma.

CHAPTER 5

What is Hate?

To HELP us with later detailed analysis of cultural works it will be valuable to ponder further the nature of hate. As we have seen, from the object-relations point of view, hate does not emerge from any primary 'animal' aggression, id-impulses, or a 'death instinct' – but from frustrated love and the inevitable imperfections of our formative environment. It is a manifestation of the need to survive, and yet may be directed against the need to survive itself, as manifest in the libidinal ego. It can thus be both a life-seeking and an anti-human force; hence its lures and its tenacity. It is worth considering this fact in a world in which there are so many arguments put forward in favour of the free expression of hate because it is a 'natural' expression of our 'real' bestiality.

The discovery of 'concern' for others, or ruth, is at one with our growth to human maturity, and to a natural moral sense on which civilisation can be based. Ruth is a positive and normal achievement, and its pains are the normal anxieties and guilts of being human. If we are without the guilt and pain of ruth, we may be in a less-than-human state. As Winnicott says:

> . . . No one can be ruthless after the concern stage except in a dissociated state. But ruthless dissociation states are common in early childhood, and emerge in certain types of delinquency and madness, and must be available in health. The normal child enjoys a ruthless relation to his mother, mostly showing in play, and he needs his mother because only she can be expected to tolerate his ruthless relation to her even in play, because this really hurts her and wears her out, without this play with her he can only hide a ruthless self and give it life in a state of dissociation.
>
> I can bring in here the great fear of disintegration as opposed to the simple acceptance of primary unintegration. Once the individual has reached the stage of concern he cannot be oblivious to the result of his impulses, or to the action of bits of self such as biting mouth, stabbing eyes, piercing yells, sucking throat, etc. etc. Disintegration means abandonment of the whole person-object to his impulses, uncontrolled because acting on their own; and further this conjures up the idea of similarly uncontrolled (because dissociated) impulses directed towards himself. (Winnicott [53], pp. 154–5.)

From such a discussion we see that the gradual discovery of the reality of one's incorporative impulses, and the reality of those at whom they are directed, helps to overcome the deep terror we have of the possible effects of such urges and the phantasies which accompany these and consequent fears. At the same time it is possible always to be driven back, or to relapse, into persecutory anxiety, and to ruthlessness.

When primitive anxieties are aroused in us, we are therefore thrust back to our deepest fears, with their roots in bodily feelings, that we shall swallow our world, or be swallowed. The exploitation of cultural trust can arouse such fears while reducing at the same time our capacities for ego-maintenance, and holding the identity together against the threat of annihilation. Guntrip, quoting the passage from Winnicott above, refers to a number of patients who expressed a horror of disintegration in various forms of oral-sadistic imagery. Guntrip says: 'This psychotic terror . . . arises as a result of fears, both of impingement and retaliation by the object of the oral libidinal ego with its biting and devouring needs' (Guntrip [26], p. 404).

In the baby this has been experienced as a 'cannibalistic ruthless attack . . . which partly is a matter of the infant's own imaginative elaboration of the physical function'. So, we can all say, 'I was ruthless then'. Winnicott adds the problem that even an adequate feed can leave the baby not only satisfied physically, but also cheated: 'often distress follows . . . if physical satisfaction too quickly robs the infant of zest. The infant is then left with (1) aggression undischarged . . . (2) a sense of 'flop', since a source of zest for life has gone suddenly.' (Winnicott [53], p. 268).

Guntrip seeks to distinguish between normal satisfactions between mother and infant and what happens when there is failure:

> . . . it seems necessary to distinguish between 'excitement' as normal and pleasurable energetic loving which is capable of leading on to a feeling of concern for the mother who is thus vigorously loved, and 'aggression' as the result of lack of satisfaction and frustration, which leads on to a morbid fear of destroying the love-object; from this arises the schizoid fear of destroying by love and later the depressive fear of destroying by hate. This could give a basis for the distinction Winnicott makes between healthy and morbid guilt. (Guntrip [26], p. 406.)

The 'fear of destroying by hate' – recognition of the problem of one's own hate – thus belongs to a normal development.

> What [Winnicott] describes is the gradual dawning on the infant of the fact that, in getting his needs met, he takes something out of the mother's body and from the mother as a person. In the absence of anger and aggression, a *concern* for the mother develops as a vital part of the process of true maturing, and it leads to the perception of the reality of both 'give and take' in a loving relationship. One does not exhaust one's love-object because it is possible to contribute as well as to get. *Fairbairn regards the process of maturing as a progress from taking to giving.* (Guntrip [26], p. 406.)

In object-relations psychology, as we can see, a process of maturation is implicit. What we call love and hate in the adult world are seen to have origins in the primitive need to survive. Love, however, is capable of growth by the discovery of the reality of the self and the object of our love, of the problems of give-and-take and of ambivalence – that is, the mixture of love and hate in human nature. It leads towards the capacity to give and meet in relation. It leads towards equality. Hate, however, is seen from this point of view as a particular form of 'strategy of survival'. It is not the opposite of love, which would be indifference. Indifference would manifest our lack of need for the object. Where there is hate there is obviously an *excessive need* for the object. Hate is thus seen as a manifestation of ego-weakness and immaturity, of over-dependence, and of unsatisfied hunger for sustenance – ultimately hunger for sustenance for the identity. It leads towards exploitation. Because it belongs to 'taking', hate inevitably involves the depletion of others and so to ethical problems. Ethical shortcomings in man can thus be seen as consequences of a failure to achieve maturity, or of the stalemate which results from the internal directing of hate at the libidinal ego. Hate belongs to false solutions, the desperate strategies of the False Self, however heroic: our primary libidinal goal is the realisation of the True Self by love.

If we accept the theories of Fairbairn, the human individual has a 'Pristine unitary ego' from the start, which is whole, however primitive. From the first, 'love' is the infant's quest for the satisfaction of needs from the mother. This love will, of course, be experienced by the child's ego which at is one with intensely oral feelings when the world is experienced largely in terms of hunger and satisfaction. Henceforth forever human love is experienced in ways which derive their meaning and symbolism from deep bodily and emotional feelings at the time when 'the child's ego is a mouth ego' and the issue is survival.

From later explorations of the schizoid problem, and from Melanie Klein's investigations of the bodily sources of unconscious symbolism and phantasy, it would seem that what we are grappling with here are metaphorical ways of expressing primitive problems of identity – while the only way in which we can express them is in mouth-ego terms, or terms of bodily ingestion, from which symbols naturally arise. The first impulse to survive feels as if the self were all one hungry mouth, directed at taking the world into oneself – incorporating 'the object'. Having learnt ruth – having been through the anxiety and concern of fearing the consequences to the object of our hunger – we feel that this first 'ruthless love' must be cruel; though Winnicott also tries to suggest that cruelty is not relevant to our consideration of the very young baby, for 'whatever he does is not done in hate'. But the first *urge to survive* is felt as a voracious impulse to *ingest* by mouth-self. As we shall see, this is of fundamental cultural importance, and pervades all symbolism.

Though there are differences between the views of Winnicott and Guntrip about the origins of the infant's first libidinal hunger, both agree that *'primitive love can operate destructively'*. As Guntrip says: 'Out of this schizoid problem of libidinal needs operating destructively arises the internal situation which creates terrors of disintegration'. (Guntrip [26]).

We can put this in another way by saying that the first problem of identity is that our urge to survive by incorporation feels so voracious that it threatens to eat up the world and ourselves with it. This fear is the subject of many nursery rhymes and fairy stories, such as *Little Red Riding Hood* (see below, p. 51). But this is a problem of love – that primitive love which has yet to find an adequate sense of reality, and to modify its vulpine single-mindedness. These human qualities are found and grow through experience of the real human mother, where she can 'be' for her child: the capacity to overcome the first primitive ruthless hate comes through the maturational processes.*

Where there is failure between the processes of maturation and the environment, the individual suffers from what must be seen, from Fairbairnian point of view, as an *intolerance of his own immaturity*:

> How do fear and hate come to be permanently embodied in the personality? ... an inadequate environment, and particularly an inadequate mother, exposes the infant to steadily increasing awareness of his smallness, weakness, and helplessness. He will be what Winnicott calls 'a collection of reactions to impingement'. But somewhere in the midst of that chaos, the psyche, the basic subject of experience, who is a potentially whole self and owns these reactions, is unable to grow a secure sense of his wholeness, but can feel acute states of fear. . . . Gradually the child must grow to feel, if he could put it into words, that it is too frightening to be weak in an unfriendly and menacing world, and also that one cannot afford to have needs that one cannot get satisfied. As he grows steadily out of earliest infancy and becomes more acquainted with his outer world he must realise that such needs make one dependent, and if you cannot change your world, you can try to change yourself. Thus he comes to fear and hate his own weakness and neediness: and he now faces the task of growing up with an intolerance of his own immaturity. (Guntrip [27], p. 186.)

Hate then emerges from *weakness* and it is in this light it will be examined in the present

---

* Occasionally we see, with horror, what happens when the processes fail to complete themselves, as with the child-murderer, or the child who is a murderer. There are special circumstances when people seem capable of reverting to primitive ruthlessness, e.g. in battle, as air-raid pilots, when surprised in criminal acts, or in domestic violence of a psychopathological kind, such as the 'battered baby syndrome'.

work. These insights are further illuminated by Balint's essay on hate to which I have already referred. Balint believes that only love is capable of growth: 'there is both a mature and a primitive form of love, whereas anxiety (and to some extent hate) exist only in primitive forms.' (Balint [1], p. 123.)

He stresses the '*weakness of the ego* in the infantile form of love', and this is obvious from what we have seen from Fairbairn, Winnicott, and Guntrip above. Obviously, where the identity feels insecure and is desperate to survive, total demands of a voracious kind are made. The environment, it is felt, *must* provide the confirmation and sustenance that is so desperately needed. Where such needs are intense, no real environment can ever satisfy such demands. In normal maturity, as ego-strength builds up, so love can become both independent, and able to accept dependence upon the (ambivalent) object without either fear of going to pieces, or fear of destroying the object from excessive need.

Where love is infantile, 'Because of this weakness the individual is unable to bear any serious frustration and has to mobilize all sorts of defensive mechanisms against it, especially anxiety. But, if we accept this, should hate be considered also as a mechanism of defence?' (Balint [1], p. 123.)

This kind of defence mechanism against frustrations Balint links with 'strong . . . sadistic tendencies' . . . 'as the result of which no safe fusion with libidinal tendencies develops'. Here we touch on the fear of love in an individual of weak identity, and the consequent sadism in him. He is only safe when he is hating: and one form of this hating is linked with splitting:

> Such people can only have ambivalent relations to their objects, their love being easily smothered by their destructive ideas or their sadism. Another attempt also based on the idea of strong sadistic tendencies answers our question by stressing the importance of splitting processes both in the mind and (especially) in regard to objects. The love-objects of such people are easily split and/or changed from extremely good to extremely bad; these latter are then pictured as indifferent, heartless, hateful and cruel, or in one and, persecutory, giving rise in the individual to feelings of hatred and anxiety in place of love. (Balint [1], p. 123.)

We are beginning to see connections which will appear increasingly significant between various hate mechanisms: ego-weakness, the inability to accept others as they are; defensive mechanisms against frustration which cannot be borne; splitting, sadism and paranoia.

The essay by Balint from which these theories develop begins with a discussion of the case of a woman who idealised the visit of some friends to a new home she had established: when the visit became a reality the actual independent reality of these friends could not be tolerated. A blissful 'angel-winged' expectation that 'this time she will be really loved and she will be able to love *safely*' because of an inability to *come to terms with reality*, turns to hate. She had no sense of the reality of these people, but projected over them an ideal object: later, of course, truth will out, and so her pure love turns to pure hate. Hate is thus related to an inability to accept others and oneself as they really are – a pattern we shall find relevant in culture.

Balint adds further concomitants to the complex patterns of hate. He relates the inability to maintain loving relationships for any length of time to 'strong narcissistic tendencies'. And he combines with this an explanation of the inability of such an individual to love in terms of their incapacity to 'bear "normal" inevitable depressions'. 'Such an individual cannot accept as unavoidable even the slightest amount of frustration by reality; and must resort to hatred and anxiety, whereas a normal individual, although aggrieved within reason, can bear it'. (Balint [1], p. 123.)

This observation, I believe, we shall also find of considerable cultural significance. A truly creative culture is one which can 'bear' the 'normal frustrations of reality' – and the pains of recognising ourselves as human (ambivalent, weak, mortal). The appeal of the kind of false culture with which I am dealing with in this work is that it '*must resort to hate and anxiety*' because it 'cannot bear even the slightest amount of frustration by reality' – i.e. it is a culture of *flight from life*.

Balint indicates some oral-sadistic elements in hate which, as we shall see, confirm observations made by Fairbairn. He refers to the connection between hate and oral greed. But he believes that such greed is essentially a manifestation that 'the object and the gratification are all-important' while 'hardly any allowance can be made in their respect': '*The object is indeed only an object*, and must be treated as such, i.e. no consideration or regard can be paid to its interests, sensitivities, or well-being; it must be, and in fact is, simply taken for granted' (Balint [1], pp. 124–5).

What Balint is surely referring to here is the tendency in the individual who has substituted hate for love to have such *absolute dependence* on the object that it becomes depersonalised, a partial object, to be taken from only, and treated with contempt. 'Our attitude is simple: we need it, and therefore it must be there for us all the time.'

This attitude is, of course, a prevalent 'hate attitude' found in the symbolism of our culture at large – as, for instance, in common attitudes to woman (as a dish, dollie, bird, bunny, crumpet, etc.). The psychoanalytical view has, I believe, established that such an approach is fundamentally a manifestation of over-dependence and weakness rather that what it seems to offer itself as – a show of strength. This 'sucking' attitude to sex is a desperate way of feeling real necessary to the individual of weak identity.

One further valuable point about the patterns of hate made by Balint is that of the presence of what has been called 'omnipotence' or 'infantile omnipotence'. This has meant a certain kind of feeling in the infant that he can control the world by magic. Balint usefully points out that:

> In fact 'omnipotence' never means a real feeling of power; on the contrary, a desperate and very precarious attempt at overcoming a feeling of helplessness and impotence. We call such an attempt 'omnipotence' if the following conditions are present: (a) certain objects and satisfactions can be taken for granted; (b) no regard or consideration need be paid to the object, the object can be treated as a mere object, a thing; (c) there is a feeling of extreme dependence, the object and the satisfaction by it are all important. (Balint [1], p. 125.)

The importance of these attitudes will become apparent when we explore the symbolism in the work of Ian Fleming. The 'omnipotence' of his hero in the face of his adversary, for instance, can be seen essentially as symbolising a 'desperate and very precarious attempt at overcoming a feeling of helplessness and impotence'. This predicament was probably that of Fleming himself, whose attitude to women (for example) was that of taking them 'for granted', treating them as 'things' 'which must be there for us all the time' – an attitude revealing 'extreme dependence'. As Balint goes on to say, 'primitive' object-relations tend to take a form in which '*only one partner is entitled to make demands*' – a form of immature relationship, belonging to the syndrome of hate, which has been elevated in our culture, by the symbolism of writers like Fleming and Kingsley Amis (his admirer) to a norm or even a positive value. We can also apply these mechanisms to that element of the exhibition of perversions which is a staple of our *avant-garde* literature and other art forms: both the perversion and its exhibition are both ways of avoiding 'emotional surrender' and yet of manifesting extreme dependence.

Evaluative concepts are thus emerging from psychoanalytical thought by which the modes of hate are seen to belong to ego-weakness, immaturity, dissociation, and false solution, while the ways of love are seen to belong to natural processes of integration towards maturity, strength of identity and realisation of the True Self.

In so far as our world itself is one which has become dehumanised, and dwarfs us so that we find it hard to discover our unique humanness, and a world in which the 'being' experience has become minimised, its effect upon all of us is to inhibit our realisation of our true selves, and encourage us to assert our sense of identity by 'false male doing'. We thus all share the predicament of the schizoid individual. But such a person especially may be able only to feel real at all in so far as he can maintain an activity of intellectual hate and the 'false male doing' of 'bad thinking'. His first voracious hungers having never been met, they may remain unmodified as by the acceptance of the 'give and take' of love – so they remain in the form of primitive hate, in a 'taking' attitude to the world, together with an inability to accept ambivalence in himself and others. His world becomes divided in consequence between 'objects to be consumed and enemies to be attacked'. There is no progress towards reality, towards, the acceptance of being weak, ambivalent and human. There is no essential 'conquest' as Balint calls it:

> The basis of all such pregenital or primitive object-relations is faulty reality testing, either still un-developed (in infants) or stunted (in adults like my patient). That is why this 'omnipotent' or 'greedy' love is unstable, doomed to meet with frustration and to lead on to hate. In order to change to a more mature relation we need much more reliable reality testing. We have to realize that our needs have become too varied, complicated, and specialized, so that we can no longer expect automatic satisfac-tion from our objects; we must be able to bear the depression caused by this realization; and we must accept the fact that we have to give something to our object, something that he expects from us, in order to change the object into a *cooperative partner*. The object can no longer be taken for granted, it must be induced to enjoy giving satisfaction to us, i.e. must come to have his or her satisfaction at the same time, in the same *mutual action*. To establish this mutuality, to change a reluctant and uninterested object into a cooperative partner, means both tolerating considerable strains and maintaining a steady and reliable reality testing. I have called this *the work of conquest*. . . . If the work of conquest has been successful, and the subsequent work of preserving is adequate, love and harmony may develop on the basis of mutuality. (Balint [1], pp. 126–7.)

Besides the implicit contrast here between maturity and immaturity there is also an implicit concept of equality. *Equality between persons only becomes possible on the basis of love.* Here there are many important political, ethical, and cultural implications. Where culture is based on hate it inevitably threatens democracy because it undermines mutual-ity. A 'sexual revolution' based on hate, for instance, can never promote essential equality between men and women because it will fail implicitly to recognise their essential mutuality and integrity. An approach to ethics based on hate can never prosper because it will inevitably undermine equality and there will be the attitude 'only one partner *is entitled to make demands*'.

There is a very definite basis for ethical discrimination inherent in Balint's distinction between love and hate. And when we apply these discriminations to our culture we can see its faults quite glaringly. One of these, indeed, is that which so prevalently prevents us from seeing the problem itself. Balint says that as we mature we become able to see that 'we can no longer expect automatic satisfaction from our objects . . . we must be able to bear the depression caused by this realisation . . .'. But this is just what in our prevalent Western ethos we cannot bear and are persuaded that we need not bear. Our environ-ment is so barren of creative opportunities, vital community life is largely absent in it, and it is increasingly dehumanised. In such a situation it is hard to 'bear depression' because there is so little available *symbolic* sustenance at hand by which to work on our inward problems, towards reparation, either in life, work, or culture. There are too few opportunities to give, symbolically, to those for whom we feel human concern or to build up within ourselves a deep sense of inner goodness.*

Meanwhile the whole burden of our economy, our acquisitive system, and its symbolism (as in advertising) encourages us to feel that we *should* expect '*automatic satisfaction from our objects*'. Automatic is the keyword. The efforts of love – of giving and coming to terms with – are everywhere devalued. Prevalent commodity attitudes to sex, for instance, belong essentially to this mode. ('Candy' as the name implies, in *Candy*, is an object providing 'automatic satisfaction'.) It is this that is meant here by saying that our culture is the culture of hate and so delusory. Because in truth our adult needs are 'varied, complicated and specialised we can no longer expect automatic satisfaction'. We cannot, in fact, have automatic satisfaction, but, rather, satisfactions involve the pain of concern. But the masks which the culture of hate wears, from the glamorous images in the mass media to the philosophical arguments of some forms of 'enlightenment' (which recommend pornography and 'release', etc.), imply, falsely, that we *can* have 'automatic satisfactions' *for the taking*, while our sense of identity depends upon easy ingestion. The extremest forms of hate, as we shall see, imply that the preservation of our ego demands that we must exploit others as less than persons. Such delusions cause much of the profound unrest in our civilisation, which expresses the deepest frustrations and 'ontological insecurity'. Our superficial hedonism is essentially based on 'taking', and fails to recognise that our deepest satisfactions, our deepest sense of identity, are to be found in giving, 'finding', and meeting – which are not acquisitive at all but belong to a maturity which has learned to create rather than incorporate, and which wants to be more rather than less human.

There is, as Balint insists, a healthy form of hate, but this kind of hate is potential or incidental, and realistic: 'when a really serious reason for it is present, strong or even vehement emotion should arise and be maintained. But it should be more like acute anger; in contrast to love, hate should easily and speedily dissipate of the situation changes for the better.' (Balint [1], p. 128.)

Love, by contrast, 'ought to be fairly constant, steady, unchanging, almost unshakeable . . . '.

But the kind of hate we are preoccupied with here, that hate which has become a substitute for love, is defined by Balint as 'the last remnant, the denial of, and the defence against, the primitive object-love (or the dependent archaic love)' (Balint [1], p. 128).

This means, he says, that 'we hate people who, though very important to us, do *not* love us and refuse to become our cooperative partner despite our best efforts to win their affection.' 'This stirs up in us all the bitter pains, sufferings and anxieties of the past and we defend ourselves against their return by the *barrier of hatred*, by denying our need for those people and our dependence on them.'

While (as in the 'James Bond' myth) hate may mask itself as super-human, in fact it is a manifestation of a *denial of dependence* – because the ego is too weak to accept the need for others. As Balint says, his theory 'enables us to understand why hate, especially persistent hate, makes us suspect a somewhat immature ego'. (Balint [1], p. 128.)

The intense unconscious hatred of woman expressed so widely in our culture is from this point of view a mark of radical immaturity.

* This theme is explored in *Love, Hate and Reparation* by Melanie Klein and Joan Rivière [39].

Psychoanalysis has always tended, Balint says, to reveal hate as a 'derivative of frustrated love'. Applying this to the hate abroad in our world, from race riots to violence in culture, we may conclude that these indicate weakness of the sense of identity and some universal problem of the frustration of love. By contrast it is the strong who can love – and 'incidentally' hate when they need to in a natural way.

Hate can thus be useful. According to Balint 'incidental hate is a . . . not-too-expensive guardian of our maturity, preventing us from sliding back into the infantile dependence on the affection of our environment'.

But, while those who are strong may hate,* their essential strength is in being able to love. 'Love has no bounds, everybody and everything can be loved that has ever satisfied our needs, or from whom we may expect any satisfaction in the future. . . '. (Balint [1], p. 128.)

Love can extend its scope from the mother to the whole earth. But it is the weak who find their main strength in hate, and in this show their dependence and inability to find human equality. 'Hate has the . . . condition that only people and things on which we depend can be hated. Hate is a measure of inequality between object and subject. . . .'

From Balint's approach we can begin to see how hate is essentially a defence mechanism – *against* growth, *against* reality, *against* being human. From Winnicott and Guntrip we have seen how, in certain circumstances, an individual has to base his very survival on hate. Here we approach the crux of our problem, which is that where his sense of identity is under the threat of annihilation, man is capable of surviving in a fashion by completely inverting the human truths which are recognised in Balint's theory. That is, the human psyche is capable of believing that all those manifestations which Balint recognises as signs of immaturity and weakness are in fact signs of strength. An obvious example, splitting, to the racialist, is a device which must be maintained at all costs as the only means to preserving strength and 'purity' of identity – at the expense of others over whom the split-off hate has been projected. Or to the Marxist it is strong to believe in one's 'correct' purity while the enemy will be an 'incorrect' Marxist, a 'counter-revolutionary' or 'filthy revisionist swine'.

Such splitting, projection, and paranoia seem to be the ultimate consequence of False Self activity, for they are ways of avoiding integration and recognition of one's essential weak mixed humanness. Here we engage with the ethical cultural problem presented by the fact that there seems to be in human life a fundamental choice between following the solutions of the True Self or pursuing the solutions of the False Self, which are the solutions of hate.

We can now, I believe, see the connection between Balint's distinctions between love and hate and Winnicott's distinctions between 'being' and 'doing'. If there is a core of 'being' this enables development to establish the capacity for *concern*, while 'false doing', on the other hand, tends to involve the subjection or victimisation of others and a 'diminution of affect': that is 'loss of feeling tone', or callousness towards others. 'Being' leads towards the discovery of humanness by love; 'false doing' towards hate and the denial of humanness.

We can see that the problems of distinguishing between love and hate, between 'being' and 'doing', and between False Self and True Self are inextricably bound up with the

---

* Balint quotes as an example a conversation between a group of Jews about Hitler. One speaker says that what he would like best as an outcome of the war would be for his friend to say to him, 'That's Adolf Hitler over there', and he could then say, 'So what?' This seems to Balint acceptable 'incidental' hate.

problems of identity and of the meaning of existence. These can also be seen to be bound up with the ethical energy in man, by which he seeks the feelings of 'gratitude' and 'continuity' only to be found by 'reparation': that is, giving creatively sufficiently to feel that the world as object has been made 'good' against the threats of destructiveness and ego-loss within. 'Concern', which is the basis of our capacity for 'living ethics', is the discovery of the reality of others in complex with the discovery of ourselves.

The problem is that, while they are the only real path to deeper joy and satisfactions and to effective dealings with the world and our only way to become fully human, 'creative' solutions involve us in pain and despair – the recognition of our tragic condition.

How different this is from the attitude to culture which is currently fashionable should be evident. There are those in this ethos who are prepared to argue that it is brave to defy our inward needs – and admirable to deny the truth that we are human. Thus, Christopher Ricks, reviewing Kingsley Amis's novel *The Anti-death League*, commends him for his strength in rejecting such positives: 'It is still one of Mr. Amis's strengths that he is so suspicious of that maturity which "comes to terms with life": he is not afraid to being accused of infantility, simple-mindedness, or even superstition' (*New Statesman*, 18 March 1966).

But surely Mr. Amis's novel tends rather to involve the reader in a paranoid phantasy, in which malevolent forces are to 'blame' for the harm in the world – and so is likely to encourage them to believe that the problem of life is not the hate or emptiness in themselves, but something 'out there'? Won't this perhaps make them more likely to deny their responsibility for their own destructiveness, and more likely to project more hate into the world? The choice in cultural expression is necessarily between one solution or the other.

Here, again, the worlds of education and culture at large clash. The teacher believes it is valuable to 'come to terms'; the commercial writer does not. But what is Mr. Christopher Ricks now doing as a Professor of English if he commends as a strength the failure to come to terms? The grave exploration of human truth by philosophical anthropology exposes his endorsement of Amis as an act of *trahison des clercs*. It is this connivance in the hatred of being human which the present work is concerned to resist – as an act itself of 'incidental hate'.

CHAPTER 6

'Evil be Thou my Good'

A MAJOR problem which liberal thought fails to see realistically arises from the fact that many of those who are influential in our culture are schizoid individuals to whom normal ethical considerations are meaningless or irrelevant. We need, therefore, to examine carefully the nature and origins of their predicament so that we can reject their approach to human experience, while seeking some more effective means to defend our culture from their perverse destructiveness. (Moralising is irrelevant because it has no meaning to them.)

In order to understand the strange logic by which values can be inverted by the schizoid individual, we shall find the meticulous analysis of schizoid conditions by Fairbairn of great importance. It will therefore help us to summarise here briefly for the present purpose his important chapter 'Schizoid Factors in the Personality', in *Psychoanalytical Studies of the Personality* [18], although this chapter has already been discussed in detail in a previous work.

From Fairbairn's point of view, as we have seen, the ego has an integrative role, while the libido has an aim which is relationship with the object: 'The individual in his libidinal capacity is not pleasure-seeking but object-seeking'. This approach led him to problems of identity, and so to a special attention to schizoid characteristics.

Schizoid persons, Fairbairn showed, have great psychological insight because they are so introverted and do not have the 'depressive' inhibitions. From them we can learn a great deal about the deeper psychological processes.

When we take into account in this way all those whose character traits are considerably influenced by underlying schizoid factors what Fairbairn calls the 'schizoid group' becomes 'a very large one' and 'includes a high percentage of fanatics, agitators, criminals, revolutionaries', and other kinds of individual who seem unable to find a sense of human identity by normal means. Schizoid characteristics, Fairbairn says, in a less pronounced form, are also common among members of the intelligentsia. 'Thus the disdain of the highbrow for the bourgeoisie and the scorn of the esoteric artist for the philistine may be regarded as minor manifestations of a schizoid nature.'

Fairbairn points out that ' . . . intellectual pursuits as such, whether literary, artistic, scientific or otherwise, appear to exercise, a special attraction for individuals possessing schizoid characteristics to one degree or another'. (Fairbairn [18], p. 6.)

Among the various characteristics of those who come into the schizoid category are these: '(1) an attitude of omnipotence (2) an attitude of isolation and detachment (3) a preoccupation with inner reality.' These may be conscious and overt, but not always, for often they are unconscious and also complicated by compensations and such manifestations. Thus the attitude of omnipotence may be over-compensated and concealed under a superficial attitude of inferiority or humility; and it may be consciously 'cherished as a precious secret'. Similarly, the attitude of isolation and detachment may be masked by a 'façade of sociability' and such false conformities. The most important characteristic is the 'preoccupation with inner reality', and this is, nonetheless, present 'whether inner reality be substituted for outer reality, identified with outer reality or superimposed upon outer reality'.

If Fairbairn's categories are to be accepted, then everyone can be said to be in a sense schizoid – a criticism which he accepts. The problem is the depth of the splitting of the ego. But, as he points out, schizoid tendencies reveal themselves in the most integrated persons under extreme hardship or deprivation ('under conditions of grave illness, or or Arctic exploration, or of exposure in an open boat in mid-Pacific, or of relentless persecution, or of prolonged subjection to the horrors of modern warfare'). But generally it is true to say that, just as Winnicott speaks of us as 'those manic-depressive people whom we call normal', so, by Fairbairn's account, we are *all* to some degree schizoid, while '*the basic position in the psyche is invariably a schizoid position*'. The schizoid individual thus has (and states) our universal existence problems in an acute way: the trouble is that his urge towards false solutions is also more acute.

Fairbairn believes that 'the problems involved in splitting of the ego deserve much more attention than they have so far received', and he sees a connection between splitting and a 'libidinal attitude of oral incorporation', – a problem we have already touched on. Here we may remind ourselves of comments by Melanie Klein on 'some Schizoid Mechanisms': the libidinal urges here referred to as bodily feelings:

> The phantasied onslaughts on the mother follow two main lines: one is the predominantly oral impulse to suck dry, bite up, scoop out and rob the mother's body of its good contents. . . . The other line of attack derives from the anal and urethral impulses, and implies expelling dangerous substances (excrements) out of the self and into the mother. Together with these harmful excrements, expelled in hatred, split-off parts of the ego are also projected on to the mother or, as I rather call it, into the mother. . . . In psychotic disorders this identification of an object with the hated parts of the self contributes to the intensity of the hatred directed against other people. (Klein [35], p. 300.)

I quote this to remind us here that in considering, with Fairbairn, libidinal and splitting aspects of schizoid characteristics, we need to do so with a sense of these not being only philosophical concepts but deep bodily feelings with considerable symbolic qualities in phantasy – which are most relevant to considerations of symbolism and culture. We also encounter here the ethical problems of our relationship with others, since this impulse to *empty others* is fundamental to our living energies and has obviously come to be modified for civilisation to exist.

Moreover, as Guntrip says:

> The schizoid phase has its own characteristic form of aggression. The frustrated hungry infant does not *aim* to destroy the breast but to possess it. He may however . . . in phantasy see himself destroying it in the act of seeking to possess it. . . . One of my schizoid patients woke up in terror one night feeling herself nothing but one big hungry devouring mouth swallowing up everyone and everything. (Guntrip [26], p. 342.)

These 'mouth impulses' represent the 'libidinal orientation' of the schizoid attitude: Fairbairn insists on the need to examine not only the 'incorporative' characteristics deriving from the 'schizoid position' – which have their origins in the 'early oral phase' of Abraham – but the associated problems of splits in the ego and its capacity for object-relations.

> The ego of the infant may be described as above all a 'mouth ego'. . . . So far as the infant is concerned, the mouth is the chief organ of desire, the chief instrument of activity, the chief medium of satisfaction and frustration, the chief channel of love and hate, and, most important of all, the first means of intimate social contact. (Fairbairn [18], p. 10.)

The mother's breast and the infant's mouth are the focal points of his libidinal object and his libidinal attitude. If there is a libidinal fixation in this early oral phase, then the features which characterise this phase persist in an exaggerated form in the individual's attitudes and modes of behaviour throughout his life (as in a 'sucking' attitude to sex, in which the partner is a 'breast' rather than a person).

The nature of the far-reaching effects of 'libidinal fixation in the early oral situation in question' are that 'The libidinal object tends to assume the form of a bodily organ or *partial object* (in contrast to that of a person or whole object).' Also, 'The libidinal attitude is essentially one in which '*taking*' predominates over 'giving', so that 'The libidinal attitude is characterised not only by taking, but also by *incorporating and internalising*,' while 'The libidinal situation is one which confers tremendous significance upon the states of *fullness and emptiness*'.

All these reveal, among other things, that the preoccupation in our culture with the breast and woman-as-breast is a *schizoid* manifestation. What is not realised in 'enlightened' attitudes to such manifestations as pornography are less to be seen as representing a new 'freedom' but rather as existential fear and anxiety about relationship. They are a mark of *deprivation* in the light of Fairbairn's analysis.

> In circumstances of *deprivation* emptiness comes to assume quite special significance for the child. Not only does he feel empty himself, but he also interprets the situation in the sense that he has *emptied his mother* – particularly since deprivation has the effect not only of intensifying his oral need, but also of imparting an aggressive quality to it. Deprivation has the additional effect of enlarging the field of his incorporative need, so that it comes to include not simply the contents of the breast, but also the breast itself, and even his mother as a whole. The anxiety which he experiences over emptying the breast thus gives rise to *anxiety over destroying his libidinal object* . . . the fact that his mother customarily leaves him after suckling must have the effect of contributing to this impression. (Fairbairn [18], pp. 11–12; *my italics* except for the last phrase italicized in the original.)

It is important to note here that to the schizoid individual at this stage, because he 'empties the breast' (and because his mother leaves him after feeding him), 'the libidinal attitude' acquires the implication that it involves the 'disappearance and destruction of the libidinal object'. This implication 'tends to become confirmed at a later stage, when he learns that food which is eaten disappears from the external world, and that he cannot both eat his cake and have it'.

As we have seen, this anxiety belongs to the schizoid fear that *love is destructive*. In our society, in which ingestion is so largely made the basis of identity, there seems to be a prevalent symbolism which arises from our apprehensions that, applied to the sphere of relation, *acquisitiveness* may make the object disappear. Fairbairn's insights illuminate the exploitation of sex in our culture and suggest that it is perhaps a play on anxiety about destroying our objects while yet offering a manic sense of being alive *because we feel appetite*. (These fears are played upon by, for instance, the use of naked women in advertisements.)

Fairbairn next tackles the above headings one by one, and in following his analysis of these features of the early oral attitude we can see their cultural relevance. Since these features are embodied in phantasy and approaches to life, and since they are in all of us (because we all have schizoid problems), they have a universal *symbolic* relevance.

The next problem Fairbairn examines is 'the schizoid tendency to treat other people as less than persons with an inherent value of their own . . .' (Fairbairn [18], p. 12).

This obviously links with what I have said about equality above. Fairbairn discusses some cases. One patient 'treated other people more or less as though they were animals', which meant, as animals are often symbols in dreams of bodily organs, as we have seen, that he was treating them as 'bodily organs' or 'partial objects'. Fairbairn concludes that these cases 'illustrate the tendency in those with schizoid characteristics to treat libidinal objects as means of satisfying their own requirements rather than as persons possessing inherent value' (Fairbairn [18], p. 15). (In our culture the 'bunny' girl is exactly that!)

There are other implications: one of 'contempt for the object' because it does not have 'inherent value' as a whole person. The other is the 'sense of superiority' to others which is a schizoid characteristic: contempt and scorn for others can be schizoid characteristics.

This orientation towards partial objects Fairbairn characterises as regressive and determined by unsatisfactory primary relationship – where in the earliest stages 'the mother . . . fails to convince her child of spontaneous and genuine expressions of affection that she herself loves him as a person.'

This 'renders it difficult for him to sustain an emotional relationship with her on a personal basis; and the result is that, in order to simplify the situation, he tends regressively to restore the relationship to its earlier and simpler form and *revive his relationship to his mother's breast as a partial object* . . .'.

This situation may arise worst of all from a mother 'who conveys the impression of both possessiveness and indifference'.

Here Fairbairn explores the nature and origins of behaviour and symbolism generated by the urge to regress to relationship with a 'partial object'. In truth such behaviour displays *contempt* for the object, and a regressive need to return to the breast which simply gives satisfaction. What is revealed by such behaviour (as Balint's interpretation also reveals) is weakness of identity and overdependence, together with the attempt to compensate for the failure to discover mature independence in relationship 'with persons with an inherent value of their own' (i.e. there is a failure to find equality).

Fairbairn's clinical reference here is to the case of a schizophrenic youth who had the 'bitterest antagonism towards his actual mother' while dreaming at the time of lying in bed in a room from a ceiling of which poured a stream of milk – the room in question being one just beneath his mother's room. This dream symbolised not only regression to the need for a partial object but also a need to remove all dangers belonging to relationship with a person from the object:

> This type of regressive process may perhaps be described as *Depersonalization of the Object*; and it is characteristically accompanied by a regression in the quality of the relationship desired. Here again the regressive movement is in the interests of simplification of relationships; and it takes the form of a substitution of bodily for emotional contacts. It may perhaps be described as De-emotionalisation of the Object-relationship. (Fairbairn [18], p. 14.)

This example, and Fairbairn's interpretation of it, will be found to have great significance in our exploration of the schizoid elements in present-day culture. There we find a great deal of emphasis on the need for 'regression in the quality of the relationship desired', and exploitation of the 'simplification' of substituting 'bodily for emotional contacts': fundamentally a desire to have satisfaction from objects which do not involve the complexities of being human. Moreover, these insights explain the origins of the contempt found in, say, advertising and the *avant garde* as manifestations of a hatred of being human.

Fairbairn next explores the consequences of the schizoid tendency in giving rise to a *predominance of taking over giving in the libidinal attitude*. Schizoid individuals find 'giving', in the emotional sense, very difficult because they are 'fixed' in the oral (incorporative) phase. Here again, in order to understand we must find our way back to the bodily feelings of the very young child whose ego is a mouth-ego and whose concepts centre round its alimentary functions and its survival.

While the oral incorporative tendency, as Fairbairn points out, is the most fundamental of all tendencies, the next in importance is the excretory functions. As does Melanie Klein, Fairbairn sees these as underlying modes of dealing with the world in the symbolism of phantasy and action. Though biologically speaking the aim of the excretory activities is the elimination of useless and noxious substances from the body, the child 'soon learns to regard them as the classic means of dealing with bad libidinal objects' and, moreover, 'their earliest psychological significance for him would appear to be that of creative activities'. 'They represent the first creative activities of the individual; and their products are his first creations – the first internal contents that he externalises, the first thing belonging to himself that he gives. In this respect the excretory activities stand in contrast to oral activity, which essentially involves an attitude of taking.' (Fairbairn [18], p. 12.)

This is also the (opposite) difference between an oral incorporative attitude which implies valuation of the object, and the excretory attitude towards an object which implies its devaluation and rejection. But 'what is relevant for the immediate purpose, however, is the fact that at a deep mental level, taking is emotionally equivalent to the amassing bodily contents, a d giving is emotionally equivalent to parting with bodily contents'. (Fairbairn [18], p. 14.)

When one sees this in the light of the 'emotional equivalence between mental and bodily contents', then one can see how one preoccupation colours the other. The individual with a schizoid tendency finds difficulty in expression emotion in social context because giving has the significance of 'losing contents'. For this reason he finds social contacts exhausting: 'If he is long in company, he is liable to feel that "virtue has gone out of him", and that he requires a period of quiet and solitude afterwards in order that the inner storehouse of emotion may have an opportunity to be replenished.' So 'In the case of those with whom the schizoid tendency is marked, defence against emotional loss gives rise to *repression of affect** and an attitude of detachment which leads others to regard them as remote – and, in more extreme cases, even as inhuman' (Fairbairn [18], p. 15).

Fairbairn explores the predominance of taking over giving in the libidinal attitude by examining two techniques by which 'individuals with a schizoid propensity' overcome difficulties involved for them in emotional giving. These are (a) the technique of playing roles and (b) the technique of exhibitionism. These, again, have considerable cultural implications.

By the 'technique of playing roles', says Fairbairn,

> The schizoid individual is often able to express quite a lot of feeling and to make what appears to be quite impressive social contacts; but, in doing so, he is really giving nothing and losing nothing, because, since he is only playing a part, his own personality is not involved. Secretly, he disowns the

---

* *affect*: the feeling (and emotional) aspects of experience.

part which he is playing: and he thus seeks to preserve his own personality intact and immune from compromise. (Fairbairn [18], p. 16.)

Closely related to the question of role-playing is that of exhibitionism. Here again there is a direct application to the cultural sphere: 'The attraction of literary and artistic activities for individuals with a schizoid propensity is partly due to the fact that these activities provide an exhibitionistic means of expression without involving direct social contact' (Fairbairn [18], p. 16).

Exhibitionism is a way of 'giving without giving', 'by means of a substitution of "showing" for "giving".' The danger here is that 'the anxiety originally attached to the act of giving is liable to become transferred to the act of showing with the result that "showing up" . . . "being seen" at all may then give rise to acute self-consciousness . . .' (Fairbairn [18], p. 17).

Thus the work of those who exhibitionistically 'show' depersonalized sex, oversimplified and separated from aspects of relationship, in cultural works such as plays, novels, or films, are also notoriously anxious to defend their work and its 'freedom'. The original anxiety about 'giving' becomes transferred to the 'showing', and these writers fear (as it is, indeed, often so) that their exhibitionism may 'give them away' and may 'show them up'. They thus become more dependent than ever on 'False Self thinking' and on the activity of intellectual hate, such as the confession of perversion (see Khan in the next chapter). They thus become extremely active (as are the sex emancipationists) both as propagandists for schizoid attitudes and in the creation of a whole ethos of 'demoralisation' or 'sophistication', acclaimed as larger than life, 'superior', more alive, more 'free', more truthful and realistic, more rational, less troubled by guilt and bourgeois conscience, and so forth. (I should perhaps make it clear that these applications of Fairbairn's analysis to schizoid individuals in the cultural sphere are mine and not his.)

Fairbairn retraces the origins of the 'taking' impulse in schizoid individuals as 're-gressive reinstatement of the early oral attitude', which is brought about by a 'situation of emotional frustration' in which the child comes to feel

(a) that he is not really loved for himself as a person by his mother
(b) that his own love for his mother is not really valued and accepted by her. (Fairbairn [18], p. 17.)

This is a 'highly traumatic situation' giving rise to further complexities:

(a) The child comes to regard his mother as a bad object in so far as she does not seem to love him.
(b) The child comes to regard outward expressions of his own love as bad, with the result that, in an attempt to keep his love as good as possible, he tends to retain his love inside himself.
(c) The child comes to feel that love relationships with external objects are bad, or at least precarious. (Fairbairn [18], p. 12.)

The effect of this infantile logic is that the child tends to transfer his relationships with his objects to the realm of inner reality. As Fairbairn says, the mother and her breast as object have already been internalised and this internalisation is further exploited. Since this internalisation coincides with the oral stage (and has all bodily feelings which we have discussed above) and 'the inherent aim of the oral impulse is incorporation', an excessive need to incorporate can become 'woven into the structure of the ego'.

In the case of individuals with a schizoid component in their personality, accordingly, there is a great tendency for the outer world to derive its meaning too exclusively from the inner world. In actual schizophrenics this tendency may become so strong that the distinction between inner and outer reality is largely obscured. . . . Such extreme cases apart . . . there is a general tendency . . to heap up their values in the inner world. (Fairbairn [18], p. 18.)

Obviously, from this account, this tendency accounts for much in creative and intellectual activity, and casts light on much symbolism. But we shall also find in Fairbairn a clue to possible ways of judging the value of schizoid culture itself. Where there is an excessive concern with internal objects, there may be a tendency to depreciate values, *deterioration*, and a kind of sterility:

> In the case of individuals whose object-relationships are predominantly in the outer world, giving has the effect of creating and enhancing values, and of promoting self-respect; but, in the case of individuals whose object-relationships are predominantly in the inner world, giving has the effect of depreciating values, and of lowering self-respect. When such individuals give, they tend to feel impoverished, because when they give, they give at the expense of their inner world. (Fairbairn [18], p. 18.)

There is a variant of this, however: individuals with schizoid attributes may regard what they have produced as if it were still part of themselves, and so its part in the world may have a related symbolism.

Associated with these problems is the characteristic schizoid feature of intellectualization.

'Intellectualization', says Fairbairn, 'implies over-valuation of the thought processes.'

> . . . this over-valuation of thought is related to the difficulty which the individual with a schizoid tendency experiences in making emotional contacts with other people . . . he has difficulty in expressing his feelings naturally towards others, and in acting naturally and spontaneously in his relations with them. This leads him to work out his problems intellectually in the inner world. . . .'

This is an attempt (so far as conscious intentions go) to 'pave the way for adaptive behaviour in relation to external objects'. But 'since emotional conflicts springing from deep sources in the unconscious defy solution in this way', 'he tends increasingly to substitute intellectual solutions of his emotional problems for attempts to achieve a practical solution of them within the emotional sphere in his relationships with others in the external world' (Fairbairn [18], p. 20).

As Fairbairn says, the consequences of this overvaluation of the thought processes are:

> (1) The thought processes become highly libidinized; and the world of thought tends to become the predominant sphere of creature activity and self-expression.
> (2) Ideas tend to become substituted for feelings and *intellectual values for emotional values*. (Fairbairn [18], p. 20; my italics.)

With schizophrenics there is a manifest split between thought and feeling: the name itself means a split in the mind. But Fairbairn insists that 'the split in question is fundamentally a split in the *ego*', a split between superficial and lower levels, the latter being 'the source of affect' – the area of feeling.

This division, I believe, can be related to Winnicott's distinction between True Self and False Self, between 'female element being' and 'pseudo-male doing' and to the division, caused by 'impingement' between intellectual activity that has to stand in lieu of the good mother, and the psyche-soma as a whole, when there is a failure of integration. The division may be linked with the whole problem of a widespread shrinking from the free flow of human feelings in our world and the 'taboo on weakness'.

Schizoid individuals are often more inclined to construct intellectual systems of an elaborate kind than to develop emotional relationships with others on a human basis. There is a further tendency ' . . . to make libidinal objects of the systems they have created'. Fairbairn draws an analogy with the phenomenon which we all know in adolescence of 'being in love with love'. But he goes on to say:

Infatuation of this kind may lead to unpleasant enough consequences for the ostensible love-object; but, when we find a really schizoid personality in love with some extreme political philosophy, the consequences become more serious, because the toll of victims may then run into millions.

When such a fanatic has the inclination and the capacity to impose his system ruthlessly upon others the situation may become catastrophic – although at times it may admittedly be potent for good as well as evil.

Written in 1940 this obviously referred to both fascism and communism: the danger is still underrated. There are further prevalent intellectual systems which demand the selfless surrender appropriate to love, while their essential inhumanity (as in sexology, the cult of hallucinogens, Sartre's belief in 'endless hostility' as the basis of our freedom, or political extremism) is masked.

The more common position of the schizoid intellectual, however, is to stand aside and look down upon the everyday world from their intellectual world from a superior attitude of detached hatred and sense of omnipotence.

A sense of 'inner superiority' is always present in individuals with a schizoid tendency, even when this is unconscious, says Fairbairn. This is based upon:

(1)   a general *secret* overvaluation of personal contents, mental as well as physical; and

(2)   a narcissistic inflation of the ego arising out of *secret* possession of, and considerable identification with, internalised libidinal objects (e.g. the maternal breast and the paternal penis).

These discoveries have great cultural relevance as we shall see.

The internalized libidinal objects which the schizoid individual has taken into himself have, he feels, been 'stolen'. For him to lose contents by giving feels like being emptied: so, if he has taken libidinal objects into himself, then he feels guilt at having emptied others. This accounts for the need for 'secrecy' and the secretive and mysterious air Fairbairn associates with 'markedly schizoid individuals'.

The internalised objects feel infinitely precious – as precious as life itself, and their internalization is measure of their importance. This obviously links the secrecy to anxiety about the identity: and because of his secret possession of these internalized objects the schizoid individual feels 'different' from other people the 'odd man out', the 'outsider', the 'rebel', the person who is 'left out'. This associates with the schizoid individual's difficulties in emotional relationships in the group. Such an individual will often try to circumvent such difficulties by attainment within the intellectual sphere. But these attainments may suffer from the same withdrawal from the human which prompts the 'outsider' syndrome.

At this point Fairbairn summarises the characteristics of the schizoid individual of which, most significant here, is 'the libidinal attitude accompanying this fixation was one not only characterised by extreme dependence, but also rendered highly self-preservative and narcissistic by anxiety over a situation which presented itself as involving a threat to the ego'. That is, the schizoid individual tends to feel paranoic.

This anxiety, to which we have already referred, about the possible 'disappearance and destruction, not simply of his mother's breast, but of his mother herself is much increased by the effect of deprivation in imparting an aggressive quality to his libidinal need' (Fairbairn [18], p. 24).

This anxiety, Fairbairn points out, finds classic expression in the myth of Little Red Riding Hood: 'the little girl finds to her horror that the grandmother she loves has disappeared, and that she is left alone with her own incorporative need in the form of a devouring wolf.'

Only through love and experience of the real mother do children come to establish confidence in continuity of existence against such threatening phantasies. In the discovery of the real mother, through experience of her loving management, the child builds up a reassurance of his continuing existence. So, in adult relationship 'finding' and 'meeting' establish a sense of confidence in continuity of existence despite the threats of destructiveness and hate within.

'But the anxiety attached to this situation persists in the unconscious, ready to be reactivated by any subsequent experience of an analogous kind.' Primitive anxieties of an existential kind can always be aroused. In the schizoid person it is this anxiety which is particularly liable to be reactivated and may involve him in forms of response to his environment symbolising these anxieties about the object. Since we are all schizoid to an extent, we can all be 'reactivated' in this way – an important point for culture, as we shall see.

Fairbairn ends his essay on Schizoid Factors in the Personality by examining the underlying logic of the schizoid condition. This arises from the child's feeling when mothering is 'not good enough' that 'the reason for her apparent refusal to accept his love is that *his own love is destructive and bad*' (Fairbairn – [18], p. 25; my italics). 'This is an infinitely more intolerable situation than that of a child fixated in the late oral phase', Fairbairn goes on. The child fixated in the late oral phase ('biting' phase) 'being essentially ambivalent, interprets the situation that it is his hate, and not his love, that has destroyed the mother's affection. It is then in his hate and his badness seems to reside; and his love is thus able to remain good in his eyes. This is the position which would appear to underlie the manic-depressive psychosis, and to constitute the depressive position.' (Fairbairn [18], p. 25.)

But where the child remains convinced that his own love is bad, this, Fairbairn says, represents an 'essentially tragic situation', and generates the strange inversions of values in the schizoid individual. He develops another motive for 'keeping his love inside himself' besides that of feeling it is too precious to part with. 'He also keeps his love shut in because he feels that it is too dangerous to release upon his objects. Thus he not only keeps his love in a safe, but also keeps it in a cage.' (Fairbairn [18], p. 25.)

So, too, he feels that the love of others is bad. Thus a schizoid individual erects defences not only against his love of others but also against their love for him. (A patient of Fairbairn's used to say, 'Whatever you do, you must never like me'.) So, when a schizoid individual makes a renunciation of social contacts, it is because he feels he must neither love nor be loved. Indeed, he will take active measures to drive his libidinal objects away from him. He draws on the resources of his hate, and by quarrelling with people draws their hate instead of their love on him. 'All this he does in order to keep his libidinal objects at a distance.' He can only permit himself to be loved from afar off. 'This is the second great tragedy to which individuals with a schizoid tendency are liable. The first is, as we have seen, that he feels his love to be destructive of those he loves. The second arises when he becomes subject to a compulsion to hate and be hated, while all the time *he longs deep down to love and be loved.*' (Fairbairn [18], p. 26; my italics.)

Fairbairn finally unravels some of the most complex motives of the schizoid by which he substitutes hate for love:

There are two further motives, however, by which an individual with a schizoid tendency may be actuated in substituting hating for loving – curiously enough one an immoral, and the other a moral motive . . . the immoral motive is determined by the consideration that, since the joy of loving seems hopelessly debarred to him, he may as well deliver himself over to the joy of hating and obtain what satisfaction he can out of that. He thus makes a pact with the Devil and says 'Evil be thou my good'. The moral motive is determined by the consideration that, if loving involves destroying, it is better to destroy by hate, which is overtly destructive and bad, than to destroy by love, which is by rights creative and good. (Fairbairn [18], p. 27.)

'When these two motives come into play, therefore, we are confronted with *an amazing reversal of moral values*'; as Fairbairn says: 'It becomes a case, not only of "evil be thou my good" but also of "Good be thou my evil".'

This third great tragedy to which individuals with a schizoid tendency are liable as we shall see, is of particular relevance to our theme.

What Fairbairn shows is that, in his urgent efforts to survive, the schizoid is impelled not only to rely on 'False Self activity' but also *to invert all normal positives and values*. Essentially, he has not been able to develop an identity in the context of love, and to him love is too dangerous – so, he must substitute hate for love and bad for good. He needs to feel real by such desperate measures as alienation, perhaps by 'bad thinking' as a form of 'False Self activity', by an empty but compulsive 'doing', or by living at the expense of others.

All these 'hate' activities can be carried on in the cultural and intellectual sphere – and our problem in these spheres today is that at a time when the problem of identity is acute and when culture requires the exploitation of the coarsest emotions through crude media, *schizoid phenomena are at a premium, and the false success of the schizoid individual is pre-eminent and often greatly rewarded by an acquisitive society*. Culture in a society of economic 'drive' thus tends naturally to become schizoid – or anti-human. The effect is to spread abroad paranoia and persecutory anxiety, and to thrust 'persecutory elements' into us, deepening the taboo on weakness and the flights from reality into an inner world of anti-human phantasy.

The consequence which concerns us here is that our culture becomes permeated with 'false solutions' to the problems of life, even under the disguise of 'enlightenment'. While seeming to be larger than human, many such manifestations are in fact rather making a hidden attack on human 'being'. Even while seeming to be revolutionary, and thus ways of resisting a dehumanizing society in the name of a new 'freedom', schizoid expression can in fact be leading us towards 'deterioration' – a lessening of our humanity, and towards the forfeiture of our human potentialities. It can seem to offer a new 'purity' and 'strength' when there seems so little to rely on so that we may confront the problem of existence. Schizoid hate seems, like the phalanxes of Nazi Blackshirts at Nuremberg, a new and 'vital' order – yet, as we have seen, this strength is essentially false because it ha turned its back on humanness.

CHAPTER 7

Perversion, Confession, and the Right of Others to Live

I<small>F THE</small> schizoid individual – who is drawn towards exhibitionism and intellectual pursuits – is capable of such inversions of normal values, such callousness, and such a capacity to substitute hate for love, impelled by what are for him deep *moral* reasons, obviously the liberal mind which believes fervently in universal tolerance is no match for him. Yet at the moment 'enlightenment' basks in a self-congratulatory haze, believing that we live in times of a new freedom and realism without 'hypocrisy'.

Alas, there is a greater hypocrisy in our hypomania, and there are many fallacies in the permissive position.

For instance, Kenneth Tynan says (discussing a play by Osborne): 'the Freudian approach to sexual deviation (as a disorder to be cured by analysis) is not only pointless but reactionary, since it transfers the responsibility for homosexual unhappiness from society to individual upbringing, thereby confirming society in its belief that queers have only themselves to blame.' Tynan seems unable to accept the view that if homosexuality is an accident of identity formation in early infancy, then it is possible for a deeper compassion to develop in individuals because they can see that it is pointless to blame 'society' or the individual himself, and indeed that 'blame' is pointless, and a mere defence reaction. From such a non-sentimental point of view it would be possible for a humane policy towards homosexuals to be developed on a realistic basis, but certainly not by regarding homosexuality as 'normal', or 'perversion' as a cruel term.

If we merely accept perversions as 'normal', false solutions become true solutions, while the 'confessions' of false solution becomes the highest truth. Pornography by the same argument becomes beneficial. Mr. John Mortimer, the playwright, argued at an Arts Council conference that 'A man is never more innocently occupied than in reading hardcore pornography' (7 June 1968). Yet those who have compulsive obsessions and fetishes often turn to the therapist to rid them of these, while pornography is occasionally found to be associated with the most tormented identity problems.

However, kinds of behaviour which to object-relations psychology would appear to manifest ego-weakness and relational inadequacy, possibly attended by deep suffering, have come to be presented in today's modish London culture as perfectly acceptable, while it is 'realistic' to see these as valid modes of self-expression. Moreover, it is 'progressive' to suppose that social tolerance will overcome all the problems inherent in sexual difficulties. All we have to do (as Mr. Wayland Young argues) is to 'include' perversions which will then cease to be perversions.

54

If this is so, then why is the therapist's continual experience that of helping individuals whose perversions have at last become recognised by them as desperate false solutions which can no longer sustain a sense of identity or offer hope ? The pervert or compulsively promiscuous individual goes to the psychotherapist *because* the therapist does not condemn. But his withholding of condemnation does not heal the underlying existential frustration. From clinical evidence comes the human truth that, implicitly, it is the patient who is condemning his own perversion – because he feels there must be another (true) need, another path to meaning. In the light of intimate personal knowledge of many perverted or promiscuous individuals in therapy, the therapist knows, if no one else does, that sexual deviations are compensations for deep problems of identity which have their origins in the first beginnings of the formation of a human personality. There is no question of 'blame', but it is as false to suppose that 'society' is to 'blame' as it is to condemn and attack unhappy individuals.

Where there are egocentric false solutions which involve living at the expense of others, however, normal ethical considerations must be invoked (as against the rapist or child molester). Sexual deviation must be understood as being linked to a 'flight from life', and it is true that it has its own positive symbolism and aims. But it is also important to insist that even the confessions of perversions need sometimes to be understood as subtle manifestation of the deviant's need to make use of others – at their expense if need be. There is thus a cultural element in perversion, and an element of perversion in our culture, both of which involve the exploitation of others by a minority who need to do this.

I have discussed above the problem of the abuse of the element of trust in culture and the need of certain individuals to thrust harm into others. Recent psychoanalytical thought has done much to illuminate further the reasons why some individuals need to *make use of others*, not least through forms of 'acting out' in sexual activity and in the use of culture in certain forms of False Self activity.

Here we may consider links between certain well-known perversions of notorious writers, their criminal acts (Genet, de Sade), their confession of these acts, and their related problems of identity. Most relevant here is a recent paper by Masud R. Khan, 'The Function of Intimacy and Acting out in Perversions' [32].

Khan's paper is based on clinical experience of the psychoanalysis of perverts and on the penetration by psychoanalytical theory to the schizoid origins of perversion. These origins spring from 'disturbed infant–mother relationship', and Khan mentions, among others, Winnicott's view that 'if the integration of the ego-functions is disturbed through inadequate holding [maternal] environment, then what in normal childhood development are transitional objects turn into the perverse sexual relationships to objects, human and non-human, in adult life, (Khan [32]' p. 399).

The 'transitional object', as we have seen, is both the symbol of the internalisation of the mother and also the child's first cultural object: thus the insight that sexual perversion has its origins in failure in transitional object phenomena with schizoid individuals obviously has important cultural implications.

In the normal individual, sexual give-and-take is an important source of feeling real and 'confirmed', and so is all that personal culture which begins with the transitional object. But if transitional object phenomena becomes the focus of an intense identity need, so will the culture of such an individual. And in so far as transitional object phenomena becomes translated into perverted forms of adult sexuality, so will the individual's adult culture come to be used in the service of his identity needs. Where these became perversions, so does the culture.

Khan sees adult sexual perversion as a social acting out of infantile neurosis. 'The technique of intimacy re-enacts the infantile neurosis':

> Through this technique another object is appealed to, involved, seduced and coerced to share in the enactment of the developmental arrest and cumulative trauma resulting in identity diffusion which constitutes this infantile neurosis. This technique of intimacy, of which acting out is the mechanism, combined in a subtle balance the defensive exploitation of regressive satisfactions of a pregenital instinctual nature as well as mobilisation of archaic psychic processes in the hope of enlarging the ego into an independent and coherent organisation and achieving a sense of identity. (Khan [32], pp. 399–400.)

Thus there is 'hope' in perversion since it is a quest for a sense of identity. But the 'fixation is not on an object but generally on an *activity*' – a truth that is celebrated in numerous obscene jests and rhymes about public figures believed to be exceptionally libidinal. Cultural 'confession' of perversions belongs, too, to this 'hope' and the attempt to feel real. Obscenity can thus even be presented to us as highly moral. For this reason a critic can see (for instance) the work of Genet in terms of a search for a 'moral order' (Robert Nye writing in *The Times Saturday Review*): but the trouble is that this moral order tends to be a *schizoid* one, based on an inverted ethic (hate = love).

For the problem of perversion is its narcissism, and this arises out of the characteristic difficulty which the individual of weak identity has in distinguishing between *me* and *not-me*. It is not that psychoanalysis accuses such an individual as Genet of 'selfish self-absorption' (as Nye implies), but that his problem is that he does not know where self begins and ends, while he is 'callous' in that he is incapable of essentially recognising the reality of others.

When he enters into the sexual activity, the pervert's relationship with the 'object' in it belongs to the stage of early infancy before the object is wholly recognised as existing in its own right.

> In perversions the object occupies an intermediary position: it is not-self and yet subjective; registered and accepted as separate and yet treated as subjectively created; it is needed as an actual existent not-self being and yet coerced into complying with the exigent subjective need to *invent* it. Spatially it is suspended half-way between external reality and inner psychic reality. The narcissistic magical exploitation of the object is patently visible. . . .

Meanwhile, says Khan, there is an inevitable deficiency in the pervert's capacity to focus emotionally on a real object of relationship. Taking an emphasis from Anna Freud, Khan believes that the crucial problem of perversion is '*the incapacity to love and the dread of emotional surrender*'. He speaks of a 'basic incapacity in the ego' to sustain relationship to an object and its internal representatives. This fundamental incapacity to relate impels the 'technique of intimacy' which perverts employ.

This technique Khan investigated both in heterosexual patients with 'a schizoid type of character disorder' and homosexuals. He refers also to accounts of perverts among writers (de Sade and Genet being specifically mentioned). And he defines this 'technique of intimacy' in terms of what Laing would call a 'strategy of survival' based on a concern to preserve 'inner contents':

> Through the technique of intimacy the pervert tries to *make known* to himself and *announce and press into* another something pertaining to his inmost nature as well as to discharge its instinctual tension in a compulsive and exigent way. . . . This impulsion to announce and communicate himself in a bodily way relates to a pressing crisis of diffusion of self and identity. . . .

Khan quotes the *Oxford English Dictionary* definitions of the verb *intimate* ('to put into, drive or press into, to make know, announce') and the adjective *intimate* ('pertaining to the inmost thoughts and feelings; pertaining to and connected with the inmost nature or character of a thing').

The outstanding feature of the technique of intimacy is the attempt 'to establish a make-belief situation involving in most cases the willing seduced co-operation of an external object'. Khan says that 'in certain sadistic criminal instances the object is coerced against his or her will, as in the case of de Sade . . .'. But 'even in de Sade's case the unconscious cooperation of his victims must have played an important part. This is very clear in the naive, delusional negation and denial by his fictional characters as victims of what is in store for them.'

The pervert has such a need to be confirmed by the exercise of his 'technique' that his need to draw into 'make-belief'* and to draw out unconscious cooperation in his victim is a life-and-death matter for him:

> The capacity to create the emotional climate in which another person volunteers to participate is one of the few real talents of the perverts. This invitation to surrender to the pervert's logic of body-intimacies demands of the object a suspension of discrimination and resistance to all levels of guilt, shame and separateness. A make-belief situation is offered in which two individuals temporarily renounce their separate identities and boundaries and attempt to create a heightened maximal body-intimacy of orgastic nature. (Khan [32], p. 402.)

Here there are cultural concomitants. There are many manifestations in our culture of the impulse to reduce us to 'the pervert's logic', involving the 'suspension of discrimination'. In a culture which so largely depends upon the 'make-belief' of perverts there naturally arise forms of 'philosophy' of a schizoid kind which seek to persuade us to forfeit our 'resistance to all levels of guilt, shame and separateness' – in the name of a new 'freedom'. The 'amoral' critic and the advocate of 'frank expression' may be seeking to create an ethos in which it is easier for some to exploit us by a 'make-belief situation' in which we can be lured to renounce our 'separate identity', and thus renounce, indeed, our human self-respect and sense of our own value in the boundaries of our unique being.

As in the advocacy of sexual 'enlightenment', this is often done in the name of the 'orgastic', which sounds (by Freudian – or perhaps rather Reichian – theory) like the 'release' of instinctual life. Khan, however, indicates that in sexual perversion there is one significant – and crippling – proviso: 'The pervert himself cannot surrender to the experience and retains a split-off, dissociated manipulative ego-control of the situation. This is both his achievement and failure in the *intimate* situation. It is this failure that supplies the compulsion to repeat the process again and again, (Khan [32], p. 402).

From the point of view of psychotherapeutic knowledge of the deeper problems of individuals who are attached to perverted sexual activity, then, we can see that it is their *failure* which impels them to make conquest after conquest, while making no essential conquest of life. We can also understand how it is necessary for the homosexual to be a predator, and what drives him to seek to involve others in his capacity for 'make-belief' leading towards seduction. We can also see how in such accounts of perverted sexual activity as those of Henry Miller the account is itself a measure of the 'manipula-

---

* The 'make-belief' situation, and the element of unconscious cooperation obviously make such a trial as that of Ian Brady, for the 'Moors' child murders, so fascinating to the public. Brady had read de Sade and M. Khan's analysis obviously fits his perversions. Public fear of child murderers is also a (quite justified) fear of the pervert's 'magical' power to delude his intended victim into make-belief.

tive ego-control of the situation'. Miller's cold phrase 'now and then one or other of us had an orgasm' sums up the whole detached ethos of schizoid sex, in which the refusal to surrender to sexual 'meeting' is preserved by a 'split-off, dissociated, manipulative' control of the sexual activity by the same intellectual hate that generates the books themselves, as 'confessions'.

Our *avant-garde* cultural ethos seeks to persuade us, by its preoccupation with depersonalised sexual activity as if this were 'larger than life' and a mark of freedom, that 'frank' accounts of physical intimacy record 'the truth'. From such an account as that of Khan we see that essentially the pervert is less than a man, while his 'confessions' have the function of disguising this by compensatory exaggerations. 'The nearest that the pervert can come to experiencing surrender is through visual, tactile and sensory identifications with the other object in the intimate situation in a state of surrender.'

This, perhaps, accounts for the intense and idealising preoccupation with the physical minutiae of sex in the modern novel and film and its compulsion to repeat*. This only *stands for* emotional surrender between persons, while in truth there is a dread of this:

> Hence, though the pervert arranges and motivates the idealization of instinct which the technique of intimacy aims to fulfil, he himself remains outside the experiential climax. Hence, instead of instinctual gratification or object-cathexis, the pervert remains a deprived person whose only satisfaction has been of pleasureable discharge and intensified ego-interest. In his subjectivity the pervert is *un homme manqué*. (Khan [32], p. 402.)

Perversion is essentially narcissistic and an inherently unsatisfying activity. But though dissatisfaction generates the impulse to repeat, the energy which goes into the make-belief of seduction is taken by the pervert as a mark of his own superiority: 'The pervert's talent at enlisting reality and external objects as an ally in the service of his ego-needs and instinctual exigeancies is what gives him a spurious and exaggerated sense of his own sensibility and its potentialities' (Khan [32], p. 402).

The 'pervert's subjective experience of the technique of intimacy and its achievements' says Khan, can be categorised as follows:

1. Overvaluation and idealization of self and object 'in lieu of true object cathexis'.
2. Insatiability. 'The sense of insatiability derives from the fact that every venture is a *failure* for the pervert.'
3. 'A solitary game'. 'Even though two persons are involved in a heightened instinctual modality essentially it is all the invention of one person. *There is no object-relatedness; hence no nourishment*' [my italics].
4. Envy, which 'derives from the actual perception and suspicion that the other person has got more out of it than the self. It is this element of envy which makes most perverts behave viciously and meanly to their object and compels them to jilt and hurt.'

An idealized and overvalued 'taking' sexual activity is hallowed by our modish culture. Yet from Khan's account this can be seen as an attempt to hide the failure, the insatiability, the solitariness, and the envy and meanness in it.

Khan sees 'confession' as another basic function of the technique of intimacy. We may recall that the purpose of this technique is to attempt to solve the pervert's identity problems by *making known, announcing*, and *pressing into others* something pertaining to his inmost nature. We can, I believe, in the light of Khan's insights, describe one element of confession as an attempt to *thrust hate into us*. Although the technique of intimacy is an attempt at self-cure, its cycles are self-enclosed and self-defeating: the confessions of the pervert can never '*meet and make known the true ego-need and the latent distress in the pervert*'

---

* Several films now consist of virtually nothing but scenes of simulated or real sexual intercourse.

because they are part of his technique of intimacy. In this we can detect the roots of the essential falsity of much modish present-day 'sex' literature, such as that of Henry Miller. Though it postures as 'true confession', in truth it belongs to the hallucinations of self-deception which are spun from the same intense need to seduce others into the idealisation of an essentially mean, empty, and 'failed' activity.

Khan says: 'It is a remarkable feature of the pervert's behaviour that he confesses with a singular unrestraint, lack of shame and guilt – both to the social object [i.e. audience] and in the clinical situation.'

He mentions the 'intensity and absoluteness' of writers such as Gide, Miller, Wilde, and Genet. But from his own knowledge of perverts Khan sees this 'absoluteness' as a form of hallucination itself. 'My clinical material leads me to infer that this confession through body-intimacies and retrospective verbalizations is nearer to dreaming and a hallucinatory mode of psychic activity than an organized ego-activity.'

This is a penetrating insight which I believe we can apply to the whole area of 'confessional' preoccupation with sexual activity in our culture, and especially to the intellectual sexuality which pervades American literary culture. Rather than representing a new realism it is rather a new form of self-delusion and sentimentality.

Khan adds the perception that the 'freedom' of the pervert from guilt and shame (possibly akin to the schizoid individual's comparative freedom from repression) is no 'true innocence' but is but an aspect of the hate-cycles of his 'insatiability'. Culturally, we can see that where an audience is lured into the delusions of sexual confession to believe that here is a larger-than-life sexual mode, it has become involved in 'overvaluation and idealization . . . in lieu of true object-cathexis'. The audience becomes the 'envious collaborator of the pervert', and at the same time becomes involved in an hallucination that disguises true human needs. The need of the pervert to 'abandon ego-controls' does not belong to a freedom in uninhibitedness, but belongs to his own ego-centric purposes: 'It is precisely this partial capacity to abandon ego-controls and repressively invoke and express modalities of sexual and psychic experience that make so many victims the envious collaborators of the pervert.'

In our cultural world, when we read of the sexual activity of Violette Leduc, 'La Bâtarde', in our morning newspaper (if it is *The Guardian*), or in the latest modish novel about her protagonist's sexual prowess by a lady novelist, we are all made into 'envious collaborators' of the pervert. But the 'confession' achieves nothing by way of the discovery of oneself in true object cathexis, such as it seems to offer. The pervert, in his hallucinations, may be seeking cure: but his confession hides his latent distress. He offers instead the 'charade' of intimacy whose failure to bring satisfaction will lead on to hate.

> But it is a confession doomed to failure because the accomplice can only help to dramatise the theme, give it a concrete reality in behavioural experience and a body-compliance without being able to meet and make known the true ego-need and the latent distress in the pervert. Hence the inconsolability of the pervert, and his addiction to the *charade of intimacy*. The pervert tries to use the technique of intimacy as a therapeutic device and all he accomplishes is more expertise in the technique itself. His failure to achieve any form of ego-satisfaction is then compensated by idealization of instinctual processes, which in turn lead to a sense of depletion, exhaustion and paranoid turning away from or against the object. This vicious circle gradually reduces the positive strivings and expectancies implicit in the technique of intimacy. Clinically we see perverts only when their auto-therapeutic attempts have totally failed. . . . (Khan [32], p. 404; my italics.)

As in the cycles of the anguished attempt of the pervert to find a sense of being real, this tendency in our culture leads towards 'a sense of depletion' – at large, a depletion of the sense of being human. It is already being recognised at large that as a means to find a sense of security of identity this preoccupation with idealised sexual functions has 'failed totally', while in our cultural ethos there is a 'feeling of exhaustion and paranoid turning away from or against the object'. The 'frank sex' 'vitality' of our culture is already showing itself as a 'charade' – and the next step seems to be towards a greater exploitation of hate and violence, and a deeper preoccupation with a sense of ugliness and futility in the sphere of personal relationships. The new 'enlightenment' is turning to a bitterly sterile conclusion and to further cycles of hate.

Khan, of course, is dealing with the *clinical* problems of handling perverts. These patients he finds ultra-sensitive to any failure of understanding on the part of the analyst because they 'project their well-founded despair' over him. The same despair impels the pervert to put forward in public the strongest arguments in favour of tolerance of the 'freedom' he must have to exploit others. He also seeks to create an atmosphere in which sexual activity which regresses to something like masturbation seems more 'alive' than normal sexuality which does satisfy and is the expression of relationship.

In analysing the aetiology of perversion Khan approaches it as 'auto-eroticism *à deux*' and so different from infantile auto-eroticism, but yet 'an engineered re-enactment of masturbatory practices between two persons as a compensation for . . . insufficiency of maternal care' (Khan [32], p. 404).

Khan examines the earliest forms of relationship between the infant and his own body at the time when the identity, 'when its sense of [body] ego boundaries', is being formed. And he seeks to explain perversion by reference to Winnicott's concept of the 'transitional object'.

Khan quotes Winnicott on the various features of the infants' relationship to this 'transitional object'. He has rights over it; 'the object is affectionately cuddled as well as excitedly loved and mutilated'; 'it must never change unless changed by the infant'; it must survive loving and hating; it must seem to give warmth, to move, to have texture – 'or do something that seems to show it has vitality or reality of its own'. It does not really 'come from without' nor from 'within': it is not something we have given the child, nor is it a hallucination: he has made it by endowing it with special qualities. And eventually it becomes diffused, into the whole cultural field: 'It loses meaning, and this is because the transitional phenomena have become diffused, have become spread out over the whole intermediate territory between "inner psychic reality" and "the external world as perceived by two persons in common . . ." ' (Winnicott, quoted by Khan [32], p. 406.)

The object of a pervert's sexual attention stands in relation to him as an infant's piece of rag stands to him, as the primitive focus of his capacity to become an independent human being and as a meeting place between himself and his culture. As the infant exercises all kinds of symbolism and acting out on this transitional object, in growing towards independence, so, too, does the pervert hope that his victim as 'transitional object' can be a focus of his solutions to the problem of identity. His 'confessions' obviously represent an aspect of this interplay with the transitional object.

A culture which belongs to the 'transitional object phenomena' belongs thus to primitive stages of play rather than to that complex culture which lies with the adult between psychic reality and the perceived outer world. This accounts for the whole 'infantile primitive' aspect of modish culture in which there seems to be so little of substance for the adult sensibility.

Khan argues that the pervert's 'victim' lends himself to being treated as a 'transitional object': 'Through its (his or her . . .) readiness to comply it lends itself to be invented, manipulated, used and abused, ravaged and discarded, cherished and idealized, symbolically identified with and deanimated all at once . . .' (Khan [32], p. 406).

The similarity between this kind of object of perversion and the depersonalised partial object desired by the schizoid individual will be obvious. But though he wants it to, his object can never do for the pervert what the transitional object does for an infant: 'What it cannot do for the pervert is to cure him of his developmental deviations in ego-integration resulting from failures of maternal care and provision.'

By analogy I believe we can say that the culture of the hallucinations of perversion can do little for us either.

Khan next analyses some of the more negative elements in the 'technique of intimacy'. One significant element is the attempt by play, make-belief, omnipotence, and manipulation, to guarantee against the acceptance of dependence, against genuine object-relationship, and against *surrender to emotional experience*. 'This self-protective vigilance and negativity in the ego also provides a screen for the basic mistrust and suspicion with which the pervert treats both his inner need to be related to an object and the object's emotional demands on him.'

This Khan links with 'manic defence' – the reassurance against depression, death, and chaos by the denial of inner reality, and a concentration on 'lightness and humorousness'. This manic glitter of the false attempt to feel alive conceals a fundamental denial of the underlying mistrust and suspicion of one's deeper needs.

Khan's final remarks confirm surprisingly the critics' image of such an individual as Jean Genet: 'the ego of the pervert is more like a collage than an integrated coherent entity. . . .' Yet the pervert is a combination of 'resistive manipulative strength', on the one hand, and 'panicky vulnerability', on the other. We may perhaps here apply Winnicott's terms 'False Male Doing' and 'Female Element Being' here – the pervert likely to have an identity held together by fragmentary 'activity' and 'bad thinking'. 'Through the mechanism of acting out and the technique of intimacy, the pervert's ego concocts for itself a *pleasurable negative identity*. In no other character disorder do we meet such a consistent idealization of the reactive defensive self-image as in the pervert.' (Khan [32], p. 409.)

Our modish culture, I am trying to argue, is largely predominated at the moment by this 'idealization of the reactive defensive self-image' of the pervert. The predominant figures in it tend to be those who have a 'resistive manipulative strength' in the realm of 'pseudo-male doing' in cultural expression, and conceal by their manic denial their essential 'dread of ego dissolution and disintegration' – and their fear of being human. Our culture seems often to offer us only a 'pleasurable negative identity' (Pinter's STOTT: see below).

Khan's last paragraphs are on 'acting out' and its positive elements as a 'strategy of survival'. 'Acting out' seems to be primarily a clinical term, meaning the resort to symbolic 'equation' behaviour as an alternative to insight and awareness. 'Acting out' Khan believes to be an element of the technique of intimacy in perversions. I believe we can extend this to include certain forms of symbolic 'equation' activity in culture. Many of the aspects of 'acting out' which Khan discusses are very complex, but one of the most important elements is that by externalising his intrapsychic problems by activity with another person the pervert seems to retain 'executive capacity' in the ego: he seems to be in command of his experience. The threat of 'passive surrender' is transformed into 'active mastery' of the impulse and object.

Because there is some sharing, guilt and shame are neutralized, and because there is pleasure, depression and psychic pain are held off. Where there is sharing there is a positive meeting of a kind: 'The mechanism of acting out by introducing the elements of play, imaginatively shared activities and through mobilising ego-interest mitigates the deadness in the internal world of the pervert.'

Acting out does provide the pervert with an opportunity for reparative efforts towards a *real* object. There is never a pure situation in which the object of a living pervert can be a mere transitional object: his 'victim' is also a person, and in this there is a chance of meeting. So, for the 'confessional' writer, as with Genet, the audience is real – and responds in such a way to 'confirm' his existence. Giving pleasure to a real person helps the pervert to overcome to a degree his 'futile relations to internal parental figures': and, at a deeper level still, acting out can help him to 'avoid total ego collapse and an irreversible regression to psychotic states'.

So, as Khan says, perversions are closer to psychoses than neuroses. The activity of perversion is a way of not collapsing into madness. This explains the desperate need in the pervert to maintain and develop the technique of intimacy: seduction becomes for him a life-or-death matter. However narcissistic or hallucinatory his relationship to his 'victim', the rudimentary element of communication in perversion is a life-line of contact with reality. The rudimentary quality of the pervert's object-relationship belongs to an infantile stage at which 'there is little meaningful communication between the child as a separate person and self and the significant parent. Acting out through the technique of intimacy breaks down this primary sense of isolation and establishes contact with an object, and through an object with the self. Here the anti-social factor in perversion offers a vehicle for hope, appeal and help.'

In perversion and the confession of perversion we find the same 'hope' that Winnicott finds 'locked up in wicked behaviour'. It is for this reason Sartre regards Genet as a saint and martyr: by his confessions he found contact with an object, and through the object with a self (a self which is now content without the life and death struggle of confession and antisocial activity).

It is this hope and element of quest for identity that we respond to at best in that culture which springs from the 'technique of intimacy'. We respond to the 'ego-syntonic' element as it is exerted against 'dissolution and disintegration'. But we need to remember the essential futility of the technique of intimacy. It is anti-social, and hallucinatory. As Khan concludes: 'The ego of the pervert acts out his dream and involves another person in its actualization. It is possible to argue that if the pervert dramatizes and actually fulfils his body-dreams with a real person, he also cannot wake out of them.'

The object of a pervert's technique is 'only a sort of thing in his dreams' (Khan is quoting Lewis Carroll). In the cultural sphere the audience is for the confessing pervert 'only a sort of thing in his dream'. *And the essence of the dream is that we shall not wake to find ourselves human.**

The elements in perversion and the culture of perversion, which Khan notes, are seen from a different angle, but in much the same terms by Albert Camus, in the chapter 'The Sons of Cain' in *The Libel*, where he discusses de Sade. For Sade

. . . enjoyment must be prevented from degenerating into attachments, it must be put in parentheses

---

* In a later paper Khan distinguishes between benign and malignant perversion: Sade and Genet being malignant: Rousseau, Sacher-Masoch, and Wilde benign. In malignant perversion the 'basic relationship to the self and object is hostile, destructive and nihilistic' (Khan [66], p. 92).

and tempered. Objects of enjoyment must never be allowed to appear as persons. If a man is an 'absolutely material species of plant', he can only be treated as an object and as an object for experiment. In Sade's fortress republic, there are only machines and mechanics. . . . His infamous converts have their rule . . . the libertine indulges in public confession. . . . (Camus [10], p. 40.)

The insatiableness and envy of perversion are apparent in Sade's symbolism: 'the maximum of enjoyment coincides with the maximum of destruction. To possess what one is going to kill, to copulate with suffering – those are the moments of freedom towards which the entire organization of Sade's Castles is orientated.' (Camus [10], p. 40.)

This is a form of primitive play with the transitional object: the essence of such play is that it must remain in a state of primitive incapacity to relate to a human object – hence its 'insatiableness': 'from the moment when sexual crime destroys the object of desire, it also destroys desire which exists only at the precise moment of destruction. Then another object must be brought under subjection and killed, and then another, and so on to an infinity of all possible objects. . . .' (Camus [10], p. 40.)

Behind this kind of phantasy is the magical and omnipotent power of the baby and the problem of 'flop' inherent in satisfaction and 'finding'. But, as Camus sees, the insatiability expressed here is the insatiability of a quest which can never find its goal: 'When the accounts are closed, when all the victims are massacred, the executioners are left face to face in the deserted castle. Something is still missing. The tortured bodies return, in their elements, to nature and will be born again. . . .' (Camus [10], p. 40.)

Sade's 'endless hostility' and his consuming appetite manifest the desperate need of the schizoid to begin to find an identity and the hope expressed by the pervert's hate. But, by the inverted logic of the schizoid, this need threatens to consume the whole world:

> I abhor nature . . . I would like to upset its plans, to thwart its progress, to turn the stars in their course, to overturn the floating spheres of space, to destroy what serves nature, and to succour all that harms it, in a word, to insult it in all its works, and I cannot succeed in doing so. It is in vain that he dreams of a technician who can pulverise the universe; he knows that, in the dust of the spheres, life will continue. (Sade, quoted by Camus [10], p. 41.)

In Sade's cosmic hate we have the extreme expression of the schizoid's 'immoral motive' – 'may as well give oneself up to the joys of hating.' And we have the impulse of the pervert to reduce everything to his play-object, taken to its ultimate conclusions in destruction. We also have the expression of ultimate insatiability, envy, and futility for 'The attempt against creation is doomed to failure. It is impossible to destroy everything, there is always a remainder . . .'. It is the ultimate attempt of the pervert to feel real – in terms which may remind us perhaps of the figure above of a *sexe-bombe* fused with the ultimate weapon of destruction: 'when crimes of passion no longer measure up to our intensity, we could, perhaps, attack the sun, deprive the universe of it, or use it to set fire to the world – those would be real crimes. . . .' (Sade, quoted by Camus [10], p. 41).

Sade died in a lunatic asylum, acting plays on an improvised stage with other lunatics: a predicament which has become celebrated in a significant dramatic work in the modern *avant garde*. Sade's identity existed only in his activity as a pervert – and in his hate-writings. As Camus says: 'A derisory equivalent of the satisfaction that the order of the world failed to give him was provided for him by dreams and by creative activity . . . he created a fable in order to give himself the illusion of existing. . . .'

Camus shows insights into the negative elements of the 'technique of intimacy' in Sade's work: his impulse to 'thrust harm' into us, his hallucinatory power to seduce us. Sade, he says, put 'the moral crime which is committed by writing' above everything else. Through his 'accumulated rage' his 'rebel's logic' led him to seek to promote 'hermetic totalitarianism, universal crime, an aristocracy of cynicism, and the desire for an apocalypse'. As Camus says:

> He himself is one of those writers of whom he says, 'their corruption is so dangerous, so active, that they have no other aim in printing their monstrous works but to extend beyond their own lives the sum-total of their crimes; they can commit no more, but their accursed writings will lead others to do so, and this comforting thought which they carry with them to the tomb consoles them for the obligation which death imposes on them of renouncing this life.' Thus his rebellious writings bear witness to his desire for survival . . . the immortality he longs for is the immortality of Cain. . . . (Camus [10], p. 42.)

Sade aspired to the survival of his hate. And Camus attributes his success in our day to the 'dream he had in common with contemporary thought' – a dream we can see in the light of Khan's analysis, as belonging to the hate-cycles of the pervert: 'the demand for total freedom and dehumanization coldly planned by the intelligence. The reduction of man to an object of experiment, the rule which specifies the relation between the will to power and man as an object. . . .'

Our time, says Camus, has blended his dream of universal republic and his 'technique of degradation'. Camus means, I believe, the police state. But I believe we may interpret the lesson of Sade in another way – in what Camus calls a world 'intoxicated with nihilism'. For the 'technique of degradation', as I hope I have shown, springs from the need of the pervert to live at the expense of others, in his sexual activity, and in his 'confession' of perversion, by which he involves others in his dream, his flight from being human, and his hate. Though this syndrome dominates our culture, we do not see it, or believe it points to a new 'freedom'. Yet, as Camus says: 'The moment we recognise the impossibility of absolute negation (and living is a matter of recognising this) the very first thing that cannot be denied is the right of others to live' (Camus [10], p. 15).

It is this fundamental ethical truth our culture seems to have forgotten, since it has become so overwhelmed by the influence of the schizoid minority. Below I shall discuss a number of individuals who have, for one reason or another, and sometimes for the highest moral reasons as it seems to them, become seduced into the schizoid ethos of our time and its cultural modes. How can we ever find a way out of such a dilemma?

PART II

The Problem of Hate in Culture

A. *Ian Fleming's* Goldfinger

'James Bond is himself again . . . and very good it is to see him there . . . the character remains true to form, and the actor also . . .

"Don't you want to get something off your chest?" asks Bond of a pretty girl before strangling her with the top of her Bikini . . . (the world is saved) . . . a good deal of fun is found in the process . . . a light touch . . . the delectable Tiffany, who certainly knows what dresses show off her going points . . . Lana Wood is such a pretty thing I was glad she landed in a swimming pool after being thrown out of a tenth-storey window . . .'

Patrick Gibbs, film critic of
The Daily Telegraph, reviewing
Diamonds are Forever, 30 December 1971

CHAPTER 8

Unconscious Meaning in the 'Spy' Story

AT THIS point it will serve my purposes to turn to the detailed analysis of a popular work of symbolism representative of our time.

The work I intend to take is Ian Fleming's novel *Goldfinger* [24], a commercially successful work of the 1960s. Here we shall apply the 'schizoid diagnosis' in literary criticism in order to find the deeper sources of the appeal of such a work which are not evident at the conscious level.

What is it in Ian Fleming's work that causes so many millions of people to be engrossed by it so that the actor who plays '007' becomes the favourite film star of the year? What enables the films to be made the biggest box-office ever? Some of this can no doubt be attributed to enormous promotion investment. But even promotion must have something to work on, and the film industry obviously saw potentialities in Fleming. Allowing for the differences between the books and the films – what were these? What causes intellectuals to write books on the 'James Bond dossier' and to take up space in weekly journals and radio programmes applauding his achievement? What brings the monarchy to the première of a Bond film? What makes for that awed adulation in the Press?

It cannot, certainly, be the quality of the writing. It is interesting to hear from teachers of slow adolescent readers that despite the lure of the cult these pupils find Fleming's prose boring. When I first read *Goldfinger* myself I found it tedious. The action is at the level of a boy's adventure paper: the same melodramatic gestures by the same paper supermen. There are the same clichés of action writing one finds in a 'Biggles' book. The crises are essentially those of the ancient staple of 'adventure' stories with the heroine tied to the rails or the hero sewn up in a sack, albeit in a new guise. The poise of the hero, with his 'equable' voice in danger, his 'quick' 'penetrating glances', and his perpetual readiness, have a long, lame ancestry. And as for 'realism' – even the dullest and most insensitive war book or 'escape' story seldom sinks to the level of such a series of stereotype phrases as Fleming's 'action' prose. Consider, in the following typical passage for instance, the phrases 'all hell broke loose', 'He called out triumphantly', 'A quick glance showed him', and so forth:

> 'You see, Mr. Bond. You were wrong and I was right. Ten more minutes and I shall be the richest man in the world, the richest man in history! What do you say to that?' His mouth spat out the words.
> Bond said equably, 'I'll tell you after those ten minutes are up.'
> 'Will you?' said Goldfinger. 'Maybe.' He looked at his watch and spoke rapidly into his microphone. The Goldfinger squad loped slowly through the main gate, their heavy burden slung from four shoulders in a cradle of webbing.
> Goldfinger looked past Bond at the group on the roof of the second diesel. He called out triumphantly, 'Another five minutes, gentlemen, and then we must take cover.' He turned his eyes on Bond and

added softly, 'And then we will say goodbye, Mr. Bond. And thank you for the assistance you and the girl have given me.'

Out of the corner of his eye, Bond saw something moving – moving in the sky. It was a black, whirling speck. It reached the top of its trajectory, paused and then came the ear-splitting crack of a maroon signal.

Bond's heart leapt. A quick glance showed him the ranks of dead soldiers springing to life, the machine guns and the locked armoured cars swinging to cover the gates. A loudspeaker roared from nowhere, 'Stand where you are. Lay down your arms.' But there came a futile crackle of fire from one of the rearguard covering party and then all hell broke loose.

The gestures at 'vitality' in the depiction of violent events here would hardly serve for a paragraph of war reportage in a newspaper; it depends so much on outworn conventions: 'Bond's heart leapt', 'His mouth spat out the words', 'ear-splitting crack', 'crackle of fire', 'springing to life', and so on.

The concept of 'manliness', as shown in battle, is as embarrassingly unreal, not least to anyone who has experienced the sympathy that springs up between men in war. 'Action' here has the pasteboard quality of a boy's phantasy of heroism:

The Bazooka shuddered slightly and the ten-pound armour-piercing rocket was on its way. There was a flash and a puff of blue smoke. Some bits of metal flew off the rear of the flying engine. But then it had crossed the bridge and taken the curve and was away.

'Not bad for a rookie,' commented Leiter. 'May put the rear diesel out, but those jobs are twins and he can make it on the forward engine.'

Bond got to his feet. He smiled warmly into the hawklike, slate-grey eyes. 'You bungling oaf,' he said sarcastically, 'why in hell didn't you block that line?'

'Listen, Shamus. If you've got any complaints about the stage management you can tell them to the President. He took personal command of this operation and it's a honey. There's a spotter plane overhead now. They'll pick up the diesel and we'll have old Goldilocks in the hoosegow by midday. How were we to know he was going to stay aboard the train?' He broke off and thumped Bond between the shoulder blades. 'Hell I'm glad to see you. These men and I were detailed off to give you protection. We've been dodging around looking for you and getting shot at by both sides for our pains.' He turned to the soldiers. 'Ain't that right, men?'

They laughed. 'Sure is, Cap'n.'

Bond looked affectionately at the Texan with whom he had shared so many adventures.

The writing gives us no inward feel of the experience of human beings in action or danger. Instead, there is an attempt to establish 'realism' as by the borrowed details of weapons: 'the ten pound armour-piercing rocket' and so forth. This is exactly how a small boy backs up his 'war' writing when he has no experience to go on, and needs desperately to try to convince us. 'So in America three weeks later 8 Dakota D.C.7's towing Horsa gliders took off for Burma with mustang escorts. They were carrying Chindit troops . . .' (Boy of 13).

Surely, for instance, a bazooka does not merely 'shudder slightly'? The impression of the flight of a missile is hardly conveyed by the hack phrase of the war story 'on its way'. Any actual explosive impact is always something more interesting and unique than 'a flash and a puff of blue smoke'. Conrad, Graves, Barbusse, and David Jones can convey the experience of violence and explosion with that intensity of perception which is impelled by dread. This particular heightening of response makes every actual act of projecting a missile in action a unique and memorable occasion. Fleming cannot realise this inwardness of experience of violence in action, and so he cannot lead us imaginatively into his episodes in a humanly 'felt' way. I am not saying that we would expect this of a commercial writer. I am saying that Fleming would have had to do more for us if he was as good a writer as some intellectuals tell us. As for his vast popular success, we need to look elsewhere for its basis than in the quality of his style.

'Not bad for a rookie' is the kind of 'in talk' which might be said by soldiers in training believing they were talking like old soldiers: from the point of view of common experience of army life it is not 'in' enough. The subsequent technical-aggressive talk ('May put the rear diesel out . . .') is like the talk of a small boy imagining what it is like to talk as a man (just as Fleming's sex is like the sex a small boy imagines himself having as a man).

If a character comes on to the stage in an imitation Victorian melodrama and says 'You bungling oaf' 'sarcastically' the audience would surely groan at such lame attempts to amuse them. If a boy in school writes this kind of dialogue in a story about America: 'Ain't that right men?' They laughed. 'Sure is, cap'n'– his classmates would groan at the stereotype. They would groan, too, at the lukewarm ineptitude of 'Bond looked affectionately at the Texan with whom he had shared so many adventures'.

Considered as novels, or even as entertainment, the books are so poor in the writing that even by the standards of detective or adventure stories their quality cannot explain their world-wide appeal. When Fleming turns from adventure and action to the novelist's sphere and seeks to convey a manly 'knowingness' about human affairs in this cliché-ridden prose, this writer must surely hardly convince the kind of pupil, of average academic ability, who can yet write with clarity and sincerity in school.

> Bond said thoughtfully, 'I wouldn't get anywhere sucking up to him, asking him for a job or something of that sort, sir. I should say he's the sort of man who only respects people who are tougher or smarter than he is. I've given him one beating and the only message I got from him was that he'd like me to play golf with him. Perhaps I'd better do just that.'
> 'Fine way for one of my top men to spend his time.' The sarcasm in M.'s voice was weary, resigned.

The morality would hardly serve for an adventure story in the Biggles mode, while the language it is couched in would hardly pass in a boy's story when he reads it aloud to his class. 'Fine way for one of my top men to spend his time', is dilute *Boy's Own Paper*. 'Weary, resigned' is an old boy's adventure story tag, too. The adventure books I read as a boy, and the stories in *The Gem* and *The Wizard* were full of this kind of heavy-handed opening: 'James Bond booked in at the Hotel des Bergues, took a bath and shower and changed his clothes. He weighed the Walther PPK in his hand and wondered whether he should take it or leave it behind. He decided to leave it.' And how often did one find this kind of chapter ending: 'Goldfinger, lit with glory by the setting sun, but with a long black shadow tied to his heels, followed Bond slowly, his eyes fixed thoughtfully on Bond's back'.

The next chapter opens with phrases which are portentously 'philosophical' with similar origins: 'There are some rich men who use their riches like a club. Bond, luxuriating in his bath, thought that Goldfinger was one of them. He was the kind of man who thought he could flatten the world with his money, bludgeoning aside annoyance and opposition with his heavy wad'.

This has the tone of a 'man of the world' who is capable of making wise comments on human affairs. This pseudo-philosophising manner enables the reader to feel that he is somehow concerning himself with the 'welfare of society,' whereas in truth he is rather indulging himself in primitive phantasies, the tension of anxiety aroused by which helps him at least to feel alive in a manic way. Here, under the surface, there is an unconscious threat evoked by the unusual words 'flatten', 'bludgeoning', and 'wad'. But we have not yet found the essential Fleming.

Even when 'tense' 'dramatic' moments occur the prelude to action is developed in the language of stock cliché:

'That's quite all right.' Bond felt there was something fishy in this. He couldn't put his finger on what it was.

'Well then, au revoir.' Goldfinger went to the front door. 'But I must give you some light. It's really very dark in here.' Goldfinger brushed his hand down a wall-plate of switches and suddenly lights blazed all over the hall – from standard lamps, wall brackets, and four clusters in the ceiling. Now the room was as bright as a film studio. It was an extraordinary transformation. Bond, half dazzled, watched Goldfinger open the front door and stride out. In a minute he heard the sound of a car, but not the Rolls, rev up noisily, change gear and go off fast down the drive.

On an instinct, Bond walked over to the front door and opened it. The drive was empty.

'There was something fishy . . .', 'on an instinct'; any efficient schoolboy writer has his quiver full of such phrases from his lighter reading.

By contrast with all the commonplace staple modes in Fleming's work there is one kind of writing which stands out as peculiarly his. It may be represented by this:

> Bond watched, fascinated. Now the slanting eyes in the flat yellow mask were glinting with a fierce intentness. Faced by such a man, thought Bond, one could only go down on one's knees and wait for death.
>
> Goldfinger lifted his hand. The bunched toes in the polished soft leather shoes seemed to grip the ground. The Korean took one long crouching stride with knees well bent and then whirled off the ground. In mid-air his feet slapped together like a ballet dancer's but higher than a ballet dancer's have ever reached, and then the body bent sideways and downwards and the right foot shot out like a piston. There came a crashing thud. Gracefully the body settled back down on the hands, now splayed on the floor, the elbows bent to take the weight and then straightened sharply to throw the man up and back on his feet.
>
> Oddjob stood to attention. This time there was a gleam of triumph in his flat eyes as he looked at the three-inch jagged bite the edge of his foot had taken out of the mantelpiece.

There is a particular phantasmagoric quality in such an incident: it is like a nightmare, or an insane delusion. The environment is full of menace, and the threats are enacted in a strange balletic slow-movement like those of a dreadful hallucination. We seem to be in a familiar world – the 'Sussex country house' setting of the run-of-the-mill crime story. But there is a particular intensity in the writing – 'bunched toes in the polished soft leather shoes' – which contrasts disturbingly with the reassuring setting. It has something of the trick with sudden horrifying incidents in a conventional setting of Edgar Wallace – the viper crawling up the bellrope – but there is a deeper fascination. This arises from a special preoccupation with the *surfaces, skins, outsides of the body, its softness or hardness, and the effect of various forms of impingement of limbs or projectiles on the external world.* Fleming's writing, as I shall argue, is most effective in a certain way when it is engaged in an obsessional preoccupation with the body, inner contents, the 'shell' of the identity, and the effects of aggression in defending or attacking this tegument of identity. It is the prose of 'anxiety over a situation . . . involving a threat to the ego' – or paranoid–schizoid prose.

It is by no means an adequate critical objection to say of Fleming that he was consciously exploiting sadism. The anxiety and suspense which his underlying symbolism arouses goes far beyond the kind of anxiety aroused (say) by an Edgar Wallace. It gains its special hold over us by arousing our fascination with depersonalised or non-human entities which threaten to invade our inner substance like disembodied projectiles, and to 'take us over'. As Winnicott has pointed out, our fear of being 'infinitely exploited' is our deepest fear of all, and we have looked at the connection between primitive anxiety and the fear of annihilation. Fleming's kind of entertainment is based on such fears, on primitive hate.

Fleming's achievement was to get such essentially deranged and primitive phantasies accepted socially as entertainment: he managed to get hate tolerated in this sphere. He seems to have managed this by various masks – techniques of charm and appeal which disguise hate, and which we can understand in the light of Khan's analysis of the 'technique of intimacy' of the pervert. Fleming's work is a cultural expression of his own use of charm for sexual purposes, while avoiding 'emotional surrender': it represents the same kind of 'narcissistic magical exploitation of the object' whose purpose is to preserve 'inner contents'. He makes us feel, for instance, that he is a man of the world in a larger-than-life way: how could such a sophisticated person be indulging in infantile phantasies?

These phantasies, of course, include phantasies of sex as well as violence. 'Heightened instinctual modality' and 'idealization of instinct', at the expense of genuine 'meeting', characterise a particular perverted development in our culture, influenced by such figures as Fleming and Amis, leading to an increased social acceptability for obscenity in our 'enlightened' culture. By influences such as theirs, aggressive oral utterance has become acceptable in our time as a mark of 'adult' maturity. We have been led to feel, How can someone who is so uninhibited be full of hate? But this is a disguise beneath which a great deal of destructiveness may be indulged in a hidden form: the depersonal-isation of sex seems an assertion of vitality, but is in fact a manifestation of flight from life. As Khan points out in a later paper, the actual predicament of the pervert, while not yet fully understood, is very different from that conveyed by the 'mystifications of . . . the envious adulation of the seemingly liberal social approach' (Khan [66]).

Fleming did a great deal to get the misrepresentation of 'the charade of intimacy' socially acceptable at a popular level, as 'sophistication'. Without batting an eyelid the respectable housewives under the driers read the coarse obscenities in which a society wife will calmly remark, in a London glossy: 'We went to the West Indies for the screwing', how everybody knows that the atmosphere there makes you 'randy', and so forth. In Fleming, as we shall see, there are from time to time extraordinarily coarse outspoken comments on subjects to do with sex. Today, the common reader does not reject such 'frankness' from his own good sense and dignity and from a disinclination to have the area of the 'most intimate dialogue' violated. He is cowed: and persuaded that it is the Flemings, Amises, Henry Millers, and Brophies who have sophistication, maturity, and wisdom. Yet, as we have seen, their very shamelessness manifests fear and forms of compensation for psychic impotence.

In consequence, examined in the light of such disinterested disciplines as object-relations psychology, many such expressions of 'knowingness' are exposed as showing lamentable ignorance, and, moreover, often full of startlingly irrational and anti-human elements.

Fleming's worldly wisdom is, of course, often something more like the boyish bravado of a naughty school-child: 'Bond said politely, "then you can go and —— yourself." He expelled all the breath from his lungs and closed his eyes. "Even I am not capable of that, Mr. Bond," said Goldfinger with good humour.'

It is believed, in the *New Statesman* milieu, that there is a new 'freedom' in our ability to print and read such a reference to an obscene phrase. Indeed, today, matters have gone further: when Wayland Young urged in *Eros Denied* that we should use the 'short words' for sexual matters, Amis purred, 'This is right'. Yet from the object-relations point of view the need to be obscene would seem to arise from anxiety, existential frustration, and the hatred of being human.

When we find sexual symbolism used in such compensatory ways we may perhaps detect those elements Khan discovers in the pervert's technique of intimacy – 'self-protective' negative, and mistrustful elements directed against the recognition of genuine ego-needs. From the point of view of the 'schizoid diagnosis' our cult of 'frankness' may belong to 'bad thinking' as a form of false solution to the problem of identity in the face of inward insecurity. If so, it is no real freedom. And, as we shall see, Goldfinger's remark really arises out of the unconscious primitive symbolism of the book.

Fleming managed to get such use of primitive symbolism accepted as a pastime, and with the primitive symbolism he managed to make the 'man-of-the-world' obscenity acceptable too, though this is but a way of disguising the infantile nature of the day-dream. Goldfinger's expression disguises the fact that he is a symbolic embodiment of the paternal penis. With this 'sophisticated' disguise has gone a whole process of reversal of values, so that obscenity, instead of being recognised as a regression to primitive oral-aggressiveness, is admired as a manifestation of uninhibitedness, and is worn as a mark of modish cultivation.

Beneath the surface of these gambits is a ruthless primitive hate, and it is really this unconscious element which carries the reader through the comparative tedium of the prose. Fleming's success thus depends upon schizoid–paranoid phantasies which relieve the existential anxiety of the modern reader albeit in a false way. They thus match the 'Great Fear' by which, as Professor Jules Henry points out, sustains Western society in the international sphere. For such reasons, a book like *Goldfinger*, will stand, I believe, as representative of much else in our culture. (Today, I see, the photograph of the girl coated by poisonous gold is replaced in a shop window by a naked girl in a coffin decorated with flowers. The essential symbol of a fear and hatred of our vulnerable 'being' remains the same. Since this book was written the attack has escalated towards such viciousness that woman is humiliated on the London stage nightly, and raped (even with a false nose) in every cinema in the country.)

CHAPTER 9

The Taboo on Weakness

I chose Fleming's *Goldfinger* as an example because all its symbolism is manifestly that of primitive schizoid hate. It is about getting and protecting gold as 'inner contents', 'taking' sex, aggressive action and counteraction, eating, and death. Above I have discussed Balint's view that 'hate is the last remnant, the denial of, and the defence against the primitive love-object.'

As we have seen, Fairbairn links the paranoia and aggression of the schizoid individual with overdependence and unsatisfied love needs. We can approach Fleming's work as an attempt to protect himself against the recognition of profound ego-weakness by this symbolism.

Hate, as we have seen, is a manifestation of the inability to tolerate dependence because dependence in infancy has proved to be intolerably dangerous. Experience of reliance on the female element has been so unreliable that the whole area of 'being' of love and relationship cannot be accepted as a primary need. It is impossible to accept that one is human, and that as a human being one needs relationship with others. This predicament, as we have seen, involves an individual in a need to base his continuing existence on alienation, paranoia, and other aggressive mechanisms.

A useful starting point in unravelling the hate mechanisms of Fleming's book is to take his attitudes to sex. Sex is the realm of experience in which we enter most deeply into 'female element being'. If I am correct in believing that Fleming's symbolism is the symbolism of hate, then we would expect to find the denial of dependence expressed most energetically in his dealings with sex. We would expect to find there a hatred of the female element – a hatred of woman. Since this fear is a projection of one's own fear of the female element in oneself, this implies a fear of one's own humanity. Where we find a fear of being human, we are likely to find solutions to the problem of life which are likely to be socially and politically dangerous.

All these are, in fact, what we do find in Fleming, though, again, hate here is heavily disguised. How successful the disguise is we shall see when we look at Fleming's life and the interpretations of his behaviour and attitudes made by his biographer.

The truth, as we glimpse it from his biography, would seem to be that Fleming was hardly able to find sexual reality in terms of 'being' with a woman at all. What is in consequence so astonishing is the way in which he is commonly believed to be an expert on sex. This, despite the fact that in any explicit comment on sexual matters Fleming reveals the crassest prejudices of a second-rate mind. For instance, he actually attributes the prevalence of 'sexual misfits' to emancipation and to the giving of women equal votes.

> Bond came to the conclusion that Tilly Masterton was one of those girls whose hormones had got mixed up. He knew the type well and thought they and their male counterparts were a direct consequence of giving votes to women and 'sex equality'. As a result of fifty years of emancipation, feminine qualities were dying out or being transferred to the males. Pansies of both sexes were everywhere, not yet completely homosexual, but confused, not knowing what they were. The result was a herd of unhappy sexual misfits – barren and full of frustrations, the women wanting to dominate and the men to be nannied. He was sorry for them, but he had no time for them. Bond smiled sourly to himself as he remembered his fantasies about this girl as they sped along the valley of the Loire. Entre Deux Seins indeed!

This extraordinary paragraph gives a momentary glimpse of a mind filled with contempt for others, and their weakness ('he had no time for them'), and with the capacity to make crude rationalisations to vindicate his hate. In this we may suspect that Bond was Fleming's *alter ego* more than his biographer admits. Fleming's achievement was to get us to accept such contempt from a 'loyal' member of the Secret Service – and to find such anti-human attitudes respectable. 'Entre Deux Seins indeed!' in its context is uttered as a scathing denial by Bond of his momentary lapse into accepting his dependence on another. Although, as we shall see, this phrase comes from a passage in which James Bond is calculating a technique of seduction, its rejection comes from another passage whose tone conveys a fear of relationship – and there is much in Fleming which reveals a fear of love. Bond is the *alter ego* of a man who expressed such fears by treating his mistresses with calculated indifference in public. Bond must be strong by denying he is human: like the Nazi Rauschning he cries: 'We will have no weakness or tenderness'. Pussy Galore will find Bond a 'man' 'such as she has never met' – that is a man who has successfully denied he is human – and that he is a man.

Where we find such spleen directed against 'sexual misfits' and hostility to 'being nannied' we may suspect that what is being attacked is some weakness within the author himself which he is trying to counteract by identifying with a mythical hero of superpotency. As Fairbairn would interpret such an attitude, this is a manifestation of overdependence and of an insecurity which fears emotional commitment as too intolerable to be accepted.

Bond's whole attitude to sex is that of the schizoid to whom 'the safety of his own ego is the first and only consideration'. In his attitude to other human beings, and especially to women, he can only regard them as having 'less than individual human value'. He thus has no value for human individuality and the rights of persons. To him women are essentially 'partial objects', and thus 'breasts' for his protagonist's 'taking'. There is no giving and meeting, in his novel, and so Fleming is thus quite cut off from any knowledge about *human* sex as an aspect of 'being-in-the-world' at all.

This essential ignorance naturally colours all approaches to sex in his book. We may begin our examination of *Goldfinger* with the above paragraph as something of a clue to its true nature – with an uncomfortable sense that something even more primitive lurks beneath its coarseness, stupidity, and cruelty.

CHAPTER 10

Primitive Phantasy

THE primitive elements in Fleming's phantasy may be explored further by pondering the basic symbolism of his work. What are the main symbols? Primarily there is depersonalised sex. We have said that it is sex as a small boy conceives of it: I believe we can go even deeper and say it is sex as an *infant* conceives of it – as a *form of eating* (while much of the eating in the book, as we shall see, is symbolic sex). Also significant among Fleming's symbols are his *motor-cars* of a very special kind, often used aggressively and sometimes capable of a kind of magic. From an orthodox psychoanalytical approach these could be seen as symbolic penises – but from the object-relations point of view we can see them as extensions of the *male element* or instruments of *doing*. The cars we may associate with the *guns, bazookas, radar-scanners*, and other weapons* by which Bond seeks to defend himself and also *to thrust harm into others*, and into large store-rooms (Fort Knox, the Bank of England). The latter we can interpret as wombs – 'insides' certainly.

These storerooms are often full of *gold*, and gold we recognise as a symbol of faeces or *rich inner contents*. The inner contents of the body, as we know from Fairbairn and Melanie Klein, are to the infant both something creative (a gift of achievement he gives out of himself to his mother as when she 'receives' his motions) and something to be got rid of. To the schizoid individual, as we have seen, there is a particular significance which focuses on faeces as 'inner contents'. He fears their loss, and so is impelled to hoard his inner contents. He also may feel his inner contents are 'bad', poisonous, and harmful. Yet he also cherishes them as 'golden'. He is afraid of implosion or of being invaded by the inner contents of others. All infants experience both curiosity about the inner contents of the mother, and the symbolism of this is often found in nursery rhyme and fairy-story. The mother's creativity is feared because it may produce siblings who compete for her love: hence her inner contents may be hated. Her creativity is also desired for oneself and so envied – which leads to the impulse to scoop her out and empty her, taking her 'gold' for oneself. For this envy the infant fears revenge. Thus the inner contents of the mother are the focus of both schizoid fears of the consequences of love and depressive fears of the consequences of hate.

As we shall see, these intense fears are exacerbated by curiosity in the child not only about 'what is inside mummy' but also by the excitement which the child feels when he becomes involved in phantasy in the parents' sexual intercourse. He recognises that there is some libidinal excitement between his parents which culminates in a mutual act in which powerful appetites are involved. This excites him too. But since he can only conceive of sex in terms of eating, this evokes existence fears arising from the hunger of his

* Thermite bombs, atom bombs, rifles, telescopes, trains, jet-planes, cruisers, lethal bowler hats.

own mouth-ego. Since food disappears from the outside world when it is eaten, and since appetite is associated by him with incorporation, he fears that his mother and father may eat one another.

He also fears that the father may fill the mother with rich creativity, or with poison, while she may incorporate the father's penis or 'empty' him as he phantasies emptying a breast. In so far as he has phantasied the incorporation of the maternal breast or the paternal penis (in Fairbairn we see how the schizoid individual feels he has *had to steal these*), the infant feels that in some way he has become involved in the dangerous incorporative energies of sexual excitement.

According to Melanie Klein, this gives rise to profound terrors in infantile phantasy – terrors associated with the 'primal scene' – that is, *phantasied intercourse* between the parents. Because 'the child's ego is a mouth-ego' he is excitedly involved, and sees this is a libidinal act; he desires this phantasied intercourse to be *sadistic*. His own masturbation phantasies are associated with this phantasied primal scene sadism. This is a useful way not only of approaching Fleming's sex but also the sex in much 'pop' culture from Hollywood to the Playboy Club. It is manic primal scene phantasy of the kind in which we indulged when masturbation was for us a way of feeling alive and real.*

In consequence of his involvement in such sadistic phantasy, the infant fears that in return for all the envy involved, his desires to incorporate, and to identify himself with the parents in their mutual incorporation, there will be *retribution*. (This kind of retribution is called *talion* retribution from the Latin *lex talionis*.) As a consequence of this fear of retribution for sadistic participation in the primal scene the infant fears revenge from both father and mother. The father turns in revenge from resentment at being threatened with usurpation (in the Oedipal situation) and threatens retributive castration. But in the background, much more deeply feared, lurks the *castrating mother*, whose retribution is made more complex because of the curiosity directed at her 'inner contents' and because of the child's involvement in the attempt to share the father's penetration of these for creative, 'emptying', or poisoning purposes. This phantasy of the castrating mother I believe we may associate with the underlying fear and hatred of woman and 'female element being' already referred to. But Melanie Klein discovered a yet more terrible phantasy, which is that of the *combined parents* who, having as it were mutually incorporated one another by mutually eating penis and breast, turn in hostile malignancy on the infant. This is one profound paranoid schizoid infant fear which we all have experienced in some degree. Such fears of invading and being invaded are obviously greater in those who suffer a schizoid sense of weakness of identity. Turning from Melanie Klein's account of infant phantasy we can, I believe, now see a particular significance in the symbolism of Ian Fleming's *Goldfinger*.

There is, for instance, Goldfinger himself. Interpreted in the light of Kleinan theory he is a symbol of the father's penis which seeks to thrust harm into the 'national gold-store' or to extract the gold from it. The penis is gold itself – which can be interpreted both as meaning that it is a faecal 'projectile' weapon, and that it is a valuable envied object (i.e. an internalised possession which is the focus of 'libidinal cathexis'). This would explain the strange mixture of hate and affection with which the author and his protagonist regard Goldfinger.

* The naked, writhing lovers on the covers of paperbacks on every bookstall, seen in this light, are manic Primal Scene phantasies, calculated to extract our money by playing on primitive anxiety, while also helping us to feel alive in a primitive way.

Behind Goldfinger lurks 'SMERSH' who is described at one point, as we shall see, as having 'bloody teeth'. This is surely the castrating mother who lurks behind the castrating father, while the combination of all the malignant forces, including such agents as 'Odd-job', represent the combined parents: a good deal of the activity of Bond feels like activity directed paranoically at the possibility of the parents becoming combined.

Other major forms of symbolism we can note in Ian Fleming's books include descriptions of sexual acts often carried out with the purpose of exploiting another person. In all his sex the prevalent attitude to woman is that of a *partial object* for *taking*. Here there is an obvious similarity between the symbolic woman in Fleming's books and the vision of the schizophrenic youth discussed by Fairbairn above (p. 47). The stream of milk in that patient's dream bears an obvious symbolic significance to Pussy Galore whose name means 'inexhaustible sexual organ', and who is one of those 'animals' of phantasy which are 'symbols of *bodily organs*' or *partial objects*.

These are the major symbols. There are others whose significance we shall need to examine later, such as, for instance, the *elaborate meals*, the way in which the women are *mannish*, the preoccupation with elaborate social codes and rituals, and the '*licence to kill*', or, as we may interpret it, 'licence to give oneself up to the joys of hating'.

In the light of Fairbairn's insights, I believe, we can see that the 'spy' symbolism of curiosity, secrecy, and paranoic action is itself an expression of primitive anxiety about what there is 'inside' us. Moreover, from Melanie Klein's work we can perhaps see this 'spy' theme as arising from *unsatisfied sexual curiosity* of an infantile kind, associated with a deep fear of 'bad inner contents' and of being imploded, castrated, or of being annihilated in some way by a malignant environment, while also needing to 'scoop out'. The symbolism of *Goldfinger* perhaps arose from a deep existential insecurity and a need to preserve identity and internalised objects against paranoic threats. What we shall have to decide later is whether Fleming sought, or found in any way, real solutions to such problems, or whether he was content to pursue and purvey the false solutions of primitive hate as exemplified in the infant's aggressive phantasy.

The fundamental symbolism in *Goldfinger* is certainly that which centres around the horror of *being emptied*, and the obsession with what there may be 'within oneself'. When James Bond has killed the Mexican, he reflects: 'What an extraordinary difference there was between a body full of person and a body that was empty. . . .'

The story centres round attempts to get valuable stuff out of something (e.g. the vaults of 'the Old Lady of Threadneedle Street'), or to thrust something malevolent into hidden places (thermite bombs). Bond is the agent of the collective need to preserve 'national order' against such threats. The identity is thus identified with the 'nation', and the solutions of the identity with 'security'. Goldfinger himself is the enemy who is an agent of SMERSH, who seeks to get good stuff out and to thrust harm in. While staying alive seems in the phantasy to depend upon omnipotence in the struggle to preserve 'inner contents', Bond's capacity to be strong enough to survive is implicitly shown to depend upon regular episodes of *taking* from *partial objects* which have inexhaustible resources (or Pussies). There is, meanwhile, a definite implication that in such taking any real mutual 'meeting' would threaten survival: the object must give 'automatic satisfaction', and any genuine love would threaten annihilation. The preserving of the tegument of the self is achieved by moving as far as possible from human relationship and towards the non-human. Bond has an 'attitude of omnipotence', 'cherished as a precious secret' – which, in the light of Balint's insights, appears as a compensation, a 'precarious attempt to overcome feelings of hopelessness'.

There is also another important aspect of the sexual relationships in *Goldfinger* which will be discussed in detail later. The women who are 'taken' are, first of all, 'made into men', while some sadistic encounters with men are obviously sexual episodes in disguise. The sex in *Goldfinger* thus seems to be disguised homosexuality. Meanwhile, woman as woman does not really appear, and if she threatens to show her face she is annihilated, controlled, subject to contempt, humiliation, or death.

In the background, Goldfinger himself paints girls with gold paint and has sexual intercourse with them. Tilly *Master*ton experiences this in such a way that she is murdered by being completely covered in gold. In this I believe we may find a symbolism of *enclosing the female element entirely in hate, disguised as love, and destroying it thus*. In so far as it is Goldfinger who does this, it is what (the infant fears) the father does to mother. But, while the infant fears this act, he also wants to participate, since this seems a way to feel alive. The strange appeal of a book like *Goldfinger* therefore lies in involving us in the desires of such a primitive phantasy. Fleming wants us to hate – and he also seeks to make hate, as an attack on female element being by faecal attack, socially acceptable. Even the cover of his book is covered with gold. In so far as we pick it up, we are defiled and involved in the false solutions of hate ourselves.

In contrast to this 'poisoned' female element, the mother lurks in the background heavily disguised, both needed and feared. She is the 'Old Lady of Threadneedle Street' whom Bond is protecting. But in her talion form she is also SMERSH. It is apparently true that such an organisation exists or existed. But the name has obvious unconscious fascination as the name of an unseen enemy in a paranoid–schizoid sadistic phantasy since it is virtually a portmanteau word comprising *mère, merde, shit, smash*, and *merge*. This deeply feared mythological mother–woman, however, is significantly *not* 'in' the other women, who are elaborately made into not-women (lesbians, storm-troopers, gangsters, and everything that mother is not). Symbolically, this means that 'female element being' derived from the mother is not 'in' the self, which is to be all 'pure' false male doing (or hate).

So, we begin to make interesting discoveries about the unconscious meaning of Fleming's symbolism once we suspect that if our attention is held it must be something other than the quality of the writing that is holding us. The torture scene in *Goldfinger*, for instance, looked at as 'adventure' writing, is poor imitation Poe: there is no need to labour examination of the clichés here. But what is peculiar is the genital element, evoking talion fear of a primitive kind, while the solution to the paranoid seems to be to cultivate one's inner vacuum and to dissolve oneself in it:

> The lever on the table moved across iron teeth. Now Bond could feel the wind of the saw between his knees. The hands came back.
> Bond counted the slowly pounding pulse that utterly possessed his body. It was like the huge panting power plant in the other part of the factory but, in his case, it was slowly decelerating. If only it would slow down quicker. What was this ridiculous will to live that refused to listen to the brain? Who was making the engine run on although the tank was dry of fuel? But he must empty his mind of thought, as well as rid body of oxygen. He must become a vacuum, a deep hole of unconsciousness.
> Still the light burned red through his eyelids. Still he could feel the bursting pressure in his temples. Still the slow drum of life beat in his ears.
> A scream tried to force its way through the clamped teeth.
> Die damn you die die damn you die damn you die damn you die damn you die. . ..

The saw is to begin by castrating Bond (inevitably) as a penance.

> 'Mr. Bond, the word "pain" comes from the Latin *poena* meaning "penalty" – that which must be paid. You must now pay for the inquisitiveness which your attack upon me proves, as I suspected, to be inimical. Curiosity as they say. . . .'

The word 'curiosity', as we shall see, is revealing. Such a scene is captivating, despite the poverty of invention, because of its play on vestiges of our infantile fear of curiosity and our unconscious dread of its consequences.

As Melanie Klein points out, the paranoic phantasy of the infant is a 'manifestation of talion fears' of a monstrous ruthlessness. In such a scene infantile curiosity meets its feared fate. It is highly significant that Goldfinger threatens to give the girl to 'Odd job' to *eat*. For most of us it is a long time since we were liable to be overcome by primitive fears that arose from the infant 'mouth-ego', so that our world was full of penises or vaginas with mouths and teeth, and cannibalistic faecal projectiles. Goldfinger has already given a cat-sibling pet to 'Odd job' to be eaten: now the girl who is the object of Bond's sexual taking is to be eaten by a faecal emanation from the talion father's penis. It is this underlying primitive symbolism which is mingled with an old-fashioned novel-ette situation of the hero tied to the train lines. Fleming's achievement is to arouse in us such very early primitive fears of parental imagos which threaten revenge for our involvement in libidinal excitement.

> There was nothing else to help him through the pain barrier before the blessing of death. For death was the only exit. He knew he could never squeal to Goldfinger and live with himself again – even in the unlikely event that Goldfinger could be bought off with the truth. No, he must stick to his thin story and hope that the others who would now follow him on Goldfinger's train would have better luck. Who would M. choose? Probably 008, the second killer in the small section of three. He was a good man, more careful than Bond. M. would know that Goldfinger had killed Bond and he would end with Bond's enquiry about the Entreprises Auric. Yes, fate would catch up with Goldfinger if Bond could only keep his mouth shut. If he gave the least clue away, Goldfinger would escape. That was unthinkable.
> 'Now then, Mr. Bond,' Goldfinger's voice was brisk. 'Enough of these amiabilities. Sing, as my Chicago friends put it, and you will die quickly and painlessly. The girl also. Sing not, and your death will be one long scream. The girl I shall then give to Oddjob, as I did that cat, for supper. Which is it to be?'

In the end, as in the old melodramas of early cinema, the hero is rescued – by magic. The lamest excuse for the escape is given – a lameness we recognise from our own child phantasies as belonging to dream omnipotence.

> 'You suggested that you and Miss Masterton would work for me. Normally I would have no use for either of you, but it just happens that I am on the brink of a certain enterprise in which the services of both of you could be of a certain minimal assistance. So I took the gamble. I gave you both the necessary sedatives. . . .'

But the weakness of the magic solution escapes our attention because our attention has been successfully held by the evocation of unconscious fears of castration. Because he is so captured by this unconscious appeal even the intelligent reader is willing to put up with the clumsiest lapses. Unconsciously, perhaps, he recognises that the whole episode was merely an excuse for the play on primitive symbolism, and now that is done with, the plot needs to be cleared up quickly, ready for the next episode. The plot was never the point, anyway.

But this leads to crude blunders at the level of 'adventure story' – as here. Bond and Tilly are imprisoned by Goldfinger. Bond feels he must get her to 'go along':

Why had Goldfinger made that cryptic remark about her 'inclinations'? What was there about her that he himself felt – something withdrawn, inimical. She was beautiful – physically desirable. But there was a cold, hard centre to her that Bond couldn't understand or define. Oh well, the main thing was to get her to go along. Otherwise life in prison would be intolerable.

Bond went back into her room. He left both doors open so that he could hear. She was still sitting on the bed wrapped in a coiled immobility. She watched Bond carefully. Bond leaned against the jamb of the door. He took a long pull at his whisky. He said, looking her in the eye, 'You'd better know that I'm from Scotland Yard' – the euphemism would serve. 'We're after this man Goldfinger. He doesn't mind. He thinks no one can find us for at least a week. He's probably right. He saved our lives because he wants us to work for him on a crime. It's big business. Pretty scatter-brained. But there's a lot of planning and paperwork. We've got to look after that side. Can you do shorthand and typing?'

'Yes.' Her eyes were alight. 'What's the crime?'

So engrossed is Fleming here with his unconscious preoccupations that he even forgets the realism demanded of crime fiction. The ubiquitous and powerful Goldfinger would hardly be living up to his image if he had not had that room bugged. But the writer's need here is to enact (as in a boy's erotic dream) the *symbolic* 'softening up' of the woman who otherwise – if she were left out of control – would be too dangerous. Once this magic power over the dangerous woman is established, we can revert to the 'Biggles' way of talking to her in the protagonist and to the cliché of the magazine story ('Her eyes were alight'), which is the staple

CHAPTER 11

Pecunia Non Olet

THE play with motor-cars and other vehicles in Fleming's work becomes more significant if we examine it in the light of Melanie Klein's observations on the play of young children with toy cars or on their drawings and other phantasies. Cars and bicycles, etc., are often used by children to represent sexual intercourse and interactions of other kinds, often aggressive, between members of the family. Keeping our analytical eye open, then, we can read Fleming's novel as if we were a psychotherapist watching a child of an age between 2 and 6 playing with his Dinky cars.

Interestingly enough, Fleming himself makes the sexual symbolism of his car-play quite explicit in places. In *Goldfinger* Bond deliberately rams a girl's car with his own, and makes the obscene jest, 'If you touch me there again you'll have to marry me' – a remark which is not only intended to convey worldly wiseness about sex, but which is in fact a joke because it obliquely refers to *the kind of belief about sex play a child of about 6 might have.*

We have here a hint from the author himself that such an incident is symbolic of sex play belonging to that age. So we may legitimately compare the phantasies of little Fritz – Melanie Klein's patient aged 6 – who spoke of

a big motor that looked just like an electric car. It had seats too and there was a little motor that ran along with the big one. Their roofs could be opened up and then shut down when it rained. Then the motors went on and ran into an electric car and knocked it away. Then the big motor went on top of the electric car and drew the little one after it. And then they all got close together, the electric car and the two motors. The electric car had a connecting-rod too. You know what I mean? The big motor had a beautiful big silver iron thing and the little one had something like two little hooks. The little one was between the electric car and the motor. Then they drove up a high mountain and came down quickly again. The motors stayed there in the night too. When electric cars came they knocked them away and if any one did like that (with an arm) 'they went backward at once'.

Melanie Klein comments:

(I explain that the big motor is his papa, the electric car his mamma and the little motor himself, and that he has put himself between papa and mamma because he would so much like to put papa away altogether and to remain alone with his mamma and do with her what only papa is allowed to do.) After a little hesitation he agrees but continues quickly, 'The big and little motors then went away, they were in their house, they looked out of the window, it was a very big window. Then two big motors came. One was grandfather, the other was just papa. Grandmamma was not there, she was' (He hesitates a little and looks very solemn) '. . . she was dead.' (He looks at me, but as I remain quite unmoved, he goes on.) – 'And then they all drove down the mountain together. One chauffeur opened the doors with his foot; the other opened with his feet the thing that one turns round' (handle). 'The one chauffeur became sick, that was grandpapa' (again he looks at me interrogatively but seeing me undisturbed continued), 'The other chauffeur said to him, "You dirty beast, do you want your ears boxed, I will knock you down at once".' (I enquire who the other chauffeur was?) He, 'Me. And then our soldiers throw them all down: they were all soldiers – and smash the motor and beat him and smear his face with coal and stuff coal in his mouth too'; (reassuringly) 'he thought it was a sweetie, you know, and that is why he took it and it was coal. Then everyone was a soldier and I was the officer. I had a beautiful uniform and' (he holds himself erect) 'I held myself like this, and then followed me. They took his gun away from him; he could only walk like this' (here he doubles himself up).

The light this casts on Fleming's phantasies will be obvious: chauffeurs, cars, violence, smearing with stuff, uniforms – all have in Fleming's phantasy world the same kind of phallic and cloacal symbolism as they do here for Fritz, and are associated with the same fears of castration and other talion harm. This is the kind of unconscious phantasy that lies behind such episodes as this:

'Don't you dare touch my car! Leave it alone.' Angrily the girl climbed back into the driver's seat. She pressed the self-starter. The engine fired. Metal clanged under the bonnet. She switched off and leant out. 'There you are, you idiot! You've smashed the fan.'
Bond hoped he had. He got into his own car and eased it away from the Triumph. Bits of the Triumph, released by Bond's bumper, tinkled on to the road: He got out again. The crowd had thinned. There was a man in a mechanic's overalls. He volunteered to call a breakdown van and went off to do so. Bond walked over to the Triumph. The girl had got out and was waiting for him. Her expression had changed. Now she was more composed, Bond noticed that her eyes, which were dark blue, watched his face carefully.

For the child the conflict of motor-cars expresses in a symbolic way conflicts between members of his family in sexual ways, in which he is involved, with consequent threats to his identity. The same symbolism underlies Fleming's episode. With sexual under-currents he introduces the episode to bring about the girl's submission by magic to the omnipotence of Bond's 'False Male Doing' eminently manifested by his motor-car prowess:

Bond said, 'It really won't be too bad. Probably knocked the fan out of alignment. They'll put temporary headlamps in the sockets and straighten up the chrome. You'll be off again by tomorrow morning. Now,' Bond reached into the pocket for his notecase, 'this is maddening for you and I'll certainly take all the blame. Here's a hundred thousand francs to cover the damage and your expenses for the night and telephoning your friends and so on. I'd love to stay here and see you get on the road all right tomorrow morning. But I've got an appointment this evening and I've simply got to make it.'
'No.' The one word was cool, definite. The girl put her hands behind her back and waited.
'But. . . .' What was it she wanted, the police? Have him charged with dangerous driving?
'I've got an appointment this evening too. I've got to make it. I've got to get to Geneva. Will you please take me there? It's not far. Only about a hundred miles. We could do it in two hours in that.'' She gestured at the DB III. 'Will you? Please?'

'Only a blazing need' reveals the wish-fulfilment that generates the phantasy. Though the girl's request to rely on a stranger in such circumstances is utterly unreal, it is true to the nature of the phantasy. She must be defenceless, and so controllable. She must ride in his vehicle and be subdued in the same way that little Fritz subdues others ('if anyone did like that . . . they went backwards at once'), as a safeguard against talion fear.

Of course, for an adult writer, even of phantasies full of magic, there must come times when the story approaches reality. What happens if a woman becomes real?

Although she was a very beautiful girl she was the kind who leaves her beauty alone. She had made no attempt to pat her hair into place. As a result, it looked as a girl's hair should look – untidy, with bits that strayed and a rather crooked parting. It provided the contrast of an uneven, jagged dark frame for the pale symmetry of the face, the main features of which were blue eyes under dark brows, a desirable mouth, and an air of determination and independence that came from the high cheek-bones and the fine line of the jaw. There was the same air of self-reliance in her figure. She held her body proudly – her fine breasts outthrown and unashamed under the taut silk. Her stance, with feet slightly parted and hands behind her back, was a mixture of provocation and challenge.
The whole picture seemed to say, 'Now then, you handsome bastard, don't think you can "little woman" me. You've got me into this mess and, by God, you're going to get me out! You may be attractive, but I've got my life to run, and I know where I'm going.'

Bond weighed her request. How much of a nuisance would she be? How soon could he get rid of her. . . .

As soon as Tilly became 'real', the inevitable reaction is to find her dangerous – and to get rid of her.

In her therapy Melanie Klein was striving towards something creative – to get Fritz to come to terms with the actualities of adults as real people and real sex. Fleming, by contrast, is using infantile phantasy for quite the opposite purpose – to pretend that real people and real sex can be avoided by resort to the mechanisms of the primitive magic of hate.

Little Fritz had to be brought out of his predicament by being brought to face his fears of the father's penis. Here the paranoic symbolism may be compared with the appeal of *Goldfinger*, which is that the long finger of the talion father may reach the protagonist:

> . . . a dream that had frightened him very much and of which he was still afraid even by day. He had been looking at picture-books with riders in them and the book opened and two men came out of them. He and his brother came to the door of the house and there a woman said to them, 'You can't hide here.' But they did hide all the same so that the men could not find them. He told this dream in spite of great resistances that increased so much when I began the interpretation that, not to over-stimulate them, I made it very brief and left it incomplete. I got little in the way of associated ideas, merely that the men had had sticks, guns and bayonets in their hands . . . I explained that these meant his father's big wiwi that he both wishes for and is afraid of, he retorted that 'the weapons were hard but the wiwi is soft.' I explained, however, that the wiwi too becomes hard just in connection with what he wishes to do himself, and he accepted the interpretation without much resistance. He then further related that it seemed to him sometimes as though the one man had stuck in the other and there was only one man!

This symbolism revealed Fritz's 'homosexual component' – as the gun symbol in much modern advertising and phantasy entertainment reveals the same elements of fear and hatred:

> Undoubtedly the hitherto little noticed homosexual component was now coming more to the fore, as is shown too in his subsequent dreams and phantasies. Here is another dream that was not, however, associated with feelings of fear. Everywhere, behind mirrors, doors, etc., were wolves with long tongues hanging out. He shot them all down so that they died. He was not afraid because he was stronger than them. Subsequent phantasies also dealt with wolves. Once when he was frightened again before falling asleep, he said about it that he had been frightened of the hole in the wall where the light peeped in (an opening in the wall for heating purposes) because on the ceiling it looked like a hole too, and a man might get up there with a ladder on to the roof. He also spoke about whether the devil did not sit in the hole in the stove. He recounted that he saw the following in a picture book. A lady is in his room. Suddenly she sees that the devil is sitting in the hole in the stove and his tail is sticking out. In the course of his associations it is shown that he was afraid that the man with the ladder might step on him, hurt him in the belly and finally he owns up that he was afraid for his wiwi.

Here there is a continual symbolism of paranoic fear, of having the identity penetrated by a 'goldfinger'. So, in Fleming's work not only the father, but the castrating mother, too, is seeking James Bond's 'wiwi': so the women Bond meets, as we have seen, have to be disarmed – by Bond's omnipotent charm – and kept in their place by his acts of hatred. Later, the woman who has been enjoyed in the train now has such danger in her inside that she must be enclosed in faeces-poison: painted with gold.

The other girls who gave themselves to Goldfinger had their backbones left uncovered: but the Masterton girl does not. Poison is sealed in her because Bond has been inside her. The danger from inside the woman is paralleled symbolically by the danger inside Fort Knox and the Bank of England: both represent what little Fritz fears as 'cold in the belly', essentially the emptying of the identity in retribution for envious curiosity about

the inside of the mother and being internally poisoned by coition (a fear of great signi-
cance to a schizoid person).

> Not long afterwards I heard the expression, now become infrequent, of 'cold in the belly'. In a con-
> versation about stomach and belly in connection with this, he related the following phantasy. 'There
> is a room in the stomach, in it there are tables and chairs. Someone sits down on a chair and lays his
> head on the table and then the whole house falls down, the ceiling on to the floor, the table too tumbles
> down, the house tumbles down.' To my question, 'Who is the someone and how did he get inside?' he
> answers, 'A little stick came through the wiwi into the belly and into the stomach that way.' In this
> instance he offered little resistance to my interpretation. I told him that he had imagined himself in
> his mamma's place and wished his papa might do with him what he does with her. But he is afraid (as
> he imagines his mamma to be too) that if this stick – papa's wiwi – gets into his wiwi he will be hurt and
> then inside his belly, in his stomach, everything will be destroyed, too – Another time he told about the
> dread he had for a particular Grimm's fairy-tale. It was the tale of a witch who offered a man poisoned
> food but he hands it on to his horse who dies of it. The child said he was afraid of witches because, all
> the same, it might be that it wasn't true what he had been told about there not being any witches
> really. There are queens also who are beautiful and yet who are witches too, and he would very much
> like to know what poison looks like, whether it is solid or fluid. When I asked him why he was afraid of
> anything so bad from his mother, what had he done to her or wished about her, he admitted that when
> he was angry he had wished that she as well as his papa might die and that he had on occasion thought
> to himself 'dirty mamma'. He also acknowledged that he was angry with her when she forbade him to
> play with his wiwi.

We can see now how the witch = mama = SMERSH, while Goldfinger = the
father's wiwi, while 'cold in the belly' = death by being 'Goldfingered'. At the same time,
as Fritz identifies with mama, so, too, does Fleming feel the danger of 'goldfingering'
(dirtying) to be directed at him: the 'spy' paranoia is an attempt to counteract this, as is
the hatred of women ('he was angry with her'). The compulsive fear of 'what the poison
looks like' lies behind many paragraphs of Fleming's about gold: sometimes the account
is obviously given its strange fascination from unconscious anxiety and the schizoid
preoccupation with 'inner contents' ('the person in the body').

This symbolism of 'inner contents', of the fear of 'cold in the belly', we may associate
with the symbolism of *gold* in Fleming's work.

Fleming's gold symbolism emerges from a schizoid preoccupation with what is
'inside' the identity. And since the schizoid has the problem of needing to overcome his
feeling that his 'inner contents' are *bad*, the one problem that emerges is that of making
bad inner contents 'pure'. Gold as 'inner contents' needs to be conceived of here in such
terms as a child feels about these, at a time when the ego is a 'mouth-ego'.* As Ferenczi
says:

> It only needs one more step for the identification of faeces with gold to be complete. Soon even stones
> begin to wound the child's feeling of cleanliness – he longs for something purer – and this is offered to
> him in the shining pieces of money, the high appreciation of which is naturally also in part due to the
> respect in which they are held by adults, as well as to the seductive possibilities of obtaining through
> them everything that the child's heart can desire. Originally, however, it is not these purely practical
> considerations that are operative, enjoyment in the playful collecting, heaping up, and gazing at the
> shiny metal pieces being the chief thing, so that they are treasured even less for their economic value
> than for their own sake as pleasure-giving objects. The eye takes pleasure at the sight of their lustre and
> colour, the ear at their metallic clink, the sense of touch at play with the round smooth discs, only the
> sense of smell comes away empty, and the sense of taste also has to be satisfied with the weak, but
> peculiar taste of coins. With this the development of the money symbol is in its main outlines complete.
> Pleasure in the intestinal contents becomes enjoyment of money, to be nothing other than odourless,
> dehydrated filth that has been made to shine. *Pecunia non olet.* . . . (Ferenczi [20], pp. 326–7.)

---

* Perhaps this is the place to explain that although the child's ego is a mouth-ego, in its phantasy 'mouth'
is associated with the other gates of the body. In Kleinian analysis of symbols, mouth, anus, and vulva relate
as gates of the body, while penis, and breasts relate too, while faeces, urine, semen, spit, and unborn siblings
merge as 'inner contents', and can also become phantasy weapons detached from the self, as can parts of
the body.

Relating this to social problems Ferenczi says:

> . . . It is . . . not improbable that the capitalistic interest stands not only at the disposal of practical, egoistic aims . . . but also that the delight in gold and in the possession of money represents the symbolic replacement of, and the reaction-formation to, repressed anal-erotism. . . .
>
> The capitalistic instinct thus contains, according to our conception, an egoistic and an anal-erotic component. (Ferenczi [20], p. 327.)

Anal-erotic phantasy seems particularly appropriate for a manifestation of commercial popular culture in a capitalist acquisitive society. From later theorists than Ferenczi we have seen that the egoism and anal-eroticism have deeper connotations. From the work of Melanie Klein we see how such anal-erotic symbolism is associated with intense aggression and sadism of a cannibalistic kind, with fearful anxiety about the inside of the mother's body and fear of castratory retribution from the parents in return for sexual curiosity, all these problems being related to anxiety about surviving. As Frankl says, the will-to-money is a form of compensation. Amassing gold can be seen as a guarantee against annihilation and against loss of inner contents – and this explains the symbolism of ambition and at the same time indicates the dangers of attaching identity to acquisitiveness as our society does at large.

These insights of Ferenczi's may, perhaps, explain Fleming's purpose as a writer. As a way of making money, his writing in itself could be a means to amassing gold as a security against schizoid ego-weakness and fear of loss of identity. In the symbolism of the 'spy' story, gold may be taken as the focus of various enactments of the author's schizoid preoccupation with whether he 'had anything inside him'. Moreover, making faeces pure by turning them into gold could have the additional value for Fleming, by the success of his work, of making hate socially acceptable – and so filth, clean. At an even deeper level this has the 'curative' meaning of an attempt to make a weak and empty identity strong by the false solution of taking from other at their expense and 'filling' oneself.

There are strange words about gold by Fleming in which he links it with fear:

> '. . . There's no end to its uses. But it has two defects. It isn't hard enough. It wears out quickly, leaves itself on the linings of our pockets and in the sweat of our skins. Every year, the world's stock is invisibly reduced by friction. I said that gold has two defects.' Colonel Smithers looked sad. 'The other and by far the major defect is that it is the talisman of fear.'

Here gold has affinities with the strange stuff inside one that is likely to leave one's identity an empty bag if it is given out or is taken out (faeces or semen). At other times this disturbing symbolism is disguised by compulsive glosses, presumably taken from the *Encyclopaedia Britannica* or some such source:

> 'There were the great gold treasures of Egypt and Mycenae, Montezuma and the Incas. Croesus and Midas emptied the Middle Eastern territories of gold. Europe was worked for it – the valleys of the Rhine and the Po, Malaga and the plains of Granada. Cyprus was emptied, and the Balkans. India got the fever. . . . Just to show you, from 1500 to 1900, when approximate figures were kept, the whole world produced about eighteen thousand tons of gold. From 1900 to today we have dug up forty-one thousand tons.'
>
> 'At this rate, Mr. Bond,' Colonel Smithers leaned forward earnestly, – 'and please don't quote me – but I wouldn't be surprised if in fifty years' time we have not totally exhausted the gold content of the earth!'

The preoccupation with 'loss of inner contents' is obvious, as is the libidinal attachment to secret internalisations which are threatened – not least by the teeth of SMERSH, gnashing here with frustrated envy:

Then, quietly, discreetly, the Bank of England would freeze Goldfinger's accounts all over the world and perhaps, already tomorrow, the Special Branch of the Swiss police would be knocking on the door of Entreprises Auric. Extradition would follow, Goldfinger would go to Brixton, there would be a quiet, rather complicated case in one of the smuggling courts like Maidstone or Lewes. Goldfinger would get a few years, his naturalization would be revoked and his gold hoard, illegally exported, would trickle back into the vaults below the Bank of England, and SMERSH would gnash its blood-stained teeth and add another page to Bond's bulging zapiska.

The blood-stained teeth of the thwarted SMERSH *merde–mère*, full of poison, complement those of the protective teeth of the Old Lady of Threadneedle Street as contrary aspects of the castrating mother. Wherever we find the 'Old Lady' she has teeth in her 'head' – or, more accurately perhaps from a psychoanalytical point of view, in her *vulva dentata*: ' . . . now that he had been inside the place he decided that the Old Lady of Threadneedle Street might be old but she still had some teeth left in her head.'

Bond displays both 'narcissistic inflation of the ego arising out of secret possession of, and considerable identification with internalised libidinal objects (e.g. the maternal breast and the paternal penis)' – and also paranoic fears because these have been 'stolen'. So, where the father is concerned, the gold is a focus of envy of the power of secretion. (Cf. little Fritz's desire to 'know what poison looks like'):

> The finely chiselled lips pursed into a thin, beatic curve. 'Mr. Bond, all my life I have been in love. I have been in love with gold. I love its colour, its brilliance, its divine heaviness. I love the texture of gold, the soft dimness that I have learnt to gauge so accurately by touch that I can estimate the fineness of a bar to within one carat. And I love the warm tang it exudes when I melt it down into a true golden syrup. But, above all, Mr. Bond, I love the power that gold alone gives to its owner – the magic of controlling energy, exacting labour, fulfilling one's every wish and whim, and, when need be, purchasing bodies, minds, even souls. Yes, Mr. Bond, I have worked all my life for gold and, in return, gold has worked for me and for those enterprises that I have espoused. I ask you,' Goldfinger gazed earnestly at Bond, 'is there any other substance on earth that so rewards its owner?'

On the same page Goldfinger calls it his 'golden compost', thus revealing the cloacal symbolism. Bond, rather wistfully, says: "Many people have become rich and powerful without possessing an ounce of the stuff but I see your point. How much have you managed to collect and what do you do with it?'

The trite gesture to conventional morality obviously means less here than the compulsive presentation of the immense and dangerous power of gold which is faeces, semen, poison, and goodness all at once.

The book, being an output from 'inner contents', is itself a kind of excretion, so book = faeces = gold, and on its cover is the woman stifled in gold:

> 'I don't know. Jill told me he's mad about gold. I suppose he sort of thinks he's that sort of possessing gold. You know – marrying it. He gets some Korean servant to paint them. The man has to leave their backbones unpainted. Jill couldn't explain that. I found out it's so they wouldn't die. If their bodies were completely covered with gold paint, the pores of the skin wouldn't be able to breathe. Then they'd die. Afterwards, they're washed down by the Korean with resin or something. Goldfinger gives them a thousand dollars and sends them away.'
> Bond saw the dreadful Oddjob with his pot of gold paint, Goldfinger's eye gloating over the glistening statue, the fierce possession. 'What happened to Jill?'
> 'She cabled me to come. She was in an emergency ward in a hospital in Miami. Goldfinger had thrown her out. She was dying. The doctors didn't know what was the matter. She told me what had happened to her – what he had done to her. She died the same night.' The girl's voice was dry – matter of fact. 'When I got back to England I went to Train, the skin specialist. He told me this business about the pores of the skin. It had happened to some cabaret girl who had to pose as a silver statue. He showed me details of the case and autopsy. Then I knew what had happened to Jill. Goldfinger had had her painted all over. He had murdered her. It must have been out of revenge for – for going with you.' There was a pause. The girl said dully, 'She told me about you. She – she liked you. She told me if ever I met you I was to give you this ring.'

Bond closed his eyes tight, fighting with a wave of mental nausea. More death! More blood on his hands. This time, as the result of a careless gesture, a piece of bravado that had led to twenty-four hours of ecstasy with a beautiful girl who had taken his fancy and, in the end, rather more than his fancy. And this petty sideswipe at Goldfinger's ego had been returned by Goldfinger a thousand, a millionfold. 'She left my employ' – the flat words in the sunshine at Sandwich two days before. How Goldfinger must have enjoyed saying that. Bond's fingernails dug into the palms of his hand. By God, he'd pin this murder on Goldfinger if it was the last act of his life. As for himself . . .? Bond knew the answer. This death he would have to live with.

The symbolic Oedipal replacement of the father by Bond with the mother in coition Fleming offers as a mere 'petty sideswipe' at Goldfinger's ego. Interestingl ' enough, Bond's coition with Tilly is shown here to have been only made possible by being an act of revenge in hate on the father rather than an act of love: it is a primal scene in which the symbolic self is involved (as in 'dirtying mummy'). It is thus also masturbatory, and has also all the dangers of the incorporative excitement of sex-as-eating which the child fears – 'the dreadful Odd job with his pot of gold paint', 'Goldfinger's eye gloating,' 'the fierce possession'. . . . Here the envy is dwelt on. More dire consequences come when the girl 'takes more than his fancy' and becomes more than a partial object. But what the paranoic infant in Fleming chiefly fears is that this 'petty sideswipe' will be 'returned . . . a thousand, a millionfold' in talion retribution. Against this fear every ritual compulsion is exerted, and all this paranoia focuses on the symbolism of gold. No wonder Fleming's books became the myths of a capitalist world.

CHAPTER 12

Homosexuality and Curiosity

As WE continue to read *Goldfinger* with our minds alert to the play on underlying primitive symbolism, relationships between the symbols establish themselves and begin to lead us in a significant direction in our interpretation. The schizoid fear of 'implosion' of the identity we have linked with the symbolism of outer 'casings' of the body and the pre-occupation with 'inner contents' which have been stolen or amassed in some other way which others are trying to extract, so that these must be defended, and so on, we have seen associated with toothed orifices. We have seen that these inner contents are symbolised by gold which can be hoarded, stolen, or used in aggressive ways, not least sexually. We have seen how strong are the associations between symbolic faeces and incorporation. All these elements surely lead to a recognition of *anal sadism*.

At a recent film première a few seconds of obscenity were deleted for the purposes of a royal première. It would be difficult to delete the anal and cloacal elements from a Bond film – though, of course, the attendance of royalty at 'Bond' premières endorses by totemism such play on primitive elements in commercial culture, making filth *pure* 'by appointment . . .'. So, sadism is now family viewing.

In little Fritz's discussion of his phantasy with Melanie Klein we read: 'They spit on him, do wiwi and kaki on him, put him in the closet and do everything on top of him.'

In this book there are Pussy Galore's coarse remarks 'That thing smells like burning wrestlers' trunks' and other quite clear faecal hints: 'Know what Jacko? I could go for a he-man like you. Matter of fact I wrote a song about you the other day. Care to hear its title? It's called, "If I had to do it all over again, I'd do it all over you".'

One fundamental impulse of Fleming, we may say, was to drown the world in faeces, the faeces of primitive hate – and in a way he succeeded.*

The gangster's conference in *Goldfinger* is virtually a device to enable the writer to indulge in infantile phantasies of anal-sadistic play related to the final 'plan' in the plot which is a massive anal-sadistic phantasy, of the 'finger' going into the mother's body to draw out its gold. The phantasy is very close to one of Fritz's: 'He screams and the wiwi goes right into his mouth. One soldier goes away and another asks him, "Where are you going?" "To look for manure to throw on him." The naughty man does wiwi on a shovel and it is thrown in his face.' (Klein [34], p. 40ff.)

This kind of phantasy links anal aggressiveness with *secrecy* and *curiosity*: the faeces are projected to stave off talion retribution for phantasy stealing and scooping out. These elements in turn lead us to a consideration of homosexuality in Fleming's work. How the

* There are other grotesque cloacal symbols in Fleming's other work which the reader can amuse himself by pondering.

phantasy of *Goldfinger* and its parallels with the phantasies of little Fritz may be linked with adult homosexuality may be seen through an essay by Ferenczi on 'The Nosology of Male Homosexuality'. Ferenczi says of the object-homo-erotic (the 'man' in a homosexual relationship): 'Apart from aggressivity . . . their constitution is characterised by unusually strong anal-erotism and coprophilia' (Ferenczi [20]).

Associated with this is 'their impulse for knowledge created a number of infantile sexual theories; this forms also the foundation of their later obsessional thinking' (Ferenczi [20]).

Little Fritz, in his curiosity, had a birth theory:

> His birth-theory too, however, the idea that he conceives and bears his father (at other times his mother) by the anal route, is also at work in this dream. At the end of this dream he is able to fly alone, and with the help of the other people who have already got out of the train, he locks the giant into the moving train and flies away with the key. (Klein [34]).

In Fleming there is much symbolism which arises from 'unsatisfied infantile curiosity' of a similar kind. Of course Fleming 'knew' where babies came from. But his symbolism shows that there was a sense in which he remained unconvinced, while his infantile birth theories still remained as part of his unconscious phantasy, bound up with all kinds of dangers. In this light some of Fleming's phantasies of special cars and aeroplanes may well be phantasies of birth by the 'anal route' – so that even Bond and Pussy find their union through being reborn by the anal route, in which the father is throttled. In the previous episode Goldfinger was locked in a train while Bond has intercourse with the girl in a compartment: all these are perhaps infantile phantasies of seeking to overcome the threat of the father's penis by some such phantasy magic.

His phantasies of omnipotence may perhaps be associated with an infantile desire to be as potent as the father, such as were found in Fritz:

> . . . there were little laden waggons that ran in and out of it on narrow rails – again the wish to do to mamma simultaneously with papa what the latter does with her, in which however he fails, whereupon he projects upon his father his own aggressiveness against the latter. Here too it seems to me that very powerful anal-erotic and homosexual determinants (indubitably present in the numerous devil-phantasies of where the devil lives in cavities or in a peculiar house) are at work. (Klein [34]).

It is from similar phantasies that the imagery of Goldfinger springs: the desire for potency is expressed in Fleming's tall story, just as little Fritz's desire for a 'long wiwi' was conceived by him as a long story.

> He accounted for the impossibility of telling it by saying it was such a long one, he would need the whole day to tell it. I replied that then he would just tell me part of it. 'But it was just the length that was horrid,' was his reply. That this 'horrid length' was the wiwi of the giant about whom the dream was concerned soon dawned on him. . . . (Klein [34]).

The long, gold finger reaching into Fort Knox makes a story with obvious parallels to Fritz's devil-phantasies about the devil in 'cavities' or in a 'peculiar house'. The aggressive 'hate' stores of Fleming themselves are a symbolic attempt to have a giant wiwi, and to thrust a certain hateful potency into the world.

The spy theme we have linked with curiosity about the 'inside of mummy', and the consequent talion fear of the castrating mother. Later we shall discuss further the underlying fear and hatred of woman already noted which pervades *Goldfinger* (and, indeed, a great deal else in commercial culture of which this is a representative sample). We have also noticed the affinities between sex and eating in the book. When we examine the sex we shall find it is with women who have been divested of their femininity and turned into men. When we examine the eating we shall find it is eating between men, and full of ritual and lore which could be interpreted in the light of Khan's phrase 'a technique of intimacy'. And we may note the curious love–hate relationship between Bond and Gold-finger which culminates in hand-to-hand conflicts in which great satisfaction is felt.

All these elements confirm the underlying homosexuality in Goldfinger. This 'camp' quality is, of course, recognised in the world at large. But what the world at large does not recognise is that Fleming's story is appropriate to the phantasy life of a boy of 6 in what Melanie Klein calls the 'homosexual position'. In the cultural sphere the implica-tions are that *what can be exploited by commercial culture are the paranoid-schizoid phantasies of a mentally disturbed infant in the homosexual position*. It is significant that the study of little Fritz by Melanie Klein on which I have been drawing is a study of *the origins of homo-sexuality*. Melanie Klein found the origins of homosexuality associated with the *repression of sexual curiosity*. I suggest that from this arises both the 'spy' theme and the exploitation of sexual depiction in this book, and in much other 'hate culture'.

According to Melanie Klein the origins of the homosexual position in a boy of the age of 5 or 6 arises from the fears of retribution from the parents for curiosity and sadistic phantasies directed in envy at their mutual satisfaction, a manifestation I have discussed. A great deal of work has been done by other psychoanalytical writers since Melanie Klein on homosexuality, and this has tended to place a greater emphasis on homosexual-ity as a problem of the whole identity. It will help, I believe, if we try to relate Melanie Klein's insights to the larger view, for these relate them to schizoid problems which are crucial here.

Where the mother has failed to establish a core of identity in her child in terms of 'female element being' the female element in the child's self feels catastrophically un-reliable. Women are hated because dreaded, and they threaten to become the castrating mother. True sexual giving, which involves the recognition of femininity and woman's creativity, is full of danger. Behind the sadism which he feels to be inherent in sexual excitement (sex being like eating) lurks talion retribution threatening annihilation. It would seem to be likely that it is for some such reason that sexual curiosity becomes inhibited, yet compulsive. We may also conjecture, I believe, that this curiosity is unlikely to find what it seeks, because of the need in such an individual to deny the existence of the realms of 'being', and so is devoted to *not* finding the female element. The whole identity then becomes based on a False Male Doing that denies this whole vulnerable realm.

The sadism in Fleming's work and its preoccupation with depersonalised sex (seen 'from the outside' as in sexology) can thus be seen to spring from his *preoccupation with the primal scene*, his *unsatisfied sexual curiosity as a child*, and the *fear of the castrating mother* and the 'combined parents' who will revenge his compulsive curiosity. His symbolism arises out of infantile paranoid phantasies of terrible parental imagos.

As Winnicott points out, the normal way out for the child in life is to modify his obsessional attempts to counteract paranoic fear by becoming increasingly aware of his parents as real persons who are far more human than the phantasied and threatening imagos of his terrified phantasy. The child thus discovers what it is to be human. What Winnicott calls the 'innate' moral code is 'crippling'.

> In the beginning, before the body is separated from thought, phantasy from reality, self from object, the child feels his frustration and anger as if they threatened to destroy the whole world and existence. Your adult moral code is necessary because it humanizes what for the child is subhuman. The infant

suffers talion fears. The child bites in an excited experience of relating to a good object, and the object is felt to be a biting object. The child enjoys an excretory orgy and the world fills with hate that drowns and with filth that buries. These crude fears become humanized chiefly through each child's experience in relation to the parents, who disapprove and are angry but who do not bite and drown or burn the child in retaliation related exactly to the child's impulse or phantasy. . . . (Winnicott [57], p. 101.)

If creative work is 'real reparation' it can lead towards the discovery of ourselves as we really are, the discovery of our essential humanness. Fleming, however, chose to employ his phantasy for a different kind of solution. Its whole impulse is *not* to find 'real persons' and their nature: not to find humanness. He sought another kind of success by taking the 'hate cycle' path of the paranoid phantasies of a child unable to emerge from the burden of his primitive fears associated with sexual curiosity, basing his solutions on these as 'bad thinking'. Thus his symbolism has the effect of reversing processes of growth, and pushes us back to the primitive. Inevitably, this has a dehumanising effect and thrusts us back to a primaeval 'morality' which is 'crippling'.

In her essay on the origins of homosexuality* Melanie Klein discusses the predicament of the child whose natural curiosity about the sexual life of the father and mother is experienced in these terms:

> . . . phantasy and intellectual development in a very small child are inhibited by the repression of sexual curiosity. . . . The curiosity develops over four questions: (1) where do babies come from? (2) what are babies made of (food, faeces, etc.)? (3) what is the difference between male and female? (4) what part does the father play in the making of a baby? (Guntrip [26], p. 196.)

As Melanie Klein indicates, the enlightenment of such a child as Fritz, whose questions have remained unanswered, is very difficult: the inhibition is most unyielding. It could thus persist as an unsolved 'felt' preoccupation in an adult who, of course, knows the 'answers' rationally. 'It is evident that a specially intense anxiety maintains a heavy repression on this disturbing matter of the father's role in the genital sexual relationship between him and the mother, i.e. the Primal Scene.'

The reason for the heavy repression is *anxiety and guilt concerning aggression*. Melanie Klein discovered this in her analysis of Fritz, and in doing so came to emphasise phantasy processes of the child:

> As little Fritz consciously accepted and absorbed the knowledge of the Father's sexual role, his Oedipus complex became fully conscious, bringing out a flood of aggressive phantasies in this hitherto very unaggressive little boy. . . . Oral, anal and genital sadism and general aggressiveness were exposed against the father and symbolic father figures in his phantasies, followed by clear primal scene phantasies in which Fritz showed himself to be involved in identifications with, and displacings of, both parents . . . in the form of a fear of his father's penis and of castration. It is evident that the child must be a victim, not aggressor, in the face of his own anxiety and guilt. Finally it emerged that it was anxiety over his mother's fate in the sadistic hetero-sexual situation that dictated his flight into the homosexual position. For ultimately the fear of the castrating mother emerged from behind the fear of the punishing father, related to the child's own hate and aggression against his mother which he turned back on himself. (Guntrip [26], p. 97.)

Fleming's phantasies I believe to stem from the 'monstrous ruthlessness' of these early phantasies in the child. The basis of his appeal is in his own hate against women 'turned back on himself'. All the elements we find in little Fritz's phantasies in his case history as we have seen are found in Fleming's work: oral, anal, and genital sadism; primal scene phantasies; and fears of castration which are symbolised in various forms – as in the scene in which Goldfinger demonstrates the power of his Oddjob to 'bite' pieces out of

---

* I discuss this essay in terms of the account in Guntrip [26], pp. 196 ff. This makes the account simpler and briefer.

the woodwork and to employ his 'bowler-boomerang' to kill. In the scene in which Bond is tortured (along with the girl) the 'child's own hate and aggression' is 'turned back on himself'. The hate and aggression against the mother are evident in the phantasies in which Bond disarms Tilly Masterton, consumes her (by sexual 'eating'), and then manifests contempt at her death, and in his controlling and 'taking' approach to Pussy Galore.

Fundamentally, the infantile conflicts examined by Melanie Klein in the homosexual position are *identity* problems. The child fears that his own aggression and sadism may destroy him from within. Melanie Klein's term 'position' here means a whole complex of inner problems, for what is involved is not only a suppressed desire for sexual relations with the same sex because woman is too much feared (which is also, as Ferenczi saw, a form of narcissism – and thus 'symmetry' to use a word Fleming used of his own life), but the whole underlying involvement with the parents, and the failure of processes of identification by which the child forms his own identity by 'taking his parents into himself'.

As we learn by comparing Fleming's phantasies with those of Fritz, the aggressive content of these phantasies is often so violent that they seem to threaten not only the individual's existence but the whole world (as SMERSH threatens the world.) The need to preserve existence is engaged with powerful symbols of energies associated with excretion, sex, and incorporation. All the symbols in *Goldfinger* resemble the symbols in the phantasies of little Fritz and other child patients of Melanie Klein, which are embodiments of this primitive symbolism by which the child strives in his phantasy to deal with identity fears. Somewhere (as the child thinks) in this puzzle of conflict over inner contents lies the answer to the question of the difference between male and female – and thus of identity.

Interpreting the symbols involves us in making conjectures which seem 'mad' at first, but which gradually become confirmed by other elements in the phantasy, which is no less 'mad'. For instance, 'Odd job's' *bowler hat* boomerang. The French name for a condom, *capot anglais*, links the bowler hat with the penis. It is black, so it is a hate-missile. 'Job' is a child word for faeces. Odd job is a lump of (worthless) faecal matter employed for distorted aggressive purposes ('odd' = inverted = hate) to which one is ruthlessly indifferent. They are just 'odd jobs', like killing and eating a cat-sibling; 'odd' also conveying the implication that one does not give them one's whole attention, i.e. they are 'diminution of affect' jobs. The bowler-hat boomerang is a missile which is made of the faeces inside mummy which may be a sibling but has been put there by the incorporation of the father's penis as a lump of faeces and is now ejected in a talion way for deadly purposes to which one is callous. They are carried out by a detached part of oneself – split off.

If such an interpretation seems far-fetched, then let us look at some of the other mad and dream-like moments in the book. What, for instance, of the mewing babies in the world poisoned by Goldfinger? These babies in their prams are supposed to have survived the disaster because they drink *mother's milk* and not *the water poisoned by Goldfinger* (*the father*):

> The train trundled through Brandenburg Station. Now there were scores of bodies – men, women, children, soldiers. The platform was scribbled with them, faces upwards to the roof, down in the dust, cradled sideways. Bond searched for movement, for an inquisitive eye, for a twitching hand. Nothing! Wait! What was that? Thinly through the closed window there came a soft, mewing wail. Three perambulators stood against the ticket office, the mothers collapsed beside them. Of course! The babies in the perambulators would have drunk milk, not the deadly water.

It is as if the author of the phantasy feels he has destroyed the whole world to no avail, since the threatening siblings survive the attack because the mother has preserved them. The attack in any case turns out to be not 'real'. The episode is like a disturbed child's nightmare. The dreamlike sequence resembles the way such events are phantasied by a child but not allowed to be real, and are magically changed – to avoid recognition of the reality of destructiveness. But the symbolism of the babies and the mother's milk has its own unconscious significance.

The single word 'mewing' gives us the clue: Goldfinger gives his own cat to his Korean odd-job man to kill and eat and he threatens to do the same to Tilly. Here, again, is a wish-fulfilment symbol of the desire that the ruthless father shall use his disembodied faecal power (odd job) to 'eat up' a sibling (of which the pet is a symbol) from inside the mother, by sadistic intercourse. Elsewhere in the book Goldfinger covers the woman who has had intercourse with Bond with gold paint (faeces) in revenge, and she dies. Surely we can say that she *has* to die because, having had intercourse with Bond who is, in the phantasy, the son opposed to the Goldfinger father whose woman Tilly was, *she might have babies*. She dies virtually because of guilt arising from Oedipal feelings about incest with the creative mother and the dire consequences. As Bond's love-object she is replaced by Pussy Galore, whose name now takes on a strange ambiguity. She is a pet part-object; 'ample genital' ('pussy' being a cant word for the female genital), and also 'fecund with babies' (*mewing* pets). She is the focus of the question Where do babies come from? and of the dangers felt to be in the father's role which, at the end, can Bond assume with her, but only once Goldfinger is dead. She is the castrating mother, made safe by a process involving the death of the father, being made into a man, and lastly being controlled by 'tender loving care'.

Here it seems appropriate to consider the name of this 'routine' which Bond applies to his objects. (It is, significantly, now the name of a cosmetic.) From the point of view of object-relations psychology I believe TLC could be given a number of other names. For one thing, it seems like a procedure detached in a schizoid way from spontaneous 'giving' in love: it sounds like a mechanical form of love-play which is gone through by an individual, as if he were an automaton (cf. Sylvia Plath's *The Applicant*: 'You have a hole? It's a poultice').

It might almost be called after Khan's 'Technique of Intimacy', TOI, because it is designed to prevent 'meeting' the discovery of the 'other', true mutuality in love, and emotional surrender.

To Fleming, as we shall see, lust is preferable to love, being more 'pure': in this I believe we can see the schizoid fear of love, which impels such an individual to substitute hate. The object in consequence must not be recognised in her own independent right, but is subjected to *contempt* and *control*. We could therefore call the procedure 'tender hating care' or 'tender hating control' or 'contempt disguised by a technique of intimacy'. An obvious affinity links TLC with the gold with which Goldfinger painted his objects: those who use the cosmetic are virtually baptising their identities with the faecal projectiles of hate: they are applying the pure 'mask of hate' to their surfaces. There are also '007' shaving lotions which baptise the man in ruthless egocentricity. To be painting with hate-gold is thus an obvious symbol of the kind of combination of idealization and exploitation of the object explored by Khan.

CHAPTER 13

Variations on the Primal Scene

ACCORDING to Ferenczi [20], in the homosexual the Oedipus conflict is especially pronounced; in this there is an attempt to 'restore the original relation to the mother'. Here, perhaps, we may speak rather of an attachment to the internalised breast-mother. This, I believe, is symbolised in *Goldfinger* by (a) the theme of protecting the 'gold' inside the Old Lady of Threadneedle Street, and (b) the need to destroy Goldfinger who is trying to get in there and, after his death, to take Pussy Galore for oneself. Many homosexual men are intensely attached to their mothers, and perhaps we can explain this in terms of their failure to feel secure enough in their own 'female element' as an integral aspect of their adult make-up in order to be able to meet an independent member of the opposite sex as an equal. Their over-attachment to the mother is thus an expression of over-dependence and ego-weakness, and they cannot risk relationships with another woman because this would demand a degree of self-reliance and independence which they dare not venture. They would have to 'find' the other – who might turn out to be as unreliable as the first object, and might turn out to be the castrating mother. It would also demand an acceptance of their need for dependence on a woman, which they can only tolerate in a perpetuated form of the infant–mother relationship. And so they seek to 'restore' the original relationship because it was not good enough and needs still to be completed. The elements of such an attachment will include hatred of the father and consequent Oedipus guilt, ruthless egoism, and the narcissism of an unwillingness to 'find' anyone other than oneself or any sex other than one's own.

As we shall see, in his personal life Fleming exhibited an arrogant egocentricity whose essence was the 'symmetry' of narcissism. Ferenczi finds the same symmetry as the basis of homosexuality: 'Homosexuals are only more strongly fixed than other people in this narcissistic stage; the genital organ similar to their own remains throughout life an essential condition for their love.'

So, in the end, Pussy Galore seems to have a penis too, for the phrase 'its point was hard with desire' evokes a penis more than a breast. And she is only acceptable because sex for her is essentially False Male Doing:

> She said, 'I never met a man before.' The toughness came back into her voice. 'I come from the South. You know the definition of a virgin down there? Well it's a girl who can run faster than her brother. In my case I couldn't run as fast as my uncle. I was twelve. That's not so good, James. You ought to be able to guess that.'
> Bond smiled down into the pale, beautiful face. He said, 'All you need is a course of TLC.'
> 'What's TLC?'
> 'Short for Tender Loving Care treatment. It's what they write on most papers when a waif gets brought in to a children's clinic.'

'I'd like that.' She looked at the passionate, rather cruel mouth waiting above hers. She reached up and brushed back the comma of black hair that had fallen over his right eyebrow. She looked into the fiercely slitted grey eyes. 'When's it going to start?'

Bond's right hand came slowly up the firm muscled thighs, over the flat soft plain of the stomach to the right breast. Its point was hard with desire. He said softly, 'Now.' His mouth came ruthlessly down on hers.

The reference to 'waif' is significant. Fleming's attitudes emerge from inverted love, and 'deep down' even the schizoid individual wants to love and be loved. We stop at the moment when 'Tender Loving Care' is to start. But there is little indication that there is going to be anything we may call love, in terms of the discovery of another being, in mutual independence.

To become acceptable Pussy Galore must be shown as having been made into a non-female woman by being raped as a child by her uncle. She must be under the control of TLC, given to a 'waif' as at a clinic, i.e. sex for her must be de-emotionalized and depersonalized, and she, a raped, crushed, 'waif', must submissively need TLC, so there is no question of her exerting her own independent feminine need in the sexual act (Fleming essentially believes that 'only one partner is entitled to make demands'). To guarantee against any feminine weakness or tenderness, Bond's taking mouth must be 'cruel' – which is how the infant maltreats his transitional object, and the pervert his object.

What is missing is the female element of 'togetherness' in sexual experience between independent beings. Bond and Pussy are in one sense a mouth-ego taking from a partial object equipped with a penis, and in another a part of the self engaged libidinally with an internalised breast-mother – a masturbation phantasy whose aim is to merely enable the dreamer to feel alive in a manic way.

Because of this such an erotic scene is quite unreal in any human terms. There are no real ambivalent persons involved in love, and so there is nothing conveyed to us of the truth of being human in love. No girl could recover from such horrific experiences as precede this scene soon enough to want to make love (the capacity for love-making being the first impulse to fall victim to distress). No one ever became a lesbian by being seduced by her uncle. No lesbian was ever cured by 'finding a real man'. Bond is not a 'real man' because he has no human feelings. Of course, as we make such objections we can feel the irrelevance of making them of such a novel. But we have to object in some such terms when we are told so widely that Fleming is a 'successful' writer, working from an 'arcane' store of sexual 'wisdom'.

Moreover, such analysis helps us to discover what the real appeal is – which here is to primitive anxiety related to sadistic phantasies of the primal scene. What is being evoked is our fear of woman, which makes us prefer to establish our sense of identity on 'False Male Doing' sex to avoid the risks associated with that whole sexual experience which includes the vulnerable female element. A great deal of the sex in our culture is 'False Male Doing' sex. Hence here the compulsive sex-switches, by which the womanly Goldfinger, the *Masterton* girl, her *mannish* sister, Pussy Galore looking like an 'SS trooper', are transfigured. Such 'symmetry' reveals fear of mature sex and is a mark of 'regression'. At the end 'Pussy' appears in a *fisherman's* jersey, to become 'as obedient as a child', lying (like a baby) in the crook of Bond's arm:

The connecting door with the next cabin opened and the girl came in. She was wearing nothing but a grey fisherman's jersey that was decent by half an inch. The sleeves were rolled up. She looked like a painting by Vertes. She said, 'People keep on asking if I'd like an alcohol rub and I keep on saying that if anyone's going to rub me it's you, and if I'm going to be rubbed with anything it's you I'd like to be rubbed with.' She ended lamely, 'So here I am.'

Bond said firmly, 'Lock the door, Pussy, take off that sweater and come into bed. You'll catch cold.'

She did as she was told, like an obedient child. She lay in the crook of Bond's arm and looked up at him. She said, not in a gangster's voice, or a Lesbian's but in a girl's voice, 'Will you write to me in Sing Sing?'

Bond looked down into the deep blue–violet eyes that were no longer hard, imperious. He bent and kissed them lightly. He said, 'They told me you only liked women.'

Pussy Galore appears eminently here as the depersonalised stream of milk in the symbolism of the schizophrenic patient's dream – a part-object ready to provide automatic satisfaction ('decent by half an inch', 'she looked like a painting by Vertes'). By the death of Goldfinger the way is now clear for her to be transformed from the castrating mother ('hard, imperious') into an object for taking. But she does not become a woman, only a kind of transitional object. Sex with her remains de-emotionalised – it is a 'being rubbed with' – symbolically equivalent to being painted with gold paint or subjected to the 'technique of intimacy'. There is 'a reduction in the quality of the relationship desired', implicit in the way she is 'no longer' 'hard, imperious' – no longer herself. Courtship for Fleming is devoid of all dangers of affection: his tone is 'cool': 'come into bed. You'll catch cold'. Pussy is safely controlled and made by regression into a child ('like an obedient child', 'She lay in the crook of Bond's arm'). She remains an object of 'make-belief' and predatory 'technique' rather than an equal partner in sexual meeting.

While sexual experience with a woman is thus so carefully controlled that the dangers of mature independent relationship and emotional commitment are avoided, elsewhere in his relationship with the world Bond relies for ego-strength upon paranoia.

Some forms of paranoia are classically associated with homosexuality. Ferenczi sees some forms of paranoia as being a complicated way of disguising homosexuality. It thus could be that Fleming's paranoia in his work and the acts of violence in them could be a further indication of unconscious homosexuality. As with one of Ferenczi's patients:

> No female person was *ever* accused or complained of, he constantly fought and wrangled only with men, for the most part officers or high dignitaries, superiors. I interpret this as projection of his own homosexual delight in those persons, the affect being preceded by a negative sign. His desires, which have been cast out from the ego, return to his consciousness as the perception of the persecutory tendency on the part of the objects that unconsciously please him. He seeks until he has convinced himself that he is hated. He can now indulge his own homosexuality in the form of hate, and at the same time hide from himself. The preference for being persecuted by officers and officials was probably conditioned by the fact of his father having been an official and his brother an officer; I surmise that these were the original, infantile objects of his homosexual phantasies. (Ferenczi [20], p. 17.)

In one case Ferenczi records how his housekeeper's husband developed severe paranoic phantasies and would 'hurry into the closet immediately after me, to see whether I had "properly rinsed everything away" '. In *Goldfinger* there is James Bond's anxiety about the SOS message he hides in the plane lavatory and other cloacal references, as we have seen. This patient of Ferenczi's combined actual disinclination for sexual intercourse with elaborate boastings about his sexual prowess: and at the same time, even as he failed to proceed with intercourse, he would attribute his own (homosexual) desires, which he could not acknowledge, to his wife, in fits of mad jealousy.

We have a similar mechanism in the symbolism of the James Bond phantasy. The violent episodes can be seen as a form of indulged homosexuality. And we often follow

Bond through a train of thought which vindicates his hate and moves on to phantasies of sexual prowess:

> Bond looked down at the weapon that had done it. The cutting edge of his right hand was red and swollen. It would soon show a bruise. Bond flexed the hand, kneading it with his left. He had been doing the same thing at intervals through the quick plane trip that had got him away. It was a painful process, but if he kept the circulation moving the hand would heal more quickly. One couldn't tell how soon the weapon would be needed again. Cynicism gathered at the corners of Bond's mouth.
>
> The death of the Mexican had been the finishing touch of a bad assignment, one of the worst – squalid, dangerous and without any redeeming feature except that it had got him away from head-quarters.
>
> . . . Should he transfer to another flight to spend the night in Miami? Bond had forgotten his drink. He picked it up and, tilting his head back, swallowed the bourbon to the last drop. The ice tinkled cheerfully against his teeth. That was it. That was an idea. He would spend the night in Miami and get drunk, stinking drunk so that he would have to be carried to bed by whatever tart he had picked up. He hadn't been drunk for years. It was high time. This extra night, thrown at him out of the blue, was a spare night, a gone night. He would put it to good purpose. It was time he let himself go.

Instead of 'saddling his wife with his desires' in jealousy, Bond (in the author's phantasy) 'calms his mind' by an assertion of 'colossal potency' ('good purpose' in hate-sex). From this he slips naturally into a cosmic paranoia, that seems to justify the indulgence, as in Ferenczi's patient, of suppressed homosexual urges:

> He was too tense, too introspective. What the hell was he doing, glooming about this Mexican, this capungo who had been sent to kill him? It had been all the time, all over the world. People were using their motor cars to kill with. They were carrying infectious diseases around, blowing microbes in other people's faces, leaving gasjets turned on in kitchens, pumping out carbon monoxide in closed garages. How many people, for instance, were involved in manufacturing H-bombs, from the miners who mined the uranium to the shareholders who owned the mining shares? Was there any person in the world who wasn't somehow, perhaps only statistically, involved in killing his neighbour?

Such wild paranoic phantasies disguise homosexual feelings associated with fear of woman and of one's own feelings.

Despite all the assertion of Bond's male potency he can in fact only treat women either with 'chivalry' (i.e. control in hate disguised as 'care') or with contempt, as by consuming them as partial objects. He can never accept a woman as a real object of love or as a human being with value in her own right to be 'met' and given to.

Here we have clues to the strange 'camp' atmosphere of the world of Fleming and some of his admirers. As Ferenczi says:

> The false, magnified potency of the alcoholic delusional patient and the hypocritical nymphomania of the jealous paranoiac correspond with the exaggerated chivalry here and with the delicate feeling that he demands from men towards women. I have found this with most manifest homosexual men. This high esteem is one reason why homosexuals, like many psychically impotent men, are unable to take a woman as an object of love. Homosexuals esteem women, but love men. Thus also our para-noiac, only that his love has been transformed through reversal of affect into a persecutory delusion and hate. (Ferenczi [20], p. 20.)

In the Bond phantasies . . . by 'reversal of affect', the fights with men in Fleming's books may be taken to be symbolic of sexual intercourse with the men Fleming uncon-sciously desired. This explains their sexual undertones and their sadism whose origins we have seen:

> But then his knee thudded into Goldfinger's groin. . . . For the first time in his life Bond went beserk. . . . Almost indifferently Bond slashed sideways. . . . He threw all his weight forward, gasping for breath. . . . Would he black out before the other man died? Now the tongue came out and lolled from the open mouth and there came a terrible gargling from deep in the lungs. Bond sat astride the silent chest. . . . Bond gave a deep sigh. . . .

It is the unconscious appeal of such an account which makes it so fascinating to the reader. As a description of a violent death it is poor, as is evident if we compare it with an account of death in such a work as *Women in Love* or *The Secret Agent*. What we have here is less an attempt to realise death than to phantasy an act of homosexual hate-sex associated with the primitive anxieties we have examined above.

CHAPTER 14

The Need to Hate

THERE are two compulsive ways of dealing with the world whose origins would seem to lie in the 'homosexual position' and the problems of identity associated with it. One is to give way to the *need to hate* and to maintain an intense and compulsive paranoid antipathy to woman and the female element.

The second is the need to establish one's 'all-rightness' by fragmentary externals, rituals, techniques, secrets, and forms of magic, as forms of 'doing' activity. Both are obsessional: the former is the basis of Fleming's manic–paranoic myth: the latter of his style.

In his clinical discussion Ferenczi divides homosexuals into two types, one of which

> swarms with obsessions, and with obsessional procedures and ceremonies to guard against them. A more penetrating dissection finds behind the compulsion the torturing doubt, as well as that lack of balance in love and hate which Freud discovered to be the basis of the obsessional mechanisms. The psycho-analysis of such homo-erotics as only feel abnormally in reference to their love-object, and are otherwise of a purely masculine type, has shewn me plainly that this kind of homo-eroticism in all its phenomena is itself nothing else than a series of obsessive feelings and actions. (Ferenczi [20], p. 306.)

The 'torturing doubt' in Fleming is expressed by the symbolism of the 'spy' story ('must he live in this life and death struggle?'). Fleming feels safe when engaged in False Male Doing of an obsessional kind: Bond's 'home' is in the aggressive activity of seeking to counteract the dangers of attack from Goldfinger. He is like the kind of man who only feels real in war. Even the solution of his identity is itself deathly:

> The sweat of pain began to form pools in the sockets of his closed eyes. The shrill whine of the saw was getting louder. It reminded Bond of the sawdust-scented sounds of long ago summer evenings at home in England. Home? This was his home, this cocoon of danger he had chosen to live in. And here he would be buried 'in some corner of a foreign blast furnace that is for ever two thousand degrees Centigrade'. God rest ye merry gentlemen of the Secret Service! What should he give himself as an epitaph? What should be his 'famous last words'? That you have no choice about your birth, but you can choose the way you die? Yes, it would look well on a tombstone – not *Savoir vivre* but *Savoir mourir*.

The acts of violence and the killings are themselves obsessional symbolic acts of trying to hold the identity together by 'bad thinking' as a form of 'doing' while seeking to hold off by hate those paranoic fears which seem to threaten the identity. The link between the schizoid fear and the possible loss of identity is made clear throughout *Goldfinger* by imagery of death emptying the bag of the self:

> James Bond, with two double bourbons inside him, sat in the final departure lounge of Miami Airport and thought about life and death.
> It was part of his profession to kill people. He had never liked doing it and when he had to kill he

did it as well as he knew how and forgot about it. As a secret agent who held the rare double-O prefix– the licence to kill in the Secret Service – it was his duty to be as cool about death as a surgeon. If it happened, it happened. Regret was unprofessional – worse, it was the death-watch beetle in the soul.

And yet there had been something curiously impressive about the death of the Mexican. It wasn't that he hadn't deserved to die. He was an evil man, a man they call in Mexico, a *capungo*. A capungo is a bandit who will kill for as little as forty pesos, which is about twenty-five shillings – though probably he had been paid more to attempt the killing of Bond – and, from the look of him, he had been an instrument of pain and misery all his life. Yes, it had certainly been time for him to die; but when Bond had killed him, less than twenty-four hours before, life had gone out of the body so quickly, so utterly, that Bond had almost seen it come out of his mouth as it does, in the shape of a bird, in Haitian primitives.

What an extraordinary difference there was between a body full of person and a body that was empty! Now there is someone, now there is no one. This had been a Mexican with a name and an address, an employment card and perhaps a driving licence. Then something had gone out of him, out of the envelope of flesh and cheap clothes, and had left him an empty paper bag waiting for the dustcart. And the difference was the thing that had gone out of the stinking Mexican bandit, was greater than all Mexico. . . .

The killing is a hate-solution, and a symbolic act of homosexual love (inverted to hate): it is also a desperate attempt to hold the identity together by 'compulsive procedure'. The 'black' truth of this symbolism, however, is disguised by insistence on Bond's integrity and his highly moral justification (the 'licence to kill'): 'Evil be thou my good' is the necessary basis of his identity. The insistence on the characteristic schizoid inversion has its own compulsiveness:

> For the equivalent of a thousand pounds a trip, every month one of the diplomatic couriers of the Ministry of Foreign Affairs carried an extra suitcase to London. The price was reasonable. The contents of the suitcase, after the Mexican had deposited it at the Victoria Station left-luggage office and had mailed the ticket to a man called Schwab c/o Boox-an-Pix, Ltd, W.C.1, were worth twenty thousand pounds.
>
> Unfortunately Schwab was a bad man, unconcerned with suffering humanity. He had the idea that if American juvenile delinquents could consume millions of dollars' worth of heroin every year, so could their Teddy boy and girl cousins. In two rooms in Pimlico, his staff watered the heroin with stomach powder and sent it on its way to the dance halls and amusement arcades.
>
> Schwab had already made a fortune when the CID Ghost Squad got on to him. Scotland Yard decided to let him make a little more money while they investigated the source of his supply. They put a close tail on Schwab and thence to the Mexican courier. At that stage, since a foreign country was concerned, the Secret Service had had to be called in and Bond was ordered to find out where the courier got his supplies and to destroy the channel at source.

Much of Fleming's writing is given to such elaborate 'justifications' of the acts of hate about which he seems to feel his hero should have 'torturing doubt' – while the whole basis of his dealings with the world is to have no human feelings. The moral effect is confusing and leads towards ethical inversion.

The compulsive 'procedures and ceremonies' which Ferenczi found in the 'object-homo-erotic' explain the basis of Fleming's appeal: 'Bond broke into the warehouse one night and left a thermite bomb . . .'. The implication of his whole paranoid–schizoid phantasy is that one should deal with the world by an aggressive thrusting of harm into others before they thrust it into oneself.

Another aspect of this compulsive paranoic aggression is its association with an intense hatred of woman, expressing a primitive fear of the female element in human beings. Here, perhaps, nothing is more revealing in Fleming's novel than his comments on lesbianism.

In the superficial 'permissive' ethos of our world it is easily possible to miss the hatred of woman that often lurks behind pornography, voyeurism, and such obsessions. For instance, we may invoke here a case quoted by Dr. Hannah Segal of a middle-aged man voyeur who needed to see a penis on the woman he observed through his binoculars.* Perhaps the impulse to deny the female element may be so strong that there is a need to annihilate woman as woman altogether. Fleming often seems to express such a desire: he was perhaps fascinated by lesbians because they are 'non-women' (as he was a 'non-man'). Perhaps when woman is a 'lesbian' it is possible to feel less afraid of her, superior to her, and justified in the attempt to control such a dangerous creature by hate. The lesbian is also possibly a woman who is living by 'False Male Doing'.

> Miss Galore held his eyes. She said 'Pardon my asking' with the curt tone of a hard woman shopper at the sales.
> Bond liked the look of her. He felt the sexual challenge all beautiful lesbians have for men. He was amused by the uncompromising attitude that said to Goldfinger and to the room, 'All men are bastards and cheats. Don't try any masculine hocus on me. I don't go for it. I'm in a separate league.' Bond thought she would be in her early thirties. She had pale Rupert Brooke good looks with high cheekbones and a beautiful jawline. She had the only violet eyes Bond had ever seen. They were the true deep violet of a pansy and they looked candidly out at the world from beneath straight black brows. Her hair, which was as black as Tilly Masterton's, was worn in an untidy urchin cut. The mouth was a decisive slash of deep vermilion. Bond thought she was superb and so, he noticed, did Tilly Masterton who was gazing at Miss Galore with worshipping eyes and lips that yearned. Bond decided that all was not clear to him about Tilly Masterton.

To Fleming a lesbian is simply a woman who fails to respond to the ultra-masculine Bond. Careful examination reveals the underlying hate and sadism associated with unconscious homosexuality. The girl looks like 'Rupert Brooke', and the man is 'challenged'. A heterosexual man is surely not 'challenged' by a homosexual woman? Perhaps a man who has also split off and denied his own female element may be. Fleming's generalisation – 'the sexual challenge all beautiful Lesbians have for men' – would no doubt be taken by some to spring from his 'arcane hoard' of wisdom. But it seems to have no basis in truth, while the sophisticated air only serves to hide the underlying primitive phantasy. 'Urchin', 'slash of deep vermilion', suggest a desire to attack a woman as if she were an object of homo-erotic sadistic phantasy, while the 'true deep violet of a pansy' is a strange phrase in this context. It all combines the odd spinsterish aestheticism of a male homosexual with the 'toughness', cruelty, and destructiveness underlying the 'camp'. Whatever we have here, it is not wisdom or insight. The reader is, of course, less concerned to see how empty is Fleming's 'knowingness' than to gloat on such pornographic hints as he can give – ('the search was expert'), or to be rapt by the vague romanticism of magazine language ('She looked incredibly beautiful').

To pause is to become aware of the hate under the surface and its counterpart – emotional immaturity and ineptitude. Consider, for instance, the embarrassingly boyish clichés of 'sophisticated' talk among Fleming's 'wrong side' characters: 'move over handsome', 'whispered adoringly' and so forth:

> They all rose and gathered round the buffet. Bond found himself between Miss Pussy Galore and Tilly Masterton. He offered them champagne. Miss Galore looked at him coldly and said, 'Move over, Handsome. Us girls want to talk secrets. Don't we, 'yummy'?' Miss Masterton blushed and then turned very pale. She whispered adoringly. 'Oh yes please, Miss Galore.'
> Bond smiled sourly at Tilly Masterton and moved down the room.

The concepts of gangsters, 'lesbians', spies, sex, and of what is smart and slick talk are essentially those of a small boy. Here it is typical of Fleming that in *Exciting Cities of the World* his most memorable experience in New York was to visit the offices of *Playboy*

* On a recent voyage through London by Underground I noticed that nearly every woman in the salacious posters on the escalators had had a graffiti penis added.

and dictate a letter to the 'prettiest secretary he had ever seen'. His world – the world of the Playboy Club – is a world in which it has been made socially acceptable for men to indulge contempt for women as a source of ego-strength while hiding their weakness and fear of being human under a pretend-tough exterior.

The concomitant contempt for others (such as Balint detects in such an individual) is obvious in such a passage as this:

> Ned Midnight had witnessed the snub. He got close to Bond and said earnestly, 'Mister, if that's your doll, you better watch her. Pussy gets the girls she wants. She consumes them in bunches – like grapes, if you follow me.' Mr. Midnight sighed wearily. 'Cheesus, how they bore me, the lizzies! You'll see, she'll soon have that frail parting her hair three ways in front of the mirror.'
> Bond said cheerfully, 'I'll watch out. There's nothing much I can do. She's an independent sort of a girl.'
> 'That so?' said Mr. Midnight with a spark of interest. 'Well maybe I can help to break it up'. He straightened his tie. 'I could go for that Masterton. She's sure got natural resources. See you around.' He grinned at Bond and moved off down the room.

Women are for the taking, and we need have no respect for their human value. This is even reflected in some costume fashions of our time,* and in many aspects of our culture we have a symbolic attack on her which manifests a prevalent fear of woman.

The fear and hatred of woman so widely exploited in our culture is not to be taken lightly. Since it manifests a symbolic fear of our vulnerable and sensitive feminine element, it inevitably spreads abroad a hatred of being human, and the false solutions that go with this – of which the most terrible historical example is Nazism. This fear of woman is perhaps what drives men to put themselves under the dominance of a dictator as a relief from the fear of dependence on Woman. As Winnicott says of the psychology of the dictator

> who is at the opposite pole to anything the word democracy can mean. . . . One of the roots of the need to be a dictator can be a compulsion to deal with this fear of woman by encompassing her and acting for her. The dictator's curious habit of demanding not only absolute obedience and absolute dependence, but also 'love' can be derived from this source.
> Moreover, the tendency of groups of people to accept or even seek *actual* domination is derived from a fear of domination by a *phantasy woman*. This fear leads them to seek, and even welcome, domination by a known human being, especially one was has taken on himself the burden of personifying and therefore limiting the magical qualities of the all-powerful woman of fantasy, to whom is owed the great debt. The dictator can be overthrown, and must eventually die; but the woman figure of primitive unconscious fantasy has no limits to her existence or power. . . . (Winnicott [56], p. 165.)

There, perhaps, we can see a relationship between Fleming's contempt for woman, his emphasis on unfeeling aggression justified by paranoia, and his unconscious homosexuality, and see how these may be linked with similar elements in Nazism. Indeed, Fleming makes this connection himself, as here, when a mystical seriousness comes over his phantasy. There is a note here which belongs to the False Solution magic of schizoid 'purity' – as of the Nazi fanatic, who is enacting his infantile hate-phantasies: 'They were all different now – no smart remarks, no unnecessary talk. These were men who had gone to war. Even Pussy Galore, in a black Dacron macintosh with a black leather belt, looked like some young S.S. guardsman. . . .'

The 'loyalty' of 'M.' and Bond is akin to the dictator's 'love', 'acting for' woman.

It is this hate which the fashionable world of the 'lively mind' in our culture seems to admire – without perhaps realising what the implications are.

* This is even noticed by popular writers, e.g.: 'I know earlier dress designers made outrageous clothes too, and they had their tongues in their cheeks and probably hated us. But at least these clothes were, for want of a better word, coherent. Modern clothes, to my middle-aged eye, are not only hideous, but chaotic. They and their wearers seen to be so abnormal. . . .' (Virginia Graham, *Homes and Gardens*, March 1967, p. 61.)

CHAPTER 15

The Prose of Paranoic Ritual

FERENCZI's exploration of homosexual characteristics enables us to connect Fleming's paranoia with those compulsive 'procedures and ceremonies' that form the basis of his style. As Pearson says, 'no-one who mattered' complained of the coarseness of Fleming's work, and certainly no-one said they were psychopathological, wrong, disgusting, cruel, or offensive to human nature. How could they be when the author demonstrated such 'taste'?

> The wide spaces surrounding this spark of life were crowded with massive Rothschildian pieces of furniture of the Second Empire, and ormulu, tortoiseshell, brass and mother-of-pearl winked back richly at the small fire . . . Bond walked up the steps and through the fine bronze portals and into the spacious, softly echoing entrance hall of the Bank of England and looked around him. Under his feet glittered the brilliant golden patterns of the Boris Anrep mosaics. . . . Now there was a long panelled corridor ending in a tall Adam window. The floor was close-carpeted in beige Wilton.

Everything reads like a caption in *House and Garden*. The air of sophisticated worldliness and acquaintance with the 'correct' things is evidently sustained from encyclopedias. (On the same page, incidentally, Fleming demonstrates his contempt both for woman and for genuine learning: 'A grey-haired woman was sitting at a desk. She looked as if she had once taken a double first. . . .')

One of the important aspects of his obsessive knowingness is that it must never allow itself to be confronted with genuine knowledge or intelligence – certainly never in a woman.

So obsessional does the detailed ritual of description become that everything seems to be described as if it was offered for sale.

> Bond watched the old Silver Ghost sweep majestically up the drive towards the club. She was a beauty! The sun glittered off the silver radiator and off the engine-turned aluminium shelf below the high perpendicular glass cliff of the windscreen. The luggage rail on the roof of the heavy coach-built limousine body – so ugly twenty years ago, so strangely beautiful today – was polished brass, as were the two Lucas 'King of the Road' headlamps that stared so haughtily down the road ahead, and the wide mouth of the old boa-constrictor bulb horn. The whole car, except for a black roof and black carrosserie lines and curved panels below the windows, was primrose yellow. It crossed Bond's mind that the South American president might have had it copied from the famous yellow fleet in which Lord Lonsdale had driven to the Derby and Ascot.

We may connect the knowingness with the snobbery, and recognise both as the kind of confidence trick we find in the journalism of the glossy magazines, in which commercial hedonism reaches its acme – 'civilised taste' disguising the fundamental willingness of the advertiser to exploit human needs, even at the expense of civilisation (the *avant-*

garde advocacy of the 'derangement of the senses' receives no more enthusiastic response than in the cultural pages of *Vogue*).*

How could such a sophisticated *gentleman* really be exploiting his primitive phantasies to make money and to satisfy his own hatred of being human?

> He sat by the window and drank Enzian washed down with Löwenbras . . . Enzian the firewater distilled from gentian that is responsible for Switzerland's chronic alcoholism, was beginning to warm Bond's stomach and melt his tensions. He ordered another double and with it a choucroute and a carafe of Fondant . . ..
>
> The Hotel de la Gare was all he had expected – cheap, old-fashioned, solidly comfortable. Bond had a hot bath, went back to his car to make sure the Rolls hadn't moved, and walked into the station restaurant and ate one of his favourite meals – two *oeufs cocotte à la créme*, a large *sole meunière* (Orleans was close enough to the sea. The fish of the Loire are inclined to be muddy) and an adequate Camembert. He drank a well-iced pint of Rosé d'Anjou and a Hennessy's Three Star with his coffee. At ten-thirty he left the restaurant, checked on the Rolls and walked the virtuous streets for an hour.

Such phrases as 'responsible for Switzerland's chronic alcoholism' or 'the fish of the Loire are inclined to be muddy' have obviously been taken from Baedeker or from travel books. In the world of popular culture such tags, and such menu knowingness are taken by many as evidence of the author's wisdom – and this wisdom is supposed to extend to knowledge of human nature. Even Pearson, who admits how false most of Fleming's know-how is, believes his knowledge about sexual matters to be authentic. What are perhaps authentic are the strangely feminine, even spinsterish, observations about details of dress, with oddly erotic undertones:

> The cuffs of the shirt protruded half an inch below the cuffs of the coat and showed cabochon crystal links containing miniature trout flies. The socks were charcoal grey silk and the shoes very old. Like many very rich men he considered that showing his money, letting someone see how much he tipped, amounted to indecent exposure. He thrust his roll back into his trousers pocket (the hip pocket is not the place among the rich) and took Bond by the arm.

We may here, however, glimpse something more than unconscious homosexuality and the compensatory obsessive need to appear 'all right' and worldly wise ('not the place among the rich'). The observation also perhaps reveals the symbolic significance of wealth to Fleming – why he had to write for money, why he is obsessed with spying and gold. To Fleming a rich man sometimes seems symbolic of a man full of rich anal promise, rich inner contents. If we study Fleming's descriptions of meals too I believe we may see them as symbols of sexual intercourse. Here Bond even feels guilt:

> With ceremony, a wide silver dish of crabs, big ones, their shells and claws broken, was placed in the middle of the table. A silver sauceboat brimming with melted butter and a long rack of toast was put beside each of their places. The tankards of champagne frothed pink. Finally, with an oily smirk, the head waiter came behind their chairs, and, in turn, tied round their necks long white silken bibs that reached down to the lap.
>
> Bond followed suit and proceeded to eat, or rather devour, the most delicious meal he had had in his life.
>
> The meat of the stone crabs was the tenderest, sweetest shellfish he had ever tasted. It was perfectly set off by the dry toast and slightly burned taste of the melted butter. The champagne seemed to have the faintest scent of strawberries. It was ice cold. After each helping of crab, the champagne cleaned the palate for the next. They ate steadily and with absorption and hardly exchanged a word until the dish was cleared.
>
> With a slight belch, Mr. Du Pont for the last time wiped butter off his chin with his silken bib and

---

* There is also the effect, noted by D. W. Harding, of 'providing a daily contrast with the relative tedium of unphotographed existence.' (On McLuhan, in *The New York Review of Books*, 2 January 1969).

> sat back. His face was flushed. He looked proudly at Bond. He said reverently, 'Mr. Bond, I doubt if anywhere in the world a man has eaten as good a dinner as that tonight. What do you say?'
> Bond thought, I asked for the easy life, the rich life. How do I like it? How do I like eating like a pig and hearing remarks like that? Suddenly the idea of ever having another meal like this, or indeed any other meal with Mr. Du Pont, revolted him. He felt momentarily ashamed of his disgust. He had asked for it and it had been given. It was the puritan in him that couldn't take it. He had made his wish and the wish had not only been granted, it had been stuffed down his throat. Bond said, 'I don't know about that, but it was certainly very good.'

The homosexual content is perhaps evident from the guilt and fear of contact which can perhaps be associated with the schizoid fear of giving ('suddenly the idea of ever having another meal like this, or indeed any other meal with Mr. Du Pont, revolted him . . . '). As we shall see, in life Fleming was extremely mean over meals.

This need for compulsive commentary also extends to Fleming's descriptions of games, his accounts of which are as tedious as those interminable compulsive war stories of small boys referred to with ennui by Melanie Klein. Just as every cigarette must have its brand name given, every dish its menu name, every cuff-link its outfitter's name, so there are obsessional descriptions of the rules and development of every contest:

> Mr. Du Pont sat with his back to the hotel. Goldfinger took the seat opposite and cut the cards. Du Pont won the cut, pushed the other pack over to Goldfinger, tapped them to show they were already shuffled and he couldn't bother to cut, and Goldfinger began to deal.
> Bond sauntered over and took a chair at Mr. Du Pont's elbow. He sat back, relaxed. He made a show of folding his paper to the sports page and watched the deal.
> Somehow Bond had expected it, but this was no cardsharp. Goldfinger dealt quickly and efficiently, but with no hint of the Mechanic's Grip, those vital three fingers curled round the long edge of the cards and the index finger at the outside short upper edge – the grip that means you are armed for dealing Bottoms or Seconds. And he wore no signet ring for pricking the cards, no surgical tape round a finger for marking them.
> Mr. Du Pont turned to Bond. 'Deal of fifteen cards,' he commented. 'You draw two and discard one. Otherwise straight regency rules. No monkey business with the red treys counting one, three, five, eight, or any of that European stuff.'
> Mr. Du Pont picked up his cards. Bond noticed that he sorted them expertly, not grading them according to value from left to right or holding his wild cards, of which he had two, at the left – a pattern that might help a watchful opponent.

The compulsive connection here between obsessional ritual and guarding against danger is obvious.

The same kind of ritual care is taken over describing how Bond takes a photograph, and exactly what steps he takes to prepare himself for a crisis:

> Bond took the elevator up to his suite. He went to his suitcase and extracted an M3 Leica, an MC exposure meter, a K2 filter and a flash-holder. He put a bulb in the holder and checked at the sun to estimate where it would be at about three-thirty and went back into the sitting-room, leaving the door to the balcony open. He stood at the balcony door and aimed the exposure meter. The exposure was one-hundredth of a second. He set this on the Leica, put the shutter at full, and the distance at twelve feet. He clipped on a lens hood and took one picture to see that all was working. Then he wound on the film, slipped in the flash-holder and put the camera aside.
> Bond went to his suitcase again and took out a thick book – *The Bible Designed to be Read as Literature* – opened it and extracted his Walther PPK in the Berns Martin holster. He slipped the holster inside his trouser band to the left. He tried one or two quick draws.

All these elaborations have the air of ritual magic like little Fritz's endless phantasies of counteraction. Often these are directed against the long-range magic of the omnipotent father-image:

> Bond turned and looked back down the roof towards the two Canasta players beneath the cliff of the hotel. So Goldfinger liked to face the hotel. Or was it that he liked Mr. Du Pont to have his back to it? And why? Now, what was the number of Goldfinger's suite? No. 200, the Hawaii Suite. Bond's on

the top floor was 1200. So, all things being equal, Goldfinger's would be directly below Bond's, on the second floor, twenty yards or so above the roof of the Cabana Club – twenty yards from the card table Bond counted down. He closely examined the frontage that should be Goldfinger's. Nothing. An empty sun balcony. An open door into the dark interior of the suite. Bond measured distances, angles. Yes, that's how it might be. That's how it must be! Clever Mr. Goldfinger.

As with small boys in Fritz's position the driving and handling of cars has its own obsessional rituals: so, too, in Ian Fleming, there is an obsession with carmanship that cloaks 'wiwi 'anxiety and makes it look 'adult':

> James Bond flung the DB III through the last mile of straight and did a racing change down into third and then into second for the short hill before the inevitable traffic crawl through Rochester. Leashed in by the velvet claw of the front discs, the engine muttered its protest with a mild back-popple from the twin exhausts. Bond went up into third again, beat the lights at the bottom of the hill and slid resignedly up to the back of the queue that would crawl on for a quarter of an hour – if he was lucky – through the sprawl of Rochester and Chatham.
>
> Bond settled back into second and let the car idle. He reached for the wide gunmetal case of Morland cigarettes on the neighbouring bucket seat, fumbled for one and lit it from the dashboard.
>
> He had chosen the A2 in preference to the A20 to Sandwich because he wanted to take a quick look at Goldfinger-land – Reculver and those melancholy forsaken reaches of the Thames which Gold-finger had chosen for his parish. He would then cross the Isle of Thanet to Ramsgate and leave his bag at the Channel Packet, have an early lunch and be off to Sandwich.
>
> The car was from the pool. Bond had been offered the Aston Martin or a Jaguar 3.4. He had taken the DB III. . . .

The 'cover' for the identity includes space for hidden resources. We are perhaps reminded of Freud's patient little Hans who desired a 'widdler' as potent as his father's. The wiwi is full of concealed power – so, too, is the identity:

> Either of the cars would have suited his cover – a well-to-do, rather adventurous young man with a taste for the good, the fast things of life. But the DB III had the advantage of an up-to-date triptique, an inconspicuous colour – battleship grey – and certain extras which might or might not come in handy. These included switches to alter the type and colour of Bond's front and rear lights if he was following or being followed at night, reinforced steel bumpers, fore and aft, in case he needed to ram, a long-barrelled radio Colt- .45 in a trick compartment under the driver's seat, a radio pick-up tuned to receive an apparatus called the Homer, and plenty of concealed space that would fox most Customs men.

Here the aggressive assertion extends to methods of warding off 'danger' by an attack on others (as we know from windscreen stickers, motorists in real life identify with 007 and act in paranoic ways on the road.)

> Bond saw a chance and picked up fifty yards, sliding into a ten-yard gap left by a family saloon of slow reactions. The man at the wheel, who wore that infallible badge of the bad driver, a hat clamped firmly on the exact centre of his head, hooted angrily. Bond reached out of the window and raised an enigmatically clenched fist. The hooting stopped.

This car-assertiveness has affinities with the assertion of super-potency which Ferenczi found in patients suffering from relational inadequacies. A 'real man' asserts himself thus but the real impulse is infantile envy of the father's big penis:

> 'You want to get cracking. This pedalling along ages one. One of these days you'll stop moving altogether and when you stop moving is when you start to die.'
>
> Leiter laughed. He said, 'See that green light ahead? Bet I can make it before it goes red.' The car leapt forward as if it had been kicked. There was a brief hiatus in Bond's life, an impression of snipe-like flight and of a steel wall of cars that somehow parted before the whiplash of Leiter's triple klaxons, a hundred yards when the speedometer touched ninety and they were across the lights and cruising genteelly along in the centre lane.
>
> Bond said calmly, 'You meet the wrong traffic cop and that Pinkerton card of yours won't be good enough. It isn't so much that you drive slowly, it's holding back the cars behind they'll book you for. The sort of car you need is a nice elderly Rolls Royce Silver Ghost with big plateglass windows so you

can enjoy the beauties of nature' – Bond gestured towards a huge automobile junk heap on their right. 'Maximum fifty and it can stop and even go backwards if you want to. Bulb horn. Suits your sedate style. Matter of fact there should be one on the market soon – Goldfinger's.'

As with the small boy, self-assertion of this kind is linked with obsessional preoccupation with the 'proper' details of every external interest. Thus a major element in Fleming's style is this self-preservative cataloguing of 'right things', page after page, like a necromantic spell recited to hold off paranoic fears.

> At the seventh, five hundred yards, they both hit good drives and Goldfinger's immaculate second lay fifty yards short of the green. Bond took his brassie. Now for the equalizer! But he hit from the top, his club head came down too far ahead of the hands and the smothered ball shot into one of the right-hand bunkers. Not a good lie, but he must put it on the green. Bond took a dangerous seven and failed to get it out. Goldfinger got his five. Two down. They halved the short eighth in three. At the ninth Bond, determined to turn only one down, again tried to do too much off a poor lie. Goldfinger got his four to Bond's five. Three down at the turn! Not too good. Bond asked Hawker for a new ball. Hawker unwrapped it slowly, waiting for Goldfinger to walk over the hillock to the next tee.

The know-how here is associated with the threat to identity from Goldfinger: the brand names, rules, and proper argot are obviously a way to sustain the identity by magical fragments of intellectual certainty – in lieu of other deeper assurances:

> Olympic-length swimming pool. . . .
> Dressed 'for the beach' by Abercrombie and Fitch. . . .
> King-size Chesterfields. . . .
> 'Where do you play?'
> 'Huntercombe.'
> Gunmetal case of Morland cigarettes. . . .
> Four Penfolds – with hearts on them. . . .
> This time it was a dunch. . . .
> They were a brand new set of American Ben Hogans. . . .

These tags of know-how extend to obscene asides which are intended to establish a manly knowingness in the sexual sphere:

> The sixth, appropriately called 'The Virgin', is a famous short hole. . . .
> '. . . Probably just some chorine he's brought down for the ride.' He smiled wetly. 'I mean the daily ride. . . .'

This hard-bitten sex wit as I have suggested earlier has the ulterior motive of seeking to persuade us that it is admirable to promote a false 'toughness' of feeling.

There is even an obsessional compulsiveness that finds a strength in detecting weaknesses in the obsessions of others. Bond is more than aware of what is 'correct': he can even detect false snobbery. So we can doubly rely on his man-of-the-world qualities and even feel confidently that Fleming is wise and *comme-il-faut*, despite his primitive phantasies:

> Goldfinger had made an attempt to look smart at golf and that is the only way of dressing that is incongruous on the links. Everything matched in a blaze of rust-coloured tweed from the buttoned 'golfer's cap' centred on the huge, flaming red hair, to the brilliantly polished, almost orange shoes. The plus-four suit was too well cut and the plus-fours themselves had been pressed down the sides. The stockings were of a matching heather mixture and had green garter tabs. It was as if Goldfinger had gone to his tailor and said, 'Dress me for golf – you know, like they wear in Scotland.' Social errors made no impression on Bond, and for the matter of that he rarely noticed them. With Goldfinger it was different. Everything about the man had grated on Bond's teeth from the first moment he had seen him. The assertive blatancy of his clothes was just part of the malevolent animal-magnetism that had affected Bond from the beginning.

The 'malevolent animal magnetism' reveals that much of this compulsive 'knowingness' is an attempt to have a larger potency than the father. In the homosexual position the boy hates the father and so can have an inward joy at trying to fault his manliness as Bond faults Goldfinger here – and shows him to be vulnerable. In this, too, we may suspect an assertion of a schizoid 'sense of superiority' where there is no true sense of value but rather fear.

For all the compulsiveness indicates that Fleming can find no essential integrity in himself and no essential human value in others. There is only a ruthless concern to preserve the ego. It is this ruthlessness that Bond's Bulldog Drummond kind of 'loyalty' disguises:

> 'Of course you understand' – Colonel Smithers looked over Bond's right shoulder 'that most of what I shall have to say will be confidential.' The eyes swept quickly across Bond's face.
> Bond's face was stony.
> Colonel Smithers felt the silence that Bond had intended he should feel. He looked up, saw that he had put his foot in it, and tried to make amends. 'Obviously I needn't have mentioned the point. A man with your training. . . .'
> Bond said, 'We all think our own secrets are the only ones that matter. You're probably right to remind me. Other people's secrets are never quite as important as one's own. But you needn't worry. I shall discuss things with my chief but with no one else.'
> 'Quite, quite. Nice of you to take it that way. In the Bank one gets into the habit of being over-discreet. Now then. . .' Colonel Smithers scurried for cover into his subject.

Bond's integrity does not extend to his relationships with women. It does not extend to 'fair play' in human relationships. It is on a different plane from the need to drive a car safely or otherwise modify one's aggression in a sociable way. It is reconcilable with a licence to kill. This 'licence' is an attempt to vindicate pure hate as the only way of life. If only hate can be kept 'pure' enough the individual can avoid recognition of his deeper needs to love and his dependence upon others.

The need for 'obsessions' and 'procedures and ceremonies to guard against obsessions' thus parallels the need to phantasy stories of attempts to rob or guard gold, to get bombs inside impregnable fortresses, and so on. But the fact that paranoid ritual is so egocentric accounts for the peculiar tedium of Fleming's style: it is the prose of compulsive 'False Male Doing'.

Fleming obviously felt that it was important to be impeccable in the choice of wine or cuff-links (though from his biographer it is clear that all his 'correct' knowledge here was second-hand). Yet, while all this is offered as 'etiquette' and 'good manners', the fact that the way human beings treat one another in the book, even when these ways are most endorsed by the author, are completely deficient in manners in the old-fashioned meaning of the word if we take it as implying that the basis of manners is the recognition of the needs, feelings, and integrity of others. Bond's behaviour both in sex and his 'spying' is so far from being 'all right' that it is virtually psychopathological: he lives entirely at the expense of the rest of humanity (though this is, of course, taken to be vindicated by the fact that he is also preserving humanity).

Humanity is in urgent need of preservation. But this can only be achieved by human means. Bond's means are anti-human. It is this that the ritual snobbery disguises: the lack of any real respect for persons. The concern with 'what is right' in dress or behaviour is thus not a sign of any genuine concern with human potentialities, but merely a self-defensive defence mechanism, concerned with the 'ruthless preservation of one's own ego', while for others one exhibits only contempt.

CHAPTER 16

Compulsive Sadism in Action

FORTIFIED by his contempt for woman, Bond (like Fleming) can hold off any danger of real relationship and love. As Bond says, coldly, of the girl with whom he has had intercourse: "Oh, I must get in touch with her again. Where did she go?"*

While sexual taking is an important compulsion, it may be confidently separated from anything human and from the emotional life and 'meeting'. The object must be reduced to the status of an object, to invoke Balint.

The compulsive ritualistic masquerade of Fleming's sexual descriptions is paralleled by his accounts of violence. The style here belongs to the detailed compulsiveness of 'thinking bad thoughts' as a form of 'False Male Doing' to sustain the identity:

> Almost automatically, Bond went into the 'Parry Defence against Underhand Thrust' out of the book. His right arm cut across, his body swivelling with it. The two forearms met mid-way between the two bodies, banging the Mexican's knife arm off target and opening his guard for a crashing short-arm chin jab with Bond's left. Bond's stiff, locked wrist had not travelled far, perhaps two feet, but the heel of his palm, with fingers spread for rigidity, had come up and under the man's chin with terrific force. The blow almost lifted the man off the sidewalk. Perhaps it had been that blow that had killed the Mexican, broken his neck, but as he staggered back on his way to the ground, Bond had drawn back his right hand and slashed sideways at the taut, offered throat. It was the deadly hand-edge blow to the Adam's apple, delivered with the fingers locked into a blade, that had been the standby of the Commandos. If the Mexican was still alive, he was certainly dead before he hit the ground.
>
> Bond stood for a moment, his chest heaving, and looked at the crumpled pile of cheap clothes flung down in the dust. He glanced up and down the street. There was no one. Some cars passed. Others had perhaps passed during the fight, but it had been in the shadows. Bond knelt down beside the body. There was no pulse. Already the eyes that had been so bright with marihuana were glazing. The house in which the Mexican had lived was empty. The tenant had left.
>
> Bond picked up the body and laid it against a wall in deeper shadow. He brushed his hands down his clothes, felt to see if his tie was straight and went on to his hotel.

Here the need to think bad and sadistic thoughts to overcome the fear of inner weakness is masked by the detached and even polite references to 'unarmed combat' methods as if these were socially acceptable forms of aggression, and to the clinical accounts of the effects as if the writer were giving a medical account of injuries in court. The detachment is also schizoid and inhuman, and has the effect, by its kid-gloved calmness, of making violence acceptable. This violence is yet another form of 'detached stream of milk' – a form of 'taking hate'. The phrase 'the tenant had left' indicates the underlying schizoid fear of emptiness of identity, for which the violent phantasy compensates. Perhaps even

---

* This is almost as callous as the manner caricatured by Mark Twain:
'Anybody hurt?"
'No, Mum. Killed a nigger.'
To Fleming a woman is nobody, as a Negro is to a Southerner.

the touch on the tie is for Bond to reassure himself he has not been castrated: the tie is perhaps here a wiwi symbol as it is for little Fritz.

This need to think 'bad' violent thoughts and have violent phantasies is embodied by Fleming in his portrayal of the thoughts of Bond, which are often active with contempt for others who do not share his own methods of solution – which are those of a psychopath:

> The last light of the day had gone. Below the indigo sky the flare paths twinkled green and yellow and threw tiny reflections off the oily skin of the tarmac. With a shattering roar a DC7 hurtled down the main green lane. The windows in the transit lounge rattled softly. People got up to watch. Bond tried to read their expressions. Did they hope the plane would crash – give them something to watch, something to talk about, something to fill their empty lives? Or did they wish it well? Which way were they willing the sixty passengers? To live or to die.
> Bond's lips turned down. Cut it out. Stop being so damned morbid. All this is just reaction from a dirty assignment. You're stale, tired of having to be tough. You want a change. You've seen too much death. You want a slice of life – easy, soft, high.

We have a continual sense in reading Fleming of an identity which exists only like an inflated bag sustained from the inside by the pressure of thoughts of compulsive aggression, vindicated by paranoia. The paranoia is directed against forces which threaten to implode the identity such as the power of 'looking magic' in the talion father. We are repeatedly told of Goldfinger's X-ray eyes:

> Bond took the hand. It was hard and dry. There was the briefest pressure and it was withdrawn. For an instant Mr. Goldfinger's pale, china-blue eyes opened wide and stared hard at Bond. *They stared right through his face to the back of his skull.* Then the lids drooped, the shutter closed over the X-ray, and Mr. Goldfinger took the exposed plate and slipped it away in his filing system. [My italics.]

The description of Goldfinger is especially interesting. Goldfinger is a symbol of an 'internalised object' which is the subject of intense libidinal attention. So the description has its own compulsive quality:

> Goldfinger was short, not more than five-feet tall, and on top of the thick body and blunt, peasant legs, was set almost directly into the shoulders, a huge and it seemed exactly round head. It was as if Goldfinger had been put together with bits of other people's bodies. Nothing seemed to belong. Perhaps, Bond thought, it was to conceal his ugliness that Goldfinger made such a fetish of sunburn. Without the red-brown camouflage the pale body would be grotesque. The face, under the cliff of crew-cut carroty hair, was as startling, without being as ugly, as the body. It was moon-shaped without being moonlike. The forehead was fine and high and the thin sandy brows were level above the large light blue eyes fringed with pale lashes. The nose was fleshly aquiline between high cheekbones and cheeks that were more muscular than fat. The mouth was thin and dead straight, but beautifully drawn. The chin and jaws were firm and glinted with health. To sum up, thought Bond, it was the face of a thinker, perhaps a scientist, who was ruthless, sensual, stoical and tough. An odd combination

Goldfinger is the internalised father's penis – a part-object which has had to be stolen because what should have been given was not given: 'on top of the thick body . . . a huge and it seemed exactly round head . . . under the cliff of . . . carroty hair . . . The mouth was thin and dead straight . . . ruthless, sensual. . . .' 'An odd combination' indeed; because as an internal imago he has been put together from scraps of 'pseudo-male doing', he seems to be 'put together with bits of other people's bodies'. (The same is true of the prose of compulsive detail.)

The imago of the internalised father is likened to Napoleon and Hitler as is the same kind of 'colossus' in the poetry of Sylvia Plath. The penis-symbol of pure (gold) hate also has vitality and is a 'misfit', hated by the True Self. The contrast with Sylvia Plath comes out sharply, however, for whereas she has great sincerity and many profound insights, Fleming has neither insight nor intelligence, and is content to make this strange phantasy acceptable by a knowing pretence at sophistication: 'inferiority complex', 'One could certainly feel the repressions', and so forth. He is a psychologist!

> What else could he guess? Bond always mistrusted short men. They grew up from childhood with an inferiority complex. All their lives they would strive to be big – bigger than the others who had teased them as a child. Napoleon had been short, and Hitler. It was the short men that caused all the trouble in the world. And what about a mis-shapen short man with red hair and a bizarre face? That might add up to a really formidable misfit. One could certainly feel the repressions. There was a powerhouse of vitality humming in the man that suggested that if one stuck an electric bulb into Goldfinger's mouth it would light up. Bond smiled at the thought. Into which channels did Goldfinger release his vital force? Into getting rich? Into sex? Into power? Probably into all three. What could his history be? Today he might be an Englishman. What had he been born? Not a Jew – though there might be Jewish blood in him. Not a Latin or anything farther south. Not a Slav. Perhaps a German – no, a Balt! That's where he would have come from. One of the old Baltic provinces. Probably got away to escape the Russians. Goldfinger would have been warned – or his parents had smelled trouble and they had got him out in time. And what had happened then? How had he worked his way up to being one of the richest men in the world?

While Goldfinger represents the internalised penis of the father, this internal object, as we have seen, is the subject of intense libidinal cathexis which may be linked with the kind of envy for the father's powerful penis such as Melanie Klein found in little Fritz. Obviously, the penis has been stolen because it is so valuable and powerful (a *gold*finger). It was the 'short men' (cf. 'short arms') which 'fill the world with trouble. . . . There is some dangerous hidden power, like a torch. . . . *Into what channels does (the penis) release (its) vital force?*' The phrase 'his parents had smelled trouble and they had got him out in time' and 'he had worked his way up to being one of the richest men in the world' take on an unconscious significance – revealing both the fear of the father's creativity, and the envy of the 'wiwi' that has stolen 'golden richness' from the mother's inside, and is capable of spawning all manner of poisonous dangers.

Ferenczi, as we have seen, speaks of the 'dread of women' in the homosexual, and this 'dread of women' recurs and recurs throughout *Goldfinger*. Ferenczi also speaks of the 'revenge phantasies' associated with this fear of woman, and so here sexual intercourse can only take place as revenge, in disguise as violence, or in some other totally de-personalised form:

> The body under the tree moved, shifted cautiously to a new position. A breath of wind whispered in the tops of the trees. The moonbeams danced quickly across the body and then were still. There was a glimpse of thick black hair, black sweater, narrow black slacks. And something else – a straight gleam of metal along the ground. It began beneath the clump of black hair and ran past the trunk of the trees into the grass.
>
> Bond slowly, wearily bent his head and looked at the ground between his spread hands. It was the girl, Tilly. She was watching the buildings below. She had a rifle – a rifle that must have been among the innocent golf clubs – ready to fire on them. Damn and blast the silly bitch!
>
> Bond slowly relaxed. It didn't matter who she was or what she was up to. He measured the distance, panned each stride – the trajectory of the final spring, left hand to her neck, right to the gun. Now!
>
> Bond's chest skidded over the hump of the buttocks and thudded into the small of the girl's back. The impact emptied the breath out of her with a soft grunt. The fingers of Bond's left hand flew to the throat and found the carotid artery. His right hand was on the waist of the rifle's stock. He prised the fingers away, felt that the safety catch was on and reached the rifle far to one side.
>
> Bond eased the weight of his chest off the girl's back and moved his fingers away from her neck. He closed them softly over her mouth. Beneath him, he felt the body heave, the lungs labouring for breath. She was still out. Carefully Bond gathered the two hands behind the girl's back and held them with his right. Beneath him the buttocks began to squirm. The legs jerked. Bond pinned the legs to the ground with his stomach and thighs, noting the strong muscles bunched under him. Now the breath was rasping through his fingers. Teeth gnawed at his hand. Bond inched carefully forwards along the girl. He got his mouth through her hair to her ear. He whispered urgently, 'Tilly, for Christ's sake. Stay still! This is me, Bond. I'm a friend. This is vital. Something you don't know about. Will you stay still and listen?'

> The teeth stopped reaching for his fingers. The body relaxed and lay soft under his. After a time, the
> head nodded once.
>   Bond slid off her. He lay beside her, still holding her hands prisoned behind her back. He whispered,
> 'Get your breath. But tell me, were you after Goldfinger?'
>   The pale face glanced sideways and away. The girl whispered fiercely into the ground, "I was going
> to kill him."
>   Some girl Goldfinger had put in the family way.

Here a number of points seem relevant. As so often, the actual physical details seem extraneous to the adventure. The need which is being met in the reader is for him to be captivated by 'bad thoughts' about sadistic intercourse. As do the child's sadistic phantasies of the primal scene, these enable him to feel alive. Moreover, the violence represents a way of controlling 'dangerous' woman. Notice how Bond has to 'wearily' bend his head before undertaking his wrestle with the girl: here again is the 'primitive woman figure' to subdue whom it is Bond's mythical fate. His contempt for her is expressed in the phrases 'Some girl Goldfinger had put in the family way.'

The way in which Bond exerts himself is also a frenetic display of potency the origins of which may be in compensation for homosexuality. Ferenczi records how one object-homo-erotic patient sought desperately to find heterosexual potency. 'In . . . another patient puberty set in with an absolute frenzy of heterosexuality; he had to have sexual intercourse every day for a year, and obtained the money for it, if necessary, in dishonourable ways.'

This kind of desperate heterosexuality is significantly depersonalised – but yet only brings further danger. In the episode just quoted, significantly, no sooner is the violent sexual act begun than Goldfinger's long omnipotent penis begins its dangerous X-ray looking: since contact with a woman involves recognition of the female element, it immediately exposes the self to the father's talion hate-looking. Since sexual activity involves the female, it arouses Oedipal fears.

If we look at the incident in terms of any possible reality, it is lame and ridiculous (cf. the inept dialogue). As an infantile phantasy of talion fear it makes a grotesque kind of sense, leading on to the symbolism of anal sadism and related threats to identity:

> His eyes carefully went over the peaceful, unchanged scene below. Unchanged? There was some-
> thing. The radar thing on the cowl of the chimney. It wasn't going round any more. It had stopped
> with its oblong mouth pointing in their direction. The fact had no significance for Bond. Now the girl
> wasn't crying any more. Bond nuzzled his mouth close to her ear. Her hair smelled of jasmine. He
> whispered, 'Don't worry, I'm after him too. And I'm going to damage him far worse than you could
> have done. I've been sent after him by London. They want him. What did he do to you?'
>   She whispered, almost to herself, 'He killed my sister. You knew her – Jill Masterton.'
>   Bond said fiercely, 'What happened.'
>   'He has a woman once a month. Jill told me this when she first took the job. He hypnotizes them.
> Then he – he paints them gold.'
>   'Christ! Why?'

The radar scanner is the father's omnipotent eye, threatening revenge for phantasy indulgence in the sadistic satisfactions felt by the child to be in parental intercourse. (Note the phrase 'Oblong mouth', with its suggestion of oral incorporation.) The gold is the father's capacity to destroy by faecal or seminal poison.

It is a moment of intensification of those Oedipal fears which are associated with the 'homosexual position'. Approach to the normal sexual role, even distantly, brings paranoic anxiety. So there is a confusion of roles here which we can link with the strange ambivalences and duplicities in Fleming's work – the theme of duplicity being an aspect of the whole 'spy' genre: one suspects every new character of being a double agent, and so forth. (This confusion of roles, and the possibility of having a reversed role which is endorsed by society ('a licence to kill') perhaps explains the preponderance of homosexuals in actual espionage work.) Ferenczi gives us some illuminating clues here from the analysis of object-homo-erotics, of switches and transversions consequent upon fears of accepting their true sexual identity and role:

> In the object-homo-erotic's unconscious phantasy the physician can represent the place of man and woman, father and mother, reversals* of the most diverse kind playing a very important part in this.
> *[*Footnote in the original*] The dreams of homo-erotics are very rich in reversals. Whole series of dreams have often to be read backwards. The symptomatic action of making a slip of the tongue or pen in the use of the gender of articles is common. One patient even made up a bisexual number: the number 101 signified, as the context shewed, that for him 'backwards and forwards were the same'.
> (Ferenczi [20]).

There is possibly here some significance in the number 007 (a magic or secret number hiding behind double false identities?) But certainly there are many reversals and switches in *Goldfinger* which reveal schizoid reversals and evasions – Goldfinger is strangely feminine in places, being described wearing a 'bikini slip', for instance, while the women are made into men, as we have seen.

The attack on Goldfinger serves (in the phantasy-indulgence) as a 'paederastic act:' as Ferenczi says: 'the paederastic act serves the purpose of the original Oedipus phantasy and denotes the injuring and sullying of the man.'

In the books Fleming indulges 'forbidden . . . desires' in terms of hate-action. Once Goldfinger is ultimately 'sullied', and Pussy Galore made into a man, there is no 'further bone of contention between father and son' so the book can end. 'The homo-erotic obsessional idea unites in a happy compromise the flight from women, and their symbolic replacement, as well as the hatred of men and the compensation of this. Women being apparently excluded from the love-life, there no longer exists, so far as consciousness is concerned, any further bone of contention between father and son.' (Ferenczi [20]).

As we have seen, this leaves Bond able to have sexual intercourse with Pussy Galore, albeit switched into a fisherman's jersey.

But the explorations in this chapter would tend to imply that in the descriptions of sexual intercourse nowadays obligatory in prose fiction there may be a paranoic element by which the writer and reader are seeking to control, by 'bad thinking', a sphere of experience which is felt to be threatening, as it belongs to the realm of being.

CHAPTER 17

Contempt for Woman is
Contempt for Being Human

ONE of the elements of his work arising from unconscious homosexuality in Fleming needs further consideration: the hatred of woman. Melanie Klein said of Fritz: 'he considers little girls and also grown-up women with an unreasonable antipathy. This second female imago that he has split off from his beloved mother, in order to maintain her as she is, is the woman with the penis through whom, for him also apparently, the path leads to his now clearly indicated homosexuality.' (Klein [35]).

This 'female imago' in *Goldfinger* is Fleming's Pussy Galore. Because of this 'split' way of dealing with woman, anything approaching a real woman can never be recognised by such a writer. Every episode in Fleming involving a woman enacts the process of submitting her to magical control, eating her, or annihilating her. Whatever happens, she cannot be allowed to exist as a person in her own right. The inability to find woman is an inability to find oneself, one's 'female element being' self. Yet this conditions all Fleming's dealings with sex.

Take the first episode in *Goldfinger*, for instance. Bond finds his way into Goldfinger's flat: the latter's secretary is helping him by signals in a large-scale criminal swindle at cards.

> Even before he could see what he expected to see he could hear the voice. It was a low attractive girl's voice, an English voice. It was saying, 'Drew five and four. Completed canasta in fives with two twos. Discarding four. Has singletons in kings, knaves, nines, sevens.'
> Bond slid into the room.
> The girl was sitting on two cushions on top of a table which had been pulled up to a yard inside the open balcony door. She had needed the cushions to give her height. It was at the top of the afternoon heat and she was naked except for a black brassiere and black silk briefs. She was swinging her legs in a bored fashion. She had just finished painting the nails on her left hand. Now she stretched the hand out in front of her to examine the effect. She brought the hand back close to her lips and blew on the nails. Her right hand reached sideways and put the brush back in the Revlon bottle on the table beside her. A few inches from her eyes were the eyepieces of a powerful-looking pair of binoculars supported on a tripod whose feet reached down between her sunburned legs to the floor. Jutting out from below the binoculars was a microphone from which wires led to a box about the size of a portable record player under the table. Other wires ran from the box to a gleaming indoor aerial on the sideboard against the wall.
> The briefs tightened as she leant forward again and put her eyes to the binoculars. 'Drew a queen and a king. Meld of queens. Can meld kings with a joker. Discarding seven.' She switched off the microphone.
> While she was concentrating, Bond stepped swiftly across the floor until he was almost behind her. There was a chair. He stood on it, praying it wouldn't squeak. Now he had the height to get the whole scene in focus. He put his eye to the viewfinder. Yes, there it was, all in line, the girl's head, the edge of

the binoculars, the microphone and, twenty yards below, the two men at the table with Mr. Du Pont's hand of cards held in front of him. Bond could distinguish the reds and the blacks. He pressed the button.

It is noticeable how Fleming labours at extraneous hints at the girl's 'attractiveness' – *as if he himself did not find women attractive* and really hated them: 'attractive girl's voice,' 'The briefs tightened'. The emphasis is never on a person but on the 'edible' features of a depersonalised partial object. The protagonist is magical: he 'slides' into the room, and exerts his omnipotent power over the woman at once:

> The sharp explosion of the bulb and the blinding flash of light forced a quick scream out of the girl. She swivelled round.
>
> Bond stepped down off the chair. 'Good afternoon.'
>
> 'Whoryou? Whatyouwant'? The girl's hand was up to her mouth. Her eyes screamed at him.
>
> 'I've got what I want. Don't worry. It's all over now. And my name's Bond, James Bond.'
>
> Bond put his camera carefully down on the chair and came and stood in the radius of her scent. She was very beautiful. She had the palest blonde hair. It fell heavily to her shoulders, unfashionably long. Her eyes were deep blue against a lightly sunburned skin and her mouth was bold and generous and would have a lovely smile.
>
> She stood up and took her hand away from her mouth. She was tall, perhaps five feet ten, and her arms and legs looked firm as if she might be a swimmer. Her breasts thrust against the black silk of the brassière.
>
> Some of the fear had gone out of her eyes. She said in a low voice, 'What are you going to do?'
>
> 'Nothing to you. I may tease Goldfinger a bit. Move over like a good girl and let me have a look.'
>
> Bond took the girl's place and looked through the glasses. The game was going on normally. Goldfinger showed no sign that his communications had broken down.
>
> 'Doesn't he mind not getting the signals? Will he stop playing?'
>
> She said hesitatingly, 'It's happened before when a plug pulled or something. He just waits for me to come through again.'

The last sentence of dialogue is as inept, as impossible to accept as 'real', as a sentence of dialogue in any imaginative work could be. The situation itself it is impossible to accept as developing in a real way, a *human* way. This, surely, is the answer to those who proclaim Fleming a 'good' writer – he has no sense of how people actually would behave in such a situation, and nor does he ever bother to try to make such situations convincing. For this there is an unconscious reason – the partial-object woman (whose mouth is 'generous', of course, and 'who would have a lovely smile') is still dangerous, and *must be kept in control* in case she is the castrating mother: so she must be kept out of any situation that might threaten to become real. The dream must be preserved as make belief. As in the attitude of the pervert to his object, the woman must never become a human person.

She must therefore never be allowed to act as an uncontrolled woman – who would have been angry, surly, dumb, rigid with fear. In any such situation, with a real person these would have *some* reaction.

The girl is entranced by Bond's 'chivalry' and his 'technique', controlled by the magic omnipotence of his hate. She has no integrity of her own, and does not react as an individual at all. What follows is conversation which belongs not to an adult novel but from a child's wishfulfilment dream. A possible comparison is with James Barrie when he is enacting a child's 'ideal' talk – split-off, pure – to mummy or daddy.*

> Bond smiled at her. 'Well, let's le[...]r [...]ew for a bit. Have a cigarette and relax,' he held out a packet of Chesterfields. She took one, [...] s time you did the nails on your right hand.'

---

* Cf. HARRY: I can understand that. And now you would like to go away and play.
  MARY ROSE: Please . . .
  HARRY: . . . You're a pretty thing. What beautiful shoes you have, etc. (Barrie [3], p. 136.)

A smile flickered across her mouth. 'How long were you there? You gave me a frightful shock.'

'Not long, and I'm sorry about the shock. Goldfinger's been giving poor old Mr. Du Pont shocks for a whole week.'

'Yes,' she said doubtfully. 'I suppose it's really rather mean. But he's very rich, isn't he?'

The girl is impossibly manageable – and childishly naïve in revealing secrets to a stranger in consequence of which indiscretion (as an adult woman would know) she might almost certainly lose her life. The episode is enchanted out from reality by wish-fulfilment – which is associated with the magic of gold. It is make-belief in which the sexual object is at the protagonist's mercy, and it is important for the enchantment to work because of the danger to the self if it does not.

' . . . Anyway, he's a millionaire himself. Why does he do it? He's crawling with money.'

Animation flooded back into her face. 'I know. I simply can't understand him. It's a sort of mania with him, making money. He can't leave it alone. I've asked him why and all he says is that one's a fool not to make money when the odds are right. He's always going on about the same thing, getting the odds right. When he talked me into doing this,' she waved her cigarette at the binoculars, 'and I asked him why on earth he bothered, took these stupid risks, all he said was, "That's the second lesson. When the odds aren't right, make them right".'

Bond said, 'Well, it's lucky for him I'm not Pinkertons or the Miami Police Department.'

The girl shrugged her shoulders. 'Oh, that wouldn't worry him. He'd just buy you off. He can buy anyone off. No one can resist gold.'

Here gold is linked with love: under the surface is Fleming's phantasy investigation of what the father does to the mother, in infantile symbols.

'What do you mean?'

She said indifferently, 'He always carries a million dollars' worth of gold about with him except when he's going through the Customs. Then he just carries a belt full of gold coins round his stomach. Otherwise it's in thin sheets in the bottom and sides of his suitcases. They're really gold suitcases covered with leather.'

'They must weigh a ton.'

'He always travels by car, one with special springs. And his chauffeur is a huge man. He carries them. No one else touches them.'

'Why does he carry around all that gold?'

'Just in case he needs it. He knows that gold will buy him anything he wants. It's all twenty-four carat. And anyway he loves gold, really loves it like people love jewels or stamps or – well,' she smiled, 'women.'

Bond smiled back. 'Does he love you?'

She blushed and said indignantly, 'Certainly not.' Then, more reasonably, 'Of course you can think anything you like. But really he doesn't. I mean, I think he likes people to *think* that we – that I'm – that it's a question of love and all that. You know. He's not very prepossessing and I suppose it's a question of – well – of vanity or something.'

'Yes, I see. So you're just a kind of secretary?'

'Companion,' she corrected him. 'I don't have to type or anything.' She suddenly put her hand up to her mouth. 'Oh, but I shouldn't be telling you all this! You won't tell him, will you? He'd fire me.' Fright came into her eyes. 'Or something. I don't know what he'd do. He's the sort of man who might do anything.'

'Of course I won't tell. But this can't be much of a life for you. Why do you do it?'

She said tartly, 'A hundred pounds a week and all this,' she waved at the room, 'Doesn't grow on trees. I save up. When I've saved enough I shall go.'

Bond wondered if Goldfinger would let her. Wouldn't she know too much? He looked at the beautiful face, the splendid, unselfconscious body. She might not suspect it, but, for his money, she was in very bad trouble with this man.

As we have seen, the 'splendid, unselfconscious body' is to be painted with gold (dangerous faeces), possessed by Goldfinger, and so poisoned. But this woman is here already under a control which has no intention of ever letting her go free. She is as much held in control by Bond as she is by Goldfinger who in turn expresses his contempt by paying her £100 a week for her to be his gilded partial object. As the dreaded primitive female she must be subjected to the humiliation of being covered, like Belle de Jour in the film, symbolically with faeces:

> The girl was fidgeting. Now she said with an embarrassed laugh, 'I don't think I'm very properly dressed. Can't I go and put something on over these?'
> Bond wasn't sure he could trust her. It wasn't he who was paying the hundred pounds a week. He said airily, 'You look fine. Just as respectable as those hundreds of people round the pool. Anyway.' he stretched. 'it's about time to light a fire under Mr. Goldfinger.'
> Bond stepped back. 'Neat little machine,' he commented. 'What are you transmitting on?'
> 'He told me, but I can't remember.' She screwed up her eyes. "A hundred and seventy somethings. Would it be mega-somethings?'
> 'Megacycles. . . .'

The girl is so devoted to Goldfinger that she almost offers her sexual favours to defend him from danger. Here the excitement belongs to the kind of sexual make-belief phantasy in which others are subject to our will as transitional objects. As with the stream of milk in the dream of the schizophrenic patient, the partial object here is separated completely from the person. A real woman would have been suspicious and hostile. But the 'breast-object' of phantasy raises no such problems: 'I like you. . . . It's a long time since I've seen someone like you. . . . I'd do *anything*.' The phantasy breast is at once ready to satisfy, and offers immediate love and recognition of value – in a world in which 'only one partner is entitled to make demands'.

> Suddenly she reached out and put a hand on his sleeve. There was a Claddagh ring on the middle finger – two gold hands clasped round a gold heart. There were tears in her voice. 'Must you? Can't you leave him alone? I don't know what he'll do to me. Please.' She hesitated. She was blushing furiously. 'And I like you. It's a long time since I've seen someone like you. Couldn't you just stay here for a little more?' She looked down at the ground. 'If only you'd leave him alone I'd do – ' the words came out in a rush – 'I'd do *anything*.'
> Bond smiled. He took the girl's hand off his arm and squeezed it. 'Sorry. I'm being paid to do this job and I must do it. Anyway – ' his voice went flat – 'I want to do it. It's time someone cut Mr. Goldfinger down to size.'

Despite its utter unreality, as being in any sense experience between adults, such a scene seems to be accepted at large as 'sophisticated' and 'wise' writing.

Seen from my perspective, it merely reveals Fleming's immaturity. He wants a woman who comes to him not as a person but as one who automatically offers him depersonalised sex, makes no demands, and is at his mercy. But there is a deeper appeal, which is that Bond is here phantasied as being able by magic to cheat Goldfinger of his partial object. Between mother and father there is the 'gold finger' and the activity which threatens so many things – siblings, annihilation, emptying, even destruction of the world. If we identify with Bond, we can phantasy ourselves dealing with these threats, and for the talion dangers inherent in our curiosity about the 'combined parents' sex – by stealing and internalising a 'partial object' stolen from the father. We become excited by the magic power by which our paranoic fears could perhaps be overcome:

> 'Just a moment, Goldfinger, you're not through yet.' Bond glanced up at the girl. She was looking at him strangely. There was misery and fear but also a look of submissiveness, of longing.
> 'What's your name?'
> 'Jill Masterton.'
> Goldfinger had stood up, was turning away. Bond said sharply, 'Stop.'
> Goldfinger stopped in mid-stride. Now his eyes looked up at the balcony. They had opened wide, as when Bond had first met him. Their hard, level, X-ray gaze seemed to find the lenses of the binoculars, travel down them and through Bond's eyes to the back of his skull. They seemed to say, 'I shall remember this, Mr. Bond.'
> Bond said softly, 'I'd forgotten. One last thing. I shall be taking a hostage for the ride to New York. Miss Masterton. See that she's at the train. Oh, and make that compartment a drawing-room. That's all.'

Bearing in mind Fairbairn's discussion of the symbol of the 'stream of milk' we can see that the sexual episode which follows is a 'phantasy feed'. Not only does it bear no relationship to real adult sex but Fleming is very careful to make it not real. It is sex not as experienced as the expression of relationship but as phantasied for the purposes of revenge on Goldfinger – a 'side-swipe at Goldfinger's ego'. The woman, characteristically, has no say, no essential equality, no value: she is but a hostage, and subject entirely to Bond's magic. To be a good feed, however, she has to be 'starved of physical love', and in so far as even the 'stream of milk' dream expresses a yearning for love (from the mother), so there is an element here of the impulse to experience love with the mother at the expense of the father who has so 'starved' her.

But a great deal of care is taken to ensure that the sex is safely not real and personal: even the fact that it takes place on a train may be a precaution to avoid being found and exposed to talion attack. All reality of relationship and meeting must be denied because it is too dangerous. And yet this 'partial object' sex of 'psychic impotence' must, for purposes of preservation of the identity, be made to seem larger than life:

> It had been a wonderful trip up in the train. They had eaten the sandwiches and drunk the champagne and then, to the rhythm of the giant diesels pounding out the miles, they had made long, slow love in the narrow berth. It had been as if the girl was starved of physical love. She had woken him twice more in the night with soft demanding caresses, saying nothing, just reaching for his hard, lean body. The next day she had twice pulled down the roller blinds to shut out the hard light and had taken him by the hand and said, 'Love me, James,' as if she was a child asking for a sweet.

Such assertion of 'colossal potency' disguises the terrors of the 'homosexual position', as with Ferenczi's patients.

There can, of course, be no texture of genuine affection in the writing (as there is in Fleming's own letters). Bond merely says: 'I shall never forget last night and today. . . .' But he quickly dismisses the woman in a de-emotionalised way: 'Kissed her once hard on the lips and had gone away.'

Here Fleming offers us his schizoid reversal of values in an apophthegm: lust is pure. Hate-sex is virtually the purest love: 'It hadn't been love, but a quotation had come into Bond's mind as his cab moved out of Pennsylvania station, "Some love is fire, some love is rust. But the finest, cleanest love is lust." '

For a moment Fleming confronts, in a clumsy way, conventional moral doubts. Characteristically he can find no *inward* doubt since he has no experience of genuine love and meeting by which to judge. Depersonalisation and de-emotionalisation involve a 'regression of the quality of relationship desired' – towards the non-human and anti-human: yet how could Fleming see this? 'Neither had had regrets. Had they committed a sin? If so, which one? A sin against chastity? Bond smiled to himself. There was a quotation for that too, and from a saint – Saint Augustine "Oh Lord give me Chastity. But don't give it yet." '

But the suavity of tone, so often heard in 'sophisticated' culture today, is essentially a mask. It disguises the psychic impotence and the essential inability to find meaning in relationship. The individual holding such attitudes to relationship must preserve his narcissistic egocentricity and hide his hatred and contempt. What is missing here is any recognition of the woman's human quality. The pose of sexual sophistication hides the essential meanness of the attitude, its mechanical concern with 'automatic satisfaction', and the fundamental failure to find the other.

The attitude of course fits in well with the hedonistic ethos of an acquisitive society.

The world exists for Bond to enjoy his streams of milk: the Loire is 'dressed' for him to take any woman he happens to fancy. He will 'run her down' as a quarry, and after a certain sequence of manoeuvres carried out with cool detachment and in the absence of all emotion, eat her in a final diaresis:

> Bond motored comfortable along the Loire in the early summer sunshine. This was one of his favourite corners of the world. In May, with the fruit trees turning white and the soft wide river still big with the winter rains, the valley was green and young and dressed for love. He was thinking this when, before the Chateauneuf, there was a shrill scream from twin Bosch horns and the little Triumph tore past. The hood was down. There was the blur of a pretty face hidden by white motoring goggles with dark blue lenses. Although Bond only saw the edge of a profile – a slash of red mouth and the fluttering edge of black hair under a pink handkerchief with white spots, he knew she was pretty from the way she held her head. There was the authority of someone who is used to being admired, combined with the self-consciousness of a girl driving alone and passing a man in a smart car.
>
> Bond thought: That *would* happen today! The Loire is dressed for just that – chasing that girl until you run her to ground at lunchtime, the contact at the empty restaurant by the river, out in the garden under the vine trellis. The *friture* and the ice-cold Vouvray, the cautious sniffing at each other and then the two cars motoring on in convoy until that evening, well down to the south, there would be the place they had agreed on at lunch – olive trees, crickets singing in the indigo dusk, the discovery that they liked each other and that their destinations could wait. Then, next day ('No, not tonight. I don't know you well enough, and besides I'm tired') they would leave her car in the hotel garage and go off in his at a tangent, slowly, driving to the west, away from the big road. What was the place he had always wanted to go to, simply because of the name. Yes, Entre Deux Seins, a village near Les Baux. Perhaps there wasn't even an inn there. Well, then they would go on to Les Baux itself, at the bouches du Rhone on the edge of the Camargue. There they would take adjoining rooms (not a double room, it would be too early for that) in the fabulous Baumanière, the only hotel-restaurant in France with Michelin's supreme accolade. They would eat the *gratin de langouste* and perhaps, because it was traditional on such a night, drink champagne. And then. . . .

The prose has the quality of the cold 'camp' writing one finds in *Vogue* and the commercial glossies and supplements. Knowing the right places and the right things to order (*gratin de langouste*) are far more important than respecting the uniqueness of another human being or respecting the most intimate realm of I–Thou relationship.

The excitement is not in establishing a relationship with a woman as a person with whom one might share love, but that of out-manoeuvring her, in contempt, and finding some way of subduing her and forcing her into the role of giving gratification as a part-object.

Here we may invoke Khan's exploration of the 'charade of intimacy' in perversion. Bond's attitude to sex, however much accepted in our world, is, by Khan's analysis, perverted. It is a 'solitary game'. 'Even though two persons are involved . . . essentially it is all the invention of one person. There is no object-relatedness; hence no nourishment.' From Khan's knowledge of the pervert in his anguished needs when he turns to seek therapy, we can see that Fleming–Bond's attitude to sex is an expression of a need to exploit another narcissistically, for his own ego-needs, and with undercurrents of envy and meanness. This can be related to all we know of Fleming, and all we have said about Bond. The woman only resists the man with 'excuses' for which he has derision and impatience: his needs are paramount – they must be met, for only he is 'entitled to make demands'. She must simply give herself in exchange for his trouble and his outlay – which also serve to guarantee that the sexual exchange is not in any sense a meeting – mutuality cannot be tolerated. The essential meanness is disguised by the sophistication ('not a double room . . .') while the seduction is calculated, like Bond's murders, with egocentric detachment as a technique ('it would be too early for that'). The egocentricity gores with a 'highly preservative concern': there is a 'threat to the ego' if the 'taking' is not successful. As Fairbairn reveals, this egocentricity is a mark of 'extreme over-dependence' – as symbolised by the name *Entre-deux-seins* which Bond later rejects with contempt.

Ferenczi says that the paranoia of the homosexual is sometimes found associated with early incidents of compulsive curiosity (e.g. touching a girl indecently). On such an occasion, 'which was often repeated', they had to suppress an outburst of intense rage. This kind of compulsive combination of contempt and curiosity, with deep feelings of hate under the surface, recurs in Fleming's phantasy: as in the episode where Bond jeers 'If you touch me there again you'll have to marry me.'

Again, we find in *Goldfinger*, this exchange: 'The girl, her face tense with anger, had one beautiful silken leg on the road. There was an indiscreet glimpse of white thigh. . . . The beautiful mouth was tense with anger. . . . The words were hardly out of his mouth before the open palm cracked across his face. . . .'

In revenge for this blow Tilly Masterton, who 'didn't think much of men', later suffers decapitation by the bowler-boomerang.

Tilly seems to be punished symbolically for two reasons. One is that she does not '*respond properly*' to a man. She will not be wholly controlled as a partial object: that is, by threatening to become too much of a woman, concerned for her sister, she threatens to expose the dangers of real relationship. The contempt of Bond's angry snarl '*entre deux seins* indeed!' is enacted finally thus: 'The little figure still lay sprawled where she had fallen. Bond knelt beside her. The broken-doll angle of the head was enough. He felt for her pulse. He got up. He said softly, "Poor little bitch. She didn't think much of men." He looked defensively at Leiter. "Felix, I could have got her away if she'd only followed me." '

Interestingly enough Tilly's fatal fault was to become devoted to Pussy Galore. I think this may symbolise the possibility to Fleming of his coming to accept the split-off feminine element in himself and to accept it as an internalisation of aspects of the mother: naturally Tilly, as a focus of this, has to perish. But the other reason is that, while she too is 'faintly mannish', she also comes a little into focus as a real person, and so threatens Bond–Fleming's need to deny dependence. She is virtually annihilated because she is on the verge of becoming human.

So, in Fleming's work, we can detect a vibration directed against woman which is an energy directed at our own humanity. Close examination of Fleming's work reveals an existential insecurity so deep that it impelled him, from the depths of his own anti-libidinal hatred of himself, to express and spread abroad a detestation of being human, with human feelings, as a false solution. Yet we sometimes catch a glimpse of the insecurity through the mask.

At one point in *Goldfinger* Bond regresses to the nursery world where perhaps the infant Fleming yearned to be loved for his own sake. Indulging in this phantasy he finds himself confronted with playmates: the little girls appropriate as phantasy objects for a small boy, fairies almost, from the world of Peter Pan. But, of course, these are Bond's 'multiple objects' whom he thinks of as pets (Pussies Galore) from whom in the past he has had 'automatic satisfaction'. This 'multiple object' phantasy, so prevalent in our cultural ethos, is a symbol of super-potency (from the film *What's New Pussycat?* to Amis's poem *A Tale of Fair Women*) is a phantasy whose origins are in the nursery daydreams of the insecure child.

The wings of a dove, the heavenly choir, Hark the Herald Angels Sing – what else ought he to remember about Paradise? It was all so exactly like what he had been told in the nursery – this sensation of flying, the darkness, the drone of a million harps. He really must try and remember the dope about the place. Let's see now, one got to the Pearly Gates. . . .

A deep fatherly voice said, almost in his ear. . . .

Would Tilly be on the same trip? Bond squirmed with embarrassment. How would he introduce her to the others, to *Vesper* for instance? And when it came to the point, which would he like the best. But perhaps it would be a big place with countries and towns. There was probably no more reason why he should run into one of his former girl friends here than there had been on earth. But still there were a lot of people he'd better avoid until he got settled in and found out the form. Perhaps, with so much love about, these things wouldn't matter. Perhaps one just loved all the girls one met. Hm. Tricky business!

The pathetic boyishness is almost engaging (though an actual child could write much more effectively about feelings on the approach of death). But Fleming's boyish attempts to confront the mortal condition ('Hm. Tricky business'), like those of Sir James Barrie, are deeply embarrassing because they reveal such pathetic inability to tolerate such disturbing areas of human experience. In the heart of 'camp' toughness we find the sentimentality which hides a powerful and destructive hate on the other side of the split.

Little girls in Bond's vision of heaven, of course, would be those towards which, as a boy in the homosexual position, he would have exerted, like little Fritz, 'unreasonable antipathy.' It is this 'unreasonable antipathy' which is indulged in Bond's kind of 'taking' attitude to sex, an attitude obviously widely endorsed by Fleming, as it is by his admirer Kingsley Amis.

The influence of such hate symbolism I have tried to expose as anti-human. If I am right it will not do to say, as Lord Hill of Luton did at the beginning of 1969, that we have no 'concrete evidence' that the exploitation of violence and sex by commercial culture has no effect on the actual lives of individuals. In the field of racial relationships it is quite clearly recognised that it is possible to spread hatred abroad by irrational emotional appeals. From subjective evidence it seems obvious that if entertainment phantasies are based on hate, they will spread hate abroad in the same way, and thus inevitably affect attitudes to life and modes of behaviour at large.

Surely from my analysis of the primitive elements in *Goldfinger* it will seem likely that such work as Fleming's must inevitably spread hate abroad in our society. This hate, however, is disguised because what is inculcated in us is *hatred of woman* and hatred of the *female element in ourselves* – and to this we are unusually prone, since one possible solution to life is to avoid humanness if we can.

Detection of the origins of Fleming's hate reveals it as originating in the 'homosexual position'. A study of the elements and origins of male homosexuality in its relation to problems of identity will be found rewarding in considering many manifestations of contemporary culture apart from Fleming. I am here not only trying to imply that there is something 'perverted' about commercial culture because so much of it shows elements whose origins are in unconscious homosexuality. I am rather concerned to show that where the need for considerable financial return on investment is the basis of culture, that what is successful more often than not is material that plays on primitive anxieties with their roots in such early problems of identity.*

* This accounts for the extraordinary degree of preoccupation on the television with themes of mental illness, homosexuality, and other forms of abnormality, for instance, and also with surgery ('inner contents'). Of the sexual acts depicted how many are normal acts in the context of love, expressing the primary human need for relationship? The fact that most are 'abnormal' compared with life, indicates that what we have in this trend is not so much 'realism' as a kind of 'make-belief' based on primitive phantasy, itself the expression of a need to compensate by 'bad thinking' in this sphere, for a lack of a sense of meaning in life. The increase of nudity in the theatre, film and on television belongs to the same syndrome, and the reduction of the object to the status of part-object, rather than to a new 'freedom'.

One of the most difficult problems of identity is the reconciliation of one's male and female elements: so, this problem can become the focus of anxiety aroused by contemporary commercial culture as in its obsession with 'kinky' and 'kookie' sex, which is the depersonalised sex of False Male Doing. Where a dehumanised environment offers so little help to find one's essential humanity, the false solutions of paranoia and hate can make a 'successful impact' in entertainment media. The audience may temporarily feel alive, but in such a way that a residue of paranoid anxiety and dread is left. This residue of existence-anxiety is a gift to the commercial world because it prompts not only compulsive 'False Male Doing' (which by its 'bustle' prevents us from 'confronting the problem of existence') but also a compulsive if meaningless preoccupation with externals such as we find in Fleming. From the same area of primitive existence anxiety arises the need to establish that one is really 'all right' in terms of a meticulous attention to details of dress, ritual, etiquette, class tokens, games, cars, and so on – an obsessional element to which the sense of identity in suburban life has become attached at large.

All this preoccupation with externals draws attention away from the fact that our primary problem in 'confronting the problem of existence' has to do with our inward humanness, and that one major problem here is realising the female element of being in ourselves. Where woman is attacked in cultural symbolism, it is this True Self which is under attack, and the hatred is a hatred of essential humanness. It is this self-hatred that so fascinates those picking over the wares on the railway bookstall.

CHAPTER 18

The Commander at 'Goldeneye'

ONE of the most subtle problems of present-day culture is that, by the kind of schizoid reversal of values discussed in this book, forms of behaviour in life which are manifestations of deterioration if they are found in any actual individual such as a patient under therapy, have been made socially acceptable, elevated to norms, and even made admirable. Thus to most people, from accounts of his life, Fleming's life must seem a great 'success'. In a society devoted to ingestion as the solution to problems of identity, Fleming is taken to represent one way of becoming larger than life.

From the point of view of object-relations psychology, however, it seems likely that Fleming's 'success' was of the kind a psychotherapist like Winnicott would call 'unreal'. ('Unreal success is morality at its lowest ebb.') Of course, the success was real enough in terms of acquisitive gain: but in terms of a contribution to culture Fleming's success was eminently the success of 'False Male Doing'. Yet the projection of him by acclaims seeks, under the mask of sophistication, to vindicate such ways of living at the expense of the True Self and at the expense of others.

What is so strange is how little the dichotomy troubles us. It is assumed, for instance, that Fleming had the sophistication and sexual experience of a man of the world, while his books convey the impression that he knew 'what was what' in many spheres. His knowing air obviously impresses Amis and Burgess, to mention two of Fleming's 'literary' admirers. Yet, in truth, Fleming's air of sophisticated knowingness, both in the realm of taste and that of experience, was quite false and no mark of accomplishment in living experience. The whole cultural manifestation was itself a gilded sham.

The relevant material for our critical approach, of course, is to be found in the symbolism of the stories themselves. But the very falsity of the beliefs he established in his own man-of-the-world sophistication, force us to take his own behaviour in life into account.

We have seen in Goldfinger the theme of anal sadism – and anal retention: the urge of the schizoid individual to keep his gold within its store. Fleming lived in a home called 'Goldeneye', and in this symbolism we may find a link between the phantasy and the life. 'Gold' as a symbol of retained faeces can be seen as a symbol of Fleming's meanness and narcissism (retention of inner contents felt to be both valuable and worthless) and his ambition to make a fortune. The 'eye' may be taken as a symbol of the 'spy' curiosity about inner contents, of the 'secrecy', and the exhibitionist schizoid 'showing' that is a substitute for living – whose complement is voyeurism.

Noel Coward, who belongs to the same social and cultural world, with all its detachment of feeling, was a friend of Fleming's and points out that the house was badly sited and was 'a perfectly ghastly place', while Fleming as a host was mean:

'One of the things that still make me laugh whenever I read Ian's books,' says Coward, 'is the contrast between the standard of living of dear old Bond and the sort of thing Ian used to put up with at Goldeneye. When Bond drinks his wine it has to be properly chambré, the tournedos slightly underdone and so forth. But whenever I ate with Ian at Goldeneye the food was so abominable I used to cross myself before I took a mouthful. Stewed guavas and coconut cream — salt fish and ackee fruit. I used to say, "Ian, it tastes like armpits." And all the time there was old Ian smacking his lips for more while his guests remembered all those delicious meals he had put into the books.'

The Life of Ian Fleming

Coward's theory is that the food and the discomforts of 'Goldeneye' were exactly what Fleming wanted and secretly enjoyed.

The enjoyment of the retention of 'inner contents' was perhaps more important to Fleming, and safer, than generosity: richness of giving was confined to the meals of the phantasies (by which he lost nothing, since they were 'showings' merely).

Fleming's sense of 'superiority' combined with isolation, went with private rituals in which a chief delight was to be without human company as Pearson records:

... all the other carefully prescribed ingredients of Fleming's routine at Goldeneye: the seven o'clock swim out to the reef, the shaving water brought by Violet on his return, the solitary breakfast of paw-paw, scrambled eggs and coffee beneath the sea walnut on the edge of the 'sinking garden', the humming birds he watched sipping from the hibiscus, the kling-klings that hopped around the breakfast table. Each had its place, its particular significance, and these small rituals could make Fleming appear an odd and sometimes a difficult host for those who did not understand him.

ibid.

As Peter Quennell relates, guests found themselves in a strongly egocentric environment:

... tended to be a very restless, unrelaxed person, and he could be very prima-donna-ish, relapsing into tantrums if he felt you were intruding on any of the things he enjoyed about the place. For instance, in the morning, if you went for a swim, you had to make a great detour to avoid the front of the house because the Commander's bedroom was on that side, and he had got into the habit of lying on his bed in the early morning, watching the view unmarred by mortal man.

ibid.

Fleming essentially disliked contact, was remote and 'superior', and was parsimonious with drinks and with money. He worked in Admiralty intelligence in the war, where no doubt his symbolic unconscious preoccupation with secrecy was satisfied. He received no decorations for his work, but the years in the Admiralty are said to have 'done a lot for Fleming' in terms of his own ambition: 'He had ambition now. He enjoyed power. He had influential friends. He was thirty-eight and it was time he made his way in the world.'

The same influential friends did much to help his books become popular, not least the journalists whose world he joined as News Editor for Kemsley, with two months' holiday written into his contract, during which to retire to 'Goldeneye': 'Here, as usual, he was entirely egocentric. All his life he nimbly side-stepped the drab, routine duties which exhaust ordinary people.'

His 'non-love-affairs' were conducted with the same incapacity to meet and give:

His flat in Montagu Square was comfortable, almost opulent; and here his love affairs continued with the same rapidity as before the war, although it seemed, with even less danger of his becoming seriously entangled with any one woman. More than ever now he was keeping love of any sort out of his relations with women. He could feel sentimental over their memory but he remained defensively detached in their presence. He was the most professional of professional bachelors, self-contained as a sultan, following his own strange hankerings for excitement and amusement in all he did.

If people bored him, he dropped them. If anything interested him, he pursued it enthusiastically until it, too, suddenly became boring. He played golf and bridge with almost perverse seriousness. There is something almost old-maidish about the ivory-tower existence which he now began to construct for himself.

ibid.

Here we glimpse the compulsiveness, the egocentricity, the 'diminution of affect' of a schizoid individual; we also see the paradox of the schizoid's appeal for while, surely, it manifests only 'contempt for the object', to 'remain defensively detached' in the presence of a woman with whom one is having sexual relationships – yet it seems that it is just this 'sultan'-like quality our world admires. In this paragraph we can also detect the element of homosexuality which is a significant underlying feature of Fleming's phantasy.

Schizoid secrecy and superiority are manifest in Fleming's concern with 'symmetry' – the imposition of a narcissistic pattern on life by intellectualization rather than living on terms of 'whole being': 'One of the words he was always using was "symmetry", and in the pursuit of symmetry in his own life everything was worked out – the restaurants he went to, the friends he played bridge and golf with, the women he took to his bed.'

This symmetry of narcissism may be associated with the unconscious homosexuality and the 'technique of intimacy' – the need never to find anything but one's own sexual organ on another person. Such symmetry is a defence against giving and finding. To accept 'assymetry' – individual uniqueness and sexual difference – would be to be faced with the reality of woman, and so with both one's own female element, and all the dangers of relationship. As Khan indicates, the pervert is one who cannot find another person in sexual partnership – cannot give himself in 'emotional surrender' to another recognised as another: the object is exploited as a transitional object which, to all intents and purposes, is treated as an extension of the self. The voyeur is often looking for a penis on the woman for parallel reasons of symmetry. And with 'symmetry', as we have seen, go envy and meanness – and the incapacity to find satisfaction.

While we detect beneath the surface of his biography intense problems of not feeling real and of 'False Self success', to the author of his biography Fleming is one to be envied, if not admired.

> Perhaps he was a man to be envied more than admired. For among all the anxious or ambitious men around him at Kemsley House he seemed to have his life so much better worked out than anyone else. Where they were worried he was aloof, where they were involved he seemed somehow above the battle. He had no wife to interfere with his golf, no bank manager troubled his peace of mind. . . . Urbane and irreverent, invulnerable and unconcerned, he appeared as a sort of Crown Prince. . . . That is, until disillusion set in and he lost his enthusiasm, and his lips turned down with dissatisfaction.
>
> *ibid*

But it is evident even from such a favourable biography that in the harsh world of newspaper journalism Fleming was not a success. He might be envied: yet the ruthless egocentricity ended in bitterness. He became a 'success' by transferring his energies to the exhibitionism of his meretricious phantasies when in life the first real relationship was demanded of him.

The effort had a further symbolic value. Fleming perhaps felt safe to marry his wife because she was a 'lady' who had already had two other husbands. Psychically speaking, such a woman is safer, perhaps, since others have survived relationship with her. She was both intellectual and aristocratic, and so 'ideal' rather than 'libidinal', and so – to the unconscious mind of such a man – less dangerous. But she also insisted, as his other women almost certainly did not, in being treated as a person in her own right. Fleming was forced to enter into a relationship which demanded some equality. He could no longer maintain the attitude that 'only one partner was entitled to make demands'. His schizoid attitude to relationship was now reserved for the public phantasies.

At the same time his writing took on a defensive social purpose. It would help him to maintain his social acceptibility, although he had married a divorcée. But there was a deeper purpose which was to seek to vindicate and to make admirable all those ways of dealing with the world by hate that were his false solution to the problem of feeling real. 'James Bond' is the False Self arrogantly offered as a successful True Self. And the trick worked.

As Pearson says:

> There are plenty of similarities between the author and the hero he created. But James Bond is not Ian Fleming, nor is he an Ian Fleming that ever was. He is Fleming's dream of a self that might have been – a tougher, stronger, more effective, duller, far less admirable character than the real Fleming. The greater the number of superficial resemblances he could establish between Bond and himself the more credible his daydream would become: hence the items of self-portraiture so carefully written into the books, the similarities of clothing, habits and speech. They were what carried the fantasy along for the lonely man typing his 2,000 words a day in the silence of Goldeneye.
>
> Until he wrote 'Casino Royale' his fantasy world had been a secret world, undercover, faintly reprehensible; in those few weeks of self-revelation at Goldeneye it had amused him to put some of his dreams down on paper; in a mood of longing for success he was to make public what he had written; and instead of being laughed at, instead of being publicly reprimanded for showing the tendencies of a juvenile delinquent, he was to find himself compared with John Buchan and Eric Ambler. *Nearly everyone seemed to enjoy his inventions. Nobody sniggered. Nobody who mattered complained.* With the publication of 'Casino Royale' the secret life of Ian Fleming received the stamp of public approval. [My italics.]
>
> *ibid.*

What had once been a private world of phantasy compensating for relational fear and impotence now became the path to that social relationship and social acceptance which are so difficult for the schizoid individual – albeit at a distance. Fleming could have been laughed at: but he became instead a successful industry based on hate, and he was able to involve the public in this inversion of normal values: he was able to 'press that into us'.

The actual relationship in his life took a characteristically long time to achieve: 'giving' being so full of danger:

> In later years, whenever he was asked how he come to start writing novels, Fleming would invariably say that it has been quite simply to take his mind off 'the shock of getting married at the age of forty-three.' It was the sort of flip, faintly cynical remark he enjoyed making. It embodied the Old Etonian myth of the effortless amateur able to turn a casual hand to anything with equally spectacular success.
>
> *ibid*

'Myth' it certainly is, for Fleming's 'achievement' represents no essential success in terms of Balint's concept of 'conquest'. Fleming desperately needed to preserve his air of 'superiority' and 'omnipotence' (and still does by the 'hate solution' appeal of his books).

When his wife first saw him she too was impressed by this pose: ' . . . at Le Touquet, where he arrived aboard a yacht. She had thought him "god like but unapproachable".'

Of course, there was a façade of 'charm' over the hate, as there is an appeal in the 'technique of intimacy' which is the essential accomplishment of the kind of person Khan discusses, who makes use of others.

Mrs. Fleming says:

> He was immensely attractive and had enormous charm. But it was as a character that he really interested me. He was totally unlike anyone else I had ever met. There was something defensive and untamed about him, like a wild animal. He would never do anything out of mere politeness or because it was expected of him, and he never wanted to talk about himself. Of course, I found it a great challenge to get through this barrier and find out what lay behind.
>
> *ibid.*

For some reason the defensiveness in his personality attracted Anne. But there was no question of mere schizoid 'taking' of a 'partial object' in a relationship with the real woman. She was too 'intelligent': ' . . . with her there could be no question of his behaving in his usual manner, culminating in the abrupt dismissiveness with which he treated nearly all the rest. Fleming had met his match and he knew it.'

Yet she admired his isolated egocentric world: 'Ian has devised a halcyon way of life,' she wrote, 'and only he could have done it.'

Was his wife herself the kind of woman whose 'brilliance' was combined with a willingness to be treated in terms of 'only one partner is entitled to make demands'?

> . . . and he knew that however deep their feelings for each other the fragile birdcage of his existence would never stand up to the strains of a permanent relationship. There was little either of them could do to alter things.
> 'I think Ian liked me because I amused him and because I made no real demands on him,' she says. 'He always said that I was the one person who could "kill the day" during his bouts of melancholy.'
>
> *ibid.*

Significantly, as Fleming's real need for Anne developed, his letters reveal the overdependence which the sophistication and ego-centricity sought to hide:

> When she was ill in Edinburgh he complained wretchedly of feeling 'further away than before and quite useless'. By the end of her illness Fleming knew that the one thing he had tried to avoid all his life had happened. He was involved totally with another human being and there was no going back.
>
> My darling, last night I looked round my room and saw all the bits of you. I have often looked at them before and almost counted the strings that bind my heart to yours. All the warmth in me comes from you. All the love I have for you has grown out of me because you made it grow. Without you I would still be hard and dead and cold and quite unable to write this childish letter, full of love and jealousies and adolescence.
>
> *ibid.*

He went on:

> Hell, this is a stupid letter and I am stupid to write it. I believe in my heart that we shall live our lives together because we shall both come back to a love which not many people have known.
>
> *ibid*

This is refreshingly genuine in its youthfulness for a middle-aged bachelor in love. It reveals a vulnerability at the other extreme from the 'toughness' we are asked to admire in James Bond. But such exposure of weakness and the True Self obviously would feel a threat. So the writing of the novels began as a way of sustaining a False Self not least by denying in phantasy the dependence, and the need revealed here. Pearson offers us the writing activity as a distraction from the anxieties of Anne's divorce and from Fleming's fear of the 'apprehended boredom of marriage'. But at a deeper level we can see the Bond phantasies as a defence against recognition of the human weaknesses intimate relationship inevitably exposes and its dangers.

In the sphere of the True Self, as we can see from his love letters, Fleming felt vulnerable and childish. So, in the alter-ego stories for public consumption he must seek to appear strong and sophisticated and endorse the 'taboo on weakness'. Hence he hastily assembled all kinds of scraps of apparent knowledgeability. What appears to be so 'real' in the 'spy' stories is, as the biographer Pearson reveals, either erroneous, hasty journalism, or borrowed information:

> . . . he relied on writing the entire book at full speed and then going over it later to fill in the details. It is also interesting to see just how shaky the expertise of this apparent master of certain kinds of expertise really is. For example, despite James Bond's apparent familiarity with all the byways of ballistics, Fleming's own knowledge of fire-arms was really very slight. He was a good shot and could admire guns for their workmanship and for what they symbolised, but he could never take the trouble to become an expert.
> There is surprising proof of this in a letter he wrote to Robert Churchill the gun-smith asking him to check over the names of the four different firearms mentioned in 'Casino Royale'. Only one of them, the .38 Colt Police Positive (the gun that General Donovan gave him during the war for 'special services'), did he succeed in naming correctly.
>
> *ibid.*

The 'arcane' air is that of obsessional 'secrecy' and paranoic ritual – not of real knowledge at all: 'Although later on Fleming was to appear to make something of a cult about the arcane information he introduced into his books, he knew perfectly well that it was *little more than a device for conveying credibility and carrying his readers with him.*'

This device of larding his text with 'knowing' expertise merely served to make the phantasies publicly palatable and to disguise their real nature.

It is hard to find a subject, admits Pearson, 'on which he was a genuine expert'.

> When one comes to think of it, it is hard to think of a single subject on which he was a genuine expert. His knowledge of food was erratic, of wine almost non-existent. He was a sound driver, but he relied on the advice of experts like Aubrey Forshaw, head of Pan Books, for the really detailed facts of automobile technology in his books. It was the same with weaponry, the same with high finance, the same with gambling, the same even with the Secret Service.
>
> *ibid.*

But then, incredibly, Pearson his biographer states that Fleming was an expert on *sex*! 'Only in matters of sex did he rely entirely on his own carefully guarded hoard of knowledge.'

We have seen what sex in the Bond novel represents: for Bond there is only the 'simplification of relationship' and the 'substitution of bodily for emotional contacts'. Fleming's phantasy sex in the novels is essentially based on his own cold and detached sex in his love-affairs, not on his real relationship with the woman he loved: it is hate-sex, not love-sex, and it is prompted by fear. But the element of make-belief in this essentially perverted sex has the effect of deluding us all, because of its manic appeal.

Yet it is this sex of False Male Doing rather than that love which belongs to 'being' which has become elevated to a high value in our society: it seems so 'alive' and larger than life. Yet even Pearson recognises that there is a sense in which Fleming had no deep knowledge, and was essentially superficial, his air of authority a 'varnish': 'The truth is that Fleming had neither the inclination nor the staying power of the expert. He was something different: he was a born journalist, and true to that calling he knew how to mobilise and exploit the knowledge of others. Few men were ever more adroit with the knowing phrase, the exotic-sounding fact, the lightly brushed-on varnish of authority.'

Fleming is an appropriate hero for Fleet Street and for the English upper middle class with their disastrous neglect of the realm of being, as in their child-rearing patterns, prep and public schools, and all (Cf. the revelations of the crushing of 'female element being' in the public school child in Royston Lambert's *The Hothouse Society*.) The essential untenderness of this world is surely celebrated by Noel Coward, in the verses he wrote for Ian Fleming's wedding:

> . . . a special Goldeneye Calypso in honour of the occasion. It began:
> *Mongoose dig about sunken garden*
> *Mongoose murmur, 'oh my – Oh my!*
> *No more frig about – beg pardon.*
> *Things are changing at Goldeneye!*
>
> *ibid.*

What many 'progressive' critics take to be a democratic advance in culture is often surely little more than the spread of such vulgarity over the whole population – not least by the influence of Fleming himself. This ethos is, of course, inimical to such genuine and tenderly weak feelings as Fleming himself expressed in his latters to Anne.

There the fear of relationship is expressed in a genuinely poetic form and even speaks figuratively of unconscious fears of vulnerability – 'you may munch holes in me':

> This afternoon I walked in the woods which are high and wet and full of jays and I saw you dressed up as a golden pheasant. You were nervous and preoccupied and you really hadn't got time for me, so you scurried back into the rotting rhododendron manure where you live. You thought (or rather hoped) no one was watching you, but you were such a bright light on the damp pine needles that this was silly of you and you might just as well have stayed and talked.
>
> There is an eclipse of the moon tonight and I suppose that is why I am writing to you. My love, I think you are sitting in your small room with your tiny life gathered round you like the folds of a warm and pretty skirt. I think you are a consumptive dragonfly in Hackney Marshes and, as an obstinate waterlily among the prevailing moss, I hope you will stay on my leaf and keep the flies off – even though you may munch holes in me until I wither.
>
> *ibid.*

Fleming could have written like that in his books. But the True Self did not write the thrillers. In Fleming's novels one searches in vain for what might have come from the True Self.

CHAPTER 19

The Socially Acceptable Psychopath

WE NOW have to consider the effect of Fleming's work at large. It may, of course, be objected that Fleming merely wrote for 'fun' and his books are merely a 'send-up'. But whatever a man utters, even if he has his tongue in his cheek, the content must come from 'inner' material of some kind, while possess it affects our inner life in turn and our concepts of man. What seems to have happened with Fleming is that when the impresarios of commercial entertainment approached Fleming's work they could see intuitively that it contained those elements of primitive symbolism which could be exploited for a vast popular appeal and invested in successfully with some guarantee of substantial returns *because of the hate.*

Yet, as implied in the quotation from Suzanne Langer above, such hate and its effects are not seen by 'sociologists'. Here the fallaciousness of prevalent assumptions about the relationship between man, culture, and society may be seen if we consider Amis's absurd point that in countries where Fleming's work is not known the incidence of rape is higher! There are so many complex human problems involved in differences between communities – the degree of respect for woman and for human integrity – when we consider such a fact. It would never be possible to prove anything by evidence from the realm of behaviour. What we must do is to study the subjective elements and decide upon their likely effect. What, for instance, is likely to be the effect of Fleming's paranoia? It seems not irrelevant that one of those who nearly plunged the world into disaster over Suez once stayed at 'Goldeneye'.

The harmful effect of Fleming's work may be directly related to his ruthless egocentricity and his own false solutions. As we have seen, there seems to have been a specific personal reason why Fleming took to writing these books. The Bond myth, with all its obsessional elements belonging to the need to preserve secret internal objects, was born at the moment Fleming accepted the reality of another person: 'On March 18, 1952, six days before the marriage at Port Maria, the manilla folder of the first Bond book was full . . .' (Pearson [46]).

It seems almost as if these strange phantasies were an attempt to overcome his fear and reluctance to enter into a real relationship. In this he was threatened with 'parting with something too precious to be lost'. When Fleming committed himself to a genuine relationship, he may have felt that this put his 'inner contents' in jeopardy – so that he devised the 'alter-ego' phantasies as a way of preserving a kind of 'False Self' activity to help guarantee against such possibilities.

As a schizoid person he inevitably feared a threat to his 'inner contents' in marriage. An

130

intense paranoic identity problem arises because the 'inner contents' of oneself have been 'stolen'.

Instead of feeling assured of the male and female elements within oneself, essentially felt as aspects of one's own being, he feels that he has within him merely partial objects which have had to be stolen because love was not originally given as the core of being in the first place. The preservation of these internalised objects is an urgent life-or-death matter, and so the onset of marriage perhaps impelled Fleming to write phantasies in which he hallucinates ways of dealing with the threat of their being 'taken away'.

Fleming's whole appeal, then, and that of the 'spy' myth, is based on an intense need to preserve one's inner contents by paranoia:

> Secrecy is here an important element: The inner necessity for secrecy is, of course, partly determined by guilt over the possession of internalised objects *which are in a sense 'stolen'*: but it is also in no small measure determined by fear of the loss of internalised objects which appear infinitely precious (even precious as life itself), and the internalization of which is a measure of their importance and the extent of dependence upon them. (Fairbairn [18], p. 22; my italics.)

The sense of omnipotence in the schizoid individual, as Fairbairn says, is associated with these needs. And in so far as we become involved in the delusions of the Bond myth we thus become involved in a false belief that we have good reason to fear a threat to our very existence against which we must justifiably exert aggression: 'The libidinal attitude accompanying this fixation [in the schizoid individual fixated in the early oral stage] was one not only characterized by *extreme dependence*, but also rendered highly *self-preservative* and narcissistic by anxiety over a situation which presented itself, as involving a *threat to the ego*' (Fairbairn [18], p. 23 my italics).

Such a paranoic view of the world leads to inevitable ethical problems: '. . . every *external* object tends to be unconsciously viewed as a kind of nourishment to be consumed or as a threat to be destroyed . . .'.

Bond's world is exactly this – a world of objects to be consumed or enemies to be destroyed. As Money-Kyrle puts the mechanism which Fleming's phantasy dramatises, '. . . in conflict with this completely predatory egoism, the ego has developed an opposite tendency to embrace and identify itself with other objects, which then it must as desperately endeavour to preserve. . . .'.

James Bond is a (good) Secret Service agent, devoted to preserving the contents of the Bank of England and Fort Knox, against (bad) Goldfinger and SMERSH. The phantasy world of the books is the world of what Money-Kyrle calls the 'insoluble unconscious conflict' of the individual involved in the processes of hate, whose conflict is 'averted . . . by mechanisms of splitting'. 'So that his world is divided into enemies to be destroyed and friends to be protected from the external replicas of (his) own aggression . . . '(Money-Kyrle [44], p. 110).

Because it is based on splitting, Fleming's phantasy is divided into split black and white partial aspects: no-one in his book is ever as complex or ambivalent as any real human person. In such writing there can be no discovery of that 'relief' we find as we gradually discover that real people are never as terrible as our worst primitive phantasy imagos. On the contrary, we revert to the 'crippling morality' of primitive paranoia in so far as we are influenced by such symbolism.

Such writing does not move towards 'finding' and 'meeting', but towards further splitting and paranoia and further denial of ambivalence and dependence. Rather than moving towards the human, as all good writing does, it moves towards the denial of the

human qualities in others and the self. Such solutions cannot be sustained except by
further falsification of the truth of experience: 'The solution, maintained as it is by so
denial of unlikeable qualities in the friends and likeable ones in the enemies, is stable only
as it is not too closely examined' (Money-Kyrle [44], p. 110).

Not only does such symbolism lead us further away from true satisfactions in the discovery of the True Self and our essential humanity: it promotes the cycles of hate
abroad and urges men to 'slip into the logically stabler state of complete moral inversion'
(Polanyi).

As we have seen, in his life Fleming was mean: and the effect of his phantasies is to
make us meaner. If anything, we become involved in his compulsive obsessional neurosis.
That is, such a novelist comes to be enjoyed for his unconscious homosexual content by
men who have suppressed their feelings for men and whose insistence on their heterosexual
potency (like Bond's) is a flight from their own feminine element, from their own feelings
altogether, in phantasied 'bad' activity and hatred of woman. At large, in the *Playboy*
world, we can say that this is a flight from being human. In so far as we identify with
Bond we enter into Fleming's paranoid delusions and his anti-human solutions.

Even in his protagonist Fleming allows some disgust for violence: but this is taken to
excuse his suspension of feeling altogether, on the one hand, and provides a few references
to cruelty for the reader's relish, on the other. What both Fleming and the reader require
are continual doses of bad, cruel, thinking, to feel alive.

> There was a nauseating toughness in the blunt prose the Russians used. It had brought on another
> of the attacks of revulsion of which Bond had succumbed ten days before at Miami Airport. What was
> wrong with him? Couldn't he take it any more? Was he going soft, or was he only stale? Bond stood
> for a while watching the moon riding, careering, through the clouds. Then he shrugged his shoulders
> and went back to his desk. He decided that he was as fed up with the variations of violent physical
> behaviour as a psychoanalyst must become with the mental aberrations of his patients.
> Bond read again the passage that had revolted him: 'A drunken woman can also usually be handled
> by using the thumb and forefinger to grab the lower lip. By pinching hard and twisting, as the pull is
> made, the woman will come along.'
> Bond grunted. The obscene delicacy of that 'thumb and forefinger'!

In order to survive Bond has to toughen himself: there must be no weakness, and
weakness must not be admitted. Fleming's work is thus a contribution to the prevalent
'taboo on weakness', and seems to justify this, as the Nazis did, by paranoia. Bond can
only oppose hate to hate, danger to danger. His dilemma, of course, as with the small boy
in the Oedipus situation, is that he admires his dangerous and ruthless opponent even
when he wants to destroy him. If his enemy had not been an unpleasant man, Bond:
'would have felt admiration for this monumental trickster whose operations were so big
that they worried even the Bank of England. As it was, Bond only wanted to destroy
Goldfinger, seize his gold, get him behind bars. Goldfinger's gold-lust was too strong, too
ruthless, too dangerous to be allowed the run of the world.'

The paranoid obsession with the dangers of Goldfinger's lust justifies the suppression of
feelings and the dealings with Goldfinger in inhuman ways. The illusion that one is
being persecuted vindicates one's own hate and both belong to the cycles of hate which
can reinforce the identity in what seems an admirable way: 'Bond, dredging the piece of
expertise out of dim recollections of something he had read, was rather proud of having
been able to return Goldfinger's powerful serve.'

The Koreans, an extension of the Goldfinger power, significantly seek to toughen their
outer skins into corn by beating their arms on sacks of sand. This has its own symbolic

significance for Fleming as a way of strengthening the identity by toughening the outer casing of the body. Bond is made to admire Odd-job for the purity of his schizoid detachment and for his depersonalised nature as an instrument of hate: he is 'uniquely dreadful': 'This was a living club, perhaps the most dangerous animal on the face of the earth. Bond had to do it, had to give homage to this uniquely dreadful person. He held out his hand.'

Goldfinger is all hate and attack. Dimly Fleming makes Bond aware that there are other needs and other ways of feeling real:

> What a bloody awful deathly place to live in. How did one, could one, live in this rich heavy morgue amongst the conifers and evergreens when a hundred yards away there was light and air and wide horizons? Bond took out a cigarette and lit it. What did Goldfinger do for enjoyment, for fun, for sex? Perhaps he didn't need these things. Perhaps the pursuit of gold slaked all his thirsts.

But Bond (as does Fleming) essentially admires the purity of this total hate and its cosmic posture. For similar reasons other schizoid individuals (such as Henry Williamson) admired the pure 'animal' hate of the Nazis:

> His voice became low, almost reverential at what he saw. 'Man has climbed Everest and he has scraped the depths of the ocean. He has fired rockets into outer space and split the atom. He has invented, devised, created in every realm of human endeavour, and everywhere he has triumphed, broken records, achieved miracles. I said in every realm, but there is one that has been neglected, Mr. Bond. That one is the human activity loosely known as crime. The so-called criminal exploits committed by individual humans – I do not of course refer to their idiotic wars, their clumsy destruction of each other – are of miserable dimensions: little bank robberies, tiny swindles, picayune forgeries. And yet, ready to hand, a few hundred miles from here, opportunity for the greatest crime in history stands waiting. The stage is set, the gigantic prize is offered. Only the actors are missing. But the producer is at last here, Mr. Bond' – Goldfinger raised a finger and tapped his chest – 'and he has chosen his cast. This very afternoon the script will be read to the leading actors. Then rehearsals will begin and, in one week, the curtain will go up for the single, the unique performance. And then will come the applause, the applause for the greatest extra-legal coup of all time. And, Mr. Bond, the world will rock with that applause for centuries.'
>
> Now a dull fire burned in Goldfinger's big pale eyes and there was a touch of extra colour in his red-brown cheeks. But he was still calm, relaxed, profoundly convinced. There's no trace here, reflected Bond, of the madman, the visionary. Goldfinger had some fantastic exploit in mind, but he had gauged the odds and knew they were right.

While the ruthlessness of this is meant in a way to be 'placed', the appeal of the book also lies in its fascination and in the way it becomes (paranoically) an excuse for Bond to take the psychopath's solution himself – for us to endorse while we identify with him in this.

> 'Mr. Bond – ' Goldfinger snapped his fingers for the two servants – 'it happens that I am a rich man, a very rich man, and the richer the man the more he needs protection. The ordinary bodyguard or detective is usually a retired policeman. Such men are valueless. Their reactions are slow, their methods old-fashioned, and they are open to bribery. Moreover, they have a respect for human life. That is no good if I wish to stay alive. The Koreans have no such feelings. That is why the Japanese employed them as guards for their prison camps during the war. They are the cruellest, most ruthless people in the world. My own staff are hand picked for these qualities. They have served me well, I have no complaints. Nor have they. They are well paid and well fed and housed. When they want women, street women are brought down from London, well remunerated for their services and sent back. The women are not much to look at, but they are white and that is all the Koreans ask – to submit the white race to the grossest indignities. There are sometimes accidents but' – the pale eyes gazed blankly down the table – 'money is an effective winding-sheet.'
>
> Bond smiled.
>
> 'You like the aphorism? It is my own.'
>
> An excellent cheese soufflé came and was followed by coffee. They ate in silence, both apparently comfortable and relaxed by these confidences. Bond certainly was.

The 'relaxation' here is the kind of relaxation which the concentration camp guards managed to achieve – possibly also over an 'excellent cheese soufflé' after working on extermination. Fleming vindicates such dissociation. Through Bond, who admires Goldfinger even as he hates him, we are involved in enjoying by proxy the humiliation of woman because she is feared, which Fleming unconsciously needs to phantasy. Bond feels merely 'uncomfortable' – but also *relaxed*: he has no human feelings.*

The type of 'man without feelings' which Fleming makes his alter-ego is worth discussing. In phantasy we often assume such a type is super-tough and independent, self-reliant. This is not so in reality. In discussing the war neuroses, Fairbairn suggests that to 'like war' is the reaction of those who have not been 'successful in outgrowing the stage of infantile dependence': *it is a mark of extreme over-dependence.*

This kind of individual is unreliable, and the 'utterly callous' person easily breaks down under stress. To identify with Bond is possibly to be diverted from one's normal engagements with experience, as a way of resolving one's identity, in the direction of false solutions and attitudes which may seem strong but which in fact may be more than usually likely to prove worse than inadequate.

Judging from the 007 carstickers and shaving lotions, 'Bond-type' cars, TLC cosmetics, and such badges of identification, James Bond is (or was) a widespread focus for identifying. The effect must surely have been to promote 'False Male Doing' – towards modes of dealing with life that are doomed to inevitable failure because of their essential falsity.

For while James Bond functions under a heavy disguise of respectability, integrity, and goodness, his solutions are essentially those of a psychopath. What is made to seem 'strong' is, in fact, the mode of behaviour of one who is so dissociated as not to be human at all. As Melanie Klein says: 'In the early sadistic phase, which every individual normally passes through, the child protects himself against his fear of violent objects, both introjected and external, by redoubling his attacks upon them in his imagination: his aim in thus getting rid of his objects is in part to silence the intolerable threats of his super-ego' (Klein [34], p. 279).

The kind of 'super-ego' to which Melanie Klein refers here is the sum of the anti-libidinal rejection by the individual of his own needs. What Fleming's phantasies represent are the 'redoubled attacks in imagination' which a child makes in order to deal with his internalised bad objects. These attacks can be so powerful that they threaten to destroy all objects and thus the self and the whole world. In this vicious circle 'Bond' is both destroyer and preserver, but his contribution, in so far as we identify with him, is to contribute to further cycles of hate with social consequences: 'A vicious circle is set up, the child's anxiety impels it to destroy its objects, this leads to an increase of its own anxiety, and this once again urges it on against its objects: this vicious circle constitutes the psychological mechanism which seems to be at the bottom of asocial and criminal tendencies in the individual' (Klein [34], p. 279).

The hate-attack 'solution' can solve nothing: yet it is this kind of solution which, unconsciously, Fleming's phantasy endorses, and it is of the same kind as that which impels criminal and anti-social acts. The ad-copy elegance and knowingness with which Fleming equips Bond is, as I have suggested, a mask hiding the fact that Fleming

---

* Note the excuse for the indulgence – that they are 'street women'. Cf. Erikson on the Nazi code: 'The Aryan would not knowingly touch a Jewish girl – except in a brothel.' The same fear of women prompts Fleming's phantasy indulgence of hate here in an equally cold-blooded way.

can give us nothing of the truth of life's experience at all. But it serves another purpose. It disguises, and even covers with elegance, a kind of criminal thinking, full of cruelty, contempt, and destructive rage.

Such phantasies also inhibit the discovery of the reality of being human. In the 'normal course of development', Melanie Klein goes on, 'both sadism and anxiety diminish, the child finds better and more social means and ways of mastering its anxiety'. That is, by creative reparation and by developing inner resources and a sense of wholeness, a normal person becomes social and peace-loving, and the reality-sense grows.

But the intention of Fleming's phantasies is devoted to *keeping the sadism and anxiety open* for purposes of exploitation (by Gildrose Productions, etc.) – and in effect to undermine creative reparation.* In general, in commercial culture, more money is made by sustaining an emotional hunger by keeping primitive feelings open. Obviously, if genuinely creative fare was offered there might be no compulsive urge to return to further anxiety, and this explains the hostility of commercial culture to true culture. It might not be that people would switch off: they might never switch on. So that expensive machines can be kept running to a mass audience, culture of the mass media is thus inherently inimical to true creativity and its satisfactions, and needs to maintain a tension of anxiety about identity abroad to maintain its audience. Primitive phantasy makes the appropriate substitute culture for a dehumanized machine environment.

True creativity demands contact with reality: 'The better adaptation to reality enables the child to get more support against the phantastic imagos through its relation to the real parents' (Klein [34], p. 275).

As Winnicott says, 'relief' is found in the discovery of reality because in reality the brakes are on whereas as the child knows there are no brakes on phantasy, which is terrifying.

In the world of the false-solution symbolism of commercial culture and journalism, there must inevitably be an antipathy to 'better adaptation to reality' since this threatens the exploitation of the appeal of 'phantastic imagos' (Goldfinger is eminently a 'phantastic imago' of a 'bad' object). In such manifestations as the work of Fleming there is always detectable an absence of concern with real relationship, an ignorance of the reality of feeling, and a denial of genuine needs. Such phantasies are thus on the side of the asocial and criminal trends in our society, which reflect the failure in a minority to achieve 'better adaptation'. They dehumanise because they thrust upon us again the terrifying imagos which we may have supplanted by our discovery of real persons by our long creative efforts in seeking maturity. Of its very nature, then, such journalistic-commercial culture is inimical to confirmation in relationship, and the successful modification of inward hate and destructiveness. It is an enemy of the integrative ego on which an adequate sense of identity depends, and it promotes hate cycles at large. In the light of this analysis there should be no surprise that violence is on the increase in our society.†

The choice before each individual, at extremes, is to either solve his primitive problems and achieve the 'tendency and capacity to restitute' or to remain in a state of need to

* How such phantasies undermine true creative reparation is eminently visible in school, where children asked to invent free drama will forfeit their own imaginations for *The Man From UNCLE*, or *The Avengers*, etc. This raises the whole question of what kind of expectations are aroused by such media as television. A schizoid culture breeds schizoid expectations and these may cut audiences off from genuine creative symbolism.

† What effect, for instance, does the Saturday afternoon experience of all-in wrestling on television have on national sensibility?

express aggressive and destructive impulses which manifest severe anxiety about his relationship with his introjected objects. If the problem is not adequately solved:

> ... the individual remains under the stress of the early anxiety situations and retains the defensive mechanisms belonging to that early state. If then fear of the super-ego, either for external or intra-psychic reasons, oversteps certain bounds, the individual may be compelled to destroy people and this compulsion may form the basis for the development either of a criminal type of behaviour or of a psychosis ... thus we see that the same psychological roots may develop into paranoia, or into criminal-ity. ... (Klein [34], p. 280.)

It is at this level that Fleming's work has 'contributed to that indifference to life and brutalisation of man which have been increasing year by year since the First World War. . .' of which Erich Fromm speaks. Fromm saw this as the chief danger of our age: 'If indifference to life and destructiveness wins the upper hand, then indeed, there is no freedom to be gained, because there remains nothing but the utmost degradation of which man is capable of, to be a beast of prey. ... There is only one hope to stop the wave of violence, and that is to become sensitive once more to all that is alive' (from the text of an address at a SANE Human Rights Day Rally, 8 December 1966).

'Becoming sensitive to all that is alive', means becoming more aware of our humanness. As Melanie Klein says of criminals:

> One of the great problems about criminals, which has always made them incomprehensible to the rest of the world, is their lack of natural human good feelings; but this lack is only apparent. When in analysis one reaches the deepest conflicts from which hate and anxiety spring, one also finds there the love as well. Love is not absent in the criminal, but it is hidden and buried in such a way that nothing but analysis can bring it to light; since the hated persecuting object was originally to the tiny baby the object of all its love and libido, the criminal is now in the position of hating and persecuting his own loved object; as this is an intolerable position all memory and consciousness of any love for any object must be suppressed. If there is nothing in the world but enemies, and that is how the criminal feels, his hate and destructiveness are, in his view, to a great extent justified – an attitude which relieves some of his unconscious feelings of guilt. Hate is often used as the most effective cover for love; but one must not forget that to the person who is under the continuous stress of persecution, *the safety of his own ego is the first and only consideration.* (Klein [34], p. 280; my italics.)

In the James Bond phantasy, to the protagonist (as to the author) 'the safety of his own ego is the first and only consideration': meanwhile his deepest falsity is the denial of his own need to love. In the 'Bond' myth hate and destructiveness are 'justified' because the protagonist exists 'under the continuous stress of persecution'. It is these phantasies of infantile paranoia, in all their dehumanizing primitive effect, which we are lured into sharing by Fleming's phantasies.

In this, such a cultural artefact offends the basic ethical consideration, arising from what Money-Kyrle calls ' ... the ethical problem in its most basic form: *whether to prey on others that we may thrive* . . .'.

Fleming's phantasy is essentially an attempt to vindicate an attitude of mind and modes of behaviour by which the identity can be preserved at the expense of others. We survive, he implies, by denying our feelings for others and our dependence on them; by maintaining a continual defensiveness against a dreaded attack which will affect our 'inner contents'; by regarding others as objects for our consumption; and by refusing to admit our hate and our responsibility for our hate.

Through Fleming's paranoia we are encouraged to feel that any relinquishing of assertiveness and hate behaviour may bring about annihilation, and yet our anxiety is focused on our fear that hate will lay the world waste. Here we have the clue to the wide-spread appeal of Fleming's books to those living in a world deficient in opportunities for true solutions, and one which is full of the fear prompted by false solutions – including the confrontations of the Great Fear, and violence itself. Their symbolism of a hate that threatens to reduce the world to ashes reflects our fear that this will actually happen in human affairs. But Fleming's contribution is to make matters worse by recommending implicitly that we take to the ways of hate and contribute to those cycles of aggression, egocentricity, and destructiveness which threaten survival.

The danger of such influences revealed by close attention to the subjective elements involved explains the lengthy and detailed attention to his work which the author has felt it necessary to give here. Of course, as with any manifestation of commercial culture, by the time any serious work of this kind has been done the vogue has faded. This is of its very nature: such culture can provide no lasting satisfactions but only a temporary sense of being alive by 'bad thinking' or some other manic ploy. But a thorough analysis of one such artefact can stand for a great deal else, as will be obvious, in the false mythology of our civilisation.

CHAPTER 20

Swallowing the Gilded Faeces

WHILE intellectuals deny the adverse moral influence of Fleming and acclaim his quality as a writer, the motoring correspondents will recognise that individuals identify closely with Bond – though they see no harm in this. For instance, in *The Guardian*, we read of a new car model:

IT LOOKS A GREAT DEAL more glamorous than it really is. It is *unashamedly* modelled on James Bond's Aston Martin in exterior shape though it doesn't stretch to some of the more Exotic equipment

BOND EQUIPE
GT 4S

I found the Bond Equipe GT 4S pretty nearly the ideal car for the conditions I assume will prevail in Britain from now on. It can cope with the combination of congestion and a maximum speed limit with no noticeable strain. Beneath its swinging fibreglass exterior it is in reality only a souped-up version of the Triumph Herald and might be reckoned expensive at £843. On the other hand it has that extra push that makes all the difference on long journeys and in town congestion.

The Guardian, 17 October 1966

It may have been a mistake on the motoring correspondent's part, to believe that this car was 'unashamedly modelled on James Bond's Aston Martin'. But what we cannot doubt is the way in which many men obviously do identify, as drivers and car-owners, on Bond and his kind of 'masculine protest'. In Australia I saw a man driving a sports car with the registration number 007, and his clothes and equipment were borrowed from Ian Fleming's phantasies. The attention to detail in motoring journalism is like Fleming's – and the emphasis on power in car talk belongs to his modes:

With a compression ratio of 9 : 1 and twin SU carburettors it has a power output of 63 b.h.p. pushing a comparatively light body. The claimed top speed is 85 m.p.h. though there was no occasion when I had it up to that.

The motoring correspondent's review hints that the extra speed will be useful when flaunting the law: ' . . . Given that the 70 m.p.h. speed limit is here to stay this is just what one needs. It makes brisk and safer overtaking easier and cuts down much of the strain of waiting for a long clear stretch before lumbering out from behind the man doing 50 m.p.h. in front of you.'

There are, of course, in Fleming's books many vindications for this kind of egocentric behaviour at the wheel. The myths of such motor-car lore tend to persuade the individual in a mass society that he, too, can really have a strong identity even in a depersonalised environment – though society will give him little or no help with true resources he can at least take to false ones as a 'get-away' person: 'In all it seems to me a car that combines a basic mass-production start with an *individual finish* and gives its owner that slightly better go at both worlds than he might normally expect at the price.'

138

But while we are pursuing glamour, we seem prepared to sacrifice safety. 'There are a lot of blind spots in the Equipe'.

Even children are trained in Bond type car aggressiveness:

P O W . . . !!

A new model will be added to the most buoyant branch of the British vehicle industry today. Mettoy, whose Corgi die-cast toy cars are exported by the hundreds of thousands a month, will launch a successor to its James Bond car at the British Toy Makers Association trade fair in London. The gimmick-laden Bond Aston Martin won international awards, Mettoy sold several million, and it is still being produced in vast quantities, but the new model is expected to do even better. It is a Bat-mobile. . . . To complicate matters another 'character model', a *Man from UNCLE* car, is having a similar success. . . . (*The Guardian*).

Such eager endorsement by journalism at all levels contributes to such a commercial success as that of Fleming. Without huge investment on the part of the entertainment industry, Fleming's books might well have remained in oblivion. The press thrives on pseudo-events because it depends for them to provide that manic larger-than-life feeling for which we hunger every morning. When an artificial mountain is being built in Hollywood for a Bond film, no newspaper can fail to mention it. So, by degrees, the symbolism of hate can be made acceptable to the intellectual by the 'quality' press so long as it seems to promise manic success. In *The Guardian* of 4 May 1966, for instance, a film critic wrote up Charles Feldman and his work on the film 'of *Casino Royale* in terms characteristic of the journalistic creation of the pseudo-event – characteristically un-critical both of the work and the phenomenon. ' "Charlie Feldman", someone explained the other morning at Pinewood, "is producing 'Casino Royale' like General Groves made the first atom bomb. . . ."

The manic enterprise was under way and a great deal of money was involved: what matters in such areas is that things shall be 'successful', whatever their quality. 'Feldman knows his public: he produced "What's New Pussycat?" It received mixed notices but is now making more money than any comedy in years. When he bought up "The Group" (shortly to be released here) no distributor would touch it. Feldman poured thousands of dollars into promoting the book and suddenly everyone had heard of Mary McCarthy.'

What impresses the writer in *The Guardian* most is the money involved – 'Feldman expects to spend almost £3,000,000 but he was once a Hollywood agent and knows all about getting value for money' – and the 'names':

There has been no stinting on the personnel. Beside Ian Fleming, posthumously, there have been at least seven scriptwriters to date: they include Wolf Mankowitz, Michael Sayers, Ben Hecht, Terry Southern, and Billy Wilder. Feldman at one point promised 20 stars but the number keeps changing. Peter Sellers, Ursula Andrews, David Niven, Deborah Kerr, Orson Welles, Peter O'Toole, and Stirling Moss have been before the cameras already. . . .

The respect conveyed for this manic world of film goes with the need to convey to the reader the sense that he, too, is alive and in touch with something larger than life. This ploy is the essence of 'pop'. (It is only fair to add that when the film appeared the same newspaper pronounced it a 'mess'.)

In such a situation one expects the educated critic to be concerned with human values. However, critical attitudes in this sphere have been undermined by many influences – pseudo-scientific 'realism', demoralisation, and the manic appeal of mass culture itself. So while hard-headed observers from the world of commerce see Bond as a mere product by which the public is exploited, the fashionable critic, by treating Fleming's books with a respect they do not deserve, endorses hate and helps make it socially respectable. Here, for instance, is Malcolm Bradbury reviewing John Pearson's *Life of Ian Fleming* also in *The Guardian*:

> Like the trousersuit and Yugoslav enamelware, the James Bond novels are an international fashion and hold a striking place in the complex underdocumented history of modern taste and the way it works. Questions of directly literary merit aside (they aren't, in terms of prevailing literary-critical standards, of much merit, but prevailing standards are showing real uneasiness with such phenomena) their success in tapping a variety of *levels* of taste has been remarkable.
>
> *The Guardian*

The confusion of taste has happened. The question of 'merit' is dodgingly left aside, for there is now 'real uneasiness' about rejecting such anti-human work. In consequence the reviewer can only manifest unwilling admiration for the 'success':

> How was it done? Fleming was a materialist and moved in taste-making quarters; he was a strategist and plotted success carefully, while protecting himself against the loss of personal prestige involved in failure; he was also a fantast about adventure who had something to offer a society of confantasts. He came of wealthy background and was well-connected (his grandfather was a banking millionaire, his father a Conservative MP killed in the First World War): he had intellectual pretensions and read widely, but dreamed of a life of action. After the abortion of various hopes, he settled down in the 1930s to a stockbroking man-about-town life, as a bachelor and an amorist with a handsome profile and an engaging melancholia. . . .
>
> *ibid.*

If taste has become so uncertain, a good deal of this can be attributed to the Malcolm Bradburys who, in the face of such a cultural manifestation, can carefully adopt re-assuring tone of detached and uncritical deference. (Cf. the carefully neutral 'amorist', the sympathetic 'engaging'.) At first the books failed to go: 'Fleming's own fantasies, values and attitudes . . . seemed at first not very saleable; by mid-1954, with two Bond books out, he had made no more than £2,000, in spite of his careful exploitation of his intellectual journalist and taste-making friends.'

However, developments in the post-war world changed matters for the better:

> Sir Anthony Eden went to Goldeneye to recuperate from illness after the Suez crisis; later Fleming met Kennedy and 'From Russia, With Love' subsequently appeared in a list of Kennedy's ten favourite books. By 1960 the Bond boom was on, supported as much by chance and changes in taste as by Fleming's own deliberation. Bond's mastery of technology and the operative status symbols, his simple patriotism and his sadism, his capacity to find the up-to-date exotic, his exploitative style in sexual relationships – in all showed that the world of post-war disenchantment could be made just sufficiently palatable for the Basil Seals, the upper-middle-class romantics whose last fling had seemed to be the war and for whom there had appeared nothing but unconditional surrender. . . .
>
> *ibid.*

The most astonishing feature here is the complete lack of human concern as to the directions taste is said to have taken, and the uncritical assumptions about such infantile phantasy (how can a university lecturer believe that Bond manifests a 'mastery of technology'?)

As we have seen, Fleming's technical 'knowledge' is mere varnish, and his use of machines belongs to primitive symbolism. Bradbury's carefully non-committal (and yet respectful) review allows the false solutions which purvey such a vicious anti-human spirit abroad to be embraced by the 'lively mind' as an acceptable manifestation of the schizoid culture of the decade:

Bond's world has a certain consonance with that invented by writers like William Burroughs and Terry Southern, sadistic and technological for other reasons;* and when the Bond films injected some mild irony into the romantic dream Bond could become profitably 'camp'.

Pearson's book, though sometimes clumsily handled, is managed with enough solidity to give us the lines of a social and psychological portrait of Fleming, and thus to show in his life the roots of this profitable syndrome. In addition it succeeds in making Fleming, a man in many ways morally unattractive, into a complex, even mildly tragic figure.

The essence of current demoralisation is that such 'profitable syndromes', though they may be found 'morally unattractive', are essentially endorsed as possible personal solutions, which we must accept as socially tolerable. Increasingly today newspaper critics will pronounce that 'art has nothing to do with morality' or 'although the film is immoral, one may still enjoy looking at the pretty girls in it' – so that, today (1972) we have at last reached a situation in which sadism and perversion can be called 'brave'. The implications are that such hostile 'solutions' are socially acceptable, not only for such 'mildly tragic' figures – but for us all. But are they? And should such attitudes to life be allowed to be spread, as they are, for primarily economic reasons?

Of course, sometimes the journalist reviewer is capable of insight into the crudity of the manufactures of commercial phantasy. Richard Roud, reviewing *Thunderball* at the London Pavilion, wrote:

> It is difficult to say for sure who killed James Bond: but one thing does seem clear – he is certainly dead. . . .
>
> 'Thunderball', which opens today at the London Pavilion and Rialto, Coventry Street is gadgetry run wild. Unfortunately it isn't much of a story. Now I don't say that the plots of the first three pictures were of transcendental interest, but they were gripping enough to hold the films together.
>
> The basic error of the plot of 'Thunderball' is quite simple: James Bond has only a few days to find the two atom bombs stolen by SPECTRE, or else. Or else what? A city will be blown up – unless the Government pays out £100,000,000 to SPECTRE. Now although this might well be a serious blow to the nation's economy, it is not enough to keep one biting one's nails. I think most of us obscurely feel that the Government can always find the money somewhere.
>
> Furthermore, the scenario writers seem to have sat down, thought up a bundle of gimmicks – shark-filled swimming pools, electrified chairs, etc., and then built the script around them. This may not be literally true, but I cannot think of any other explanation for the totally indigent screenplay. One thing happens after another, seemingly without rhyme or reason, and certainly without excitement or interest, Perfunctory, listless, and tired are the three best adjectives to describe the film.

The compulsive obsessional rituals of Fleming's work, I believe, have always been boring. This is exposed here, while the *financial* impulse is allowed to be glimpsed. It is for once as if the underlying primitive symbolism was not sufficient to carry the day.

> One should not, I suppose, talk about films as if they were problems in merchandising but the Bond pictures have always been what the trade jargon so aptly calls 'products'. They have an astute collection of everything the public is esteemed to want – luxurious living, glamorous, far-off places, a bit of sex, a lot of thrills, and an invincible hero it is a pleasure to identify with, if only for the duration of the film. This time the formula has gone wrong, but there is no reason why Bond could not be properly resuscitated in the next film. At least the main pre-condition for any kind of renaissance has already been fulfilled: the subject is dead.

Roud's criticism here does not extend to any discrimination against such exploitation of sensibility. Indeed, he feels it necessary to apologise for describing any film as 'merchandising'. He seems to accept the exploitation of sensibility by such a 'formula' as normal and socially acceptable in the world of entertainment. Such acceptance paves

---

* The consonance is certainly there, only such writers are surely united by the fact that they adopt schizoid modes of culture, rather than that they are 'technological' or even sadistic. Of course, such modes tend to make people into things, by a kind of hostile technicism.

the way for a cynical violation of cultural trust at large by commerce, even if this 'depletes individual creativity', despite the critic's evident integrity.

A debate in the House of Lords on 2 February 1966 showed that the English mind now accepts the exploitation of taste as an inevitable feature of the economy. Moreover, in order to keep the film industry going, money is invested which enables American commerce to make fortunes out of exploiting the English sensibility, using English hate to do so, in an inevitable cataclysm of decadence:

> LORD WILLIS (Lab.), calling attention to the problems of the British film industry, said that the industry occupied a dominating position until about 15 years ago but since then it had been in danger of extinction.
>
> It was paradoxical that most of the film legislation had had an effect precisely opposite to its intention. Far from giving British producers greater independence and finance, it had weakened them. Far from preventing American domination, that domination had never been so overwhelming as it was today.
>
> The Americans were hard-headed businessmen. They made films in Britain because it paid them to do so. Such films qualified for the British quota and such producers could qualify for large sums from the British fund. It was an extraordinary situation that four-fifths of a fund created to help British producers should find its way across the Atlantic.
>
> Sums paid to some of the stars had reached the point of sheer insanity. Just now the Americans were providing work to British technicians and others but there was no guarantee that they would stay. For economic or political reasons they might pull out and if they did the British film industry would collapse in a month.
>
> LORD MOYNIHAN, in a maiden speech, said that the subsidy for the British film industry should be examined and, if necessary, be supplemented or reallocated to give greater support to the industry as a whole. Money was not going to British independent producers, but to the Americans.
>
> You may feel a little proud (he said) of the new craze which is sweeping the world – James Bond. One may feel that James Bond is an Englishman, that these films are English films. On the face of it one would be right in this assumption. Unfortunately James Bond is an American financially.
>
> Last year $1,500,000 was paid in Eady money to the producers of *Goldfinger* – Americans. Last year $1m. of Eady money was paid to the producers of *Tom Jones*, a typically English production. The producers were Americans. This year a predicted record of $2,100,000 of British Eady money was to be paid on *Thunderball*. This was also going to the Americans.
>
> *The Guardian*

In Parliament the only objection to Bond films seems to be that England was not profiting from them.

One of the most influential figures in support of the intellectual acceptance of Fleming as a successful writer worthy of intelligent attention is Amis. It is no doubt partly because Amis, who is taken seriously in university English departments and was a director of English studies for a time at Cambridge, wrote a book on Fleming that such a critic as Bradbury above can speak of the 'real uneasiness' of critical standards, and has to conclude that Fleming was a 'mildly tragic' figure – which virtually elevates him to the role of creative genius. (Bradbury pronounced Amis the Jane Austen of our time, reviewing *I Want it Now*.)

It may be interesting here to glance briefly at Amis's support of Fleming. As will have been seen, I do not base my objections to Fleming on the possibility that his books may have a harmful direct influence on the morals of the reader. The effect is a more subtle one of devaluing human nature and fostering false solutions to the problem of identity.

Interestingly enough, Amis takes seriously the criticism that to identify with Bond might encourage individuals to behave as Bond does with women. However, he does not answer this criticism by saying that this is unlikely but by implying that if individuals do behave in such ways, why worry – since such behaviour is perfectly normal.

It is especially worth examining the insinuating tone in which this reply to such objections is couched: 'Bond collects almost exactly one girl per excursion abroad. . . . This is surely not in advance of what any reasonable personable, reasonable well off bachelor would reckon to acquire on a foreign holiday or a trip for his firm.'

Here we need to analyse the implications of Mr. Amis's suavity of tone. For, although his manner is bland, the writing is carefully angled to persuade us by its tone that it is perfectly acceptable to reasonable people for individuals to have an acquisitive attitude to women. We are so convinced by the politeness of the prose that we do not stop to examine the implications of the terms 'reckon' and 'acquire'. The mood the prose induces is one in which we would be very surprised if 'ingestion' sex were to be declared in any way unusual – yet in fact the argument is based on an assumption that woman is essentially a 'partial object' for the 'taking'. (Cf. *Take a Girl Like You* . . .)

When this kind of tone has established a general attitude to sex, as its use in the pages of the *New Statesman* has done over the last two decades, it becomes increasingly impossible to try to point out what is wrong with this kind of attitude, in which woman is 'collected' to reinforce man's identity. It becomes impossible to point out that the norm here is an attitude to relationship is one in which there has been a 'regression in the quality of relationship desired', and a degree of de-emotionalisation and depersonalisation. Although Amis's tone implies that he is speaking as one who seeks sexual liberation, his way of writing makes it more difficult for us to point out that no freedom can be based on a situation in which 'only one partner is entitled to make demands'. It also becomes increasingly difficult to point out the gulf between this novelist's view of life in his work and arguments, and that of the world of E. M. Forster, to whom 'personal relationships' are 'everything'.

The human bachelor does not, despite the implications of Mr. Amis's way of writing, behave like James Bond, except for some bachelors who are unusually disturbed individuals. The objection to James Bond is not that he is a misrepresentation of the sexual adventurousness of bachelors, however – as Mr. Amis seems to think. The objection may be that Fleming's way of writing, and Mr. Amis's way of writing, has the effect of persuading individuals to pursue false solutions to their own problems of relationship. They may come to feel they are not 'personable' unless they 'collect'.

Sexual relationships may be taken as an index of the degree to which individuals are integrated enough to realise their libidinal goal in object-constancy. A man who 'collects' women on 'trips abroad' is manifesting relational inadequacy. Possibly he is driven to this to compensate for his essential 'psychic impotence' – and his need to continually 'find a fresh object' because he cannot find an adequate sense of goodness with any one person – because she eventually, as she becomes real, becomes the 'unsatisfactory object'. The inability to develop anything richer than the 'pick-up' relationship is a mark of being limited to 'partial object', 'taking' sex because one cannot tolerate emotional surrender. Only a minority of people, bachelors or not, are in this predicament, and it is by no means one we will benefit by emulating or supposing it to be superior to object-constancy. Indeed, from my analysis of Fleming it would seem that the kind of promiscuity Fleming endorses may be a manifestation of unconscious homosexuality and of what Rollo May calls 'psychic impotence'.

Ferenczi says of men who are afraid of homo-eroticism, because they fear their own unconscious homosexuality, in Western life

> . . . in order to free themselves from men, they become slaves to women. This may be the explanation of the 'chivalry' and the exaggerated, often visibly affected, adoration of woman that has dominated

the male world since the middle ages: it may also possibly be the explanation of Don-Juanism, the obsessive and yet never fully satisfied pursuit of continually new heterosexual adventures. Even if Don Juan himself would find this theory ridiculous, I should have to declare him to be an obsessional invalid, who could never find satisfaction in the endless series of women (so faithfully drawn by Leporello in his book) because these women are really only substitutes for repressed love-objects. (Ferenczi [20]).

Mr. Amis implies that if you are not a 'collector' like James Bond, your identity may be weak: as with Fleming, he seems to believe that lust is strong, while love is weak. Yet from the point of view of psychoanalytical studies, if we find ourselves believing such things, it may be because we are afraid of woman – and this may express our fear of our own femininity, and our more sensitive humanness.

If, in discussing Ian Fleming's works, critics encourage us to believe that it is acceptable to take up a 'James Bond' kind of strength in our approach to life, they may be persuading us to reject the promptings of our own inward needs, to behave as if we did not have a conscience – and so drive us further away from the problems of meaning in life which are bound up with sex and relationship. This I believe has been the effect of the acclaim such work as that of Ian Fleming has received in our intellectual milieux, during the last two decades.

B. Hate in High Places

CHAPTER 21

The Charming Hate of Iris Murdoch

THE problem of exploring the schizoid elements in our culture is perhaps comparatively easy when one is dealing with a writer like Ian Fleming, who lent himself so happily to commercial exploitation. The problem becomes much more difficult when one turns to individuals whose integrity is beyond suspicion, whose intellectual power is considerable, and whose character cannot really be diagnosed as 'schizoid'.

As we have seen, the schizoid impulse to invert values and to substitute hate for love has its origins in the desire to hide deep inner weaknesses, and existential insecurity. For this reason, schizoid inversion is very seductive, and beckons to us with all the allure of a 'pure' solution to all human ills. Moreover, so pure, morally, can the schizoid impulse seem that it seems impossible to bring up traditional canons to evaluate works of culture which take a schizoid path. Works created in a schizoid ethos can seem to demand completely new critical and ethical criteria.

Once this situation has been brought about, it can thus seem an act of great moral value to 'give oneself up to the joys of hating'. Such a situation has been brought about by such pieces of distinguished literary criticism as Sartre's work on Genet, by which the efforts of such an individual to establish a sense of identity on the basis of hate can seem to be the work of a saint.

We all live in a 'life-world', and dwell in an intellectual structure, by which we perceive the world, and express our view of it. When an individual is persuaded to adopt the 'schizoid' life-world, and the intellectual structure of moral inversion which belongs to it, they may well come to 'give themselves up to the joys of hating' without realising what effects their work is likely to have. They may not themselves be open to being called 'schizoid individuals', and their intentions are completely honourable. Yet, since they have adopted the schizoid pattern of thought and feeling, they have lent themselves to modes which are, by their very nature, likely to breed yet further hate.

The schizoid diagnosis, however, enables us to examine such cultural problems in a new light – which is that of the degree to which works of symbolism are an attempt to overcome problems of identity. The question then becomes – Does this work help us to feel more deeply what it is to be human? Or, Does it confuse this issue, or persuade us that we need not be human? Obviously, from this, ethical considerations follow. Moreover, we can also note that, since it offers itself as *a work of art*, a work offers to tell us something about human experience. Does what it tells us help us to be more human – or encourage us to be less human? Does it not perhaps simply exploit the area of cultural trust – and leave us even hungrier than before for sources of a sense of being human? Does it, perhaps, make our quest for humanness seem itself futile? Does it make us feel

147

that ethical considerations are irrelevant – with consequent effects on our behaviour and our feelings about life?

Here one significant figure is Iris Murdoch, Oxford don and figure of eminence. Her work has been compared (by P. J. Kavanagh in *The Guardian*) to that of the George Eliot of *Daniel Deronda*. This may not mean much in a milieu in which Malcolm Bradbury acclaims Kingsley Amis as the Jane Austen of our time: as George Eliot herself said: 'It would be better to abstain from "opinions of the press" '. But I believe that Iris Murdoch's novels are commonplace. Their appeal I believe to be due to the fact that she has in them, misguidedly, taken over certain nihilistic (or schizoid) modes from European culture – disastrously. They are thus, judged from the point of view of a concern for creativity as a means to discover our humanness, destructive. The book I shall take as illustration is *The Flight from the Enchanter*, described by V. S. Pritchett as 'easily the most brilliant and original novel that has appeared for a long time'.

As with Fleming, the first impression of a reader who turns to Iris Murdoch, perhaps impelled by widespread praise, is the dull flatness of a style. At times this flatness is so dead that her prose has none of those qualities which belong to emotional involvement. Essentially, she does not seem to care about her characters, and she does not give us anything of their inward life: there are no 'life rhythms'. She tells us 'about' her characters, but we are not taken into their beings. There is a sophisticated detachment in the account: but the author seems to have no fundamental *care* about the human life she offers to be dealing with.

> 'Rosa! Oh, good!' said Rainborough. A light gleamed in his eyes which was almost, but not quite, pleasure. Rainborough had known Rosa for more years than Saward had; and in the matter of Rosa he felt a certain resentment. Rainborough would have liked to play the role of being unhappily in love with Rosa, but it had been Saward who had set his heart upon meeting her after Rainborough had already known her some time. Indeed, it was probably Saward's passion which had first revealed Rosa's charms to Rainborough. But it would have seemed to him absurd to love Rosa vainly, since his friend already did so.

It is difficult, reading such drab writing, so rhythmless, so bloodless, to keep one's eyes open: the conscious reaction can be no more than, 'So what?' If one came upon such a passage in a personal letter, a friend writing about friends, one would find it difficult enough to sustain interest even if the subjects were known to one. It reads like rather inadequate notes for an uninteresting projected novel: and, of course, this is what it is – for the novel never comes off, never comes to be more than this schematic interplay of characters, intellectually conceived from the outside. Interest in them is driven by no felt knowledge of the human heart, no feeling for human inner realities despite the reference to 'passion'. There is no symbolic depth revealing the pressure of 'inner necessity', in the bodily life of a person and its symbolism arising from the 'psychic tissue'. Having noted this poverty of style, as with Fleming, the critic needs to look round for some other underlying reason for such a writer's notoriety.

Iris Murdoch's apparent knowingness about people is no more than the same kind of sophisticated air of being a man of the world such as we find in Amis or Fleming: 'A light gleamed in his eyes which was almost, but not quite, pleasure.' But, as with Fleming, her language never rises above cliché because there is no essential creative impulse to drive it beyond cliché towards insight. The concept of relationship between persons, and of their inward impulses, never develops into a mature interest (such as our interest in Gwendolen Harleth must be, with that of the authoress).

Strangely enough, since the author is a don, the concepts here even of the intellectual life are no more than cliché: 'Rainborough respected and envied Saward's learning, which extended far beyond the bounds of the ancient world, and he disliked and was impressed by the simplicity of his life. He also had especially admired the way in which Saward was able to harness all the resources of his intellect to a single task.'

But what is described is never 'given' us: we never feel at the level of being what 'the simplicity of his life' feels like, or how it manifests itself. The depiction of an 'intellect', 'harnessed to a single task' is conveyed in superficial terms, without a shadow of irony, nor with understanding of what intellectual passion might feel like, in terms of the whole personality. Compared with George Eliot's picture of intellectual narrowness and futility in Casaubon, or Thomas Mann's depiction of consuming intellectual energy in *Dr. Faustus*, Saward's 'learning' has no more substance, felt by the reader, than that of the commonplace 'intellectual' of a woman's magazine story. By contrast, in her book on *Sartre*, Iris Murdoch shows that she does know the intellectual life. But she seems not to be able to give it to us in a novel.

The essential superficiality and thinness of Iris Murdoch's concepts of personality, or make-up, is not disguised by an over-written portentousness of style, nor by her gestures at the *droumenon*, the thing 'done', the 'felt life' of the novelist. Under the surface there is nothing alive and nothing comes to life despite an occasional forced extravagance of words and a gesture at 'significant symbolism' of imagery with no basis in reparative engagement with the inner world:

> After the door closed, Rosa sat for some time still rubbing her eyes and rubbing her hand over her face. Peter Saward sat looking at the paper-knife. He heard her get up. Then she began to wander about the room. She always did this. It was a kind of dance. Peter Saward felt the whole room suddenly stiffen. The walls were full of consciousness and jerked themselves upright. The ceiling trembled. The space flung itself out like a fisherman's net and hung poised in an expanse of significant points. . . .

'Significant points' is a give-away phrase: the writer is herself straining after 'significant points': but there are none there despite all the straining. The symbolism of the elements of the scene could only have meaning if they were objective correlatives to the inward condition of one, or either, or both, of the characters. By contrast, for instance, in *Ulysses* we can link the things described on the seashore as objective correlatives, symbols of elements in Stephen Dedalus's subjective preoccupations in his thoughtful walk. The complex between perception and apperception in Joyce's novel is revealed by significant symbols: the feel of the mood is created in us at the depth of unconscious metaphor. Or we could take the description of the back-garden of the house, in D. H. Lawrence's short story *Odour of Chrysanthemums*. By a single phrase, such as 'the raspberry canes rose like whips', Lawrence can create a mood of menace and the expectation of cruelty related to the pregnancy of the woman, the tiresomeness she finds in her little boy's childish tricks, and the impending doom from the coalpit: all threats to the security of identity and, so, painful. Such symbolism springs from the deep inner dynamics with which Lawrence is engaged, from true creative reparation. Lawrence himself is seeking, as by trying to come to terms with death, to ask about humanness, about the point of life, which is what the widow asks as she looks at her husband's corpse. We are involved in the atmosphere and the anguish by the texture of his prose.

By contrast with such writing one finds in Iris Murdoch the 'significant points' of inward symbolism essentially *faked*: her fisherman's net is a stage-prop derived from the impulse to show two characters 'enmeshed'. As a metaphor it is extraneous to the moods of either, merely imposed on the mood she is seeking to evoke in the reader. When examined closely, this mood is one of spurious significance which the writer hopes to establish by a portentous movement: 'She always did this. It was a kind of dance.' It is the self-explanatory phrase of the affected intellectually self-conscious girl: 'Oh, I always do this, I don't know why.' And then, 'It was a *kind of* dance'. Anna's dance in her pregnancy in *The Rainbow* is also a 'kind of' dance: but to compare the two is to reveal the thinness of the gesture at passion here. Iris Murdoch makes it a 'kind of' dance because her style cannot realise exactly the bodily rhythmical movement passion could generate, as Lawrence can. She can only 'do': her writing cannot 'be'. Like a schoolgirl she has to say 'kind of' because her prose is not 'felt' enough to define the experience. So the actual portrayal of the passion, examined closely, is ridiculous. It has the air of the antics of amateur stage lovers, prosy and grotesquely 'ham':

> At last he felt Rosa's fingers touch his hair. They touched it lightly at first, like birds daring not to land. Then they came back and plunged deeply in. Rosa drew her hands down the two sides of his face and lifted his head. She was standing above him. For the first time since her arrival they looked into each other's eyes. They looked gravely for several minutes, each scrutinizing the other, not with tenderness, but with a puzzled curious intentness. . . .

Some debt to Lawrence is obvious: but her writing cannot do what Lawrence does because her writing does not have the 'felt life' of engaging with the 'rhythms of the body', as his has. So, the 'dance' is stiff and dead. Her characters are never unsure of themselves, never aware of a central weakness of being, never aware of being impelled by a range of feelings beneath the superficial mental ones. They are always 'in control' – in command by their own intellectual will: 'She always did this.' Even the trembling ceiling conveys nothing ominous, while the fisherman's net of space, however much a gesture of portentousness, is no realised impulse from the intractable areas of being, of passion. Nothing is allowed to live, to *be*, beyond control. The creatures have no inner world. They do not look at one another with tenderness – only with 'held-off curiosity.' So we either have to protest that we know nothing of what goes on inside these people in their emotional life, which the portentousness invites us to take seriously: or we have to protest that they are cardboard: perhaps clever cardboard, but cardboard all the same.

On our part, we – the readers – are told 'about' them – that they feel envy, or passion: but we are only *told*. We take in a form of thinking as 'doing' about them: nothing affects us in the realm of being, by creativity. Nothing is recreated in us of the inward contest which goes on in every human being and in every truly creative work of symbolism. So, when they go beyond the little dance in which the writer manipulates them, their antics are grotesquely ridiculous (not that the writer means them to be). ' "Hmmm!" said Rosa, and she threw away his head as if it had been a ball. Peter Saward caught her by the wrist as she was moving off . . .'.

Reading carelessly, I thought at first she said that he caught his head as she threw it away. One can, in fact, only read such writing by dulling one's response to the language. 'She threw away his head' – this is a gesture at saying more than the commonplace 'she thrust away his head': but if one allows the 'striking' image to form, it is only possible to form one that is ludicrous. No sensitive writer should allow such unhinged violence to seem to stand for 'significance': the style itself is all 'false doing'.

Iris Murdoch's writing invites no more, and gets no more, than a skippingly superficial mental engagement. One may read in her work about passion, but one feels less than lukewarm interest. Nothing touches one's feelings – and thus the writer need not involve hers: all she seeks is a kind of exhibitionism, a 'showing' in which there is no giving. She is, for the adult reader, despite the 'sordid' episodes, the adult equivalent of Enid Blyton – trivial, mushy, and 'safe': the life she fears to allow out of her control can never take over her prose.

How does such 'dead' writing have such a widespread appeal? As with Fleming, I believe this is because of the unconscious hate in the 'life – world' the writer has adopted.

In reading such a book as the one under discussion it is not long before one's expectations of having one's primitive anxieties stirred are satisfied. A particular kind of gawky and ironic tone introduces us to a grotesque preoccupation with 'sexual comedy' – ridicule, rather, of human susceptibility in 'passion'. The enigmatic character Rosa is found to be in sexual relationship with two Polish characters. Again we have the 'multiple object' phantasy which recurs in clinical histories and whose roots are in fear of relationship. As in Amis so often we have the 'stern and curious look' ('that uncertain feeling') masking the preoccupation with primal scene sex as observed or imagined with dread and curiosity by the infant. And we have the presence of the imago castrating mother. Although such elements are common in present-day sex 'comedy', from the point of view of object-relations psychology they appear as appropriate to infantile phantasies at a time when intense curiosity about adult sexuality is associated with deep anxiety about sex as a threat to existence. The mode plays on the schizoid fear that sexual contact – or indeed any kind of bodily or emotional content, threatens annihilation.

It is this fear of being human to which Iris Murdoch's enthusiastic readers are responding. And it is to disguise this primitive appeal that intelligence is in abeyance in the novel: a hatred of being human necessitates a willed detachment from 'all the life-rhythms we share with all living, breathing creatures' (Langer, [41]).

First Rosa succumbs to one Pole:

> Stefan was no longer looking elated, but was studying her with a stern curious look. 'Come and sit here, Rosa,' he said.
> She moved, and fell upon one knee beside his, looking into his face. In a moment he grasped her by the shoulder and pulled her down towards him. Rosa lay stiffly in his arms. As she lay she was looking straight into the eyes of the old woman, who watched them without any change of expression.
> 'We make love now, Rosa. It is time,' said Stefan, in a matter-of-fact tone.
> 'It's impossible,' said Rosa, in an equally matter-of-fact tone, 'because of Jan – ' She was not able to think, and she could not say anything more explicit than that.
> 'Jan is nothing here,' said Stefan. 'Now is me, not Jan. Come.' He rose to his feet, pulling Rosa with him.
> 'Your mother,' said Rosa.
> 'She not see, not hear,' said Stefan.
> Involuntarily, Rosa stepped back so as to be out of sight of the old woman round the angle of the room, and as she moved Stefan caught her off her balance and threw her full length on to the mattress. He fell on top of her, and they lay there panting. After a few minutes he was making love to her savagely.
> On the following day Rosa began to wonder what on earth she was to do.

I do not, of course, deny that in real life a woman like Rosa might be seduced by a Pole such as Stefan: but what is unreal here is the cool mask of polite schizoid indifference ('What on earth . . .'). Only in severe dissociation could a woman react with such cold-blooded aloofness as Iris Murdoch's character is made to do. But the effect of the mode is to persuade us to take this as normal, polite, self-assurance, poise: its effect is to make us feel that both in the sexual life and in bad-thinking phantasies it is better not to be human.

We know from her philosophical writing that Iris Murdoch is impelled by the most moral motives. Yet, because she has adopted a prevalent 'hate' mode in her approach to human life, her appeal becomes parallel to that of Ian Fleming. Her phantasies help us to hold the identity together by 'bad thinking'. The sense of existence-security her books provide are essentially based upon violence and hatred of human nature, and, despite her intentions of discriminating between 'the nice and the good', the effect of the literary modes she adopts is to pout into the world 'little bits of shit in China'.* And incidentally the effect is to endorse our taboos on recognition of our relational needs, and problems of 'being' in those areas of life where we feel most vulnerable.

As in *Goldfinger* we had an obession with 'inner contents' of the mother; here we have the same exploitation of fear of the castrating mother who threatens talion revenge for sexual curiosity, associated with becoming involved in the parents' sexual excitement through masturbation phantasies (Iris Murdoch's books are eminently that). The protagonists have coition in the presence of the old mother, who watches their love-making. The effects here are more serious and more damaging than Fleming's, for they tend to involve us in disgust of sexual life itself – and so to attack us more deeply in the realm of being: ' "She decay inside," said Stefan. "All is decay. I cannot explain. You smell it soon." '

There is here no reparative urge to discover the reality of suffering, as there is, say, with Raskolnikov. There is no cry of 'What is it to be human?' There is only the subtle dissociated pretence that such behaviour in such a situation has *nothing abnormal* in it: this is human 'reality'.

There is no occasion to doubt Iris Murdoch's sincerity in seeking the reality of human nature. In what possible sense, however, can we take such a grotesque scene as a confrontation with the problem of existence, at the deepest ethical level, when its presentation is carried out with such strange flippancy? Surely it is rather that the writer has been persuaded to believe in her own phantasies yet and the effect is to involve us in their anti-humanity. We are drawn in to share a schizoid detachment from all feelings by which a normal human being would react to such experiences. This means we are invited to enter into a flight from life, an anti-libidinal hate, and a denial of our own humanity. It seems good and clever not to be human. Elsewhere, in *The Nice and the Good*, Iris Murdoch implies that Freud was correct to find man's animality as the most real thing about him. Undoubtedly, man strives towards something better, but can Iris Murdoch sustain any substantial belief in the reality of civilisation – or in the values of the True Self? Can she really believe we are human, with a preponderant concern with civilised meaning in life?

In *From the Enchanter Fleeing* the episode seems to be a 'comic' portrayal of a predicament that could be ours: but in so far as Rosa is only a little bewildered, her response could be ours only if we were capable of denying all our human feelings or suffering from diminution of affect. The reactions of the protagonist are politely lukewarm in what for any living human being would be a shattering experience: 'On the following day Rosa began to wonder what on earth she was to do.' In this superficiality of tone we have an implicit reassurance that we must not take all this very seriously: whatever shall the poor little thing *do*? Nobody is to fuss. Yet the effect of this cold politeness is a deterioration of the psyche of the reader. While primitive anxieties are evoked a surface pretence is encouraged that such disturbing phantasies need not trouble a sophisticated

* See below, p. 161.

intellectual person. The effect is demoralising in that whenever we find ourselves in a situation which is likely to lower our human value, such as a seduction, we shall feel it inappropriate, or not clever, or not *comme il faut*, to react from normal good sense, as we ought to respond, as if to an outrage of our True Selves. Of course, as in Fleming, neither the men nor the women nor the sex are 'real'. Not even a Pole whose sex was so depersonalised as here, not even a man as capable of dealing with partial objects only, could throw a woman down on a mattress in the presence of his 'smelly' old mother, and 'in a few minutes' be 'making love to her savagely'. He might, I suppose, if he were psychotic, as James Bond might, if he were a real psychopath in life. In reality the woman would put up some kind of struggle and might be able to put the man off, enough to escape. If she were forcibly raped this in reality could only be seen to be a horrifying violation. If she colluded unconsciously with a rapist, Rosa could be manifesting her own derangement.

But it is not that the characters collude as human beings. We are to collude with the phantasy – in being raped ourselves. In this kind of schizoid mode, Rosa must not escape: Rosa is a vehicle for a phantasy postulation that psychopathic solutions to fear of relationship and dependence may be valid and socially acceptable.

As we expect, with mechanical symmetry, Rosa is to be seduced on the next page, by Stefan's brother Jan: 'He looked back at her, not with sternness, but with a strong fierce expression. . . .'

Again, the 'strong fierce expression'. This preoccupation with the threatening aspect of imagos surely indicates the origin of the scene in primal scene phantasies of a talion kind. The origin of this anxiety is perhaps in the need of an infant suffering deprivation to scan the mother's face. The mother's looking has not adequately confirmed identity: as Winnicott says, 'some babies, tantalised by . . . maternal failure, study the variable maternal visage in an attempt to predict the mother's mood'. They 'do all that is possible to see in the object some meaning which ought to be there'. I conjecture in the light of this insight that in the mode adopted by Iris Murdoch and Kingsley Amis sex is so meaningless as a form of 'pseudo-male doing' that people are always looking at the face of those in sexual passion hoping to see a meaning. Fearing the commitment of being 'to body gone' they wish to preserve looking as a form of scanning by intellectual hate: but the contrast between the eye of 'knowing' and the bodily doing and being is grotesque – and so they enact the destructiveness of Psyche on Cupid as bitter comedy. We know, too, from Melanie Klein that the infant wants the parental sex he phantasies to be sadistic, and yet he fears this, and fears the combined parents more than anything – because they threaten his identity. Obsessions in 'sex comedy' with looking at sex and faces in sex are therefore both sadistic (that is, full of incorporative hate) but also the exercise of intellectual will in situations in which the identity seems to be threatened especially where there is profound insecurity of 'being'.

Whatever its origins, this literary mode of play on primitive hate is one which Iris Murdoch adopted as the basis of her appeal:

> 'Now, Rosa!' he said and got up.
> 'Now what?' said Rosa, with all the sudden irritation of deep misery.

In so far as the last phrase is anything but a cliché it suggests a distrust of feeling and a defence against it: real feelings should be invoked here, but they are resented, since they must be denied:

'Now we make love'.

'O God!' said Rosa. Then she added, 'That is not possible, Jan.'

Jan looked down at her with a look of surly incomprehension. 'How not possible?' he said.

Rosa got up. They were standing very close to each other. Jan was immobile, his face stony. Rosa was trembling between anger and the grief of despair.

'You know about Stefan?' she said.

'Of course,' said Jan. 'And now is me. Come.'

Rosa's knees gave way and she sank down on to the mattress.

Rosa gives way in the same way to the Pole's omnipotent urge to incorporate her as women do to James Bond – by magic. The inward impulse of a human being to preserve herself inviolate is denied: yet any woman who behaved thus in real life could only do so because she was gravely ill, psychically. Yet the tone indicates that this is *all it is*. To give way to one man one day, and his brother the next. All that is involved is a little giving way. A little irritation of misery. What a mockery this literary mode makes of those deeply felt yearnings for dignity by which individuals feel anguish at any outrage to the True Self – even to the extent of being willing to die to avoid 'insult'.

Again, I do not deny that people can and do behave in such ways. What I assert is that their feelings must be very different unless they are suffering from some severe dissociation: even then there would be a deep sense of conflict somewhere within. The literary mode, however, because it is schizoid, disallows this inner reference of True Self integrity. The effect is surely to deepen the 'taboo on weakness' and to endorse prevailing attitudes to human nature. The effect of such work is to involve us in acceptance of a false belief that people could behave as the schizoid mode displays them capable of behaving. To take on this mode is to become blind to value in persons in their own right and to human significance in the realm of 'feminine element being' and the True Self. What is depressing is that a large intellectual minority finds the portrayal of such behaviour and such schizoid detachment acceptable, truthful, even admirable and moral.

Rosa only finds being outraged only a frightful bother.

> After that day Rosa was completely at a loss. . . . The only thing that troubled her in an immediate way was the old mother, whose presence in the room during the love-making horrified and frightened Rosa in a way that she could not get over, and whose very existence hung upon her like a threatening cloud beneath whose menace she felt herself guilty of a fearful crime . . . as the days passed she began to fear them.

The gesture at 'depth' of reaction – if we apply standards of adult emotional reality – is pathetic. Yet, from another point of view 'fearful crime' gives the clue to the unconscious sources I have suggested, in infantile anxieties.

If an adult had in fact committed such an act in reality, she could only have endured the emotional consequences by extreme measures. To have such a trivial response she could survive only by total 'loss of feeling tone' – by psychopathological dissociation. Rosa could not endure such a situation *in full realisation* of it without great anguish if she remained a normal manic-depressive person in touch with reality. But this anguish is not 'given'. No two brothers could treat a woman in such a way without deep and conflicting emotions in themselves: but this novel shows no realisation of the truth that they would be insane if they had no feeling – or inhuman. Had the episode been at all 'real' it would feel to Rosa a 'fearful crime' against her own nature. This is not realised. All we have is 'The only thing that troubled her. . . ' in a tone of tea-time conversation. Gorki or Dostoevsky would have found in such a situation, its inevitable hell, its terrible depth of dissociation of emotion and identiy, the human truth inevitably involved, in such a *mélange*, in any *real* situation. This novel's coldbloodedness, by such a contrast, seems itself psychopathological.

All Iris Murdoch can pathetically tell us is that 'Rosa was completely at a loss' – as if she had done no more than lost her purse or taken the wrong bus. The only thing she can see that is wrong in this sadistic phantasy of split relationship in partial object sex, in the obscene little chapter, is the presence of the mother. In this mode we are almost persuaded that the experience 'wouldn't be too bad' without that presence.

What is interesting is the mechanism by which, in the reader, normal apprehensions of reality and of human nature are closed down. Iris Murdoch's novel at first glance seems no more than a fashionable essay in 'sexual comedy' for the respectable suburban reader who needs to be shocked to feel viable. But in the schizoid inversion of this literary mode there is a deeper unconscious appeal to which these readers are responding. As with Fleming, this hate is – has to be – gilded by charm. Iris Murdoch's books are disguised by 'intelligence' as a witty and amusing story, of sexual 'fun' and mix-ups. They appear socially acceptable even though they contain phantasies more sordid than any commercial pulp-book writer would ever dare to devise. The reader, accepting intellectual acclaim (Iris Murdoch is, after all, an Oxford don and a member of the Arts Council Literature Panel – how long before she is a Dame?), may relax and indulge in his primitive phantasy – persuaded that he need not pay, by the degree to which he is involved in denying his own nature.

But, of course, there is a price to pay: he suffers a 'severed head'. He is that much more cut off from 'being' and the True Self. Such a work enlists us in a homunculism which manifests a hatred of 'female element' humanness. In so far as we become involved in this, we become a little more cut off from the deeper needs of the whole being – and so from sources of reassurance as to What is it to be human? and What is the point of life? To the creative–reparative quest for a sense of identity this kind of book is an offence, not only because it is grotesquely sordid but because it subtly distracts the reader from sources of realisation and meaning.

In rejecting *From the Enchanter Fleeing* as a creative human document, therefore, I am not complaining that it is immoral or obscene (though it is both). I am rather trying to suggest such writing pursues the false solutions of hate. Take the episode in which Annette is assaulted and is shut in a cupboard bare to the waist while two men discuss women outside. Is this titillating episode justified artistically? It may help Iris Murdoch's readers to feel more alive by phantasying human humiliation – significantly the humiliation of a woman. Yet the indulgence is disguised. The author tries to give point to this meaningless episode by the 'Lawrentian' symbol of a moth, which Rainborough crushes at the end, all very 'significant'. (Are we supposed to see his fumbling at her 'small breasts' as 'life'?)

But the real significance of the novel is in the false toughness by which we are turned against human vulnerability and involved in contempt for it. There is an effect of leading us to feel that bodily experience and relational experience 'don't count'. Thus, for Annette, losing her virginity is of less importance than having one's ears pierced: to her her body is 'just an exquisite machine'. She had never been in love: ' . . . although she was not without experience. She had been deflowered at seventeen by a friend of her brother on the suggestion of the latter. . . .'

Here we have a glimpse of the sadistic anti-libidinal denial of vulnerability and True Self being, beneath the 'brilliant' surface. With a witty grimace it is implied that even the fiercest voracity makes no impact on the personality. Having one's ears pierced counts more than being 'deflowered':

> 'I'm glad of that', said Annette, 'I'd hate to have any mark on my body that was there forever, or to lose anything that wouldn't come again. I'm glad I've never had a tooth out. And I've never had my ears pierced.'
> 'You don't *lose* any flesh when your ears are pierced,' said Rosa. 'The flesh is parted, but nothing is taken away.'
> 'I know,' said Annette, 'but it would make a difference to my body and it would never be the same again. It would make me feel that it was getting used up and that there was no going back.'

It is indicative, indeed, that this should come only a few pages after the indifference reference to defloration above. 'The flesh is parted, but nothing is taken away', is obviously an unconscious symbol which emerges from the primitive phantasy of curious violation. Under the surface of the exchange, in prose which looked at closely is strangely limp, one may glimpse a primitive horror of fleshly existence with its roots in the schizoid fear of 'losing inner contents': 'It would make me feel that it was getting used up.' In the exchange the novel seeks both to deny the truth of infantile phantasy about bodily incorporation and loss, and yet to encompass it: but the mortal truth is that 'there is no going back'. We exist in a unique body and soul in time, and there is an inevitable anguish in giving or love – in being human, in emotional surrender: yet this is necessary for us to find meaning.

From this existential anguish such writing flees into a denial of our emotional vulnerability, and yet transfixes us by horror of relationship. So it must always be shifting the relationships round, in phantasy, as Ferenczi's homosexual patients fled into heterosexuality, in a frantic quest for 'meeting' where none is possible. Both are symbolised by the phantasy of the Poles – who proclaim 'we share our women . . .', who have the 'smelly' old (castrating) mother in the background, and who tell a cold-blooded story of how they have 'drowned' the female element in the past. This fable is of a schoolmistress whom they both seduced and who consequently throws herself down a well but catches her foot in the rope and hangs upside down half way. The carpenter comes down the street and finds her: 'He asks her, "you want to come up or go down?" She say "Down", so he shake well rope, and she fall into well and drown for good. That was funny, wasn't it? "You want to come up or to go down?" '

The story might almost be taken as being symbolic of our culture's whole predicament: there is for culture a situation in which the choice has to be made and the choice can be to drown 'female element vulnerability' and the chances of the True Self for good. Denial of feeling in the schizoid, as we have seen, goes with a deep desire to be loved: so in such bizarre phantasies such writing seems at times to be yearning for the capacity to feel passion, anger, or fear – and to feel real by hate. Yet when she seeks to persuade us that she has found such depth of feeling, the situation is so bizarre itself and the phantasy figures are so unreal that we cannot be convinced. Here Rosa is 'given' the experience of horror: but with equal ruthlessness Iris Murdoch gives her the triumph of denying it, by intellectual effort: 'Rosa sat down on the mattress and closed her eyes. She stiffened her body and crushed down out of her consciousness something that was crying out in horror. It was nearly gone, it was gone; and now as she sat rigid, like a stone goddess, and as she felt herself to be there, empty of thoughts and feelings, she experienced a kind of triumph.'

Note again the vague 'a kind of': it is all too easy, we protest, this suppression – it is too magical, and has, instead of creative engagement with real feeling, a mere gesture of contempt and manic denial. Betrayal of the libidinal need for an object could not be so easily dealt with. But in Iris Murdoch refuge is rapidly taken in the superficial bright chit-chat of the sophisticated intellectual world, and all its defensive forms of 'pseudo-male' doing and thinking: 'where clothes were concerned inexhaustibly imaginative', 'the strange impression of a woman both elegantly dressed and naked at the same time', 'Yet she knew he was looking into her eyes', 'I am just famous'. She takes refuge, too, in the 'bad thinking' of carefully contrived erotic scenes, a kind of strip-tease of the intellectual writer, as when Mischa Fox leers at Annette while she is being fitted for a frock, or Rainborough ogles at his secretary ('silken knees downward were plainly visible, together with an inkling of underwear . . . the simpler bodily curves . . .').

In the dream relationships, magic and omnipotence are predominant, as in Fleming (and women's magazine stories). The men have strange hidden powers of compelling charm: the women are 'ready from the first to be his slave'. In Iris Murdoch's relationships people must always be in control by will – always, as with Amis, able to look at their experience with ironic 'detachment'. Of course, 'horrid' things happen – as in life, one might say. But they do not really impinge – and nothing is ever essentially mysterious, ungovernable, or beyond understanding.

So much so, indeed, that nothing ever essentially exists or is allowed to exist wholly – to be – in Iris Murdoch's world. Hers *is* the world of the severed head, or rather a world wholly withdrawn into 'inner contents' of a mental kind. But our heads are not severed – nor, really, is hers. We have to live with the whole experience and, by striving to imply that it is possible, the effect of her work is to undermine our capacities for living. Or they would if we were to give wholehearted assent to these schizoid phantasies. As it is, probably all they do is to encourage the same kind of superficial reading as, say, the thrillers of Agatha Christie, in which the somnolent reader reacts from time to time assaults on his senses, and finds in them a pale sense of being still alive, a dim substitute for meaning.

Moreover, our assent is inhibited by our alienation. The coldbloodedness and hate in this literary mode do not *allow* assent. We respond in disgust, even though this mental disgust is itself an enlistment in her anti-humanity. What is distressing is that so many individuals in culture today have become seduced into this kind of nihilism, adopting modes which, though they may involve us in hate, could hardly be said to draw us towards love – as E. M. Forster and Lawrence do. Iris Murdoch is even more perplexing, because, as she shows in her excellent book on Sartre, she sees the problem. But her work, her *écriture*, does not convince us that it conveys the capacity to care for human dignity and value.

There is little to be gained from Iris Murdoch in terms of creative achievement, in the discovery of being and realisation of the True Self. Rather, from her work we take something worse than what we absorb from Ian Fleming. He seeks to lure us into denying that we are human by offering us the false solutions of aggression and paranoia. Despite her evident humanity as a person she adopts a literary mode in her writing that is schizoid, and so assaults the very core of 'female element being'. She spreads abroad the impulse to deny our deepest needs and our most central creative potentialities while fostering a trivial attitude to the emotional life – a trivial attitude which is not mere superficiality but the exertion of a destructive hatred of all that one *is* at the core. In Iris Murdoch's work the reader is involved in 'false solution' phantasies with greater intellectual subtlety, and in prose of colder blood.

C. The Ethos of the Avant-garde

CHAPTER 22

A Little Bit of Shit in China:
The Reduction of Symbolism

THERE seem to be insights relevant to cultural problems in the comments made by a psychotherapist on the problems of running a hospital villa for schizophrenics. This doctor's method was to run the villa as a family home (for young men patients in their twenties) with the resident therapist acting as 'father', and the nursing staff acting, with some ensured permanence, as 'mothers'. Working in this way, the 'family' had to endure the anguish of responding to psyches with all the energy of the age of two or three, and all the primitive forces of that stage, in the bodies of men. The true solution of being a family for these patients was agonising – because it was human.

One of the difficulties for this doctor was that because of the painful feelings involved the hospital (as 'society') tended to retreat into a kind of *indifference* (see Conran [13]). The hospital liked it better during an earlier regime, in which the schizophrenic patients were encouraged to regard the *hospital* as the 'parental object' – and to *attack it* in order to 'find themselves'. To the therapist who took over, this seemed a false solution, akin to Sartre's solution to the problem of our freedom in 'endless hostility'. This hate behaviour included sending faeces back to the kitchen in the food trays: an act whose symbolism, in terms of 'inner contents' should be obvious. Yet the hospital 'liked it better' when this happened, because it could feel outraged, and could feel that the patients were 'bad' and only fit to be rejected. It could thus avoid the anguish involved in regarding them as fellow human beings, in despair.

The moral of this story seems to be that false solutions of hate can seem at first to be more easily acceptable than the true solutions of being human. Those trays of ordure would seem to be symbolic: the appeal of the schizoid modes I am examining lies in the strange fact that we like to be offered the chance of feeling 'a bad somebody rather than a weak nobody' in symbolic terms of 'bad inner contents'. 'Thrusting filth into others' can thus be seen not as a way of living at the expense of others but as actually a way of offering them strength and fullness.

This relationship between the symbolism of hate and problems of identity illuminates much in the realm of fashionable culture. Despite the nihilistic moral fervour of the *avant-garde*, it is important always for us to bring into the argument the ethical consideration of the problem of the degree to which individuals may live at the expense of others. Here it needs to be quite clear that there is such a fact of human life as paranoia, and that individuals who suffer from this and parallel conditions are impelled to seek to do harm in the realm of culture as much as elsewhere. Dr. Hannah Segal makes this quite plain, for instance, in her *Introduction to the Work of Melanie Klein* [47]. In her chapter on the Paranoid–Schizoid Position she gives an account of a patient who suffered from paranoid–schizoid problems.

> The method of projecting bad parts of the self split into many fragments, typical of schizoid defences, was characteristic of the patient. He once dreamt that he was facing scores of little Japanese men – his enemies. His associations showed that the Japanese represented his urine and faeces into which he put parts of himself which he wanted to be rid of – urine and faeces were then projected into his objects. On another occasion he wrote an article for a foreign paper which, as he came to realise in his analysis, he felt would have a very bad moral effect on his readers. He consoled himself with the fact that it was 'far away' and the consequences could not, therefore, reach him. In a later dream, the article was represented as a 'little bit of shit in China'. (Segal [47], p. 21.)

In many present-day debates on problems such as censorship it is assumed that there is no evidence that harm can be done by cultural influences. If we take clinical histories as evidence, however, there is observation in plenty of the need of some individuals to seek to thrust harm into others. For instance, Laing makes it clear that some schizoid patients can so fear the 'other' person and the possibility of becoming an 'object of his experience' that they may be driven to 'negate the other person's autonomy' and seek to 'kill the life in him' in order to forestall the attack they fear the other is about to make on them.

When the schizoid individuals in the hospital referred to above sent faeces in the trays returned to the kitchen, they were not performing a cultural symbolic act nor were they attacking an actual person. They were equating the hospital with the bad parent, and making an equation attack on it. They had split off and projected their own inner weakness, and hated it 'as' the hospital kitchen. As will be seen, this mode of behaviour is regressive, and essentially uncreative; it can express nothing that can yield insight (unless perhaps when interpreted by an analyst), and all it can cause is alienation and offence. It represents a reduction of symbolism to a state that comes before the development of the capacity to symbolise. This is exactly what much of our *avant-garde* art does today.

The schizoid confusion of 'equation' and symbol can be explored in the light of clinical experience. In her fascinating paper 'Notes on Symbol Formation', [48], Hannah Segal records how during her patient Edward's analysis 'a certain degree of symbol formation on a symbolic equation basis had occurred'.

'Symbolic equation', Hannah Segal believes, belongs to the earliest stages in our capacity to develop our capacity to symbolise. When the problem of ambivalence is first encountered there is a defence mechanism developed which is projective identification. 'In projective identification, the subject in phantasy projects large parts of himself into the object, and the object becomes *identified* with the parts of the self that it is felt to contain. Similarly, internal objects are projected outside and identified with parts of the external world which come to represent them.' (Segal [48], p. 383; my italics.)

Symbolism requires a relationship between the self, the thing symbolised, and the symbol itself. The first rudimentary projections and identifications to which Hannah Segal refers belong to stages at the beginning of the process of symbol formation. Hannah Segal sees the capacity to symbolise as belonging to the accomplishment of the 'depressive position' – the stage at which there first develops a firm sense of the distinction between the *me* and the *not-me*, and a concern for the effects of one's hate on others.

There is, however, a stage before this capacity to work backwards and forwards between subjective and objective worlds is developed. Hannah Segal refers to an autistic child who suffered 'a paralysis of his phantasy life and of symbol formation'. 'He had not endowed the world around him with any symbolic meaning *and therefore took no interest in it.*'

Children in whom processes of symbolisation are inhibited fail to achieve the capacity to develop a fully human identity by employing symbolism towards a sense of meaningful existence. They remain at the stage of employing equations rather than creative metaphors. These early symbols are 'not felt by the ego to be symbols or substitutes, but to be the original object itself . . .'. Thus in his analysis a child patient of Melanie Klein, when he saw some pencil shavings, said 'Poor Mrs. Klein': to him the shavings were Mrs. Klein cut into bits.

Symbolising is a *three-term* relation, i.e. a relation between the thing symbolised, the thing functioning as a symbol, and a *person* for whom the one *represents* the other.'In psychological terms, symbolism would be a relation between the ego, the object and the symbol.'

When this three-term relationship breaks down, however, as it does in schizophrenia, a different term is needed, and Hannah Segal suggests the term 'symbolic equation'.

This kind of symbolic equation is the basis of the 'concrete thinking' of the schizophrenic* who cannot symbolise but 'where substitutes for the original objects, or parts of the self, can be used quite freely . . . but . . . they are hardly different from the original object: they are felt and treated as though they were *identical* with it.'

This leads to all kinds of confusions.

> This non-differentiation between the thing symbolised and the symbol is part of a disturbance in the relation between the ego and the object. Parts of the ego and internal objects are projected into an object and identified with it. The differentiation between the self and the object is obscured. Then, since a part of the ego is confused with the object, the symbol – which is a creation and function of the ego – becomes in turn, confused with the object which is symbolised.
> *Where such symbolic equations are formed in relation to bad objects, an attempt is made to deal with them as with the original object, that is by total annihilation and scotomization.* (Segal, [48], p. 393.)

Thus if there is regression from the capacity to symbolise to this kind of primitive symbolic equation activity (belonging to the paranoid–schizoid position), there is a loss of all that richness and effectiveness in our dealings with reality which are developed along with the capacity to symbolise – and to make our links with human culture. With symbolism belongs our capacities to see the world and to give it meaning.

So when patient Edward took to symbolic equation activity, 'anxiety was displaced from the person of his analyst, felt as a bad internal object on to substitutes in the external world'.

> Thereupon the numerous persecutors in the external world were dealt with by scotomization. That phase . . . was characterized by an extreme narrowing of his interests in the external world . . . his vocabulary became very poor. . . . He forbade himself and me the use of many words which he felt had the power to produce hallucinations and therefore had to be abolished. (Segal [48], p. 394.)

If our culture, as I believe, is becoming increasingly schizoid, then this may imply, rather than 'freedom', a 'narrowing of interests' and a reduction of creative potential. There may also be a confusion of aims, as when medium or audience become confused with objects into which aspects of the self have been projected paranoically so that they seem deserving of attack since they have become *equated* with the original object.

* Another patient was baffled and confused when the therapist said, 'You want to eat your cake and have it too.' She said 'But I didn't have any idea of eating cake here in your office. Whatever gave you that idea?' Another patient said of his mother, 'I suppose she might have preferred me to be a baseball. Then she could have taken me out to the playground and bounced me on the asphalt and hit me with a bat.' (Burnham [9], p. 67.)

What seems to have overtaken our modish culture is something that can perhaps be better understood by reference to schizophrenic 'concrete thinking'.

Of the latter Hannah Segal gives as an example:

> A schizophrenic patient in an analytical situation . . . he came in blushing and giggling . . . we found out that previous to this hour he had been attending an occupational therapy class in which he was . . . making a stool . . . he could not bring himself to talk about the work he was doing. For him the wooden stool on which he was working, the word 'stool' which he would have to use in connexion with it, and the stool he passed in the lavatory were so completely one and the same thing that he was unable to talk to me about it. . . . (Segal [48]).

A similar breakdown of creative capacities to mean seems to have happened in the world of culture. The predicament of the artist is to be compared with the predicament of the child patient who experienced such distress when a pencil was sharpened because the pencil '*was*' Melanie Klein.

There are many signs in the world of culture that a schizoid minority is urging on the break-down of distinctions between acts in life and cultural acts, a confusion which surely parallels the regression from the three-term relationship of symbolism proper to symbolic *equation*, such as is found in schizophrenics. The fashionable *avant-garde*, for instance, admires the 'purity of motive' of the 'intellectual gangster' even though he becomes involved in acts of violence in the political sphere. 'Happenings' may involve the audience, as in the New York 'way out' theatre, when theatre-goers find themselves tumbled about or placed among naked lovers, or involved in 'group gropes' on the stage. Film and television drama tend to become a loosely strung series of sensations rather than a dramatic entity, as the film critic of *The Times* has pointed out at the time of writing. 'Destruction' art may involve individuals in some form of ritual with a dead animal (such an event was recently the subject of a police raid) or exploding sculptures (Tinguely). Entertainment becomes 'psychedelic' and linked with the rape of the mind by drugs, the violation of the senses by hypnotic lighting effects or high level sound, or other forms of 'derangement of the senses'. The effect of a play or film which most satisfies the creator may be that members of the audience go out vomiting, or on stretchers.

While such manifestations often claim to speak for a new 'freedom', they seem in the light of Hannah Segal's point of view, rather to represent regression, withdrawal, and a 'narrowing of interests' in the sphere of culture. Confusions of creative symbolism and 'equation' attack on 'the object' belong less to culture than to desperate attempts to act out personal dreams and to involve others in them sometimes in desperate, anti-social, or even criminal ways. There seems to be no more justification for these than for the activities of any other criminal or anti-social individual.

In all this, urgent personal needs to hate find an advantage in being able to violate 'cultural trust'. The public meets the arts supposing that they may offer something to deepen our sense of our human potentialities. Whatever ego-support he may himself gain by his antics, it is this natural creative trust which the schizoid individual who exploits hate in the cultural sphere violates. For him there are other more subtle satisfactions, for he attacks the inward life itself. He also knows that he can effectively reduce capacities to engage with reality and reduce living power by his power to thrust hate into us. To be violated thus, as by many television plays, is an anti-human experience, while at the same time objection is stifled because such exploitation is socially acceptable and even acclaimed as 'realism' or valid 'protest'.

We must allow that some schizoid expression will draw our attention to deep existential problems. But the danger of schizoid expression is that it tends towards the inversion of values, depersonalisation, 'living at the expense of others', and the attack on being human.

Here, serious problems are raised, even by the very desperateness of the contemporary artist. Because of the problem of finding a sense of meaning in a world in which solutions seem impossible, some artists drive themselves to extremes – attacking their canvas, turning on themselves, and turning on us, the audience – as if we must be sacrificed to their quest. Some artists have been aware of this problem: Mahler was worried that a work of his might drive people to suicide. Since then some artists have not only ceased to care about the effects of their work, but actually hope they can disturb the audience.

Francis Bacon, for instance, speaks of having the aim in his painting, of making 'a direct assault on the nervous system'. In his latest paintings it seems that creative symbolism itself is on the point of breaking down altogether. As Guy Brett, the Art Critic of *The Times* said (June 1967): 'In an interview with David Sylvester printed in the Marlborough Gallery's Catalogue he [Bacon] quotes Paul Valery's remark about wanting to give the sensation without the boredom of its customary vehicle, to evade the nervous system's protective padding.'

Bacon, says Brett, is 'hoping in the process and by accident to discover a hidden intuitive direction'.

> His direct assault on the nervous system was made by discovering a balance between a familiar recorded image (like a photograph) and an unstable, disorientated way of painting. The image acquired presence on the point of slipping away or being destroyed. These new paintings are an impressive display of Bacon's special technical refinements, but they are dumb in a way his paintings have not been before because one is not taken past the methods of conveyance. (*The Times*, 15 March 1967.)

With someone like Bacon, there is no doubt as to his artistic integrity. But in his work there would seem to be a movement towards some break-down of symbolic communication. It may be that the work of such a distinguished artist could, incidentally, encourage others who do not have his kind of integrity to make an 'equation' attack on the audience – and, indeed, there is much in 'underground' art today of this kind.

After looking at Bacon's pictures we feel 'maddened'. We may recognise that he is, as Winnicott puts it, 'striving to be seen'. But what happens to *us*? We may be helping *him* to be seen: but are we better able to feel 'seen' ourselves? Or does he merely undermine our security of being confirmed as human? Is what he offers 'creative reflection'? These are not easy questions to answer, and answering them involves us inevitably in the study of deep problems of identity. Some patients with schizoid illnesses can only be helped to *be* at great cost to the psychotherapist. How much can people at large afford such a cost for culture without becoming diverted or reduced in their personal lives? The disturbing manifestations of the cultural underground from the use of hallucinogenic drugs to the present pursuit of 'constructive vandalism' towards anarchistic ends in the universities will surely not allow us to answer this question glibly? We could be on the verge of yet another catastrophic assault on reason, yet coming unexpectedly from what seemed to be the source of sweetness and light – from culture itself. We may be disarmed, meanwhile, by our very willingness to give assent to culture because it is an area of trust.

Yet the consequent ethical problems are ignored by such a fashionable critic as Edward Lucie-Smith. To him there is a new departure from tradition, and we must banish old expectations from our minds. Writing about another painter, he says:

Let us suppose that we banish this tradition from our minds. What do the modern arts have to offer? Basically, it seems to me, a theatre without actors, a psychological entertainment. Recently I interviewed the young British painter John Walker on the B.B.C. Third Programme. Asked what he wanted people to feel when they looked at his pictures, he replied 'something of what I myself felt in painting them'. A reasonable enough response. But his pictures, if they are about anything, are about states of mind – not so much symbolized, as directly expressed. The spectator, to get what they have to offer, must not interpret, but simply open himself. The picture is an event which he must surrender himself to. And this is precisely the same demand that the avant-garde theatre also makes of its audience. (*The Times,*).

In the end, of course, such a critic merely finds himself in a new aestheticism – encapsulated in the limited concepts of an ethos dominated by homunculism and the limited concepts of the will-to-pleasure and self-assertion. Bantock's remarks are perhaps relevant here when he speaks of 'Minds which all too loudly proclaim their complete freedom from prejudice and convention, in the end come to accept the most boring of conventions – the convention of unconventionality; for the mind which asserts its own autonomy . . . succumbs to the deadliest of tyrannies – that of itself . . .' (Bantock [3], p. 142).

The parenthesis I omitted above links the vanity of the mind which asserts its own autonomy with the attitude to art characterised by Clive Bell: 'what civilised man needed', considered Bell, was 'complete development and self-expression'. This kind of claim for self-sufficiency we still encounter in claims for the 'autonomy of art', and it is this which has led to the acceptance of equation for symbol in art and even, apparently the artist for art. In its most grotesque form this claim is found in the point of view expressed by Lucie-Smith when he writes that, where artists are concerned,

... a particular class of people exists, who must be supported not for what they do but for what they are. They embody, and often in the most unlikely corporeal forms, some principle of refinement or civilization without which the rest of us are benighted.

In a religious society it would be perfectly possible to image a body of people among the rest, and uncomplainingly supported by them. One thinks of Zen monks in Japan. But it is scarcely possible to imagine such an arrangement at work in a thoroughly materialist Western democracy, such as our own. (*The Times* 6 December 1966.)

This precious attitude to the artist is a corollary to the prevalent concern to 'reject the imputation of meaning – emotional or other – as an insult to the Muse, a degradation of the pure dynamic forms, an invidious heresy, in the arts'. The phrases quoted are those of Suzanne Langer. She characterises the evasion of the problem of the meaning of symbolism in the arts as 'the silly fiction of self-significance' which 'has been raised to the dignity of a doctrine'. When we find this attitude, 'essentially based on a logical trick', extended to justify even the abandonment of the function of pursuing meaning by symbolism in art and then to justify artists for artists' sake, it is surely urgent to resist it – not least because the environment at large is so deficient in creative sources of a sense of significance.

What Lucie-Smith calls a 'thoroughly materialist Western democracy' suffers from a debility of attention, through creative symbolism, to problems of hate, love, and meaning in the inner life. The artist needs to be defended against a philistine, materialist society because he exposes himself to all the uncertainties and intangible depths of the inner world and the symbolising impulse wherever it may take him. He has a contribution to make to ego-maintenance, and to 'confronting the problem of existence'. Where he is worth cherishing it is because he is capable of contributing to our deeper natural energies of the creative exploration of experience, not because he embodies a refinement we cannot quite understand but must be prepared to 'uncomplainingly support.' If he is concerned to bring about a reduction of creativity in the pursuit of his own needs to feel real at our expense, we must pronounce him as philistine as the society he lives in.

How the schizoid impulse to substitute 'equation' for symbol goes with a 'narrowing of interest' and a reduction of true creativity is obvious from an interesting interview on 'Happenings' published in *Twentieth Century Magazine* [31]. This was conducted by Richard Kostelanetz with Alan Kaprow, the critic, sometime painter, and author of *Assemblage, Environments and Happenings* [30], described as the 'best book we have on *avant-garde* American art of the past decade'. Kaprow was the inventor of the term 'happening'. He is a devotee of the American tachiste painter Jackson Pollack and of the musician John Cage – who relies so widely on chance in composing. Kaprow is introduced as having a 'technique' and a 'philosophy'.

Kaprow chose the word 'happening' because it was 'neutral': 'It was a neutral word that *avoided reference to art*' (my italics). For art is substituted a kind of play:

> R.K. How did you solve the problem of involving people in a satisfactory way?
> A.K. It has since become very very clear to me how to do this: You invite people to play a game, in which the rules are explained and the expressive nature is clear. If they want to play, they will respond. Once they've made that commitment, you can play your game to your heart's content. That's why I gave up the audience.
> R.K. Let's say, I'm a friend of yours, and you are planning to have an Event. What do you tell me?
> A.K. I spent my time thinking of the game. Let's call it a game, although the analogy should not be pushed too far. I simply write down the nature of the game and send you a copy of it. If you are interested, you will come to my meeting, where we will discuss the game.
> R.K. For example?
> A.K. Hop-scotch, kick-the-can, stealing cars. Or it might say we'll do the following things: draw some lines in the ground, and we're going to jump in the following way. Then we'll kick the can across the street and hide while somebody tries to find it and find us in turn. After this we'll steal some cars in such and such a street. If you're interested in playing my game, then come and talk it over, and we'll decide who's going to do what at that time. After that, we'll do it.

What has been relinquished, obviously, is that symbolic activity of which Winnicott says: 'The interplay between originality and the acceptance of tradition as the basis for inventiveness . . .' and 'the interplay between separateness and union'. That is, what are to be avoided ('the analogy shouldn't be pushed too far' . . . 'That's why I gave up the audience') are those 'cultural experiences that provide the continuity in the race which transcends personal existence'. Art is out. 'Commitment' means 'joining in' a game rather than commitment to human experience. Cultural experiences, as Winnicott emphasises, are 'in direct continuity with play': but here there is a reversion to a kind of play which is appropriate to a stage before the emergence of a personal culture in the individual. Significantly, it takes the form of children's play which is still exploring the relationship between the *me* and the *not-me*, and making those very earliest experiments in social relationship which in insecure children tend to become adolescent delinquency.

When children steal things they may be trying to discover whether anyone loves them, so they are taking something that they feel really belongs to them. Adults taking part in such 'play' are re-enacting the child's attempt to feel real – by direct 'equation' attack on the adult world-as-object and a kind of playful criminality rather than by cultural creative effort. Such play may contribute to the sense of feeling real, but only by 'coming up against it' in an aggressive way. It can contribute nothing towards answers to the question What is life about? or What is it to be human?

Indeed, it reverts to a form of 'transitional object' behaviour, belonging to a stage at which this confrontation can be engaged upon, by cultural symbolism. Kaprow regresses as it were to the infant stage of attacking, biting, loving, and ill-treating the cuddly rag, or other plaything, which symbolises the first internalisation of the mother and the capacity for separateness. 'Society' is surely identified, however, with the 'bad' object. The capacity for separateness has not been found, and so the continuing attack on society is itself a manifestation of over-dependence. Such individuals *could not do without a society which they can feel is alienating and hostile,* nor could they do without their anti-social attacks on it. They are by no means truly concerned with transforming society to become more humane. Theirs is not art so much as a form of sentimentalised and socially accept-able criminality with a pseudo-philosophical vindication: indeed, all that is sought is a kind of distracting 'fun' which is itself the counterpart of the American hedonistic and manic 'fun' living of the commercial and advertising ethos.

The deliberateness of the regression and 'narrowing of interest' is obvious in the way in which all creative responsibilities are 'eliminated' in 'happenings'. As in children's early play, 'self-expression', 'to your heart's content', is all that matters – but there is no creative gain even over internal dissociation, and none is sought. All that is sought is the crude sense of being real and alive:

> R.K. In your pieces nowadays, the actions of the primary participants may be planned very well in advance, but they involve so many other people, often passers-by, who don't know what's going on, that the secondary actions remain unfixed. . . .
> A.K. . . . Right, that's because of the elimination of fixed space. When you have an outline around your space, in which all of your activity takes place, then you are responsible for everything that happens within it. The minute you break your space, a lot of dimensions become unpredictable. . . .

But the purpose of this 'unpredictability' is not to enlarge the scope of creativity nor to allow the creative powers of 'female element being' to take over in an intuitive way. It seems rather a compulsive quest to avoid engagement with the 'backlog' of unsolved problems of identity and relationship within one:

> A.K. The third source I very often use when my mind doesn't pour out sufficiently; that is the yellow pages of the phone book. I've used them for many, many years. I go about it this way: either I'll flip the book open to some arbitrary point and point my finger down rapidly, and I'll write what I find – it might say Vacuum Cleaners, or something like that. Or else I'll use a chance method of some kind, such as pieces of paper with numbers on them, which in turn tell me which pages to go to. *One way or another it makes no difference actually.* (My italics.)

There is a parallel here with the deliberate 'jamming' of 'systems' within the self by a schizophrenic patient of Laing's (Julie) who needed to preserve chaos against the fear of being *interpreted*. If the schizophrenic is 'heard' and responded to, then he fears, he may be 'in' the mind of others or they may 'enter' his mind. Contact is too dangerous, and leads to fears of implosion or explosion of the identity. Kaprow's schemes to avoid any kind of symbolic responsibility ('it makes no difference') may be seen as a schizoid ploy to avoid communication itself. Creativity must be 'avoided' at all costs. What he 'selects' has no difference from any collection of odd scraps of material of any kind anywhere.

In the face of such reductions of art, of course, there are critics who are prepared, in their response to this kind of schizoid ploy, to allow that an expression of any kind is acceptable whether it is meaningless or not – perhaps because by extending such an acceptance they feel they are helping the schizoid individual to complete his personality. From the point of view of the 'schizoid diagnosis', however, this is but to become involved in the distortions of the schizoid himself, who is essentially thus abusing the area of 'trust' in which cultural symbolism exists.

Kostelanetz sees something of this, and obliges Kaprow to admit that responsibility for selection which he refuses to accept:

> R.K. At this point, however, you exercise some choice, which is to say some taste. You go to the yellow pages to find possibilities; then, you choose from the examples you pick up.
> A.K. Either I choose or I subject these to chance choices, which I do not select but simply accept . . . I use as quick a bunch of methods as I can, to pull the choices out of my head; and some of these are, indeed, chosen by chance at the end. . . . In composing lately, I freely combine my own ideas with suggestions made by somebody else or by certain chance methods. These are usually mixed up in some fashion so that the result turns out to be a give and take between my preference and what's given me by my environment. I don't mean to be pure in these things; if I suddenly decide I don't like something, I'll chuck the whole chance method; if I feel chance is working for me, I'll follow it all the way. . . .

The 'chance' method is thus in a sense a way of cheating oneself, and escaping responsibility for a selection which in fact the creative worker is responsible for and must be held to be responsible.

Kaprow likes 'happenings' to take place in various cities at once because it is a 'way of feeling in touch'. We can interpret this as meaning 'if pseudo-events are happening in a number of places at once then there will be a greater sense to those taking part in them of being real than if these were happening in just one place'. What counts, obviously, is the 'touch' which is essentially no different from the kind of satisfactions obtained in, say, war, or pseudo-eventual journalism, when outward happenings seem to confirm one's existence without any essential 'inner 'gain. Of course, all art is in a sense made up of 'pseudo-events': but Kaprow's are invented simply for the sake of having them happen: not for any purpose of satisfying the human need for meaning.

> R.K. These Happenings, then, are solely for their participants. They have no large effect upon their innocently bystanding observers.
> A.K. They may although the observers may not know what they've gotten into.

Kaprow simply fails to answer the first point made by his interviewer: it means nothing to him. What has been abandoned is the concept of art as 'a man speaking to man'. Since this has been abandoned, the activity itself has no validity in the world at large, no more than any other personal and private activity which enables an individual to feel alive and real, from masturbation, or secret drinking, to crime. The 'freedom' of which Kaprow speaks is the freedom of reducing creativity to the ultimately trivial plane; and in this it complements the trivialisation of symbol and emotion throughout the world of commercial entertainment. 'In *Calling* . . . I learned afterwards, some people had a soda between events, and others went round the block five times to take up time, and at that time they saw lots of sights or amused passers-by who saw the packages of wrapped-up people. This kind of freedom therefore, I would like to amplify, and I think I'm beginning to do more of that now.'

Kaprow poses as one who is seeking to make a more 'alive' kind of art. But having sought to reduce art to something without essential creativity, he can now proceed to seek to invert all values, in his philosophy of art:

> R.K. Do you then react negatively against permanent art, even though you teach courses in it?
> A.K. No I simply react by making the kind of art which is more alive in my time. That's all, I can't make permanent art, because it is false to me to make permanent art.
> R.K. Why is it 'false'?
> A.K. It's not real.

Or, to put it into our terms, the schizoid moves towards the abandonment of symbolism because he cannot *afford* symbolism. Genuine symbolism would bring him in touch with his own humanity, and this he cannot tolerate. All he can afford is 'equation', where the 'other' is equated with the internal objects projected into the environment and attacked directly. In so far as man's need is to sustain a human identity, there is nothing more 'real' to him than his own myths, meanings, and signs: it is these which enable him to feel 'real'. But to Kaprow only 'False Male Doing' is 'real': being, creativity, the female element, humanness, *symbolism* are not.

What seems to have happened with the *avant-garde* is that they have found in commercial culture a form of exploitation of equation symbolism which provides a temporary manic sense of being 'real'. As I analyse it in this work this is the symbolism of hate – and in its aggressive assertion of the ruthless 'doing' or 'active' pseudo-male self. It seems to provide all that is necessary for ego-maintenance. It spreads abroad, inevitably, the 'taboo on weakness' ('Wham!') and an anti-human ethos (Batman, Superman) in which it is increasingly difficult for us to find true creativity and to have confidence in it. To be creative seems to be weak because it involves the recognition of one's ambivalence, vulnerability, despair, and inner needs. Normal creativity and even meaningful symbolism itself come to seem 'pallid'. Such individuals as Kaprow simply cannot accept the responsibility of genuine creativity. Yet their only hope seems to be somewhere in the field of 'expression', because as schizoid individuals they cannot feel real enough in actual life and personal relationships. They must find an activity somewhere between the two – half symbolic, but not essentially symbolic: half-life – but not actual life, rather a form of play. Like children, they live in phantasy while still living in actuality. But their creative expression is not controlled by the intuitive 'reveries' in which the genuine artist relies on his most secret areas of 'female element being'.

The result of this predicament has been that widespread seizure on the existence of 'pop' art and commercial culture as a reason for abandoning altogether the human responsibilities of creativity. There follows a most significant passage in the interview under discussion:

> A.K. . . . in Pop Art, which is largely made up of paintings and not assemblages and sculpture – in. say, a painting by Roy Lichtenstein – you have an ironic reference to a moment in the forties by the style used. It represents a kind of half-humorous nostalgia for the Boston Pops Orchestra era or the snap-crackle-pop era, the whole time of soda pop that was the childhood of Lichtenstein and almost every other pop artist. At the same moment you have an indulgence in a holocaust of commercial attention and publicity that is bound to enervate everybody shortly and cause its imminent death; so it, Pop Art, acquires a built-in obsolescence from this very faddist attraction. I don't mean that it was generated for fad reasons, but the way that it has been caught up in everybody's sensibility is bound to bring on its end.
>
> R.K. America uses up its favourites very quickly.
>
> A.K. So, since everybody participates willy-nilly in this kind of rat-race, let's enjoy the rat-race *Let's take it right by the tail and play it to the full.*
>
> R.K. Therefore, create a work of art that will make news today and will be dead tomorrow. . . .
>
> A.K. So that it can make more news in another form; as gossip, it is continually renewable by virtue of its unseizability. . . .

From my point of view the argument here could be interpreted as follows. Commercial art uses manic symbols whose basis is hate – that is, anti-human 'tough' and 'incorporative' ploys, by which the individual may temporarily suppose he can feel alive and real. Since this symbolism arises from false solutions to the problem of identity, the symbolism of 'pop' soon fades. It only enters into everybody's sensibility 'rapidly' because it is superficial, trivial, and false. Thus the modes of 'pop' culture are continually changing and becoming obsolescent.

To certain individuals, such a Lichtenstein, there will be a nostalgia for the false solution symbolism of the outer world of their childhood and adolescence. The import of their work thus tends to be, 'Would that it were possible for me to live by anti-human false solutions, instead of having to become an adult and thus be faced with the need to discover genuine solutions and satisfactions, or go under as a human being!'

The result is a kind of homunculism in art that can yet seem to be that art which is 'most alive'. But this manic art, because it is based on false solutions, is exhausted with greater speed because it is exposed to sensibility at large. Kaprow speaks as if inevitably exposing art to 'everyone's sensibility' exhausted it. (Tell that to Li Po!) This is, of course, an obviously schizoid view, as if communication threatened to 'empty' 'inner contents' – out of art as out of an individual. In truth, the exposure of genuine works of art throughout the centuries has never exhausted them, though there may be changes in valuation. Manic 'pop' art, at the hands of sensibility at large, only suffers its proper due, which is to be exhausted by exposure to the genuine needs of human beings at large. After a while everyone finds that they cannot sustain their identities by this or that form of pseudo-symbolism – they discover the falsity of each episode of false solutions for themselves, and now must find further manic ploys or discover genuine creativity in some way.

To really 'seize this situation by the tail' would be to foster and cherish genuine art, to develop education in such a way as to try to change the situation, or to find some way of protecting symbolism from misuse. The 'pop'-loving world of the *avant-garde*, however, takes the path of a *trahison des clercs*: for them to take the situation by the tail is to join it. They decide, as Kaprow does, to 'play it to the full': or, in my terms, 'give themselves up to the joys of hating'. The origin of their need to do so is made obvious by Kaprow – they cannot feel real unless they, too, rely upon the art of false solutions. Or rather it is not art at all they want but some 'real' reaction – notoriety, impact – or mere 'gossip'. To Kaprow 'art' actually becomes *renewed* by 'gossip' – thus the essential criterion for a piece of art is its news value. Art lives not in capturing universal signs and meanings but in being talked about (what a give-away!). Though he denies that 'pop' art is generated for 'fad reasons' it is obvious that the modish art of the *avant-garde* finds its justification in the way in which it is gleefully taken up by the commercial media themselves: it becomes part of the 'bustle' which distracts our world from the problem of existence itself.

Yet, in a sense, the position is an attempt to 'hold on' to creativity itself when culture itself has been replaced by dead fact.

> A.K. The current media are too full of information now for us to be stuck with one way of doing things. We're deluged by information, past and present, through our schooling and in magazines and television. These constitute such an abundance of possibilities that to stick to any one thing or any one discipline or any one developmental idea would be very hard to do; it reveals an almost obsessive discipline. That's why those who paint in certain obsessive ways are so interesting because it is not merely painting! it is a philosophical holding on – a desperation, a concentration against all odds. . .

One would expect to follow here an insistence on the I–Thou in the face of reduction to I–It. The feeling here is no doubt genuine, that in America, where man's inner life is so much held in contempt, the individual concerned with 'inner contents' and the existential problems, has somehow to hold on to what he can. Yet, of course, in so far as he 'holds on' to falsifications of the creative process, he only makes the situation worse. To encourage art to merge with the general attempt to feel real by 'equation' conflict with society merely deepens the taboo on weakness as it affects creativity:

> R.K. . . . you see a formal sympathy between Happenings and the current environment in that both force upon us such various and disparate experience within a single frame or thread.

A.K. Well, Happenings are a medium, let's face it; they've become an art form. Fundamentally, what a Happening does, which other historic arts don't do, is permit a number of moves through different media, and, moreover, through times and places that you would have to filter through another medium in the other arts . . . it achieves a liberation that no other art form has yet been able to do . . . you can see a movie and empathize, as you can read a book and empathize; but you can't actually do it – jump out of your seat and into the Vista-Vision screen and fight with the guys in the O.K. corral.

The schizoid confusion of symbol with actuality is obvious: here we have in the field of the arts that 'concrete thinking' which the schizophrenic manifests. He must 'do it' rather than 'empathize'. Creative symbolism is not a conflict with the actual world but a means of engaging with and working on inner problems of structure and content of the human personality through sign and meaning. To move out of the realm of symbolism and begin to exert one's aggression on actual people in a real setting is merely to act out one's phantasies – which is a psychopathological manifestation from which our world suffers too much already – from gangsterism and teenage delinquency to the paranoid manifestations of war. Indeed, all around us this ugly manifestation is visible in the way in which our society has attached the problem of human identity to forms of ingestion, bustling, and activity that simply cannot solve them. In devising the 'happening' Kaprow is merely complementing and endorsing the society in which it lives and selling subjective disciplines down the river to commercial enslavement itself. This is the true face of his 'freedom'.

The ultimate reduction of art in his view is revealed at the end of the interview. There is no difference for Kaprow between the mere activity of going to a supermarket and taking part in a creative activity. He seems obsessed by the supermarket, which from my point of view is a physical feature of the environment whose depersonalised nature has been created by economic ruthlessness in which human needs for 'meeting' have been denied. Kaprow sees no difference between supermarket and studio:

R.K. Do you know any unintentional creators of Happenings, whose works you find excellent?
A.K. Yes, I see them all the time. For example, there is the man who manages the Shop-Rite up there on Route 25a. He, along with many others, studies how to be a good manager of a super-market; but by the ways they arrange the products, the displays, the check-out counters, and the particular lighting effects, he promotes, in fact, an unconscious ritual every Thursday night – a ritual of buying and exchanging. I think these are perhaps magnificent quasi-Happenings.

The word 'magnificent' is significant here: to what degree is the 'magnificence' of a Charles Ives or a Gustav Mahler, for instance, implicitly reduced by comparison with the activities of a window-dresser concerned to sell corned beef and prepacked bacon to customers whom he regards only in terms of their limited functions of ingestion? (Perhaps the mis-spelling 'Rite' has misled Kaprow?)

There is surely a distinction to be made between efforts which concern themselves with survival of the human identity in its need for meaning, and those which, admirable as they may be, are only concerned with the survival of the body-system and its requirements of baked beans and corn cobs. To Kaprow there is some economic conundrum:

A.K. . . . The only differences, continues Kaprow, is his lack of attention to the fact that it might be something other than a means of making a lot of money.
R.K. Why is it a 'quasi-Happening'; because it is different from the ordinary run of things?

What follows in answer to this question may be taken as an indication of the depth and profundity of the prevalent concept of 'art' in the 'pop' *avant-garde* world:

A.K. The difference lies in the kind and amount of attention given to it. I can look at it more poetically than economically, and they look at it more economically than poetically. When I'm there I not only have a shopping list and a certain amount of money, beyond which I may not go; but I also have a sense of the spectacle, which arises partly from a detachment at the same moment that I am involved in it.

R.K. Here, however, you are seeing things that other people might not see.

A.K. Right. So, if the artist has a special function I'm not at all sure that it is better than the manager's or the car salesman's. . . . It is simply that, yes, there are differences between us human beings – between men and women, between artists and physicists and poets and ditch-diggers and all – but each of us do the best we can at our tasks. My job as an artist is to make dreams real.

How shall we ever justify the arts in a society in which their essential contribution to man's identity is suppressed under a headlong pursuit of 'external' ends – when all the individual concerned with creativity can say is that the creative individual is really no different from a shop assistant except that he has different interests?

Kaprow's 'vitality' and his sense that what he is offering is 'real', is based on no greater concept than 'making dreams real' – which we can interpret as simply meaning 'acting out my own private phantasies'. He has no concept of how, parallel to the disciplines of the scientist seeking for truth in the external world, the individual engaged upon subjective disciplines needs to accept the profound responsibility of training and using his 'female element' capacities – intuition, insights, sense of order and relevance, power of myth-making, and concern with techniques of sign and meaning, to explore the limitless realms of the inner life in the pursuit of significance.

All Kaprow can offer is a vague gesture, expressed in journalistic phrases, towards 'interest' as if life were so lacking in interest that we had to invent a game to make it interesting (Why won't Bingo do?)

R.K. This suggests the question of evaluation. In what sense is one Happening 'better' than another?

A.K. I've often wondered, because I really know that some of them flop, that some of them read better than they actually perform, and that some of them that read badly turn out magnificently in enactment, and some are just as interesting when read as they were in performance. Even within those cases, where there is an equal interest in both means of communication, some are better than others. I can usually seize on that was wrong in a particular piece; but as for making a generalisation, I confess that I don't know enough about the situation yet.

On creative matters Kaprow has only abysmal ignorance and philistinism to offer: from any exploration of the nature of subjective disciplines, he has not begun. He has only the gift for enlisting the world's faddish interest in his own private games and those of colleagues and members of the public who can be persuaded to join in. His ambitions, however, in acting out his private phantasies, are limitless, and will no doubt be fulfilled electronically: 'Hopefully, we'll be joined by Telstar and such media so that we can be in touch with one another. . . .'

But his kind of reduction of creative pursuits to trivialisation, non-symbolism, and primitive 'equation' activity offers nothing to the urgent need for an exploration of the point of life. The kind of 'communication' he offers is less in its human content than a moment's exchange at the check-out counter of a supermarket, and infinitely less than one experiences in a traditional food store, whether in Norwich, Vermont, or an English village. If, indeed, Telstar is to be enlisted in Happenings, it is a pathetic comment on the unequal development of science and art in our world that the most remarkable inventions of technology should be used for the self-encapsulated ends of those who are only concerned with the preservation of their own egos through the equation activity of anti-social *blagues*.

D.   Hate through the Machine

CHAPTER 23

Harold Pinter's Basement

A WORK of culture may have the effect of exerting on us a 'technique of intimacy' and may have the effect on us of being subjected to the 'acting out', of someone's phantasies, when we trusted it as a form of expression in which *a man is speaking to men* about human experience. I want here to explore these problems further in a television drama by Harold Pinter. If we look closely at this dramatist's work I believe we can see that there are certain essential differences between what we expect, or suppose we are watching – and what we really get, which manifests an abuse of trust.

Pinter's work is concerned with making a certain kind of impact on us at the time of performance. As one critic observes; 'For Ibsen, the past histories of the characters are the soil in which the whole plot is planted. For Pinter, the past histories of the characters, like their off-stage lives and their social backgrounds, couldn't matter less. *The only facts that he's concerned with are the facts of what is said and done on stage.*' (Hayman [28], p. 8.)

This critic admits that Pinter's settings seem very 'real'. But the reality is created only for the purpose of what the work is to do to the audience: in our terms, its effect is more 'equation' than symbol. A critic suggests Pinter is not concerned with 'human definition' and in this he implicitly denies that the writer need be concerned with 'human fact' at all – nor need he have responsibility to human truth: 'In withholding from his audiences the clear bounding lines of the definition that he knows they come for, Pinter is pursuing a deliberate policy' (Hayman [28], p. 8).

To Pinter 'There are no hard distinctions between what is real and what is unreal, nor between what is true and what false . . .'. But Hayman admits that because of the limits inherent in this there has been a decline in Pinter's later work: 'The plays are thrillers. . . . They work an audience by spreading out the mystification, enjoying it and exploring it for its own sake but never resolving it. . . . After *The Lover* what had been a means becomes an end – and the quality of the work suffers. . . .' (Hayman [28], p. 9).

Pinter's acclaim, however, is based on an insistence that Pinter *is* concerned with human truth. That he writes 'thrillers' and successfully 'exploits the possibilities of television to full' (Hayman) is taken to be an indication of this 'realism'. Along with *The Naked Ape* and *On Aggression*, Pinter's view of man is felt to be deeply and even courageously truthful:

> There is no mystification for the sake of keeping the audience guessing; what mystification there is serves the useful purpose of focusing our attention away from the surface of events and away from casual connections between them, on to the fears and anxieties and aggressions that are expressed in the actions and reactions, the playing and the fighting. We may start off by thinking 'how odd' when Jane undresses, but soon we are following each move in the manoeuvring for superiority as if we were

watching a wrestling match, and the tension is all the greater for the fact that there are no rules in the game – or if Law thinks there are, then Stott knows there is no penalty for breaking them. (Hayman [28], p. 77.)

This paragraph is about *The Basement*, the television play I propose to examine here. First let us examine the significance of the names: Hayman suggests that STOTT is meant to convey 'stoat'. STOTT is perhaps 'animal man', and LAW 'moral 'man. JANE is Lady Jane – the female sexual organ, but, of course, also 'woman' – and so the female element in us – and in Pinter. The play deals with a conflict between these three endo-psychic entities. This play is by no means realistic, and relies for its effect upon stylised symbolism, and so can be interpreted as the dramatisation of psychic entities. It thus provides a good example of the mode which Pinter adopts.

What first rivets the viewer's attention is the vision of JANE undressing, getting into bed naked, and being made love to ('*A gasp from* JANE . . . *A long sigh from* JANE'). From the TAM rating point of view success is guaranteed. But there is a deeper symbolism to Pinter's use of depersonalised sex in this way, a symbolism we can interpret as we did Fairbairn's schizophrenic patient's dream of a stream of milk. While such a symbol expresses our need to be loved and to feel real, it is only expressed in a form which makes it difficult for the need to be fulfilled in a personal way.

The main drama is between the two men. The woman is first of all left outside in the rain, and is only peripheral to their relationship. She must remain a 'partial object' – to be subjected to attack and contempt, kept under control, taken, and humiliated. Much of the exchange between the men is peripheral and trivial, too, in the Pinter fashion of 'oblique' dialogue.

> But it's not dry.
> It's very soft . . .
> I have others . . .

What Pinter captures (we are told) is the obliquity of everyday conversations – or how people 'fail to communicate'. I believe this accomplishment of Pinter's may be seen in another light. When people talk obliquely they are often filling in the exchange in other ways such as facial expression: or they are establishing some contact other than exchange by person-to-person 'frisson'.

Their dialogue is only part of a complex human contact. Pinter separates the dialogue off from this. 'Pinteresque' dialogues are based on a mode in which it is impossible to find meaning in such interpersonal life but only possible to express fear and distrust of this. He is able to recreate the way in which other people's conversations, ordinary everyday conversations, seem grotesque *to us in moments of dissociation*. For instance, if we hear on the telephone that someone is very ill or dead, for the next few minutes, hours, or days the ordinary exchanges of life may seem to us bizarre and even horrible. In the mode he adopts, Pinter 'hears' all ordinary conversations like this: at times he can make grotesque comedy out of this – but it is always cruel. And in that this is what he hears when he is 'diving' it is nightmarish and something like the threatening voices heard by the psychotic in paranoic delusions.

Pinter's accomplishment is to make ordinary conversation seem fearful, threatening, and ominous, and in doing so he adopts a 'schizoid' mode. At the opening of *The Basement* we have besides an ominousness derived from the development of the sense that the two men have shared a 'place' in the past. Here, as in Ian Fleming, there is a deeper symbolism at work: the 'place' is a place in the past of consciousness and identity: 'I was feeling quite lonely, actually. It gets lonely sitting here, night after night. Mind you, I'm very happy here. Remember that place we shared? That awful place . . . I've come a long way since then . . .' – it can be the womb – or, rather, the same origin which the True Self and the False Self, the divided selves, have shared. It is the same symbol as the 'house' or 'room' above.

For LAW Pinter expresses only contempt. He is caricatured as 'ordinary'. He is proud of having bought his flat cash down. He is proud of his high-fi. He 'unbuttons his cardigan'. This 'schizoid superiority' to ordinary life is now a convention. LAW is the human being who is capable of finding satisfaction in normal reparative activities, and he is presented in hate and fear.

In so far as LAW is a normal human being with whom STOTT has shared a place in the past we can, I believe, say that LAW is the father in this symbolic vision. Or to put it in a more useful way, he is the female element in father and mother internalised in a genuine way. He is the true human self, arousing all those problems of emotional conflict, identification, and ambivalence which the False Self seeks to deny. This True Self is the butt of hate in the play – and the subject of *abasement*. Having made this analysis, I believe we can begin to see that Pinter's phantasy is also similar in many ways to that of Fleming. Pinter's work, too, is a 'thriller', based on primitive infantile phantasy. The way JANE undresses bear an obvious relationship to the way girls are magically subject to James Bond's controlling mastery. From my point of view I see this not only as portraying 'stottness', but of subjecting woman, and our universal 'female element', to contempt and humiliation.

Because this is what is being acted out, the audience is riveted by a vision of the primal scene. But the primal scene is de-emotionalised and seen as an act of hate, while LAW remains indifferent in a studied (and schizoid) way as he continues to read his *Persian Manual of Love*. The man in bed with the naked girl is not the father (LAW) but STOTT (the 'real' animal): in this there is a 'side-swipe' at the father such as Bond's at Goldfinger, when, Oedipus-wise he steals his woman and so takes the father's place. The woman is not the object of love as the expression of a personal relationship between individuals: in 'equation' terms she is first undressed herself and shown to the audience as a partial object, and is then humiliated by de-emotionalised possession. There is no 'sharing' or 'meeting' – significantly, the woman 'sighs' – the man does not. The atmosphere is one of psychopathic diminution of affect – no one responds or is allowed to respond in a normal human way except that envy is aroused in the viewer.

Surely, all the audience can feel at such a scene, is envy, for the protagonist, who seems to be having a larger-than-life depersonalised 'feed'. He has supplanted the father with the mother; and is exulting in the triumph of dehumanisation – for not only is LAW unembarrassed: he is unmoved, unjealous, and shows his contempt by the de-emotionalised sexual activity of reading pornography.

Harold Pinter is an extremely clever and effective dramatist, and it would be impossible to cram more 'impact' into such a moment in a play. It is as if the action at this point seeks to convey to us, in the most intensive way, that False Self solutions to the problem of identity are commendable. It is as if the writer is trying to convince himself this: yet, as we shall see, Pinter is also serious enough to allow the deeper needs to lurk in the background to his drama – and the need for love breaks through with its own symbolism.

But in this scene we may find aspects of the trend which has since developed further in the avantgarde theatre, in which by nudity, stage sex, and sadism, a 'black' assault is made on the sensibilities of the audience. There is a history of this mode in the theatre, from Jarry and Artaud to today's blatant obscenities. But we must, I believe, bear in mind the possibility that such 'acting out' which is full of sadism could have the effect of prompting moral inversion: 'Evil be thou my good' – '*long shot of* STOTT *standing on a cliff top* . . .' – as Devil or Anti-hero? (It is noticeable that the Devil has very much come into his own in present-day films, books and plays).

As with Fleming's characters, STOTT is built up as having arcane qualities, conceived in terms of 'compulsive ritual' rather than genuine human qualities: 'Man of great gifts. . . . He has a connection with the French aristocracy. . . He got a First in Sanscrit . . . he owns three chateaux. . . . Have you ever ridden in his Alvis. . . . How pleased I was to see him. After so long. One loses touch . . . so easily.'

As with Fleming, human attributes are conceived of as no more than extraneous fragments of external information about them, of the kind one finds in guide-books, while any dialogue about human matters demanding any depth is flat and dead. Thrusting civilised 'trimmings' aside, what is most real about STOTT is that he is a stoat. The effect of the work is to persuade us that this posture is 'strength' and a fully justified way to sustain the identity.

The evident Oedipal conflict in *The Basement* can be related to the problem of male and female elements, discussed above, which is dramatised in this play. The male in *The Basement* seems to consist of what Guntrip calls 'False Male Doing' while the woman who can 'be' cannot be found.

There is thus great difficulty in the meaning of the play over the consequences of becoming involved in the excitement of the primal scene and in Oedipal feelings, all of which are symbolised in *The Basement* (the 'basement' being the womb, the place where one began, and the 'position' within one where the foundations of identity are.)*

In this play STOTT perhaps represents the 'False Male Doing' of the false solutions of identity based on hate – the aggression of the 'real' animal. LAW is the symbolisation of everyone's awareness that there is a True Self which yearns to be born, associated with the internalisation of the father and in the dimension of 'being'. In the Oedipus conflict there is both a talion threat from the castrating mother, but also perhaps a *fear* that the mother as object will prefer the true to the False Self – the human self to the (hate) self that deals with experience by dehumanising itself. What then? Is it perhaps such a fear that is explored here: but the play finds no confidence in any solution.

The woman begins to respond to the True or 'human' Self over the edge of the bed in which she is making love to the False Self. After all, the True Self yearns to love and be loved – and so to 'be'. So, at him, 'JANE *smiles*'.

But the humiliation of the True Self (LAW) by the False Self proclaimed to be real (STOTT–STOAT) progresses. LAW's pictures are rejected by STOTT

> STOTT *lifts a painting from the wall looks at it.*
> STOTT: No.
> LAW: No, you're quite right. I've never liked it. . . . You're right. They're terrible. . . . Take them down.
> STOTT *begins to take them from the walls.*

We can, I believe, interpret this in terms of the schizoid mode's effect, of reducing symbolism to equation and civilisation to the animal. The effect is to reduce *drama* to

* See Gaston Bachelard in *The Poetics of Space* on the symbolism of house and room, Bachelard [67].

sadistic circus. Normal creativity, which belongs to the female element of the True Self must be humiliated and destroyed. Later when the men fight they do so between bare walls. The normal exchange between the ego and cultural sources of reparation must be reduced by the schizoid mode to something simple, bare, and pure – and inhuman. Only the 'desymbolised' is 'real', as with Kaprow.

Yet, too, there is a yearning to be human. JANE is the (needed) mother: 'JANE *in the kitchen, cooking at the stove, humming,*'

But the yard is now devoid of civilised context: '*The yard is surrounded by high blank walls*'.

While everyone 'deep down' yearns for civilised human contact, as he yearns for love, nothing is more full of dread for us. So, both love and civilised attributes, as in Fleming, can be made to sound ridiculous, along with the quest for maturity, creativity, or True Self being, if we adopt the inversions of schizoid culture.

To the modish followers of his cult, no doubt, Pinter seems to have a strong and un-flinching wisdom about his view of human nature. Yet in the light of philosophical anthropology, his view seems a mark of over-dependence – looked at closely, there is something as infantile as Barrie behind Pinter's emotional coldness. There lurks behind the symbolism the need, as in Barrie, to keep the mother figure eternally within one as a little girl – i.e. in the naive state in which she was conceived in infancy. The awareness of the mother's sexuality has, after all, brought the horrors of talion fear – fear of the castrating woman, of dependence on a woman, and of the weak feminine element in oneself. The woman must be controlled by being the object of contempt – and contempt, too, must be expressed for the feminine attributes: hence the philistinism in Pinter as in Fleming.

There is thus a phantasy need to reduce relationship to that of childhood, and at the same time to portray mature adult living as ridiculous and horrible. What is 'real' is primitive aggression, and the primitive need (such as we find so embarrassingly urgent in James Barrie's *Mary Rose*). This need is, at root, a need to achieve the first stages in confirmation of identity:

> . . . JANE *building a sandcastle* . . .
> LAW: How old are you?
> JANE: I'm very young.
> LAW: You are young. (*He watches her work.*) You're a child. . . .

We may compare Harry the son with Mary Rose his mother on his lap, reduced to a child ghost:

> MARY ROSE: . . . Did you know this house?
> HARRY: When I was a young shaver.
> MARY ROSE: Young? Was it you who laughed?
> HARRY. When was that?
> MARY ROSE (*puzzled*): There was once some one who laughed in this house. Don't you think laughter is a very pretty sound?
> . . .
> MARY ROSE: You are quite old.
> HARRY: I'm getting on.
> MARY ROSE (*confidentially*): Would you mind telling me why every one is so old? I don't know you. do I?
> HARRY: I wonder. Take a look. You might have seen me in the old days – playing about – outside in the garden – or even inside. . . . (*Mary Rose*, pp. 130 ff.)

As has been pointed out in psychoanalytical studies of *Mary Rose*, the 'house' in *Mary Rose* in which the ghost wanders, and over which we have such an uncanny sense of time, can be interpreted both as the mother's body, but also thus the house of the self, the identity, in which the play, as the dramatisation of endopsychic situations and structures, takes place. In Barrie's play he is re-enacting his own relationship with his mother, whose depressions he sought to lift as a small boy by entertaining her. Her depressions seemed to have been brought on by her inability to complete mourning for a lost child, whose ghostly presence was so real to her that she would converse with him. In the play the mother's ghost becomes a powerful presence, and is given final peace by the son on *whose lap she sits as a child*. The room is thus a focus of symbols of the need to find a sense of identity within a self that feels hollow and threatened with emptiness, ghostliness, and annihilation.

Pinter's phantasy houses have something of the same meaning and his dramas generate something of the same uncanny and ghostly magic as *Mary Rose*. Between Harry and Mary there is a conversation about a 'naughty tuft' (= penis) which is heavily suppressed, but which is important in the Oedipus story of the play. Once possessed by the son, Mary is 'free' – and ultimately 'controlled'. In Pinter's play it is often urgently necessary, as Hayman points out, that a woman must be taken *in the house of a rival*, who is thereby humiliated. It is, symbolically, like filling a space that otherwise seems to threaten with deadness.

It is also important in this play that the father must masochistically condone his humiliation: he must be hurt and cringe – like the audience. As Hayman says:

> Both the aggression of the couple, who invade a man's house to make love in it, and the masochistic reaction of the victim are oddly close to what happens in Pinter's screenplay for the film *Accident*. . . . Coming back to his house after a visit to London, Stephen finds that Charlie and Anna have broken in to make love there. Stephen, who desires Anna, seems to be aware of the action as a kind of aggression and he is very angry, but we only hear the anger in the tone of voice he uses to stop Anna from making the bed. He tells her to leave it for the woman who comes in the mornings, but a moment later we see him making it himself. Then, going down the stairs with Charlie, he gives him a key of the house and invites him to use it for the weekend. (Hayman [28], p. 73.)

The 'modish' term 'make love' disguises the real nature of the sexual acts here. So prevalent is the use of primal scene phantasy in our commercial culture that we ourselves fail to see that what is being expressed is not love but hate. What we had better say is 'Charlie and Anna have broken in to make hate there'. That is, the sexual act in this play and its fetishistic objects and sex games, as in so many present-day films and television plays and in the novels of Fleming, are not the expression of a love relationship but rather the focus of intense primitive fears. Sex is a reenactment of the child's vision of parental intercourse in which there is both the manic assertion that one is alive, and yet an intense fear that involvement in the mutual incorporation will bring annihilation. In both these feelings there is a great deal of aggression, aggression which is an assertion of aliveness, and aggression exerted against the dread of going out of existence through the agency of the talion mother or the more terrifying 'combined parents'. Hate is thus thrust into others to counter a fear they will empty or implode oneself sexual aggression and 'bad thinking' will serve in this. These schizoid impulses have been adopted by our culture.

It is anxiety about this aggression, this hate, in which the problem of identity is focused, which television and cinema have learnt to exploit. Looked at in sociological terms this is disturbing because we have a society which seems to grow increasingly inhuman and in which the individual feels increasingly insignificant. In this state he feels increasingly at the mercy of his own primitive fears and of annihilation, and need to find these actual human contacts by which he can be reassured that he will not be destroyed by the phantasy 'others' of his own paranoia. He needs a deeper sense of what it is to be human – such as truly creative art can give him.

But he does not get this. Instead he gets that kind of 'impact' which writers have devised for distribution through the crude machine media – a kind of equation-symbol 'impact' that hooks into this very identity-anguish itself, drives the individual back to primitive phantasies, and impels him towards primitive solutions such as the impulse to resort to infantile aggression, to feel real by desperate means.

This regression is meanwhile vindicated by the homunculism which implies that beneath the 'veneer' of our civilised life there is only animal aggressiveness so that the expression of hate is only realistic. Hayman links the aggression in Pinter's sexual scenes with the violence in his plays, but sees this exploitation of aggression as acceptable social criticism:

> There is also a parallel between the games that are played in the film (*Accident*) and the games in *The Basement*. In both, aggressions are brought into a new kind of focus. In the tennis in the film, there is a kind of balance between the geniality on the surface and the violence which only sometimes breaks through, as if by accident, but the extraordinary game that the dinner-jacketed guests play with the cushion is openly violent. . . . The scene makes a very valid point about the aggressive competitiveness inherent in this sort of sociality. (Hayman [28], p. 73–74.)

We can, I believe, look at this in another way. The 'aggressive competitiveness' in our society can be associated with the way in which we have attached the problem of identity to 'False Male Doing' as the basis of ego-strength. But this is not all there is to be said about our kind of society, because most individuals are in touch with their True Selves and the area of being. They achieve ego-maintenance, they obtain deep satisfactions from reparation, they are able to enjoy their 'female element' despite the shortcomings of our culture. Most individuals, even in our society, and despite the prevalent existential frustration, are not living on the brink of such a threat of ego-weakness that they fear they will go to pieces or go out of existence.

In the fashionable schizoid mode, however, it is assumed that everyone is living on the brink of loss of existence, and so all those normal forms of play, aggression, contact, meeting, and symbolism by which normal (or 'manic-depressive') individuals feel real and alive seem not only irrelevant but even menacing and terrible just, as (normal) conversation seems insane. We need 'ruthless confrontation' to feel real: but it also terrifies us because we know deep down it is the expression of weakness. If we were to resort to normal exchanges, on the other hand, these might involve such terrors of loss of identity, of implosion, of aggression getting out of hand and consuming others, and of the wrecking of our world, that we must needs stave off these dreads by making an aggressive attack first.

Three major ploys in this counter-aggression are (1) to obviate normal (dangerous) symbolism by regression to symbolic equation, (2) to express contempt for normal human existence – and so (3) to seek to control others because they are dangerous. A writer like Pinter takes over these attitudes of the schizoid mode from the implications about human dialogue in the way he caricatures it in his dialogue, to his depersonalisation of sex and his implicit attitude that what is 'real' about man is his savagery. This even leads him to attempt to control others and attack and humiliate woman wherever possible because woman is the symbol of all that is vulnerable in oneself.

The Basement can be read as an enactment of these ploys, partly in symbolic dramatisation of inner conflict, partly in the regression to symbolic equation.

Subtly, human civilised achievements are derided by conversations in which normal accomplishments are reduced to meaninglessness as they might be in an insane conversation in a mental hospital:

> STOTT: She's charming, isn't she? . . .
> LAW: Very helpful, of course, around the house –
> STOTT: Plays the harp, you know.
> LAW: Well?
> . . .
> LAW: . . . You don't find she's lacking in maturity?

A London audience, brought up on Pinter, obviously, would laugh raucously and destructively. What matters is the use of the woman as partial object: the first thing she does is to undress. That she 'comes from rather a splendid family' is starkly irrelevant: all that belongs to the sphere of being human, as is being 'charming'. The cold exchanges are, of course, devoid of any human feeling – love or jealousy – and of any human meaning. Culture, the capacity to play a harp, the capacity to be domestically engaged, are reduced to a psychotic meaninglessness – we might be listening to a mental patient giving his talk on how to fly celery to London in airships. Thus 'You don't find she is lacking in maturity?' raises the biggest and most hebephrenic laugh of all, for the growth of human personality is made utterly irrelevant and futile.

The audience's attention is riveted on the sexual act with the dissociated 'stream of milk', and it seems to them only ridiculous to discuss the *human* attributes of such a partial object. The object is exposed to utter ridicule in case there be any suggestion that she could be found as human. Whether or not LAW has a harp is more important: and, of course, the harp has its own symbolism. The 'reality' is the function of the sexual organs symbolised by the harp. There is never to be any meeting of persons.

The next brief episode returns to the primal scene, but this time with LAW as the protagonist. He is resisting, because they can be *seen*.

> *Exterior. Beach. Summer. Day.*
> LAW *and* JANE *lying in the sand.* JANE *caressing him.*
> JANE (*whispering*) Yes, yes, yes, oh you are, oh you are, oh you are.
> LAW: We can be seen.
> JANE: Why do you resist? How can you resist?
> LAW: We can be seen! Damn you!

If we see LAW as the True Self or moral self, then what is happening is that this self is being seduced but resists. This could be a true recognition of the fearfulness of the True Self in making love to woman. If we see STOTT as the son-protagonist and LAW as the father-protagonist, this can be interpreted in terms of the paternal relationship being felt to be a betrayal of the son–mother relationship. Because he adopts the schizoid mode, Pinter does not accept a creative role: he dwells exclusively on primal scene anxiety and 'bad thinking', unmodified by attention to the realities of human make-up and relationship. Earlier JANE looks over the edge of the bed in which she is making love to STOTT and smiles at LAW. This conveys the schizoid view that woman is treacherous, and a confusion as to whether STOTT or LAW is the 'True Self'. But the scene that follows, in which there is an undercurrent of menace, emerges from our primitive need to phantasy the primal scene out of curiosity, as a child does. The curiosity is not only dangerous but it also contains elements of 'magical hate looking': we have considered this 'radar scanning' element in Fleming.

There follows a scene in which, again, the normal conversation is made to seem tremendously threatening, as it does, perhaps to a child involved in talion fears of its parents' sexual life. He senses the primitive emotions under the surface, so powerful that everything that is said seems both ominous and yet futile and irrelevant.

> STOTT: This was one of our old haunts, wasn't it, Tim? This was one of our haunts. Tim was always my greatest friend, you know. Always. He's marvellous. I've found my old friend again – (*looking at* JANE). And discovered a new. And you like each other so much. It's really very warming.

The unconscious elements aroused by the primal scene phantasy involve feelings about the 'True Self', and its relationship or identification with the father (LAW), which self has been 'found again'. Finding this self involves coming to terms with the father's relationship with the mother, and the relationship between male and female in oneself. But this 'reconciliation' has already been prejudged, and predetermined by a convention that must reject it. The impulse is to deny the True Self, and to turn on this 'reconciliation' the bitterest irony: 'It's marvellous . . . It's really very warming.'

Relationship between human beings, or between the genuinely human elements within oneself, must be exposed to the bitterest anti-human contempt because the prevalent mode denies our weakness of identity: LAW says 'Same again? (*To* WAITER) same again. (*To* JANE) Same again? (*To* WAITER) Same again. The same again, all round. Exactly the same.'

Life goes on in its futile way, always the same. Sexual intercourse from a point of view blind to its personal, or 'being', significance is 'the same' – a dull repetitive round, like impingement. Reparation and creative achievement, towards true strength of identity, are impossible. We drink the same again, as we function in the same way, again and again. Under the surface is the feeling continually harped on in this convention, that, while one must have recourse to sexual activity, in the absence of growing meaning in love to which this activity can contribute, the sexual activity, since it is 'taking' from a 'partial object', is always 'same again'. As with the seductions of the pervert for whom the object is never a person, never recognised outside the *huis clos* of his ego-centricity, this 'same again' feeling goes with a desperate insatiability.

The ethos obliges the writer to vindicate aggression, sadism, and 'False Self' activity, as the basis of identity. Able to portray positive human 'meeting' only with hopeless contempt he feels it hardly necessary to seek to vindicate this view, let alone search for alternative possibilities. STOTT changes his drink: he will be 'different'. And his direction is different from all those 'bouts with Laforgue', the 'great elms', the cricket and squash. As with Fleming, though Pinter does not bore us by telling us how to play them, these are but tags attached to 'civilised living' out of encyclopedias: they are essentially meaningless activities. What has meaning is the justification of hate:

> STOTT: . . . You were pretty hot stuff at squash, you know.
> LAW: You were unbeatable.
> STOTT: Your style was deceptive.
> LAW: It still is. (LAW *laughs*.) It still is!
> STOTT: Not any longer. . . . (*The* WAITER *serves the drinks. Silence.* STOTT *lifts his glass.*)

The protagonist is happy in his hate – in his hate-solutions to the problem of identity and in his schizoid sense of superiority. STOTT can triumph over LAW without rising from his seat. 'Real animal' hate can defeat 'moral' man without effort: 'we will have no weakness or tenderness . . .'. Strength can triumph over weakness: so when STOTT and LAW run a race in Pinter's phantasy LAW, 'going fast, turns to look for STOTT; off balance, stumbles, falls, hits his chin on the ground.' STOTT didn't run.

Humiliation is rubbed in:

LAW: Why didn't you run?
      Exterior. Field.)
(JANE *stands, scarf in hand. Downfield* STOTT *stands.* LAW *lies on the grass.* LAW's *voice.*)
LAW: Why didn't you run?

Such a writer as Pinter, I believe, does not even see the extent to which his adopted view of man is imprisoned in a schizoid mode. Only from philosophical anthropology can we see how his play does not give humanness a chance.

So any objections to the *ménage a trois* are ridiculed. LAW asks, 'Don't you think it's a bit crowded in that flat, for the three of us?' STOTT replies, 'Not at all'. The only objections that are allowed, in LAW's mouth, possible objections from the 'Council' while moral objections are ridiculed in an afterthought: 'The Town Council, I know for a fact, would feel it incumbent upon itself to register the strongest possible objections. And so would the Church. . . .'

Religious objections to the dehumanization inherent in the relationship between LAW, STOTT, and JANE are dismissed as ridiculous by this trick of caricature in which they are equated with pompous officialdom and the hygienic concern with overcrowding, on the one hand, and ineffectual organised religion on the other. These are the only objections. There can be no other objection.

The joke disguises the mounting aggression and menace in the subsequent bizarre sexual and aggressive phantasy. LAW suddenly throws gramophone records against the wall. STOTT and JANE '*naked, climb into bed*". We may reflect upon the nature of a cultural manifestation in which, in such an atmosphere of menacing hate, a writer–actor takes the part of a character representing animal hate and climbs naked into bed with a girl stripped of her personal qualities, while another character who seems to be full of hidden aggression, sits by and picks up the poker and pokes the dying fire.

The 'moral' man, True Self, LAW, is left only able to 'poke' embers: the False Self is the strong man, incorporating the partial object for all to see and envy.

The impact through the medium is guaranteed at every step of the hate-cycle:

(JANE *is sitting at the iron table.*
STOTT *approaches.* . . .
He bends over her, attempts to touch her.
She moves her body away from him)

– everything happens in a terrifying indifference, as if everyone were petrified and speaking only in a trance. Anything which is presented as belonging to the normal kind of development between human beings is caricatured:

Interior. Cave by the sea. . . .
(LAW *and* JANE. . . .
She bends and whispers to him.)
JANE: Why don't you tell him to go? We had such a lovely home. We had such a cosy home. It was so warm. Tell him to go. It's your place. Then we could be happy again. Like we used to. Like we used to. In our first blush of love. Then we could be happy again, like we used to. We could be happy again. Like we used to.

As with 'same again', the intention here is to make love and object-constancy seem futile and ridiculous, by the repetition, the use of 'cosy', and the vapid phrase 'In our first blush of love'. It is meant to convey something like James Joyce's (schizoid) remark 'When I hear the word love I want to puke'. At the same time it is a nostalgic retrospect, with a sentimentality evocative of Barrie, of mummy talking to daddy about the time before STOTT arrived to change everything.

Delving more deeply into the primal scene, the play now explores our dark primitive awareness of this dreadful phantasy. The father penetrates the mother, and so explores the faeces within her: so, her 'betrayal' of the son's love filthies everything. The relation of the object to the True Self involves loss of contents and other threats to the identity: so, it is far less pure than a relationship to the hate self. So Pinter makes LAW speak of defilement in betrayal.

> LAW (*whispering very deliberately*): She betrays you. She betrays you. She has no loyalty. After all you've done for her. Shewn her the world. Given her faith. You've been deluded. She's a savage. A viper. She sullies this room. She dirties this room. All this beautiful furniture. . . .

The effect of this strange speech is to suggest that any real human relationship is 'dirtying' (i.e. involving danger from the faeces inside mummy), and it also invites our sympathy for STOTT. Pinter's lack of human perspective is obvious if we compare the fact that STOTT obviously has nothing but contempt for JANE, as he shows by the way he treats her. Yet LAW says 'after all you have done for her. Shewn her the world. Given her faith.' These are strange remarks. But they serve to contribute to the Stoatman's over-valuation of his own altruism, and at the same time contribute to the need here to show all reparative activity and love as meaningless, because these were originally rejected in the mother. Moreover, the passage reveals that even LAW is capable of 'giving himself up to the joys of hating', which is the basic impulse of the schizoid mode in drama.

The effect of this revelation of the 'defiling' effects of the woman's disloyalty is shown in this primitive phantasmagoria to be fatal – or almost fatal – to STOTT – just as the infant dreads the fatal effects of parental intercourse and his knowledge of parental intercourse. But since everything in this schizoid phantasy is de-emotionalised, so is the response to death:

> LAW: And now he's dying. Are you heartbroken?
> JANE: Yes.
> LAW: So am I.
>   (*Pause.*)
> JANE: What shall we do with the body.
> LAW: Body? He's not dead yet. Perhaps he'll recover.
> (*They stare at each other.*)
> *Interior. Room. Night.*
> (LAW *and* JANE *in a corner, snuffling each other like animals.*)

When Pinter, acting 'pure' STOTT, climbs naked into bed with JANE, this is presented with a statuesque simplicity – it is hate made clean. Here the play turns a contrasting contempt – arising from fear – upon the contrasting 'animal' sex of the father and mother, of True Self and object, of normal sexuality, which repels us because of its dangerous complexity – and humanness. This hatred the play now unleashes in a sequence in which he gives free rein to symbolic equation assault on the audience. The audience by now has its primitive feelings aroused. Pinter maintains, like Fleming, a 'civilised' gloss, by his setting ('*The walls are hung with tapestries, an oval Florentine mirror, an oblong Italian master.*') – and one could be deceived into believing that Pinter is expos-ing the truth of our 'real' nature beneath the civilised exterior. But the civilised setting is a bluff: a mask of hate.

For what the play is really doing is *acting out*, as a psychotic does, the conviction that False Self activity is strength. LAW plays a flute: he is female element sensitivity. He has only this weak flute to defend himself with. LAW first '*bites into a grape*' – he is masterful (strength through joy) and then tosses the bowl of fruit across the room. 'JANE *rushes to collect it*'. She is one of those eminently controllable female acolytes in the phantasy world of those contemporary writers who fear femininity. And then, under the guise of playing cricket (civilised), STOTT hurls large *marbles*. Marbles are a child's playthings; but they are also petrified – and in terms of primitive phantasy of the infant we can say they are petrified faecal projectiles. They crash into windows and hurt LAW. LAW defends himself only to cast one into a fish-tank. '(*The tank smashes. Dozens of fish swim across the marble tiles.*)'

The dreaded creative power of the father's sexuality is destroyed: his seed is wasted. '(JANE, *in the corner, applauds.*)'

LAW, ridiculously now, 'waves his flute in acknowledgement'. STOTT bowls again: '(*Marble crashes into* LAW'*s forehead. He drops.*)'

The schizoid phantasy progresses further and drops all pretences of being about human beings interacting: '(*The room is completely bare*)' – the inner world in which this psychodrama is being acted out is devoid of all hope in terms of cultural or human solutions. There can only be ferocity between elements of the self – ruthless confrontations – in which the outcome is prejudged.

> (LAW'*s face, sweating.*
> STOTT'*s face, sweating.* . . .
> *The broken milk bottle, in shaking hands almost touching.*
> *The broken milk bottles fencing, not touching.* JANE *stirring milk, sugar and coffee in the cups.*
> *The broken milk bottles, in a sudden thrust, smashing together.*
> *Record turning on a turn table. Sudden music.*
> *Debussy's 'Girl with the Flaxen Hair'.*)

The clash of *milk-bottles* is now crosscut with the girl making milky coffee. The symbolism at this point is revealing, and recalls Fairbairn's 'The schizoid individual, deep down, needs to love and be loved'. For despite the 'lovemaking' the conflict over the girl is not a conflict between adults for a mate, but an attempt to rediscover the mother who is desperately needed. Throughout, apart from the moment with LAW when she smiles, tries to seduce him, and urges him to 'get 'rid' of STOTT, this girl never behaves like a real person at all. She is coldly indifferent, and remains as impersonal as the dream stream of milk. At the end, while the men are duelling with broken milk bottles, she is coldly standing by making a milk-feed. The broken milk bottles symbolise a desperate need for, dependence on, the stream of milk. The clashing of milk bottles symbolises the hate that must be relied upon as a source of identity which has not been developed from a genuine source of love in nourishment by a truly loving woman. The girl's milk-feed is the love deeply desired under the surface – and so the sense of the 'need to love' breaks through even the schizoid mode.

There is no resolution: after the clash of broken bottles we dissolve to a record of Debussy's *Girl with the Flaxen Hair*. Somewhere behind this music, somewhere behind the broken milk-bottles, somewhere behind the naked JANE, somewhere behind the milky coffee, there is, or should be, Pinter feels, the true object, the real feed, the real love. But it can only be gestured at and he is hopeless of ever attaining it because he is imprisoned in his chosen mode.

Rather he has settled for the false (hate) solution to the problem – and so all he can do is to expose to the *audience* the clashing broken ends of two milk-bottles. The play must expose to the audience, through symbolic equation, treachery, derision of reparation, the insolent touching of a breast, a woman climbing into bed naked, a marble smashing into the forehead of the True Self, a sigh and a gasp from a woman in a depersonalised sexual act, and other such depersonalising phantasies. They feel a 'strong' sadism.

What is extraordinary about the whole mode is its successful exclusion of all positive, or 'true self', human attributes. The possibilities of shame, pity, jealousy, modesty, love, emotional surrender are all obliterated by being submerged in the 'diminution of affect' and the denial of humanness. The mode does not even allow creative symbolism to develop: what the play must make is such an impact on the audience that they it endorses our STOTTness, and vindicates the assault on LAW, and all the human values caricature in LAW. In this conflict between True and False Self the odds are made to look even – as by the symmetry of the broken milk-bottles. There is no outcome, but only an endless conflict by violence, by which alone one can feel real. Yet, as we have seen, the play is given a considerable slant by which the False STOTT Self is felt to be the most real and is preferred. The apparent futility of the end seems not really meant. What is meant, it seems, is conveyed at the moment when the whole thing begins again. '(LAW *wearing* STOTT's *raincoat.*)'

True Self and False Self are the same. Hate is the same as love. The hated father is the same as the son who annihilates and supplants him. As in *Goldfinger*, the symbolic annihilation of the father clears the way for phantasy possession of the mother: but now the episode is to be repeated in a talion way.

But there is no possession, and no discovery of what it is to be human: there is only the futile ballet of hate and dissociation – the 'bad' dream conflict by which the False Self is sustained. *There is only the preservation of one's own ego* by ruthless confrontation, and for this it is necessary to grind the faces of others, as through television plays which exploit 'impact' to the full. Those who respond must yield up a little of their own humanness in order to confirm that our culture is right to insist that false solutions in hate are the only possible ones.

Surely the effect of such art must in the end be that we shall entirely be swallowed into its maw, in which all human values are inverted or dissolved and the anti-human is triumphant. Again we can find Winnicott's phrase apt – the success of such work represents 'morality at its lowest ebb' – not because the plays are 'immoral' but because every technique involved has the effect of turning us against our humanity and to become involved in a state of dissociation in which positive emotion, reparative effort, creative meeting, and the quest for identity and a sense of meaning seem futile and meaningless. Here is homunculist nihilism in the arts indeed.

Pinter's plays are serious works. But they have set the stage for further developments which follow him into this chosen mode, and this threatens to reduce the world to one in which there is no human truth ('there are no hard distinctions between what is real and what is unreal, nor between what is true and what false'). Yet surely this is to deny creative human realities?

From the point of view of the schizoid diagnosis we can thrust away the 'realism' of the homunculism which Pinter has taken from a schizoid culture and ask why a critic such as Hayman assumes that Pinter is correct when he proclaims there is 'no penalty' for aggressive attack. From our point of view it is not that a penalty has to be paid for violence, but that a penalty is already paid, because we have become involved in the false solutions of hate. There is another penalty which is that in so far as we cease to respond, to feel, to choose, and to act in a moral way, as LAW, we become inhuman. To forfeit belief in our potentialities – this is both the penalty Pinter has paid in his work, and the penalty we pay for Pinter, by accepting such schizoid modes in art.

Moreover, in so far as we pay Pinter the tribute of attention such as we pay to culture, we are trapped in his destructive attack, not only on human nature, *but on symbolism itself*. The work of Pinter and others who adopted the schizoid mode has led to that reduction of the theatre to the level of the brothel and sadistic exhibition such as we have now on *Oh! Calcutta! I Was Hitler's Maid, The Dirtiest Show in Town, Dynamo*, and *Do It*.

Everything that appears on the screen in *The Basement* is less a symbol in a creative work of art than a means of using the hallucinatory power of equation symbolism on an audience. Pinter is the perfect hypnotist for the TAM rating – the perfect writer for a mechanical culture – because while his work acts out hate, he is able to gain acclaim for this very hate as 'realism'. There is a sense in which the best material for television – if impact is the criterion – would be the exhibition of lunatics, and of psychopathological acts of hate such as executions – a truth which television implicitly recognises by some of its own choices and which manifestation is now invading both cinema and stage.

CHAPTER 24

The Manic and Voracious Camera:
Hate in Film

FOLLOWING my examination of Fleming and Pinter, it seems natural to go on to consider film and photography for a while. These seem to demand special attention when we are examining the nature of present-day culture, since these have become, together with television, the predominant arts of our time. They are also *machine* arts. From my point of view film is one of the most startling of all contemporary phenomena in the field of culture because, while it seems to be associated with far more than its fair share of hate, the response of the public is more inclined than with any other manifestation to accept this hate and see it as good and beautiful.

Moreover, there is a curious contradiction, as we shall see, in the attitudes of those who make films. If we attack the implications of a film about, say, human nature, they will tell us that 'this is art' – that is, they claim the autonomy of creative individuals. If, however, we examine their attitudes to their own work we often find that they take no responsibility for all that activity of selection and symbolism in which any creative person finds himself engaged. They pretend that they merely 'point the camera at life'. They do not even take the responsibility for the directions in which they point it, and the symbolism of their conceptions, cutting, and editing. Obviously, there seems to be some deep problem over symbolism in the world of film.

We can approach these problems with other questions in mind. Why should film reviewing often seem so much to belong to an ethical world of its own? Why should film magazines, for example, more than any other journals, come to contain small advertisements offering exchanges of perversions? Why should film and television be so increasingly preoccupied with the observation of physical love-making ('the bare breast has come to stay')? Why should the film world be so much one of multiple and unstable relationships and have more than its fair share of divorce and suicide? Why should the film world be so corrupt? Why should film and television focus so obsessively on the sexual act?

We can, I believe, answer some of these questions in the light of the schizoid diagnosis. The world of film – film making, film promotion, and film reviewing – seems by its nature to involve people in schizoid modes. Here, particularly, can be illustrated that exhibitionism which has been substituted for giving; here there can be portrayed that larger than life manic denial of deadness which the individual who has such difficulty in feeling real needs so desperately. Here, eminently, we find the depersonalised stream of milk instead of the person, the 'shown' partial object instead of a whole human being.

The camera seems itself to suggest schizoid modes because of the symbolism of the film's essential mechanism – the camera 'eye'. The camera is an instrument of 'taking' and a shot is called a 'take'.

The eye, as we gather from psychoanalytical case histories and theory, has a special significance in terms of that bodily symbolism which is associated in infancy with the growth of consciousness. The eye is associated with the mouth and other orifices, and is both a means of 'taking things into oneself' and a way of seeking to exert one's power over others and over the world. We talk about 'feasting our eyes' while lovers 'hunger' for the sight of one another ('Drink to me only with thine eyes').

The child feels that sex is a kind of eating, and this connection between sex and incorporation continues to be felt throughout life. Sexual hunger and eating are associated with the eye which (as Winnicott points out) is a symbolic organ of incorporation. The voyeur feasts his eyes on an 'object for consumption', and 'devours'. In the phrase 'the evil eye' we have a recognition that we have a desire that 'looks could kill' – if our hallucinatory magic could work. In some uses of film it seems possible for this visual hate to be acted out, either by 'taking' or by visual rape. (As Frankl points out in his *The Doctor and the Soul*, schizophrenic patients often have a feeling they are being filmed).

How people become involved in some strange kind of depersonalisation around a film seemed to me to be suggested in a student study of the making of a film by Harold Pinter. *The Servant* was made from a script written from a novel by Michael Anderson. From what Pinter says it is clear that no one quite knows, even when the film is finished, what the intention was:

> Q.: *When he telephones Vera, is this merely because he wants to sleep with her, or because he wants to use her?*
> PINTER: I think by far the major point there is that he wants to sleep with her. I think at the back of his mind is the possibility that she could be an ally in the house. . . .

Pinter discusses a character for whom he is responsible *as if he were a character in life whose motives he could only guess at:* 'I think . . . I think':

> Q.: *In the restaurant-scene, there are three very intense conversations going on, and yet, when the camera withdraws from each pair, and focuses on the next, we can see the pair we have just been listening to, by now seeming to speak very politely and formally and easily, despite their fraughtness. Was this what you had in mind in this scene?*
> PINTER: No, I think that's really Losey's arrangement there, which I think is indeed very fine. I only wrote the conversation between the people. *I didn't know how he was going to treat it.* As you know, I took part in the scene myself, and I didn't know what he was doing with the others. We were all rather drunk, actually, on the day we did it. The drink was real. *But I didn't know how he was going to do it.* . . . (My italics.)

The creation of a film, as so often, appears very much a spur-of-the-moment free-for-all. In the absence of a single reparative impulse in one guiding creative intelligence, those concerned seem to exploit any sensational potentiality – without accepting responsibility.

> Q.: *Were you anxious not to make the James Fox character too sympathetic?*
> PINTER: Well, I don't understand this. May I just say on it that I don't understand what the word 'sympathetic' means. I am just concerned with what people are, with accuracy. If you want to sympathize with that . . . fine, if you feel that you can merely observe it . . . fine. *I'm not concerned with sympathy.* (My italics).
> Q.: . . . *which is merely audience reaction?*
> PINTER: I must tell you one thing, by the way, which might interest you. Someone said to me a little while ago – they didn't understand the film – 'Why, after they came back from the pub, why

didn't they go out, why did they stay in the house?' And this is what you mean. They didn't. They stayed in the house. 'But why didn't they, why?' I found this very odd, actually. If you don't understand why they stay in the house, then you don't understand the film at all. They stayed because they stayed.

Q.: *Things happen because they happen?*

PINTER: That's it, you can say that again.

Q.: *There's no other reason for it. People are always anxious to interpret films, whereas they should in fact just watch them.*

PINTER: I agree. I certainly think so. No, I think Joe Losey would be the first to admit this. He has occasionally made certain statements about the film expanding it in other terms, which I think he actually thinks twice about. And I personally would make no claims for the film in other terms. I would merely say that this is a film about two men – and that this is what takes place.

Here we have a strangely withdrawn dissociation, combined with an indicative attitude of superiority to those who do not 'understand'. For us to 'understand' the film, apparently, requires that we should accept that 'things happen because they happen': that is, we must accept a perverse confusion of what is created with 'reality'. There is evident here, even, a form of 'concrete thinking'. In fact, Pinter has (as he admits) selected, altered, and interpreted the events which happen in the film ('I modified and developed to a certain extent the first script'). He is thus creatively responsible for the events, the persons, and the implicit attitude to life – the *meaning*. Pinter discusses later the differences in the economy where words are concerned, between writing for film and stage, and so shows that he recognises this fact. To disclaim responsibility on the grounds that 'things happen because they happen' when you have *made* them happen (symbolically) is untenable – except to an individual who has adopted the prevalent dissociation in cultural modes.

The situation in which such a film is made seems to provide the opportunity for a kind of conspiracy in which symbols can be exploited without any reference to human truth or creative ends: the ends are again, to do with 'impact'.

Significantly, the producer, Joseph Losey, approaches his human situation from a preoccupation with depersonalised symbols: speaking of his film *Eve* he says:

> ... seen it as I made it – but I used mirrors in *Eve* conspicuously from certain different points of view. In the first place the waters of Venice is a sexual symbol, not overtly so but it seems to me so apt a sexual symbol that it has its effect even if you're not using it as conscious symbolism. And also in Venice the water is something that is very much taken up by mirrors, it is always being reflected in the mirrors, and the broken surface of the water when it's at all rough or when there's any kind of movement in the water is reflected in the many-faceted aspects of the Venetian mirrors, in chandeliers and the Venetian glassware in general. I found that I was having an enormous number of mirror shots in *Eve* for these reasons, and also because I consciously, very consciously was trying to show the audience something about the reversal of sexes, the male element in the female, the female element in the male, and the constant reversal of male-female conventional positions and attitudes between Tyvian and Eve. So I used the mirror sometimes to continue this reversal thing, or to emphasise it, and sometimes to spin the audience around so that they wouldn't know where they were. ...

While the symbolism obviously has some meaning for Losey, the absence of creative control is obvious in his gestures '*something* about the reversal of sexes' and '*so they wouldn't know where they were*': what in fact the effect of the rather precious camera work is to involve the audience in something like depersonalisation. The same effect seems apparent when Losey makes the *house* a leading character in *The Servant*: the characters are subservient to a non-human entity: house significantly emptied of woman:

> In *The Servant* I wanted to present the house as a character all the way through the picture and I wanted to present it first as a rather naked character, naked except for the remnants of previous generations that had lived there and left their false partitions and their bits of wallpaper and their

coats of paint on the mahogany stair rail and so on. Then I wanted to show the house as he finished it, and then finally to show it as it becomes vulgarised by the servant when he exerts his own personality over it.

The character of the house surely symbolises hostility to woman and dependence? The 'room' is a symbol of the identity in which there is a clash between male and female elements:

> Q.: *Was there meant to be any relation between the pictures on the walls and the pictures on the cards?*
> PINTER: No, the house was supposed to have about it a kind of man's club feeling of leather and military prints and oil portraits, and the kind of formality and masculinity which a woman hadn't in any way invaded until she came in with her chintzes and her spice racks.

As the interview proceeds it becomes evident that the producer thinks of his art in terms of making an impact on the audience. To do is to subject his audience to 'symbolic equation' attack. The abrogation of creative responsibility goes with this, and it is as if any hate expressed is not 'his' but 'art's'. So, even in the most significant episodes, he speaks of *guessing what was in the minds of the characters*. So we have a script writer who refuses to take responsibility for what he selects as truth about what the character's intensions were and a producer who merely guesses at what is going on. Each behaves as if they were powerless before the 'life' they are recording – when in truth the picture of life is one they have created.

> Q.: *Why exactly does Susan kiss Barrett at the end?*
> LOSEY: Well I think 'exactly' is the wrong word because she doesn't kiss him exactly for any reason, she kisses him because she doesn't know what to do or what she's going to do until she does it, and when she does kiss him it seemed always to me that it was a mixture of things. In the first place it was probably a deliberate attempt to provide a reaction out of the boy, to bring him through his degradation and his lethargy by provoking him into some kind of an action, and all she gets from him is a kind of sick tittilation. It is probably also, although certainly not consciously, an attempt maybe to join him in the sense of degrading herself, and there possibly was an element of attraction-repulsion, although as soon as the kiss is joined the repulsion is the only thing that is active. I said not 'exactly' because I don't think there was any precise intention on her part, she had to do something, she was lost, she didn't know what to do: she was in physical contact with the man who had physically affronted her, blown smoke in her face, and laughed at her, and who had physically offended against every kind of decency code in relation to the fiancé. He just had humiliated him on the bed with the tie, and had been excessively insolent and rude to her: and when she's up against this kind of physical force she used a physical thing.

The woman as symbol in the imaginative work is being used to express the fashionable fear of emotional surrender, of 'giving' and relationship. They adopt a deliberate mode, but this is masked by the elaborate pretence that they are not responsible for such symbolism. They talk of her ('probably also, although certainly not consciously . . .') as if she were real. And at the same time disclaim any intentions for her – though Losey himself directed the actress ('it seemed . . . to me', 'probably a deliberate . . .' 'probably also', 'there possibly was', 'I don't think there was any precise intention *on her part*').

If the 'intentions' of a character are not defined in the novel, or by the script-writer, or by the producer, *where are they?* That is, if she is a symbol, who is employing this symbol, to what end? The mode of collaboration that is used in such a film recognises no such problems. Increasingly, we have films that are more and more disturbing – yet more and more irresponsible. The members of this team speak as though all they had to do was to film something that already existed (yet they have created it). With no controlling creative intention the audience is left in the dark deliberately in order to have its nose rubbed in the hate:

> So, a lot of people find the end sequence a bit much to take, and in a way this is what I intended because I wanted them not to be able to find any comfortable answer to the picture, not to dismiss it

simply on the grounds that it was about homosexuals and therefore didn't relate to them in any way. *I wanted to grind their noses in it in a kind of way* ... *I wanted the scene to be almost unendurable* so that there could be no easiness about the resolution in the film at all. Now I think a lot of people say they don't like the end sequence, and they wished it had stopped earlier because they can't take it, because it is too difficult, because it is too personal, because it doesn't give them any easy answers, but that's precisely what I wanted. (My italics.)

There follows some antagonism to 'intellectual' people as if there were individuals who threatened to find out for themselves what is really happening. What is interesting is what is revealed by the need to make the last scene 'almost unendurable' by 'grinding their noses in it' – with intentions about the meaning of characters and actions so vague as we have seen. There is only one guiding concern, which is to humiliate the audience, because this is the cultural mode the public is supposed to demand. In this approach humanness inevitably suffers. Relationship is presented always in a schizoid way, as if it were possible for individuals to treat one another as part objects without human value, without consequences to their essential relational needs.

> Q.: *I wasn't quite sure how Vera felt about Tony.*
> LOSEY: Well I think she thought he was a very pretty and attractive young man, and it probably gave her a slight kick to be with a man as handsome as that and as upper-class. She was slightly contemptuous of him – as she says, 'You can't have it on a plate for ever'; but I suppose in her way she probably never had it so good, as they say. And so then when they were fired – she was brought into the house as a convenience by the servant and not necessarily as a plot – Hugo and 'Alright baby, you're on your own', you know, 'go find your own food'. So she had a very rough time and I suppose she looked back on her affair with Tony as something that gave her shelter, protection, security and she wanted to come back. I never thought of her coming back as a calculated thing or as part of a plot, she was coming asking for help. She hasn't seen Hugo since he dumped her and she finds him there, and this throws her. He's going to fling her out because his first reaction is that she'll get in the light, and then when he sees that again it's going to give him more power over the master rather than less, he suddenly has the idea 'Well why not bring her back in and I can sleep with her too, and everything will be fine'. It's a further step, but none of the things that the servant does, or that she does, are really calculated. I mean he intended to bring her from Manchester because he was sleeping with her there and it was convenient that way, but I don't think that he at first anticipated that he was going to bring her into the master's bed too, though he was amused when it happened.

Towards the end of the interview what shows through is an anti-human contempt for those who are 'afraid of not being loved or not loving': those who seek to find their humanity confirmed in relationship:

> Q.: *But in fact he (Tony) is totally weak, isn't he?*
> LOSEY: Well he wasn't setting out to dominate, but that class doesn't set out to dominate, it just does, it's there. Totally weak? He was totally weak in the sense that he was totally selfish, that he was only interested in serving his own appetites, which even if he did so gracefully and elegantly it still is the same thing. I don't ever think of a character, though, as totally bad or totally good, totally weak, totally anything: I think that in this particular picture the servant, the master and the fiancé, and even the maid, are all products and victims of the same thing, and there should be compassion for each of them at various moments. It may seem strange to say so but I wanted the servant to be sympathetic on various occasions and I think he is, in other words I wanted you to understand what made him hate, what made him want power, what made him, if you like, evil. And I wanted the boy to have a certain naïveté, a certain innocence, and a certain charm. It seems to me that it's the story of people caught in the same trap although they approach it from different ends; it's a story about the trap – the house and the society in which they live. To me the film is simply about servility, about the servility of our society, of our age, the servility of the master, the servility of all kinds of people in different classes and situations who are afraid – people who are afraid of not having money, who are afraid of their wives, or their mistresses of their brothers or their fathers, or their rulers, or afraid of the atomic bomb or whatever – it's a society of fear, and the reaction to fear is for the most part not resistance and not fight, but servility, and servility is a state of mind. If I were going to define the meaning of *The Servant* as I felt it rather than saw it, and as it developed in the course of the picture, I would say that the one phrase that does it for me is that it's about servility as an attitude of mind.

Here 'servility' is virtually equated with acceptance of the need for dependence, of relational needs, and of belonging to the social community. It is 'servile' to be human. We are to sympathise chiefly with the Servant, who manifests the hate solutions of attacking and undermining others: it is as if the hero of *Othello* were pronounced to be Iago, while the point of that play were to be seen in the miserableness of Desdemona's tendency to believe in the integrity of human beings and in love.

The underlying assumptions are revealed further in an interview with Dirk Bogarde, who played the Servant, who spoke in a revealingly off-the-record manner. The disclaimers of intention now appear ridiculous, since the whole creation of the film is seen to subserve the obligations of the schizoid mode in culture. 'Joe found this ticky little volume called *The Servant* . . . it's a rather thin, boring novel . . . Someone else had already begun the project: they had been intending to make it into a huge big Hollywood picture . . . Joe got hold of Pinter's script, which was frightfully exciting' – but now the need was to capture this and 'fight the money boys.' Here we have the clue to how the schizoid mode and its reversal of moral values is so saleable – and a clue to the direction in which film must go. The collaborators begin to think of Image-women, of whom they talk thus: 'I'm a tremendous fan of Wendy Craig's, and I served her ill in a film called *The Mind Benders*. I'd got her her first screen part in it, and they absolutely screwed her silly with stupid hair and wigs, and frightened her to death. I had an apology to make there.'

There is a story about how Sarah Miles was brought in. Bogarde saw her at a première sitting with the young man who they had thought to use in the film. She was going to marry him. 'Joe came round and talked for hours. Sarah was, of course, our dream. He was frightened by the boy, by the languidness of him. Being American he was rather worried, he said, "Maybe the boy's a queer or something." It turned out the boy's father was Bogarde's agent. In the end, when he saw Sarah was determined to do it, he got hold of Leslie Grade, and Leslie gave us the money . . .'

Q.: *What's Losey like to work with?*
BOGARDE: We work together without any words ever being spoken . . . I never ask him anything, he never tells me anything. It's completely a mutual marriage of minds . . . it's an incredible thing. . . .

The language reveals how the members of such a team think of people:

He's a squalid little man, but he pretends he's a gentleman's gentleman. The first mistake he makes is when he says that he was last with Viscount Bart and James Fox corrects him, 'Oh, Lord Bart'. He admits the mistake. I make him admit it with my face, but he's annoyed because he's trying to pretend to this young boy, whom he's summing up pretty quickly as a pisspot – he knows exactly what sort of a prick he is. . . .

Making such a film obviously provides rich opportunities for the indulgence of hate, as through depersonalised sex:

Q.: *When Barrett rings up Vera do you think it's just because he's wanting to sleep with her again?*
BOGARDE: Well, I think he's no doubt got a couple of tarts on call, probably runs four or five of them. Vera's one, she's pretty, she might do for this fellow. He's young and he's nubile and he wants sex, so get her down from the North. She obviously can be passed off as his sister since they're physically more or less the same kind of colouring, and that's how he really gets her in: it all clicks very neatly – the maid's room is there, he can have her, the boy can have her, he can watch them having each other, he can have the boy, he can do anything he likes, they're there. But if he gets the boy trapped in a mesh with this girl, who he knows has got a peculiar form of strength and sex, then he'll get rid of this neat lady-dressed fiancée of Tony's. But she fights, so Barrett fights back, and his only weapon is the destruction of Tony to keep himself there, because the weaker he keeps *him* the less chance there is of being slung out. . . .

Sex, to the collaborators in the team, is 'it', and their attitudes to relationship, in so far as one can take them more seriously than sophisticated flip talk, seem far from the attitudes of the true artist. There is no recognition of human value and the view of man seems reductive and nihilistic. Persons are not persons, and sex experiences are incorporative, deprived of their emotional and personal reality.

> Q.: *What do you feel about the relationship between Tony and Vera? What is Tony's attitude towards her?*
> BOGARDE: Oh, well, there again, if you look at it objectively, he's an absolute sucker for this situation, but taking that, that's what is written and can happen, then I think it's a real sexual relationship, I mean it's just sex. I think there's something very erotic about charvering maids anyway, you know, I think there is to lots of people, and having one on your doorstep is too much, especially one who's out to get you.

A world, indeed, in which things are divided between objects to be consumed and enemies to be attacked. 'I think he really does love her in some sort of way, and he obviously thinks he's marvellous at it with her. I don't think he likes sex much with his girl-friend. I think that he's sexually conscious, which I think everybody is really.'

In a situation in which no creative control is exerted, we have a form of collaboration in which false-solution strengths become pre-eminent. These people must appear to be 'sexually knowledgeable', and to have a 'realistic' view of the 'animality' of human nature. The most important constituent of their film is the hate which can hold an audience by anxious curiosity, while involving them in the dehumanised attitudes of a schizoid culture. 'Black' attitudes to man can run riot, given the schizoid vindication. Besides the 'unknown motives' of the characters, the actor Tony Fox even speaks of 'scenes we don't see':

> I think that all the time Barrett in the scenes we don't see is saying what a bitch she is, and he's saying, 'now you've lost your balls, mate, you want to watch it because they'll really tear you apart, these little girls!', and he does say 'Slut', you know which is obviously what Barrett's told him to think, and not what he does actually think. I think he just fancies it very strongly with her.

Significantly, from each participant, as we have seen, there comes a strongly expressed attitude to human native, which is taken to be realistic, and justified (as is obvious from a reference here) by the atmosphere of the Ward trial and the degrees to which it made such views socially acceptable. The attitude to human relationships ('after you've had someone a lot, you go out and look for someone else') is that of a cultural atmosphere which holds a deeply sick view of man and which cannot find whole relationship and no goodness in any real contact. Yet this attitude is expressed as a normal and valid truth: a related need is for such individuals to seek to vindicate such 'psychic impotence' as larger than life, or the 'truth about human beings.' The 'truth' here is that human beings are all 'mad and nasty': the truth is Big, Bad and Strong:

> Q.: *The girl in the pub, was she a friend of Barrett's, or did Barrett get hold of her or what?*
> BOGARDE: This is very difficult because I don't know what was in Joe's mind here. I think I'm right in saying that it's a kind of loneliness, you know, and that after you've had someone a lot, you go out and look for someone else and this is what he finds. One had to do it quickly, so it was a girl who had had a bust-up, I think. Alison Seebohm played it, and worked out some story behind this girl, and they just happened to meet, and Tony brought her to the house and then Barrett obviously got hold of her. This is where I fall out of sympathy with the film because I don't think Barrett could have got anybody interested in those sort of parties, unless he had something that I can't see there. It seems to me that if he was snappy and really cool, like some of these people who could go into a place and just pick up people, you know, then you can believe it, but he seems so different from that. I don't think he'd go for a society matron, he'd seem much more likely to go for little boys or little girls of about twelve, these'd be the people Barrett would go for, and I absolutely disagree with Joe about that party. All the critics disagree, probably on intellectual grounds, but I disagree with his casting, because

in the novel it's very clear that it's about a twelve-thirteen year old girl who come in at the end. I think this is much more erotic and much more likely, because Barrett is the kind of person who could get girls who haven't got a penny, to do it for a couple of sweets or ten bob, or a free meal, or 'don't you want to meet a posh gentleman!' or something. He'd have much greater access to these kind of people than he would to those rather extraordinary, ritualistic characters. Obviously Joe's trying to make a point here – what he's saying is I suppose, that this is the way these privileged people do behave; they pretend to be so piss elegant, and really, you know, they like making scenes, and condemn other people who have an extraordinary sexual life. I think he's trying to make a point, but I think the real point is that they wouldn't do it . . . they might do it with Stephen Ward, but not with Barrett.

The film *The Servant* was universally acclaimed. The student paper was devoted at length to the technicalities of its filming (how 'opticals' were avoided, etc). What interests me is that, as these informal interviews reveal, despite the claim of the film to be considered intellectually respectable and creatively 'meant', it is in fact worked out as the expression of a collocation of coarse destructive attitudes to life.

The novel is described as a 'thin ticky little work': Pinter's script as 'exciting'. But Pinter disclaims creative responsibility for the world he creates. Losey speaks of the characters as if he had no idea of what the point of their existence was except to express a contempt for 'servility' and for the weakness of those who desire 'to love and be loved'.

These weaknesses are masked by the 'technical excellence', the Eastman colour, the production, and the quality of acting, etc. If these are 'outstanding' how can the essential effect on sensibility be to foster a deterioration of personal civilisation? Yet, possibly, the effect of such a film might be to convey to people a dislike of being human that might make their existence problems more difficult. Like a great deal else in today's cinema, it could thus reduce emphathy, and so make hostility and violence between men more likely.

E. The 'Amazing Reversal' in Culture at Large

Fig. 3.

CHAPTER 25

Schizoid Inversion in Culture at Large

If my analysis is accepted, it must follow that there is in our culture at large an amount of hate which, if it were devoted, to say, racial discrimination, we should see as a problem demanding our urgent attention. Because the hate is directed at targets which we are accustomed to hate unconsciously, such as woman, representing our own vulnerability, we do not see how dangerous the situation is.

How has this situation come about – so that even the Arts Council can come to declare that there is no harm in obscenity? The development has come by a myriad processes, all based on the underlying problem that we are afraid of our most vulnerable human sensitivities. Again, it is a matter of a slow collective psychopathology, developing by almost imperceptible stages. One can only approach these, by taking note of the things that arrive through one's own door – one's newspaper, the scripts one happens to come across, books one picks up. One mustn't, of course, see everyone who contributes as a 'schizoid' individual: everyone today picks up this inverted mode, as they once picked up Nazi inversions, and we are all victims of a fashion in 'black' solutions to the problems of life.

A useful first example is provided by an advertisement in *The Times*, next to the Court Circular, at the time of writing. There is, once more, a drawing of a girl gnawing her fingers. The text reads:

> You don't have to smuggle Candy through the customs any longer. The masterpiece that's sold 6 million copies and convulsed the rest of the world has arrived. . . . Follow Christian Candy on her non-stop, side-splitting romp. Through pools of sherry. Under hospital beds. In coalmines, lavatories, temples. With sick psychiatrists; Mexican gardeners; money-grubbing hunchbacks; sex-grabbing gynaecologists; uncles, gurus, fathers. Nothing cramps her style. . . . The ultimate satire on sex. . . . (*The Times*, 9 September 1968.)

'Now you can read it': the implication is that there is now a new era of liberty of expression in which even the British public is being treated as 'adult'. Such a book is presented in the heart of bourgeois respectability as both a 'masterpiece' and an 'ultimate satire'.

From the point of view of the 'schizoid diagnosis' the assertion that the book is a 'satire' on sex is merely a way of making socially acceptable its essential attack on being human. The references to sexual intercourse in 'lavatories' and with 'hunchbacks' gives us a clue to the schizoid effects, which are to de-emotionalise and dehumanise sex, to make it ugly and degraded. From the point of view from which this book is written the advertising copy may be reinterpreted thus:

> You are afraid of your own 'feminine' vulnerability, and your dependence on others. These anxieties focus on an unconscious fear of woman, because once you were totally dependent on a woman – and she was only weak and human. This woman is also a symbol of that dangerous emotional commitment which you associate with the sexual life.
>
> Here is your chance to indulge, in a socially acceptable way, your hatred of woman, of the emotional life, and of sex. Here is your opportunity to see the essential humanity in yourself attacked and humiliated – but quite safely, under the pretence of 'satire'. See this woman as a 'partial object' symbol, voluntarily expose herself to humiliation, rape, and the ugliest depersonalisation. See the sexual life treated with disdain and contempt. Join in a destruction of all human values ('sick psychiatrists', 'sex-grabbing gynaecologists') so that a mood of schizoid futility develops in you – so that you can begin to feel that it is perhaps not necessary to be human, and that your essential humanity is perhaps best denied. In exchange, you may find a new source of strength, in the false solutions of hate, and 'bad thinking'. You will feel someone – and you can even safely indulge a cruel sense of superiority to others. Besides all this you can even pretend it is all a joke, to attack and degrade your own humanity.

From this point of view such a work 'convulses' the world in a sense very different from that implied in the advertisement. For what such cultural artefacts do is to paralyse the very sense of being human.

To go back to one of the earlier moments of the 'permissive' trend in the decade, let me take, as another example, the vignette reproduced above (p. 199) which decorated a series of newspaper reports. The vignette reproduced above was printed throughout the *Evening Standard*'s reports of the trial of Stephen Ward in 1965.

The startling feature of this illustration is that it attempts to offer as a symbol of charm and vitality – as an 'ideal object' – the face of a typical defendant in the Ward trial. From the point of view of psychoanalytical theory, some of those involved in the case were unstable individuals whose desperate need to feel real took the form of promiscuous sexual activity. Incapable of relationship in any settled or positive way, they 'contracted into' society by the 'false doing' of prostitution or semi-prostitution. Besides this activity, their ways of seeking confirmation and affection included group sex, prevarication, with hints of blackmail, soft drugs, and symbolic 'acting out' (e.g. shooting through letter boxes) and the impulse to extract payments from individuals on various grounds – including payments from newspapers such as *The News of the World*.

The associated symbolism of their notoriety is strange, however, not merely because the mask of such unstable individuals was glamorised as in this vignette, but because the vignette implies that the way of life exposed by the relevations at the trial was larger than life. At least, it implies, the demi-mondaine is more alive than us. The vignette is thus a manic symbol: it invites us to share false ways of feeling real by the implication that such individuals are gay, beflowered, and beautiful. In truth, as we could glimpse through the proceedings, there was in the background a great deal of individual suffering, aggression, contempt for humanity, manifestations of the impulse to humiliate others, and a self-loathing which, in the end, brought one participant to suicide. Yet what masks the flight from life is offered to us as a vitality which 'society' thwarts.* Yet the wretched tired readers on the suburban train, thwarted by the dreary mechanical life to which 'society' has condemned them, were being invited to feel a thrill of outraged respectability

---

* In the summer of 1968 the diarist of *The Times Saturday Review* wrote up Christine Keeler as the author of her memoirs with attentive respect.

which might reassure them in a manic way that they were still breathing at least. They could identify for a moment with those larger than life individuals. Yet essentially these husbands and daughters were more real as persons while the individuals they were reading about were caught up in the meaningless cycles of hate.

Looked at from the object-relations point of view the behaviour of the individuals concerned appears as a desperate attempt to feel real – as symbolised perhaps by the 'two-way mirror' though which individuals watch others in sexual activity, and by the double life of Ward himself, split between reparative effort as a healer, on the one hand, and as one concerned to submit women to humiliation and contempt by offering them as a pimp and exhibitor of indecent shows, on the other.

As was evident from much public comment, as a consequence of such glamorisation, the individuals concerned were believed to be 'more capable of love' than normal individuals, while their sexual life was believed to be larger than life. Their subsequent behaviour surely reveals this as an 'amazing reversal of values', and exposes their projection at large as a desperate form of compensation in a world without a sense of meaning.

At the time, suddenly, came Stephen Ward's suicide. To the student of object-relations psychology this suicide could be seen as a development only too likely to follow the events. His arrest exposed Ward's agonisedly split life as a reality which could no longer be denied. His two worlds were shown, by reflection in the court revelations, to belong to the same individual. He could not longer maintain a split, and, in terror that the 'bad' should spoil the 'good' he kills himself rather than 'allow the True Self to suffer insult'. To avoid the horror of his predicament he leaves a note blaming 'them'. A number of individuals prominent at the trial, picking up this paranoid note, use it to reinforce the prevalent schizoid myth, endorsed by the philosophies of Wilhelm Reich, that 'society' penalises our 'natural' man, implying that Stephen Ward stood for 'release' and fulfilment against an 'inhibiting' society.

However one interprets Stephen Ward's suicide, from the point of view of object-relations psychology it cannot be seen as the 'enlightened' commentators saw it, as an heroic protest, against 'society' or 'conservatism'. His suicide could be seen as the last act in a life which was shown to be impelled by desperate attempts to feel real in a weak and divided self. Ward's acts in the world of upper-class sex games were *themselves* characteristically exhibitionist (substituting 'showing' for 'giving'); self-destructive (he gave himself away and seemed to seek exposure) and onanistic (as by watching others in sex, or by pimping, as at Cliveden). Menninger associates all three, and says: 'It has been observed that suicidal attempts sometimes follow the interruption of an individual's habitual auto-erotic activities. . . .' (Menninger [43], p. 61).

He associates this with the need to *feel guilty* (which by Kleinian insights could also be associated with the need to *feel real*). The auto-erotic activities indulged in are believed unconsciously to be dangerous, and the risk increases the pleasure. (There is also the risk, as with an entrepreneur like Ward, of being found out.)

> But when the process is interrupted the self-punitive and erotic satisfactions are abruptly terminated while the aggressions are stimulated by the prohibition imposed. The self-destructive tendencies are then turned on the self, robbed of some of their erotic mitigation, and suicide is resorted to, not only because it represents a more violent form of sexual preoccupation with the self, but because it also affords a device for the punishment of those whom the victim feels to be responsible for his deprivation. (Menninger [43], p. 62.)

Stephen Ward's suicide therefore could be seen as having its own complex logic: like his sexual activity it could have marked a desperate failure to feel good enough to survive. It could be seen as virtually a final sexual act, narcissistic and onanistic, which also brought the satisfaction of revenge on 'them', and so some feeling of being real in hate and self-punishment and revenge.

From an object-relations point of view there is in such individuals deep fear of the sexual act, so that they can only enter into sexual activity in a group. To be alone with one female partner is too dangerous because she might turn out to be the castrating mother. In this there is a fear of talion revenge, so that the compulsive observation of others in sexual intercourse is a reenactment of phantasies of the primal scene, but in circumstances in which the individual overcomes his fears of the castrating mother by having her under control (as a paid 'performer') and seeing her humiliated. The proxy situation and the mirror also guarantee against any close contact, so that the sexual act becomes remote from any individual person. All this points to Ward's antics as an anguished form of psychopathological behaviour in one of weak identity.

However, to the propagandists of the 'sexual revolution' Ward's anguished life had to appear as free and superhuman. So, to them, the arrest and trial of Ward seemed like a public arraignment of the very hate-solutions in depersonalised sex which were for them the chief source of meaning. In protest they must defend these compensations and proclaim their validity. Desperate sexual 'strategies of survival' must be made to seem an assertion of 'freedom' against inhibiting 'society'. In the end it comes to seem to the 'enlightened' view that it is *social disapproval of deviation* that is to blame for deviation itself and the unhappiness inherent in it – another comforting delusion. The consequence of the furore and 'frankness' round the Ward case was not only a boom in the sale of newspapers but also a startling reversal of moral values at large which effect is concealed by the smiling mask of the vignette reproduced here.

The technological advance marked by the issue of colour supplements has brought its own manic falsifications. The *Daily Telegraph* colour supplement of 16 April, 1966 provides a choice example of how values can be blatantly inverted in the need to establish this kind of vehicle for advertising which needs 'impact'.

The article in question was called: 'London, the Most Exciting City'. Among advertisements full of 'identity-boost' writing ('Don't tell me – I know!' . . . 'The kick thrust spurt of power getaway peak through deep green forest eagle sweep . . .') we have this: 'Different cities have at various periods in history . . . suddenly become magnets for talent, drawing young creative people from all parts of the world . . . living close to the revolution . . .'

Apparently: 'Eros the God of Love is still at the heart of London. . . .'

Through the cigarette smoke we glimpse 'Aristotle Onassis . . . perhaps Princess Margaret . . . a frenzy of the prettiest legs in the world . . . just ordinary English girls, a gleam of joy on their pretty faces. . . .'

Someone is quoted as saying: 'The girls are prettier here than anywhere else – much more so than in Rome or Paris.'

The writer goes on:

> They're more than pretty, they're young, appreciative, sharp-tongued, glowingly alive. Even the sex orgies among the sex-and-pot sets in Chelsea and Kensington have youth and eagerness and, in a strange way, a quality of innocence about them. In Rome and Paris, the sex orgies are for the old, the jaded, the disgusting and disgusted. Young English girls take to sex as if it's candy and it's delicious. . . .

The 'creative revolution' turns out to be one of the developments of the fashion trade and advertising.

On the one hand, the writer wishes to vindicate depersonalised 'taking' sex (sex = candy), and, on the other, wishes to make this dissociated activity and dangerous 'pot' respectable. So he picks out some of the 'successful' young who had 'suddenly' come to 'own the town': dress designers, fashion artists, photographers, models – and put them on the same level with the Beatles, and the Professor of Experimental Philosophy at Cambridge:

> This explosion of creative vitality, a sort of English renaissance, has occurred on the very highest levels, as well as the more frivolous ones. On the top-most sphere of pure thought, Fred Hoyle, the Cambridge astronomer, has just advanced a theory about the physical nature of the universe as sweeping in its implications as those of Copernicus, Newton or Einstein. . . .

The 'knowingness' about physics and astrophysics here belongs to the world of Fleming and his sophisticated acquaintance in the bright journalistic way with everything that can be a badge of acceptability. Here the reference to science is intended to endorse the 'sexual revolution'. Fleming himself contributed to the social acceptance of schizoid sex – so that we no longer see the contempt in such talk about 'pretty girls' who 'take to sex' and do not see how anti-human it is to regard others as partial objects for 'automatic satisfaction'. Because certain 'enlightened' propagandists have persuaded us to accept depersonalised sex as a new freedom, we do not see how 'pot and sex orgies' manifest a flight from relationship and an act of will inflicted on one's own humanity, in hate.

But on close examination we can see how the mask is decorated: '. . . Youth . . . eagerness . . . innocence.' These are linked with Princess Margaret, success, creativity. Most of us probably dismiss such writing at a glance. But psychoanalytical theory suggests that it has a powerful unconscious appeal, because it offers us such strong 'sophisticated' solutions to our feelings of ego-weakness. If we keep alert, we can see we are being offered a false glamour. But the general reader – the impressionable youth for instance – cannot detach himself so. An atmosphere is created in which he is encouraged to feel that it is real and alive to accept the new inverted values as by taking to 'pot and sex'. The mention of royalty guarantees respectability: the urge to harm oneself and lower one's sense of one's own value is masked by the word 'innocent'.

Protest to Fleet Street is met by blank incomprehension: the present author wrote to protest to see what reply would come:*

> I am not aware that *The Daily Telegraph* ever advocated the taking of drugs. I consequently find your letter rather difficult to comprehend.
>
> <div align="center">Yours faithfully,
MAURICE GREEN, <i>Editor.</i></div>

But the effect of the article *was* to contribute to the general ethos of demoralisation and the social acceptability of addiction. The tone of the article, definitely, at one point, accepts the taking of drugs, implicitly, as 'innocent', while the whole tenor of the article glamorizes drugs together with 'candy' sex, meaning that depersonalised sex is harmless, as 'swinging', sophisticated, and larger than life. This is but one tiny example in a whole tide of demoralisation that has flowed in the sixties. While certainly not

---

* See Professor Henry's letter protesting against the TV advertisement phrase 'once you've got this narcotic TV viewing habit you're hooked', and the reply, 'It did not seem objectionable to us', from the *New York Times* Advertising Acceptibility Department.

sharing its punitive (hypoparanoid) reaction, one can see why the Scottish Kirk speaks of a 'baleful' London culture.

Writing of such a kind conveys knowledge neither of adult sexuality nor of intellectual matters. Such rubbish would normally be dismissed as anti-human propaganda it truly is: but the danger is that practically no one – not even every member of a university staff room – essentially dissociates himself nowadays from such a level of comment – or such myths – in colour supplements and television magazine programmes.* These outlets have the prestige: there is no source of prestige other than ephemeral journalism and television entertainment since these have largely replaced serious reading and critical comment. So, inevitably, problems of identity tend to be seen in terms of the nihilism of the homunculism that pervades popular theories of human nature, the ethos of advertising, journalism, and the arts. From this view of human nature there seems no grounds for objection to the attitude to human relationships conveyed in such an article, and everyone feels a reluctance to invoke dignity or decency in response for fear of 'unpopularity' – or 'Grundyism'.

Such eulogies of orgiastic life in Chelsea and Kensington have been ridiculed in *The Guardian*. Yet this paper also implicitly endorses such 'enlightened' attitudes to the new sexual revolution – as when Christopher Driver, their then features editor, suggested that it was time jealousy was 'civilised out of existence': it was a mere hangover from property values of a bourgeois era. An enlightened married woman, in the 'open community' between the sexes, is no longer a chattel and can make her own decisions about whose bed she shares, he claimed. It seems there is to be no passion, either way!

The ethos of 'amorality' promoted abroad after the *Lady Chatterley* trial and the Ward case has been eagerly exploited by many enterprising individuals, so that a rapid transformation of our culture at large has happened with surprising speed. We now have nudity and sexual intercourse (albeit simulated) on the stage, together with various manifestations whose symbolism in the light of my analysis in this book will be obvious. At a recent production at a leading theatre a naked woman was killed, in a long and elaborate scene at the end, by having a sword thrust into her vagina. There was nothing in the text of the play (*The White Devil*) to suggest or vindicate such a horror. In other productions on stage and screen there have been scenes showing woman hanging naked on meat-hooks, raped, having their breasts cut off with kitchen knives, having their vaginas syringed to purify them of devils, and so on. Defaecation on the stage has been simulated, and in one play the three characters at the end were dead, naked, and swilled about in tanks, until, at the end, parts of them were eaten. In one film a woman was shown tied to a post while being pelted with excreta. One film director filmed himself copulating on a heap of offal: in another film we are promised 'a girl's pudenda seething with maggots'. In an American avant-garde film a girl masturbates, in a long 'clinical' scene, lasting fifteen minutes, with a bicycle wheel. Male homosexual rape has taken place on the New York stage. The effect of these psychopathological antics is not confided to the audiences who see them. They are continually described, or illustrated, in journals and magazines which undoubtedly find their way into the hands of young people and children. *The Guardian* is a family newspaper, but it contained recently an account of a man who had sexual intercourse on the stage with two women at a Film

* The approach above was later endorsed by implication by a leader in *The Guardian* which spoke with enthusiasm of 'the new amoral society we have constructed'.

Festival, and then proceeded to prepare to kill a goose and bathe in its blood, on the stage. When prevented, he defaecated on the stage, and walked off shouting obscenities. *The Observer* recently described in a recent issue the scene in a film in which a black penis was stroked with a flower, and another in which a man had a ring inserted in his nipple. In *The Times* of October 22nd, we read in the film criticism:

> For see, there's this lad ... who has trouble with erections. Not, as it turns out, quite the sort of trouble Miss Smith supposes when she first takes on a little extra-mural tuition and encouragement, but after a while and a deal of spilt milk (or at least spilt liquor from a chocolate duck) to be wept over, it all works out rather pleasantly for both of them.

These accounts, whatever the content of the films, are obscene – not maybe in the legal sense, but certainly in the sense in which I would want to use the word in a literary critical context. Moreover, as will be obvious from my analysis of schizoid symbolism, they are deeply evocative of anxieties about 'inner contents', primal scene phantasies, and 'the parts and functions'. They are perverted, and, inevitably, spread abroad a fear and hatred of being human.

The question I am concerned with here is how such material has come, between 1963 and 1971, to become acceptable, even in the English family home? How have we been disarmed, and for what reasons? We now almost subscribe to the Danish official view that there is no harm in pornography – because no statistical analysis can ever prove that delinquent or perverted acts followed from the effects of any obscene work. My study of schizoid processes in this work, I hope, will put a substantial question mark beside this ridiculous assumption. For not only does pornography have an educational effect, like every other cultural artefact. It has, because of its origins in perversion and schizoid processes of the sick imagination, a profound effect *as symbolism*, and a destructive effect on the imagination and creativity itself. (This point is argued more fully in the present writer's *Sex and Dehumanisation* and *The Pseudo-revolution*).

However, for the moment, I am concerned here with how moral values have become so amazingly reversed, in this sphere. Today the exploitation of depersonalised sex for profit is one of the features of the modern scene which the truly liberal mind is supposed to endorse. Indeed, many left-wing people have even been persuaded that there are justifications for pornography, in terms of the release or rediscovery of 'Eros' in the face of a deadening society. As soon as one questions the effects of pornography, the cry of 'censorship' is raised – or one is accused of raising trifling issues, when much more serious ones are calling for attention.

These attitudes are, I believe, the result of a long process of moral inversion, brought about by cunning individuals, to whom the development of a receptivity for schizoid moral inversion and the reduction of symbolism to the 'equations' of hate is a life-and-death matter. Obviously, it is impossible to mention any of these individuals by name, or even to describe their efforts in such a way as to enable the reader to identify them. But it will be as evident to the reader that, for instance, some of them appear on television with monotonous regularity, and are written up in magazines in terms of their life and struggles, with eulogistic praise: 'he was in business . . . it had been a long hard struggle'. Not least do we find in student magazines a profound admiration expressed for those who have become successful by exploiting schizoid sex in this way. The exploiters themselves, of course, rise enthusiastically to the acclaim: 'In the end I had to do it myself. It was only will power, sheer guts, and a good address' said one. 'With a team of top barristers . . . and I mean top . . . I designed a brochure that was bound to get shot down: strong enough to sell the magazine, not enough to put me in jail . . .' The commercial sexploiter thus puts himself on a par with the pioneers of free speech, and the liberal is taken in. In film reviews there is often great glee expressed that a particularly obscene film managed to get a licence: those who might object are ridiculed as a 'family of Grundies'. Intellectuals are disarmed by the subtle linking of 'literary names' (Henry Miller's letters, &c.) with articles on sexual perversion. The pornographer himself will proclaim loudly that he doesn't recognise the legal definition of pornography as something that is likely to 'deprave and corrupt', but that pornography only exists in 'unsophisticated' minds, on in 'the mind of the beholder'. Thus, a paralysing relativism has been impressed upon the liberal mind, while schizoid hate has managed to thrust into our culture forms of perverted dehumanisation, sadism, and anal hate (the cast in one 'sex' show shout 'Shit!' at the audience). Such an amount of all this has never been expressed in any culture of the part, except perhaps ancient Rome. But not even at the time of the most brutal public tortures and sexual humiliations did members of the public at large have such an immediate close-up view, as they are given by technology (and zoom lenses) today. Yet many intelligent people continue to assert that the most important element in all this is the primary right of every individual to have the opportunity to express himself, in an unbridled way. They would never say this about racial hatred: but with the other forms of schizoid hate that manifest themselves in sexual depiction, the dogma is unquestionable. One article I saw even spoke of 'the right to self-abuse'.

In truth, if we are to believe object-relations theory, everyone has a delicate balance to preserve between hate and love, between primitive urges to exploit others as less than persons, and finer impulses to find others by creative engagement with their reality recognised in equality. It is merely cynical to believe that we are all 'kinky' and so may as well give way to such false modes of behaviour in order to feel big and bad. By the glamour and manic charm of glossy pornography the individual can be drawn into further cycles of false solution and away from his own humanness.

Feelings aroused by the depersonalised sex of such magazines tend to be aggressive and destructive because these belong to the false solutions of 'bad thinking' and False Self activity. So it is not irrelevant that bundles of 'sex' magazines are found by the bodies of murdered children. It is not that the magazines directly prompt such murders (though this could be so) any more than sexual crimes could be prompted by a reading of Sade's *Justine* (though Sade himself thought that this was likely). It is rather that the murders and the pornography belong to the desperate compensations, involving aggressive phantasy, which some must act out. This explains why the newer pornographic magazines tend to be so preoccupied with hate in their articles and why they attract 'kinky' letters. Each of these ought to seem as repulsive as a racist paper to anyone who places a high value on human nature: but we do not see this because of the manic gloss and because the attack is on the 'female element' of which we are afraid, in ourselves.

What is called 'sophistication' here means, obviously, what Suttie meant by 'demoralisation' – the abeyance of that conscience which is the basis of identity, bound up with our sense of the value of ourselves. That we find it impossible to find effective objections to such 'business' is a mark of the same kind of delusions that blinded us in the thirties to the essential moral degeneration that led to the 'pure' inversions of Nazism. It is one of the fatal weaknesses of democracy that it tends to assume that it can tolerate schizoid destructiveness without seeking to 'contain' it – until things have been too disastrously undermined.

The world of films and film-reviewing, as I have said, arrogantly regards itself as a world apart from normal ethical considerations. It is obsessed with its own importance and brusquely disregards all traditions and criteria. Words in film reviews do not mean the same as elsewhere: for instance 'love' merely means to make love except where one is speaking of one's affection for a projected 'partial object' image:

> Much as I love Jeanne Moreau, this is definitely Miss Bardot's film, and her funniest scenes occur when she plays against the Brigitte Bardot character with which we are all familiar. For one thing, at the beginning we are asked to believe – a tall order indeed – that she is a virgin. Discontented with her lot, she more or less willingly allows herself to be carried off by three handsome caballeros. The next morning, when, hidalgo-like, they politely drop her off at her caravan, she slumps up the steps and collapses into a chair, moaning contentedly, 'I'm shattered'. Which wouldn't be nearly so funny if someone else did it, precisely because we feel sure that the Miss Bardot we know could handle (and love) twice that many Mexicans. (*The Guardian*).

On another page of the same newspaper – on the hard news pages – the rape of a woman by several men would be reported as an act of savagery and dissociation. In film it is a kind of aggressive play-activity, the indulgence in which in phantasy is made tolerable by a 'send-up'. Again, here we have a 'multiple-object' phantasy, a common element in masturbation dreams. The reviewer finds it funny that 'Miss Bardot' should be 'shattered' by being raped. What he fails to notice is that what the film invites is indulgence in a phantasy attack on our feminine vulnerability.

I am less concerned with the films in question here, than with the tone and manner of the reviewers who, week after week, are being force to lower their standards until now they have virtually given up invoking ethical values at all. Without noticing it, their flip tone, or their sophisticated manner, have had the effect of detaching from film culture the question of our attitudes to human nature altogether.

I am in great difficulties here, because I am not a film critic, and while I want to discuss the effects of film criticism, I have not seen all the films, many of which are no longer shown anyway. I thus have difficulty in making my comment fair. But what I am concerned about, I think legitimately, is the continual denial of evident human truths in film reviewing itself – a phenomenon no doubt encouraged by the films themselves.

We need to consider the predicament of the film critic himself. He must say something, to fill his columns. He must see dozens of films, and he must continually meet his colleagues. If we study his writings in our collection of cuttings, we shall see that, step by step, he tends to fall in with the persuasions of the film world: it is almost impossible for him to opt out, under the circumstances. Moreover, of course, he is continually subjected to immense pressure from the publicity departments of the industry itself. Most film critics exert an astonishing integrity and moral sense in the face of all these problems. But all the same, it is evident to me that, by degrees, film criticism has become almost entirely encapsulated in the schizoid reversal of moral values – together with a special kind of 'technicism' which belongs to the essential voyeurism of the cinema as an art form, and its deficiency of genuine symbolism in depth.

So, step by step, the critics applaud the fact that 'the naked breast has come to stay . . . no more awkward angles or illogical cuts', or that, having seen the real thing in detail, simulated sexual intercourse now looks old-fashioned. By a certain significant tone, each step towards voyeuristic depersonalisation has been hailed as a new and valuable departure. The implication is parallel to the beliefs in our economic life, that every expansion is a good thing, and every technical innovation is to be necessarily acclaimed and publicised. Step by step, human beings are reduced to the cinema to the status of objects, in a schizoid way, and each step is enthusiastically endorsed. Yet now every night thousands of people, many between 16 and 25, are witnessing sexual activity from the 'outside', much of it perverted, in a way that is completely different from anything ever experienced in the history of human civilisation. Even in the most tender moments of film, as in a dream love sequence, the camera not only follows the lovers to the wood – it follows them into the wood, unclothed, and naked, even to the bouncing buttocks of simulated intercourse. In life, if we followed lovers into a wood and spied on them, we would consider ourselves sick, and we would be treated by society as sick. But today we accept this Peeping Tom syndrome as normal, in technical culture.

To enable this 'advance' towards perversion in film, it has been necessary for a considerable change in moral standards to take place, in film criticism and social acceptance. And, at every stage, there is always some new 'film' book to endorse it. At the time of writing, a film is running which shows a boy of fifteen having sexual intercourse with his mother: yet there are 'no moral hang-ups', the reviewer says. This means that all normal moral considerations are completely in abeyance, for the purposes of film – and this is continually being offered as a good thing: 'evil be thou my good'. This extension of the desire of the liberal to be as 'guiltless' as possible, towards a situation in which 'everything is possible' without any kind of ethical discrimination being made, has now become an 'amazing reversal' indeed. We even hear film producers talking as though world over-population made murder less of a crime than previously, while I recently heard a group of intellectuals agreeing with a film which had urged its audiences to believe that, since our species is doomed anyway, we might as well have a good time, while relationships and values were less important than they used to be. Thus, the advance into 'amorality', associated with the way film presents the world is spreading abroad a dangerous and deep sense of irresponsibility, at the very moment when man requires all the powers he can summon, to create a future in which he can survive.

Early on in this process, a film appeared which presented in a very charming way a story in which a couple's relationship broke up, and the woman killed herself. The reviewer in a liberal newspaper says that it was 'not debased by nostalgia or sentimentality'. He cheerfully accepted the way in which the film presented the protagonist's infidelity: 'he feels no conflict'. One finds this said of film situations today again and again: jealousy does not bite, and splits in object-relations cause no emotional stress. In the light of the human facts established by psychoanalysis, if a man felt no conflict in such a situation he would be in such a state as would cause a psychiatrist to be extremely alarmed by his condition. In the light of clinical knowledge of human beings, if by no other light, it is impossible for human beings to deny their need for dependence and their concern for relationship unless they are psychopaths. Since the 'ultimate aim of the libido is the object', such a severe split in object relationship would be a mark of deep conflict within the self. Such indifference to the need for object-constancy would manifest some profound depersonalisation. Indeed, in 'feeling no conflict' such an individual as the protagonist would be manifesting the 'diminution of effect' observable in those who commit the most terrible crimes. As Zilboorg says:

> The dulling of emotions, the failure to feel, has nothing to do with morality or immorality. It is both a cause and a result of many severe psychopathological reactions, and I am certain that it plays a

major role in the development of all sorts of criminal personalities and their crimes. If the emotions are flattened and dull, we may understand pain in the manner that a blind man might possibly 'understand' colour – he would perceive it as something foreign to him. Under the circumstances, the aggressive drives would break through, since the barrier of feeling fails to arrest the action; the will cannot step in, as it were, and assert its control. The will can act only in that which is reason and that which is feeling and integrated. If they split off from one another even partially, the door to aggression opens to the extent of the diminution of affect. . . . (Zilboorg [62], p. 72.)

Whatever this insight reveals for forensic science, it will surely make us suspect the assumptions of the critic, and (if he is right about the film) of the film itself.

Zilboorg links integration, conscience, and sanity with the preservation of 'good feeling tone'. 'Good feeling tone' belongs to the realm of love and being. But these are so dangerous to some that they must seek to deny them, wishing to unmake man, and to dehumanise him.

That which has become known in present-day psychology as the ego – the very substance of human personality – cannot function either in the direction of conscience or in the direction of virtue, unless it is fully integrated with adequate feeling tones – which seem to be more an essential ingredient of that which makes 'man' more than mere intelligence and cold reason. (Zilboorg [62], p. 72.)

It is this kind of human fact which many a film, albeit 'beautifully', has the effect of inverting. Interestingly enough, the maker of the film discussed above said that some people might consider it 'cruel and shocking'.

Because the film world has cut itself off so much from the rest of the world, however, the critic is often left with only the 'impact' to report, and the reputation of a fashionable film maker, rather than the reputation of Man.

At worst, of course, there is no doubt of the hate expressed by this medium to what seem to me horrifying degrees. Here are extracts from a review of a film that offered a dispiriting experience.

. . . three pregnant women in the same nursing home flashing back comprehensively to their tangled and unfortunate lives as they await the arrival of the infants . . . the battery of dubious excitements in which the characters indulge or which they have pressed upon them – homosexuality, male and female, incest, seduction of minors, masturbation, not to mention minor matters like undergoing several illegitimate pregnancies, watching animals mating, and bathing nude, cover practically the whole range of the Swedish cinema's repertoire.

Even worse, though, is that nobody seems to enjoy any of it. Surely somehow, somewhere, some Swedes must snatch a little fun? From the Swedish cinema in general and this epitome in particular, you would never know it. There is, admittedly, one 'life-accepting' figure in this film, but since this means that the acts as though, and everyone takes her to be, mad, hardly counts.

Here it will be noted that the one 'life-accepting' character is mad: the film, again, seems to invert values in a schizoid way to the extent of presenting the experience of relationship as a sequence of disagreeable acts of depersonalized sex, while the emergence of new life is greeted with hostility and revulsion. Again, the symbolism of the film seems to deny dependence and its rejection of creative relationship must have been antihuman. Yet all the critic can say is that the film 'has quite a lot to be said for it'. Taken as a vision of life, it sounds like the record of compulsive obsessions of a psychopath. Compared with a sequence of psychoanalytical case histories, the preoccupation with perversion in films seldom conveys the 'hope' locked up in psychopathological behaviour in life.

It is possible that the exceptional amount of hate we find associated with film may be due to something inherent in the camera itself – as a 'taking' instrument. The camera, after all, does not give us what Hannah Segal calls '*symbols created in the inner world*' but symbols taken from the outer world that go direct through lens to emulsion. Possibly camera art has elements in it intrinsically which are like the approach of schizophrenics to reality: the camera belongs to 'concrete thinking'. Perhaps this explains the confusion between life and image in the film world, and why the world of film is so strikingly apart in its assumptions about human nature and in its ethical ethos. As I have said, film seems to impose some kind of schizoid mode on the individuals who serve it. Whether or not this theory is accepted, what certainly cannot be denied is the inordinate amount of hate in film.

An early surrealist film showed two fierce poisonous creatures biting one another to death. This image may be interpreted for its implications about human truth: man, 'really' is like that: his predominant urge is hate and this hate meets hate. Here we find, again, essentially symbolised, the view of ego-maintenance which Sartre holds, that endless clash with the freedom of others which is necessary to sustain the schizoid identity.

These philosophical justifications have enabled today's *avant-garde*, and commercial promoters in culture, to offer certain new developments with enthusiastic commendation – of manifestations which in previous ages would have been disapproved of, as they should be. For instance, we may take the tone of some remarks by a leading dramatist about his youth, in a newspaper interview: 'I was a morbid youth. But I had a remarkably enjoyable association with five other boys. It was a great relief, I remember, that they knew what I was on about. *Ruthless mutual confrontations.*' The implication here is not that extremes of mutual hate are tolerable in *art*, but that the person himself who has produced such art is commendable for having, *in his life*, experienced such impulses, 'honestly'. (Incidentally, it makes 'fair comment' almost impossible, since it is so difficult to separate the works from the man).

The effect of such continual propaganda in favour of hate is having its deep effect, and today most 'sophisticated' people, like the audiences at London theatres, take all this as 'realism'. It has immense effects at large on attitudes to life, and promotes a sense of moral futility. Such a decline of responsibility marks a contribution to the possibility that man may indeed not survive. For, as Albert Schweitzer said, the important thing about anyone's philosophy should be that it was tenable 'even if the world should end tomorrow'. To give over to despair and irresponsibility, such as our hate-culture is breeding, is to expose us to our essential 'nothingness', in a way that menaces our psychic health, and existential security.

The widespread belief that violence and sex, as they are exploited in our culture, are merely the expression of real drives, so that in recognising these we will be able to find our true nature is fallacious. Fortunately, philosophies are emerging that expose the fallacious assumptions lying behind such beliefs. For instance, Erwin Straus the phenomenologist points out that 'objectification is the . . . essentially *perverse* action of the voyeur' (my italics). Our belief that the impulse to 'look at' sex has suffered a painful restriction which benefits from 'release' is challenged by Straus, who believes that, on the contrary, voyeurism marks a particular breakdown of the whole relationship between the individual suffering from scopophilia and his world. It marks a failure of the 'communicative mode' – and it threatens creative eroticism with exposure to the 'public' in all its forms, so that it becomes 'shrunken'.

The behaviour of the voyeur is not an inherently meaningful surrender to fate, like that of lovers . . .

Voyeurism threatens to affect us with the 'shrunkenness' of those who are no longer capable of being touched, and who cannot give themselves over to creative fate. Shame is a protective device, that defends our capacity to find meaning, in love in privacy, from the intrusions of the schizoid pervert. (See *Phenomenological Psychology*, 'A Historiological Approach to the Problem of Shame' and my discussion in *Sex and Dehumanisation* and elsewhere). In the light of this, and Khan's work, the growing exploitation of voyeurism ad of sadism in our culture may be menacing capacities for creative vision at a great depth.

This raises the question of the relationship of the individual who makes shocking films, or who puts shocking scenes on the stage, and 'society'. We can perhaps envisage, as (say) Sartre cannot, other ways of finding freedom or strength of identity or meaning, in which each individual relies on his own resources of 'being', or inner security, without the need to resort to alienation or 'ruthless confrontation'. We may believe that a human meaning in life can be found through 'encounter'. But the schizoid individual needs to phantasy brutal creatures attacking one another, or to 'act out' attacks on woman, in order to feel real. So, throughout our culture, we have the image of woman subjected to humiliation and attack, as a symbol of that inner sensitive humanness that we most fear.

If we saw such scenes from the point of view of a Winnicott, we would see them with compassion. In much of today's culture we are invited to enjoy the sadistic assault – in London the audience laughs as the actress is raped, caught by the hands in the curtain rings and undressed, made to stand with her naked posterior and genitals showing to the audience, 'taken' or 'eaten'. As Guntrip says, 'the female element is the emotionally sensitive self that can be more easily hurt, and then can be felt as a weakness to be resisted, resented and hidden behind a tough exterior. Patients . . . may generate an intense hatred of their female element, project it and experience frightening destructive impulses towards . . . women.' These frightening impulses are acted out in dozens of film and stage shows today – and the effect in inevitably to make such attacks on sensitive femininity seem acceptable – together with the hate involved. It is significant that the actress is often extremely beautiful, and so the hate is disguised – and can be more sadistically (and guiltlessly) enjoyed. I was amazed recently to see a film, in which a woman is subjected to the cruellest humiliation, described as having a 'delightfully light touch' by a critic: when I challenged him he said that critical opinion seemed now to be pretty generally agreed that there was 'more than a suspicion of burlesque or parody about this film' and that it would not bear my 'serious interpretation'. Yet when the film first came out, reviewers saw it as a deep criticism of society ('about the decadence of a society in which the only way a woman can obtain sexual satisfaction is through masochism.') It contained things which, reviewers said, could not be described in a family newspaper (at that time!) yet the producer 'is not interested in why she is as she is' – 'no time is wasted on psychology.' Yet it opens with a scene in which the woman is being whipped and degraded. An intelligent woman I know was deeply offended, pained, and sickened by the film. But this very painfulness must now be hidden, first by the accounts of the beautiful quality of the filming – and now by a pretence that the film was a light-hearted take-off anyway. The Masks of Hate are well exemplified by such an example, and they are described every day in the film criticism columns.

Other film-makers justify their films under the guise of social criticism. In one of these a typically civilised couple are shown to have longed for one another's death for a long time. They pass through a scene of devastation – with shattered bodies, blood, suffering, and death. A reviewer said this represented civilised society gone mad, 'returning us to the condition of the beasts – except that beasts are seldom malicious, seldom kill just for pleasure.' But the violence of the film is, evidently from the reviewer's account, far in excess of the need to convey this criticism of society – as, indeed, is much of the violence indulged in many stage shows today. In the film referred to, the couple's alienation culminates in the woman eating her husband – a symbolic act which recurs again and again in contemporary culture.

We may reflect on the degree of creative power needed to genuinely encompass such a horrible event. But the way in which the character talked of the matter, light-heartedly and with sadistic enjoyment, had the kind of quality too often found in modern novels, or the stage plays I have referred to. It is a joke – and the flippancy reveals an essential sadism, and denial of human reality. Anyone who could joke so about such a horrible thing could only be a psychopath – and yet she is shown as normal. There is no 'psychology' and she is not a 'case'. The film, says the reviewer, is 'shot through with a Swiftean disgust at life' – and so he gets nearer the point, which is that the film is the comment of a schizoid individual who seeks, under the disguise of his 'social criticism' to express his hatred of woman, and of being human. The inner weakness that threatens to destroy from within is projected over the outer world, and hate is split off from the 'pure' self – which is held together by False Male Doing, and 'bad thinking'. To vindicate this, film-makers and reviewers bring up all kinds of fragments from revolutionary texts. But the essential basis of their art is to be found in the light of Fairbairn's diagnosis of schizoid states.

The effect of such works could be to promote further splitting, paranoia, and projection – and further attacks on 'them'. Some film-makers have actually been said to have contributed by their films to student riots and outbursts of political demonstration of a violent kind. Yet such anti-bourgeois fanaticism seems likely only to breed a futile revolt, with no sense of a possible human outcome. But intellectuals writing about such films applaud their depth of humanity. There is no doubt about the moral fervour behind them: but in the light of Polanyi's analysis of the origins and nature of 'armed bohemianism', there are many dangers – not least that suggested by the fact that 'the wave of anti-bourgeois immoralism' in the Germany of the thirties 'formed the reservoir from which the SS and the SA were recruited' (*Knowing and Being*, p. 17). As one examiner for the English Tripos said in 1971, about student essays,

> The attitudes conveyed in a surprisingly large number of the essays seemed to me to be paranoiac, in that they expressed the fear of subversion of the personality by an apparently amorphous and indefineable 'they'.

It is true that in some ways our society is like that – and our minds are conditioned by pressures which are brutal enough. But the paranoid element comes to a large extent from those schizoid revolutionaries who thrust into our culture schizoid-paranoid feelings, not essentially because they wish to make a positive challenge to the society itself, but because they need to act out their own sicknesses – at the expense of the feelings of others, and express a desperate existential frustration, to which their solutions are false-self solutions.

How possible will it ever be, I wonder, to arouse doubt about the continual erosion of values by such mass media? It is true that the UNESCO Conference on Culture at Venice in the autumn of 1970 raised this problem. But it saw the answer in terms of persuading film directors and others to take more care about offending the values of society. It seems unlikely that such persuasion can ever have an effect, while culture is so largely industrialised. An economist, E. J. Mishan, sees the process as a straightforward consequence of problems of economic growth. Writing of the abolition of censorship, he says, 'Although drawing support from writers and liberals, the steam behind the movement for the abolition of all forms of censorship, and more specifically in favour of complete freedom of erotic subjects, is predominantly commercial.' (*The Costs of Economic Growth*, p. 155). As an economist, however, Mr. Mishan does not fall for the liberal arguments. He points out that the arguments in favour of a more mature society relying upon health and the natural functions rather miss the point that under the impact of the torrential forces of modern technology and commerce, society is 'rent apart' – and is already torn wide open by modern communications. Ours is a society 'in a state of rapid dissolution'.

In this situation, the result of the experiment of 'apparently unlimited commercial potential' in releasing pornography may not be disastrous, but 'is hardly likely to promote the happiness of mankind'.

> The rapid economic growth of the West over the last half-century and especially the last two decades, has not yet been accomplished without traumatic effects on their populations. Tension is more evident everywhere than harmony, disproportion more evident than proportion. The gross overdevelopment of the acquisitive instinct has its genesis in the industrial free enterprise system of the Classical economists. The increasing obsession with sex, and with sexual display masquerading as fashion; the technique of distilling that carnality of sex, as though it were an essence to be poured lavishly into all forms of modern entertainment, these owe too much to private enterprise and advertising. The result, today, with commerce eagerly reacting to the expectations of excitement it has done much to create, is the gross displacement of a social libido.
>
> *op. cit.* p.158

The chapter from which this note comes is called *The Weak Link Between Expanding Choice and Welfare*. If I am correct in my analysis of the schizoid origins of pornography, violence and sexploitation, then we have now in our world an unholy alliance between the liberal intellectual, with his absurd concepts of 'total freedom', and a commerce that has developed an excited acquisitiveness, in terms of the pursuit of greater and greater sensuality which is running away with it. In consequence, the whole psychic health of the community is at risk, because, as Mishan says, the flood that will follow the increasing abandonment of censorship will leave 'a morally fragile and edgy society to cope with the flood as best is can.' (p. 159.)

In the face of such a situation, the general connivance of the intellectual at the spreading abroad of a schizoid hatred of being human is a *trahison des clercs* of immense proportions. Yet locally it looks continually innocent: the local film clubs is 'persuaded' by the British Film Institute to take a proportion of films which are 'spiced with sex' and 'classics' in the struggle to 'demolish censorship'. Mr. John Huntley, for instance, of the British Film Institute discussed on Woman's Hour the local reaction to the opening of a branch of the National Film Theatre in Norwich.

> In Norwich, for example, when we first opened, there were big rows in the local press. People were not only baffled by the films, but they were shocked by them – we'd rather come to assume in London that the days when you could shock an audience had gone. But not so. We found, when we opened with what we thought were very naive films ... that the columns of the *Eastern Daily Press* were packed with the wildest outcries from people who had been to see these shows and who had said, 'Is this the kind of muck which the National Film Theatre is going to bring to Norwich?' Let me hasten to add that the situation has settled down to some extent, and audiences very quickly become rather sophisticated. (*The Listener*, 20 April, 1961.)

T.M.H.—H

We may read the word 'sophisticated' here in the way the pornographer uses it – meaning 'indifferent to the expression of schizoid attitudes to relationship' – indifferent to hate, blind to human truth, demoralised, and deprived of standards of discrimination. Above I have tried to show in what spirit films seem often to be made: in the light of which offence to human nature the people of Norwich were quite possibly right to protest. But no doubt by now they have become 'sophisticated'.

The difficulty of sustaining any objections to the decline in criticism from a firm adherence to human values may be seen if we examine a page of a newspaper containing cultural criticism. Opposite is a facsimile of the review page of a staid and responsible newspaper, the Edinburgh *Evening News*. As with most newspapers, the 'criticism' of film and television picks up the style of publicity hand-outs. 'Next to Rod Steiger, a dog with the saddest eyes ever seen on TV ... took the acting honours in *Across the Bridge*. ... When you have a top-form Steiger, you don't need anybody else. ...'

The effect of this tone is to establish an ethos in which it becomes impossible to question the 'success' of the film – commercial success, as with *Candy*, being the chief criterion ('6 million readers ... this masterpiece').

On the page under discussion a dilemma arises. John Gibson seems genuinely horrified by the film *The Penthouse*. He sees through the pretence of the film to have a moral, and sees that this is but a 'flimsy excuse'. But since he cannot escape from the bright tone of film reviewing, he cannot avoid a phrase which could itself be used for further advertising: 'a positive brute of a film'. That should surely fetch the apes in?

The reviewer's account of the film makes it plain that the plot of this film is no more than a 'flimsy excuse' for indulgence in hatred. The film symbolises the rape of the secret core of being, symbolised by the woman who is attacked by those who have given themselves up to a force outside themselves (marijuana) and beyond the control of ruth. A symbolism of being 'infinitely exploited' is used to exploit the anxieties of the audience for commercial success.

The critic does well to reject the film. But he cannot discredit it; his last flippant remark about making the audience dislike the 'mixed up meter men' takes the sting out of his criticism – while the glamorous photograph alongside in fact turns his review into an advocacy of it. The pretty girl's face says to the reader, 'Come and see this beautiful woman savaged and humiliated' – or, virtually 'come and rape yourself'.

Next door to this review, with its indirect invitation to indulge in dehumanisation for entertainment's sake is a note on the presentation on television of an actual murder. This horrible incident is described in a manner equally chatty: 'looked decidedly trigger-happy', 'scared-stiff prisoner', 'a scream, a twitch, and it was all over', 'Some war'. To the student of language it is horrifying that in describing such an actual event the reviewer should use the same bubbling idiom as he is going on to use for describing the 'dog with the saddest eyes you have ever seen on TV'. Later the BBC screened the execution and it was reported that while the wretched victim was tied up waiting for the firing squad a television camera man shouted 'Hold it!' because he needed a fresh battery for his camera. Fromm's warning on increasing indifference seems increasingly relevant in a world of entertainment in which the simulated rape of a woman and the actual murder of a man are handled as if they are on the same plane as a Bank Holiday treat or an 'irresistible animal'.

One of the reasons for the confusion of values at this level is the growing nihilism in

Getting high
in the penthouse...

'The Penthouse' (ABC Ritz) has been passed for exhibition when no child under 16 is present. Personally, I wouldn't exhibit it when anyone is present.

A married man (Terence Morgan) and his mistress (Suzy Kendall) are conducting an affair in the penthouse of a London skyscraper block of flats. It's the morning after. Enter two psychopaths posing as meter men.

They tie up the man, who's a bit of a wet fish from the start, and at knifepoint force half a bottle of whisky down the woman. Then they persuade her to share a reefer.

When they are high and she's higher, one of the intruders leads her into the bedroom. When he comes out his mate takes over.

There's supposed to be a moral here. Which is worse of the two evils – adultery or rape? But this is a flimsy excuse for a positive brute of film.

Where this concoction succeeds is in making the audience dislike the mixed-up meter men, Tony Beckley and Norman Rodway.

John Gibson

■ TELEVIEW ■ DEATH COMES
THE BIAFRAN WAY

By JOHN GIBSON

How often do you witness a real killing on TV? Seldom – and I am not complaining. We can do without the blood. But I.T.N. in News at Ten were well within their rights in screening a killing direct from the mad men's war in Biafra.

Besides, viewers were warned that the next four minutes of film would be harrowing and advised to switch off if they were squeamish.

Federal troops, who looked decidedly trigger-happy, earlier in the programme were seen questioning a scared-stiff prisoner who, they claimed, was a Biafran soldier or sympathiser.

After assuring the prisoner and I.T.N.'s Michael Nicholson that they had no intention of killing him, they tied him up by the roadside and promptly riddled him with bullets. A scream, a twitch, and it was over.

'We are screening this because it provides vital evidence that there's needless brutality in this war,' said I.T.N. They stressed that the Nigerian officer who pumped home the bullets was later court-martialled and shot by firing squad. Some war.

FIG. 4.

minority culture – itself a schizoid phenomenon. Many serious works are acclaimed today *because they are about nothing*. Thus an American critic writes on Beckett:

> It is idle to ask what Beckett's novels and plays are 'about'. In any traditional or conventional sense. they are 'about nothing' . . . [but] . . . it is the most significant 'nothing' in twentieth century literature. Beckett's works are not empty intellectual exercises, but profound explorations of human intellectual dissociation. . . . (Hoffman [65], p. xii.)

Neither producer, nor author, nor actor make any claim to understand what the work is about in terms of the symbolic exploration of the nature of being human. Its effect on the audience as 'symbolic equation' is what matters. A theatre producer devoted to schizoid theatre will graduate from Beckett to Genet in the pursuit of equation symbolism. Here are some revealing remarks from an interview with Peter Lennon:

> Roger Blin, who was the first to put on a play by Beckett . . . the other night . . . sat reminiscing on the days twelve years ago when *Godot* first came into his hands. . . .
> 'What was your first reaction to *Godot*?'
> 'I was struck by its extraordinary observation of everyday life. For me *Godot* is a very "realistic" play.'
> He thought for a moment and then leaned forward and began to dismantle the play like a mechanic, twisting cupped fingers in the air as he spoke: 'I saw a marvellous economy of the means of expression and a great talent for creating a prolongation between the lines; there is a subtle relationship between what is said and what is implied and a masterly use of interrupted dialogue. . . . '
> 'I had to take over the role of Pozzo when the actor who was to have done it quit because he could not get into the part. Jean Martin played Lucky. From the first he played with that terrible, trembling shiver. It upset people. *Women would go out with a handkerchief pressed to their mouth and vomit.* Better than nothing, I thought. But the play was a tremendous success from the very first.'
> 'How did people interpret the play then?'
> 'Some people think that Vladimir and Estragon are, you know!' – he winked and stretched his arms out, in the crowded café, in an attitude of crucifixion. 'The good thief and the bad thief! . . .
> 'I think, mind you,' he said, nodding down from between outstretched hands, 'that they may well be the good and the bad thief. Godot for me,' he said, coming down to earth, 'is whatever permits us to keep on living that five minutes more. But an English lady had it all worked out. Vladimir and Estragon were England and France, always quarrelling but never able to completely break away. Pozzo was' (he articulated slowly) 'the Union of Soviet Socialist Republics which holds Lucky (Poland) in subjection. And Godot!' His eyebrows shot up. 'Godot was American aid! I asked Sam once who Godot was and he said it was a pair of old Army boots. . . .
> 'I would like to put on Genet's *Les Paravents*, but the French Army won't let me. It's banned. With Beckett it is like the work of a milliner.' He began to stitch, stitch, stitch, shortsightedly to get the point across. 'I never pronounce the word "production" in connection with Beckett. . . .
> 'I put on *Krapp's Last Tape* at the TNP. But I mistrust it a little. I think it is a little sentimental . . .' (My italics).

The 'sentimentality' Blin sees in *Krapp's Last Tape* is a sentimentality found in all Beckett whose work, when examined for its meaning, offers little but the renunciation of the need to begin to engage with life at all and a recommendation of the flight into withdrawal or inanition.* Occasionally, as in *Krapp's Last Tape*, the sentimentality shows through despite its inverted form. Victorian melodrama sought to portray life in reassuring black and white terms and to deny the complexity that struggled within each human nature – even the blackest villain could be redeemed by a passionate appeal to turn from black to white. We reject such sentimentality because it is essentially anti-human: as Winnicott says of sentimentality, there is hate in it, 'and sooner or later the hate turns up'.

Beckett's inversion of sentimentality is just as unreal and anti-human. To deny all creativity and love in schizoid futility is as gross as to deny all hate and guilt: both forms of denial are means to avoid the essential problems of ambivalence and the core of ego-weakness. A nihilistic writer like Beckett seeks to forfeit all creative effort in a fog of grey, self-pitying withdrawal. Such schizoid regression in art has been masked by forms of criticism in which humanness has been eradicated as a critical criterion. So we have a

---

* Cf. 'Peggy Guggenheim in her memoirs compared Beckett to Goncharov's hero Oblomov, who can scarcely bring himself to leave his bed, and even in those younger days Beckett rose in mid-afternoon struggling with the apathy he was to render in . . . *En Attendant Godot*' (Richard Ellman, *James Joyce*, p. 661). Beckett's work is devoted to the futility of ever being born.

cultural atmosphere in which it has become virtually impossible to draw attention to the schizoid skeleton in the cupboard of our world of art and entertainment because to do so seems to challenge art itself. This book has been an attempt to drag that skeleton firmly into view while trying to suggest that if we were not so fascinated and deceived by false postures we might be able to do something about the disastrous dearth of true creativity at large.

Criticism at the moment is prostrate before schizoid inversion. Here, for instance, is a review of a Pinter play in *The Guardian*:

> 'Tea Party' is a very good play, indeed, written with extraordinary definition and clarity, and yet with all those strange undertones of the sinister and the absurd of which he is a master.
>
> It is an advance upon his earlier play as seen on television because the area of vagueness is much less; in 'Tea Party' it is no longer possible to wonder just how or what some of the characters are or what they are up to. And yet, while all is so clear, it is clothed in the ambiguities and suspicions which Robert, the big business man, and in the end the man of tragedy, feels increasingly and which are symbolically shown in the apparent loss of his sight. His beautiful wife and her relationship to her own brother, his secretary to whom he is attracted, and the two maligned little boys of his first marriage, all are involved in a gruesome manoeuvring which has the precision of a ballet and the deadliness of a nightmare. . . . (Mary Crozier, *The Guardian*).

'All those strange undertones of the sinister and the absurd of which he is a master'. . . . 'The precision of a ballet and the deadliness of a nightmare'. Such trite adulation cloaks the perception that though Harold Pinter's 'area of vagueness' in this play is 'much less' in extent, his work has the effect of exerting hate on the audience. Yet even if the reviewer felt such misgivings, how could they be expressed when the cultural event in question was so big ('The largest theatre in the world' of the European Broadcasting Union's project) ? It seems irrelevant to ask what the art is about – and indeed, Pinter seems most anxious to thrust aside any inquiry into the human meaning and intentions of his art. All Pinter will ever express is a sense of being taken over by a particular mood: 'I've started a couple of pages of something different. A new form, and I'm diving. It's simply, as it stands, about a woman of around fifty. And she's talking. That's all I bloody well know. . . .' He speaks as if the artist had no volition: yet his interviewer indicates some conscious choice of 'impact' material: 'sexual games and fetishistic objects . . . spice the confrontation'.

An older critic, with more resources, can make reservations about a fashionable cult, as Philip Hope-Wallace so often does:

> At first and even into the second, sadder half, the relentless ribaldry and poker-faced outrageousness of Harold Pinter's new enigmatic parable ('The Homecoming' at the Aldwych) was relished by the first night audience – or most of them. Gleeful squeals of joy greeted the unvarnished home-truths exchanged by Cockney brothers in a widower's home, welcoming back a brother from America and his ex-model suburban British wife with a view to inducing her to go on the streets and keep them in comfort. But in the end I sensed some disappointment and shared. The thing is perfectly turned, but to what end?
>
> No doubt that is the wrong question to ask. These Pinter pieces, variously amusing according to taste and often fraught with that fashionable commodity, menace, are not really 'about' anything. This play is not 'about' a moral exposé as is Lenormad's 'Les Ratés' for example. The pieces are quadrilles, stylishly danced, or like the arabesques and whorls in paint to be seen on the easels of *avante garde* art dealers: superbly executed doodles.
>
> Boredom can set in fairly early with the rationalist. I enjoy myself the outrageousness and am quite happy with the baffling message of motiveless evil lurking in wait. But to me (and to me only it may be) Mr. Pinter reverses the chief pleasure in the theatre: which is to sit with fellow humans (the audience) either fully in-the-know or in keen curiosity as to the general state of affairs and then to see the players, probably not in full knowledge or in misguided expectation make a mess of or redeem events through

their 'own' devices and character. In Pinter the thing is the other way up. It is *we* who are exchanging wreathed smiles and knowing nods of complicity . . . it leaves us feeling cheated.*

But even this critic, despite his sense of a human reference, is doubtful of questioning fashion. 'No doubt that is the wrong question to ask' – because schizoid fashions have taken over the Arts today, it is no longer acceptable to invoke human values.

It is only fair to add that sometimes the mask is penetrated. Here, for instance, is the drama critic of *The Times* reviewing Edward Bond's *Saved*:

> It contains the ugliest scene I have ever seen on any stage – where a teenage gang daub a baby with excrement and stone it to death.
> One can no longer take cover behind the phrase 'bad taste' in the face of such material. But one has a right to demand what purpose it fulfils. In a recent interview Mr. Bond said that his aim was to 'illuminate' violence. One would hardly guess this from the play itself which does nothing to lay bare the motives for violence and appeals to no emotions beyond those aroused by the act itself. According to one's proclivities these may be horror, sadistic relish, or amusement: a fair proportion of last night's audience fell into the third category.
> The most charitable interpretation of the play would be as a counterblast to theatrical fashion, stripping off the glamour to show that cruelty *is* disgusting and that domestic naturalism is boring. But the writing itself, with its self-admiring jokes, and gloating approach to moments of brutality and erotic humiliation, does not support this view. In so far as the claustrophobically private action has any larger repercussions, it amounts to a systematic degradation of the human animal.

This is a most penetrating response. The critic strips away the masks to discuss the essential schizoid element in the play – the attitude of 'might as well give oneself up to the joys of hating' – as in the 'gloating approach' to moments when hate is exploited and in which humanness is being subject to attack and 'degradation'. *Saved* is one of the works around which the present-day controversy over censorship hovers. Many liberal individuals in the world of culture confess that when they seek to endorse complete toleration they find themselves defending such works as *Saved* which secretly and privately fill them with repulsion and fear. The fear is justified, for *Saved* represents the kind of manifestation of cultural hate which does not stop at the limits of art. As art loses its sense of symbolic purpose it becomes mere equation attack, whose purpose is merely to follow the schizoid mode in art. As the above critic indicates, the whole ethos of creativity and criticism is affected by erosion: one can no longer refer effectively to 'bad taste' since bad taste preponderates, while the audience largely responds by finding the violent, disgusting, and anti-human *amusing*. Again, we may distantly hear the laughter of Storm-troopers as they force a Jew at gun-point to scrub the pavements in the ghetto. The gloating laughter of the sadist manifests a false joy and derision at the symbolic humiliation of his own feared human weaknesses, projected over his victim, and attacked there. Bond's baby victim is the 'regressed ego' in each of us, and the satisfaction such a play promotes is that of seeking to crush the essentially human life in ourselves.

The same baby reappeared in 1971, on a mountainside in Persepolis, when Ted Hughes' *Orghast* was performed, a strange play which opened with a baby being stamped on. Yet this symbolic baby is, too, 'Littleblood' (or the one Sylvia Plath called 'Littlesoul') – the regressed libidinal ego that wants to be born. In his poem in *Crow* Ted Hughes writes the truth, which is that one wants this creature to

> Sit on my finger, sing in my ear, O littleblood . . .

For, like the pulse Sylvia Plath hears in her ears, he seeks to cry I am, I am:

* In *The Listener* (29 June, 1965) Mr. Hope-Wallace added: 'A gesture has been made, but what does it mean?'

O littleblood, hiding from the mountains in the mountains
Wounded by stars and leaking shadow . . .
O littleblood, drumming in a cow's skull
Dancing with a gnat's feet . . .
Sucking death's mouldy tits . . .

This essential body-assurance that one is alive can also be menacing: as Sylvia Plath cried, 'I am terrified of this dark thing that sleeps in me'. So, one can stamp it out on a mountain side, or stone it on the stage of a London Theatre.

The critic is faced continually today with postures of the rejection and destruction of this weak, inward self. So, every publisher's catalogue, and every review of a batch of novels thrusts at us grotesque manifestations of False Solution phantasy. A reviewer in *The Guardian* will cheerfully commend a novel for its 'realism', even, in presenting a hero who rapes two hundred woman. In this ethos, the novel can only be accepted as a form of destructive phantasy play – supplying a regular dose of schizoid 'bad thinking'. At least these phantasies help us feel alive in a dehumanised society that menaces our sense of identity: but they also contribute to the dehumanisation. At the same time both the status of man, and the status of the novel as art, are reduced.

Again, I am in difficulties, because I cannot mention the novelists I would most like to mention. Significantly, some of them are very attractive women. But again, there is a distressing inability for the university educated mind to escape from the pressures of commercialised culture, and condemn the moral inversions which have gradually been made to serve its need for a large return on invested money. Novelists are commended for their 'Ugly scenes of sexual seduction', and for the compelling effects of their perverted phantasies ('he doesn't sleep with her until she irritates him, when he does, and turns out to be mildly diseased, so she comes home to be cured'). These sordid episodes are written with 'beguiling grace', and there is praise for the 'sad mechanics of loveless seduction' – inevitably. The novelist is 'earnest' in postulating that an attractive unattached woman 'can only express herself through sexual relations.'

In saying this, a reviewer said that this opened a debate 'beyond the confines of a book review' – and again we have the problem of the increasing unwillingness of reviewers, as in film, to make life difficult for themselves by invoking the ethical standards of real life at a time when these have to be flouted for economic purposes by publishers and their authors. (An Australia author, Martin Boyd, to his credit, gave up writing altogether when his publisher demanded that he should spice his next work with sex).

Most novels, by reviewer's accounts, must be pretty thin creatively, to need so much hate to sustain them: but, of course, as with film, much of this hate can be made acceptable by charm. A good deal of the basis of the appeal of the popular modern novel is a form of that 'confession' which Masud Khan tells us is an aspect of the false attempts of self-cure of the pervert. Yet this, which Khan points out is a form of idealism and idolisation of the sexual functions, in lieu of genuine meeting in meaningful relationship, is taken to be 'realism'. Of course, if someone with the stature of a Camus is writing, then the negative impulses and forms of behaviour in characters can be seen as 'strategies of survival' and we may learn from the book, because we may learn how even the most destructive manifestations may have their own meaning – as they have, in the work of Jean Genet. Only because of this element which enables us to understand the world of the pervert, as Eugene Kaelin says in *An Existentialist Aesthetic,* can we accept his work as socially tolerable: otherwise we should have to reject it as outrageous pornography.

But there is no excuse for regarding ethical debate as being outside the scope of a book review. The reviewer's function is still to concern himself with the implications of a novel for human relationships. The problems of an 'attractive unattached woman' should surely be seen in the same light as those of anyone else – as problems of identity and relationship, and the need to find meaning in relationship and living. Moreover, in his selection of the behaviour of his characters, and in his presentation, the novelist must accept the heavy burden of artistic responsibility. As T. S. Eliot said:

> When we read of human beings behaving in certain ways, with the approval of the author, who gives his benediction to this behaviour by his attitude towards the result of the behaviour arranged by himself, we can be influenced towards behaving in the same way.
>
> *Religion and Literature*, quoted in *Trousered Apes*, Duncan Williams, p. 3

Literature, as Duncan Williams says, is caught up in 'the great crisis of the present' – but it is also responsible to a degree for this crisis. The increasing exploitation of schizoid hate in such things as popular novels means that even in teaching people to respond to literature we are, as Ivor Wynters has said, 'We are teaching savagery'. Students are encouraged to read books which are described as 'brilliantly dirty', or books in which a character says about sex, 'What a good, clean, busy feeling you get if you've done it to *get* something' – in a book described by the reviewer as a 'sharp little parable'. It is difficult to analyse the way in which a certain sophisticated air of acceptance in both reviewer and author manages to convey approval abroad of an essentially schizoid attitude to human nature. Sex is characteristically 'it' – as it is in the weeklies and Sundays every week, and we have ceased to flinch from the implicit dehumanisation and hate. Such writing is a form of nihilism in the arts, which conveys abroad an essential homunculism, to use Viktor Frankl's useful term. One can hardly bring oneself to protest that it is *love* they are talking about – that which can yield meaning, *sub specie aeternitatis*, at best. Every batch of novels smutches the sphere of intimate dialogue, of meeting, of our deepest need for confirmation in the 'encounter' with another, indeed, the original course of our human identity. Yet the reviewers go on giggling and saying their bright things, subservient to the commercial business on which they depend for their livelihood. Yet not only are we damaged in our sense of what it is to be human: such travesties of human truth make it increasingly impossible for such a great writer as Alexander Solzhenitsyn to assert the groping human need for 'mutual affection' and the quest for meaning against a dehumanised society in all its brutality. They contribute to the schizoid alienation of man.

From the point of view of philosophical anthropology, we can surely no longer be complacent about the effects of such schizoid modes, in prompting 'bad thinking' and moral inversion. Does the suburban novel-reader really need so many 'brilliantly dirty' compensations for existential frustration? Do they not influence him, to think of man in a certain brutal way – so that his empathy is reduced? Here is the publisher's announcement of a typical novel: *The Man who had Power Over Women*:

> Peter Reaney is probably half mad and certainly half drunk when the White Cliffs give him instant insight into English condition. . . . His head is crammed with lurid notions – one moment he is dreaming of rounding up every woman in Oxford Street for service in State Brothel Number One (the old Hilton), the next of being the last potent male on earth. The complex factor in his life is that he is no pallid neurotic but a big, burly man whose bawdy excesses could be seen as healthy counter-attacks on the futility of the life he sees around him. . . . But just who or what is Reaney? An embryo Hitler? The post-Suez John Bull? A genius without talent? Don Juan crippled by respect for people? A whisky pope? He may be all of these things. But he is certainly *alive*.

Is the state of book sales so bad that publishers have to depend upon such phantasies of compensation for existential frustration? Is it our freedom to read such matter with which the Arts Council is concerned? How has such a mere elaborate dirty joke come to be acceptable entertainment? It seems incredible that enough people are prepared to pay a pound or two for such a book. Such books are solemnly read and coolly discussed by respectable maiden ladies, widows, and other provincial library users who show no sense of a need to invoke the truth of their own experience, to reject such a view of the world as psychopathological.

But even light reading cannot go this way without involving each reader in some forfeiture of a sense of human dignity and without serious erosion of the way he conceives of himself. If we are to have confidence in human potentialities for the future, surely we need to defend symbolism from such ill-use?

It will not do to say that 'people don't take such things seriously'. We have seen that all our effective life depends upon delusions – and it is the quality of our delusions that counts in our creative living. Of course, at times the cult of hate exposes itself as a ludicrous pose. In an interview with John Horder (*The Guardian*, 26 March 1965) the Japanese novelist Jukio Mishima said:

> ... I also write light novels for women's magazines, which is the way 90 per cent of Japanese writers make a living.
> My serious novels all concern death in one form or another. Death is a most familiar concept in Japan and has much in common with child feeding at a mother's breast. No matter how ambitious or productive a person is, everything is related back to one or other of these states. In the end sex and death are rightly related in a strange way. Double suicide is our great national invention and is the perfect culmination of the two. The couple almost always have sexual intercourse before they kill themselves. This way of death flourished in the eighteenth century, and must be the highest ecstasy of human desires. ...

'Must be' is choice: certainly no one can protest from experience that it is not so! Yet such 'outrageous' play on themes of hate can be made in the absence of all protest by the shrugging aside of all human realities in the context of demoralisation. Of course, *The Guardian* might protest they published this in irony: but there was no sign of this. (Since the time of writing, this author has taken part in a group act of hari-kiri, evidently psychopathological.)

The problem here is that, as the cultural coverage of such a paper as *The Guardian* declines into *facherie* and make-belief modishness, even the atmosphere in which disciplines by which finer attitudes to human nature might be upheld is dissolved into bright nonsense while such values as human dignity are quietly eroded. Surely there are dangers in the continual erosion of reference to normal values, while abnormal values are cultivated instead? Here Anthony Burgess, again in an interview with John Horder, offers an 'explanation' of his impulse to write in 'psychological' terms:

> I write because I've a childish inability to separate fantasy from reality. It's pathological, I suppose. I do write out of high spirits but the actual business can be a hell of a chore. My wife and I are not very in love with life – we both tend to be suicidal and manic-depressive. Life is interesting as raw material but I find significance not in the world but in the imagination. Writing novels is making the world dance to your tune, you know. The world continuously fails to live up to my ideal for it, so all I am left with is what goes on in my imagination. ...

Such superficial play with psychological terms makes it even more difficult to use psychoanalytical insights seriously to see what is wrong with our culture. Because of the fashion for schizoid modes, such a writer can even offer a turning against life as the basis

of his appeal. It is as if he feels obliged to find some pathological potentiality in himself –
which is, of course, what Norman Mailer has advised writers to do.

Behind the scenes there is often honest confusion over the schizoid problem: in a
personal note to the present writer Norman Shrapnel, a novel reviewer for *The Guardian*,
reports on his response to Henry Miller (prompted by a protest from me):

> I first took ... (Henry) Miller to be a mocker, self-protective and therefore (in his terms) life-
> protective. I now think that is wrong or largely wrong. I still can't bring myself to think as you do and
> you *may* be right, that he's anti-life. Certainly he's a destroyer. Maybe I've committed the grisly and
> elementary mistake of accepting him at his own valuation – i.e. as a destroyer of life gone bad, gone
> dead (the illusion, I suppose, of all the violence-obsessed), whereas it could be that he's just a destroyer,
> point. But as I say, I can't really believe that. ...

Perhaps we could have agreed, if we had exchanged notes on such destructiveness as a
'false means of feeling real': but what lies hidden is the exploitation by Miller of culture
as an area of 'trust' in the ways indicated by Khan.

There is no doubt a deal of goodwill among those who cope with a batch of novels
every week in Fleet Street – they are so unwilling to believe in hate that they cannot see it
in the books they deal with. If the novelist abuses trust, however, the critic should surely
say so unless he is to abuse trust himself. The attitude to man expressed in his symbolism
at whatever level affects our society at its very roots, in that area of which Winnicott says:
'The potential space between baby and mother, between child and family, between
individual and society, or the world, depends on experience which leads to trust. It can be
looked upon as sacred to the individual in that it is here that the individual experiences
creative living.' (Winnicott [60], p. 372.)

There is no occasion to be merely trivial or to tacitly join the lynch-party, when our
deepest needs are at stake.

One manifestation in our culture which is all too plain to those who watch television
only on rare occasions is the amount of hate thrust into the home in order to hold a mass
audience. Yet so active have the apologists been that it seems quite eccentric nowadays
to refer to it. Once more we have here acquired 'sophistication' so that, daunted by the
gigantic size of such an industrial enterprise as the television communications system, we
are prepared to accept an amount of hate that would have been unthinkable a decade
ago. Here we may take as an example 'Steptoe and Son'. An undercurrent of hate was
the essential basis of the appeal of this programme: 'No-one is going to get me drunk on
a half-pint of cider, take me up an alley and do me. ...'

This is a typical protest by the son to his father. If we study the scripts we find that
the whole appeal of this television series is in an underplay on anal sadism associated with
Oedipal feelings in a self-conscious way which is very different from the traditional
vulgarity of a clown or a Chaplin. One episode begins and ends in the lavatory:

> ALBERT *pours some disinfectant down the pan and scrubs away ... he then pulls the chain ... he tries to open the
> door. It won't budge. ...*
> (*Shouts*) Help. help. I'm in here. ...

This begins like a Chaplin episode: the old man locked in the lavatory. Yet, if we
reflect, the incident couldn't *quite* have occurred, not in a Chaplin film, with such explicit
'sophisticated' emphasis on the lavatory and the cloacal and anal elements. Certainly,
before television, which is an *intimate* medium, no such episode would have dwelt so
insistently on such violent language with its primitive origins (from two episodes):

I'll smash his head in. . . . I'll stuff this brush right down his. . . . I'll stuff your feet in as well. . . .
Just remember the story about the little boy who stuffed his finger up the dyke. . . . (ALBERT *looks*
puzzled.)
HAROLD (*holds his finger up*): You think about it . . . that's all. . . . This house is going to be hotter than
a Beatle's earhole. Oh, up your pipe. . . .

    ALBERT: I'm not having that thing in bed with me.
    H.: What's wrong with it? It'll be like a built-in warming pan.
    A.: It's too dangerous.
    H.: Perhaps you're right. If you get those scrawny little knees stuck in the gaps, it'd be a very hard
job explaining it to the fire brigade. It'd look very kinky . . .

    (ALBERT *is asleep in the lavatory.*)
    (HAROLD *reaches up and pulls the chain.* ALBERT *leaps up in terror and yells*)
    A.: Oh . . . help . . . what . . . achh . . . ohh . . . (*feels his backside to see if it's wet*).He gets right in my
Bristols he does . . . ['Bristols' = rhyming slang for Bristol City = titty]. It would have invited a kick
up the Khyber at least . . . ['Khyber' = rhyming slang for Khyber Pass = arse].

    (HAROLD *returns with an armful of swords, and proceeds to drive them through the cracks in the* [*lavatory*] *door* . . .
we see (ALBERT) *inside the lavatory, hemmed in by swords.*

Men may talk like this – but not to their families. And few would dwell so monoton-
ously on the anus. The dialogue is not in any sense to be justified on the grounds of
'realism'. The obscenity seems to be there merely for 'impact'. This vulgarity is surely
extreme, even given the need to attract a mass audience? What is the damage to
sensibility? That the authors are intellectual shows in the explicit and knowing references
to 'kleptomania' and so forth. I quote these extracts to suggest that in 'Steptoe and Son'
we have something which is not an intuitive clowning over unconscious anxiety, like a
coarse circus turn, but represents the choice of certain cultural modes – what I would
call 'hate' modes – by 'educated' middle-class writers for a mass medium dominated
by the needs of advertisers (since the BBC is in competition with 'independent' television).

This programme, however, is given adulation that almost runs to reverence from the
cultural sociologists Hall and Whanel in *The Popular Arts* because it is about 'workers' and
is watched by 'the people'. 'We feel something indestructible about them . . .', they say.
Did the 'people' or their popular heroes ever talk like this? 'Kleptomania is not tealeafing.
It's an illness . . . this Xenophobic fixation he's got. . . .'

The 'educated' air merely masks a crude attack on human nature – something utterly
at the other extreme from the compassionate bathos of *Modern Times*.

Perhaps the indifference of readers is the most alarming aspect of the increasing exploitation of hate in our culture. Suppose one saw people calmly accepting an anti-semitic
neo-Nazi paper? Yet English middle-class wives show no recoil from articles containing
rabid hatred of woman symbolically expressed in much of the writing and many of the
illustrations. Indeed, by now (1968) the ethos of our journalistic literary world is now so
inverted that it is thought to be gay and fun to be impelled by hate. For instance,
reviewing Montherlant's *The Girls* in *The Times Saturday Review* (17 August 1968), Kay
Dick says his work is 'packed with gorgeous wisdom about love and work' – yet she
admits he 'prefers to be known as a woman-hating womanizer'. One might expect a
woman journalist to protest against the expression of hatred for women, if not against
perversion ('he has a basic taste, for juveniles'). Yet the readers of *The Times* are not at all
disturbed, and there is no protest.

Nova is a choice example of a new genre in this sphere. It exudes hatred of being human
from every page. Discussing novels, an article in it once considered women writers'
attitudes to sex.

In Brigid Brophy's *Flesh* the overbearing Nancy resolves the problem of her husband's virginity and ignorance by teaching him how. He is a willing pupil though he resents her superiority, calling her a 'careers mistress' and finally repaying her by making love to the 'au pair' on the drawing room floor. Baba, the anarchic, swinging Irish girl of Edna O'Brien's novels, marries an impotent man knowingly and then proceeds to take it rather badly, swearing at him as he sleeps in this passage from *Girls In Their Married Bliss*: 'The vote, I thought, means nothing to women, we should be armed. I got back and kept addressing curses to his big thick pyjama back. Boor.' Ellen Sage, in a passionate pilgrimage to the Riviera in Miss O'Brien's *August is a Wicked Month*, finds the sands oily with sleazy, incompetent men. But she keeps searching and finally runs a Hollywood actor to earth. He performs satisfactorily enough, though briefly: her own passion during the act appears to stupefy him: he reels away after muttering one word – 'Jesus'. This short-term pleasure is costly for Ellen. She is left with a case of clap. (Possible moral: mostly they can't do it at all – when they can, it may be tainted. Live alone. It's safer.)

This is supposed to be an exposé of the hatred of men in women writers, but, with its use of blunt, depersonalised sex terms, it is at one with the exhibition of hate-sex it pretends to deplore. Indeed, this is its appeal. The terms used for love-making are characterised by a tone of depersonalised hatred: 'it', 'they can't do it at all', 'clap', etc. This reduction of the sexual life by the language of hate is interspersed with picking from the books themselves – choice moments of exhibitionist play on anxiety, as by this vision of a 'multiple object': 'The divorcée in Edna O'Brien's next novel *August is a Wicked Month*, can state that she "longed to be naked with all the men in the world making love to her, all at once".'

'Better to be a bad someone than a good nobody' is a strategy here supported by the short story in the same number in which unconscious fear of relationship and hate of woman is displayed. Here again is the masturbatory 'multiple object' phantasy subtly mingled with syphilophobia, a common symptom of identity fear and fear of love in the adolescent. A man visits an eastern country and stays in a house in which he is unsure whether it is the mother or daughter who visits him in the night. The underlying distaste for bodily reality is allowed to break through nastily: the protagonist meets the wife:

'How very nice,' she said quietly, coming forward.
I took her hand and raised it to my lips. 'I am overcome by your kindness, madame,' I murmured. There was, upon that hand of hers, a diabolical perfume. It was almost exclusively animal. The subtle, sexy secretions of the sperm-whale, the male musk-deer, and the beaver were all there, pungent and obscene beyond words; they dominated the blend completely, and only faint traces of the clean vegetable oils – lemon, cajaput, and zeroli – were allowed to come through. It was superb! And another thing I noticed in the flash of that first moment was this: when I took her hand, she did not, as other women do, let it lie limply across my palm like a fillet of raw fish. Instead, she placed her thumb *underneath* my own hand, with the fingers on top; and thus she was able to – and I swear she did – exert a gentle but suggestive pressure upon my hand as I administered the conventional kiss.

We have the boast of super-potency, and a posture of sophistication, as in 'James Bond', disguising psychic impotence and ignorance:

Here I must pause. This is not like me at all – I know that. But just for once, I wish to be excused a detailed description of the great scene that followed. I have my own reasons for this and I beg you to respect them. In any case, it will do you no harm to exercise your own imagination for a change, and if you wish, I will stimulate it a little by saying simply and truthfully that of the many thousands and thousands of women I have known in my time, none has transported me to greater extremes of ecstasy than this lady of the Sinai Desert. Her dexterity was amazing. Her passion was intense. Her range was unbelievable. At every turn, she was ready with some new and intricate manoeuvre. And to cap it all, she possessed the most subtle and recondite style I have ever encountered. She was a great artist. She was a genius.

Note 'the great scene', 'thousands and thousands of women I have known in my time . . .', 'her range was unbelievable'. The writing belongs to the tradition of erotic suggestiveness of the Paul de Kock tradition – 'he felt the curves under her *déshabille* . . . her heaving *embonpoint* . . .', etc.: the formula has only changed a little towards 'sophistication'. But what is new is the degree of hate in the 'confession' of 'super-potency'.

While the style invites us to indulge in such phantasies, it offers us the same 'knowingness' as we find in Fleming, disguising a parallel ignorance of human truth. The 'bad thinking' seems more real than what we know to be real, like the patient of Guntrip who masqueraded his 'masculine protest' before the mirror.

Again the unconscious origin of the story is in our fear of the primeval talion woman which the writer is arousing. In magazines such as *Nova* this emphasis on the hate and fear focused on this myth-woman of our unconscious phantasy is what makes for success.

'That daughter,' he said at length, 'the one you met – she isn't the only daughter I have.'
'Oh, really?'
'I've got another who is five years older than her.'
'And just as beautiful, no doubt,' I said. 'Where does she live? In Beirut?'
'No, she's in the house.'
'In which house? Not the one we've just left?'
'Yes.'
'But I never saw her!'
'Well,' he said, turning suddenly to watch my face, 'maybe not.'
'But why?'
'She has leprosy.'
I jumped.
'Yes, I know,' he said. 'it's a terrible thing. She has the worst kind, too, poor girl. It's called anaesthetic leprosy. It is highly resistant, and almost impossible to cure. If only it were the nodular variety, it would be much easier. But it isn't, and there you are. So when a visitor comes to the house, she keeps to her own apartment, on the third floor . . .'
The car must have pulled into the filling-station about then because the next thing I can remember was seeing Mr. Adbul Aziz sitting there looking at me with those small clever black eyes of his, and he was saying. 'But my dear fellow, you mustn't alarm yourself like this. Calm yourself down, Mr. Cornelius, calm yourself down! It is not a very contagious disease. You have to have the most *intimate* contact with the person in order to catch it. . . .'
I got out of the car slowly and stood in the sunshine. The Arab with the diseased face was grinning at me and saying, 'Fan-belt all fixed now. Everything fine.' I reached into my pocket for cigarettes, but my hand was shaking so violently I dropped the packet to the ground. I bent down and retrieved it. Then I got a cigarette out and managed to light it. When I looked up again, I saw the green Rolls-Royce already half a mile down the road and going away fast.

From the point of view of object-relations psychology, what is 'new' about such writing is its 'diminution of affect' – and of extremist play on dehumanized sex and on hate. In the more sophisticated journals today we find an increasing play on negative emotions. Yet this nihilism springs from no radical principle in thought or idea. Of course, this would not work unless underlying it was a desperate need at large in individuals to feel real in a dehumanising environment. Dismayed by a world which dwarfs them and their hopes for meaning they turn in desperation to 'bad thinking'. It is, after all, indicative that the bulk of the sales of such papers as *Nova* and *Playboy* are made from railway bookstalls, to tired travellers who want to be relieved of their ennui in transit by a negative thrust to the sensibility. The reader may study the nudes and other symbols in such papers in terms of the 'schizoid diagnosis'. The motive behind all this (as E. J. Mishan has said) is economic, but it supplies a feeling of being alive in a dead society. Yet this ploy is vindicated by the advocacy of those who believe demoralisation to be the way of a new freedom.

Yet the overall picture is one of an increasing flight from being human, in a desperate exploitation of hostility and dehumanisation.

When arguments based on the theory of 'release of impulse' in favour of more violence are taken to extremes, the effect is to seem to vindicate the schizoid inversion of values of a new positive. Hate is even offered in advertisements as a new value:

> Gift books befitting the Moral Revolution that has brought a new togetherness into the American Home.
> 1. The Marquis of Sade's *120 Days of Sodom* with Dr. Iwan Bloch's equally famous *The Sexual Enlightenment of a Corrupt Society*, the most ruthless of Europe's erotic classics.
> (Advertisement in *New York Review of Books*, December 1965.)

Note here that to be 'ruthless' is a positive, while sadism is 'revolutionary', bringing 'togetherness': this is 'welfare pornography'.

The arguments of such a representative figure as John Calder are another example of the extremes to which 'impulse' theory can lead us as a basis for cultural morality. Calder claims that there is a need to provide cultural means for people to 'get violence out of their system' because this will educate them:

> Kraft-Ebbing may have written the 'Psychopathia Sexualis' for specialists, as Bach and Haydn wrote much of their music for the dignitaries of small German courts, but the spread of education and culture has today made both accessible to millions. It would be an insult to a people that likes to think of itself as free to suggest it should be any other way. Of course sadistic literature can stimulate sadistic impulses which are probably present in all of us. The answer is not to keep people in ignorance of these impulses which can lead to many other antisocial manifestations, but to allow them to develop the sophistication in facing them which . . . educated people have already developed for themselves.
> We live in an age of mass adult education by means of television, the press, the paperback revolution, and the affluence which enables more people to travel and absorb new ideas and new attitudes. Increasingly, people's moral attitudes are based on their own common sense, that is to say, that they adopt social attitudes because they understand the necessity for them rather than out of fear of hell-fire or legal chastisement.
> There will always be dangerous lunatics in our midst just as there will always be bad drivers and people who abuse such social pleasure as alcohol, sex, etc. The responsibility of society is to educate more people to face the anti-social forces that may be present in their own natures, to live with them and control them. Any attempt to put the clock back by direct or indirect censorship can only be seen as retrograde in our development as a civilised nation.
> I do not think that there is any mystical way in which people can get violence out of their system by viewing it, but the intellectual development that enables civilised people to put horror into its proper perspective can no longer be confined to a small proportion of the population and any attempt to limit this sophistication can only have the dangerous result of allowing poison to flourish while withholding the antidote. (John Calder, from a letter to *The Guardian*.)

In the light of object-relations psychology the assumptions here are invalid. Our capacity to live with our own aggression depends upon our 'healthy moral sense' and whether we can accept our human make-up at a very deep level of bodily and emotional life in complex with our psychic life and the sensitive processes of ego-maintenance. This is not a conflict of 'reason' with 'emotion' and we do not modify violence by intellect alone. 'Sophistication' is by no means the quality required to create civilisation within ourselves in terms of the True Self. Looked at more closely, I suspect Calder's 'sophistication' means 'indifference' – and a turning over to False Self activity. It may be true that 'bad thinking' about sex and violence can bring a kind of sophisticated 'togetherness' – and we have met it before in a certain morally inverted blood brotherhood. There is also the problem of the need of a schizoid individual to thrust harm into others, which we have explored, and these need their 'sophistication' limited.

In any case, does Calder's advertisement of an 'irreverent' book, reproduced below, endorse his view of himself as an educator?

ARE YOU EASILY SHOCKED?

We have seldom seen the reviewers quite so humourless as over *I Jan Cremer* the autobiography of a young Dutch topster who sold over 100,000 copies in Holland and is now moving up on the British bestseller list. The zestful, admittedly shocking but funny, readable and incredibly alive snook cast at all our taboos makes delightful irreverent reading in spite of such mixed reviews as: '*It is a shapeless rag-bag of experience and egotism, almost all of it ugly and sordid*' – Newcastle Journal. '*Written to shock, and it does.*' – The Queen. '*The filthiest book I have ever read.*' – Western Daily Press. '*This chunk of childish filth is brilliantly adroit*' – The Scotsman. '*So now Holland's most sensational book comes to Britain. It speaks with the authentic voice of chip-on shoulder youth dedicated to setting fire to everybody over the age of 35*' – Sunday Citizen. '*Dutch courage with vengeance*' – Observer. '*The ring of Henry Miller at his bawdiest*' – Sunday Times. Personally, we have of course some good reviews too, especially of Alexander Trocchi's brilliant translation. We recommend it to all anti-authoritarian adults with a sense of humour. . . . (Advertisement in *The Guardian*.)

In my last examples I wish to consider some of the implicit attitudes to personal behaviour, and especially the sexual life, to show how far these may be from the 'human facts' established by object-relations psychology. As we have seen, while reviewers occasionally protest, there is little fundamental concern shown by any of them that the exploitation of depersonalised sex in our culture offends human dignity. If there is protest, it is merely jocular:

Those old stand-bys birth, copulation, and death do heavy duty this week, the second even more so than usual so that passages read like the life and time of what were once laughably styled the pudenda. Viva Vulva! Vagina Regina! One has no wish to make a molehill out of the mons veneris, but it will be a happy day for fiction when sex finds its level as an element and not the be-all and end-all of experience. So if priority over a cluster of talented ladies goes to *The Indian Summer of Gabriel Murray* it is partly because it is not riveted entirely below the waist . . . etc. (Christopher Wordsworth, *The Guardian*, June 1968.)*

Our protest needs to be grounded on objections such as those implied by Frankl's dictum, 'sexual libido becomes rampant at a time of existential frustration'. But there is also the objection that, in the light of philosophical anthropology, so much of the sex in our culture is a ridiculous travesty of human truth, and often its complete inversion.

In a newspaper interview, for instance, a well-known young actress (said to be a 'trend-setter' in the 'sexy society') said that 'if one was in love it was difficult to be unfaithful'. She did not say that if one was in love one did not want to be unfaithful, but spoke rather as if love made it difficult to keep up with the orthodoxy of being unorthodox by sexual promiscuity.† In film, play, or novel the tendency grows to present incidents of infidelity without any investigation of the deeper causes or consequences, but in 'amoral' terms of the (acceptable) 'reality' of 'how people behave'. (In John Osborne's latest play two women share a man with no sign of jealousy.)

This amorality goes with the lack of realism. Infidelity expresses the anguish of those who find it hard to be real, and who lack capacities for object-constancy – who are thus unable to fulfil the deepest primary aim in themselves, which is to find 'creative reflection' or confirmation in meeting. Of course, such a belief depends upon accepting Fairbairn's belief that 'the individual in his libidinal capacity is not pleasure-seeking but object-seeking'. Where such aims are not being fulfilled, we encounter the deepest problems of identity. These are so painful to us that we defend ourselves against them

---

* The following week a (favourable) review by the same writer of a book by Edna O'Brien bore the heading 'Irish Jig-a-Jig'. Taste has sunk a long way since the time of Forster and Lawrence!

† Similarly, an American journal for adolescent girls said: 'Marriage was still the best solution to the problem of sex.' It is not that the primary human need for love and relationship is expressed in marriage – but marriage is a 'solution' to a 'problem' of impulse.

either by moralising against promiscuous individuals in an authoritarian way which is hypoparanoid, or take an amoral stance which is hypomanic – both ways of denying the guilt, fear, and hate aroused in us by threats to our relational goal.

In our ethos the 'amoral' stance has an additional attraction which is that it allows us to feel that such manifestations as promiscuity or adultery are larger-than-life forms of behaviour. Here we can perhaps see the connections with the 'confession' of perversion and its hallucinations. Although in fact infidelity is a manifestation of our most dreaded human weaknesses of ambivalence and dependence, we can by 'bad thinking' make it seem heroic. And this heroism of the 'false solution' is endorsed by attributing its cause to 'society'. This tendency to blame 'society' for our sexual problems can obviously be traced to the influence of Wilhelm Reich, one of the most extraordinary figures in the history of psychoanalysis. From the 'schizoid diagnosis' it now seems evident that Reich himself was a schizoid individual whose symbolic concern with 'inner contents' became manifest in many aspects of his thought and life, as, for instance, in his 'economic' theories of orgasm, and his researches into ways of conserving the amounts of energy in the body, by orgone boxes, and the rest. Such a schizoid individual might well become, as Reich did, the victim of paranoid delusions later in life. But he, too, rejected the separation of sex from the personal life which characterises the pseudo-revolution and sexology.

The greatest traumatic experience in Reich's youth was his mother's suicide, which seems to have followed her son's betrayal of a sexual infidelity. From this, perhaps a whole pattern or strategy arises with its own symbolism. Only remove social opprobrium, and the guilt of betraying the mother will be overcome and the 'good' mother restored. Reich's theories divert our attention from the essential problems of the sexual life, which are problems of meaning and identity in relationship, and by rationalisation throw the blame over 'society'. This false solution impelled Reich's programme of sex clinics for the proletariat and his impulse to bring about a social revolution through sexual 'freedom' – an enthusiasm which has been revived in our time. Yet in the light of object-relations and existential psychoanalysis, such an impulse would seem to be a mere form of compensation for existential frustration.

When *The Sexual Revolution* was examined by the *International Journal of Psychoanalysis* the reviewer said scathingly, 'the reader will be surprised to learn that the author had passed adolescence quite some time before this book was written'. Yet Reich now takes a leading place among the heroes of present-day 'enlightenment', though his social theories seem far less realistic and profound than many psychoanalysts who are neglected by popular thought, such as Fairbairn, who insisted that the primary libidinal goal was not sex, but relationship; and the existentialist psychoanalysts who insist that man's primary need is 'confirmation' and 'meaning'.

Factors which affect the degree to which an individual can achieve his relational goals include the degree to which he can tolerate dependence and bear his own weakness – that is, how much he dares to depend upon another in love, and how much he dare be human. Good relationship can be an important source of a sense of well-being, security, and richness. As Joan Rivière says:

> ... true love, as we call it, is precisely a condition in which the two factors coalesce and become indistinguishable, in which ease of mind and happiness are perpetually being derived from the fact that the man or woman is full of a love which can satisfy and fulfil the needs even of another beside himself. A mutual love serves as a double insurance against pain, destructiveness and inner destitution;

and also, in complementing and fulfilling each other's sexual needs, each transforms the sexual desire of the other from a potential pain and source of destructiveness in him or her, to an absolute pleasure and source of well-being. . . . (Klein [39], p. 44.)

In such a relationship 'the advantages of dependence' are 'used to the full'. It is important to notice the recognition here of ambivalence – of the destructive elements, and the dangers of loss, loneliness, and helplessness, inherent in our love-needs, elements against which love has to strive. Love can never exist without these problems of identity, of goodness, and reparation. It is a significant mark of much 'enlightened' comment and culture dealing with sexual matters and matters of relationship today that it ignores these problems, or seeks to pretend they 'need not matter'. Thus there is a degree of falsification which is disguised in many ways, usually by a posture of 'liberation'.

Here we may consider such a sensational paperback on sexual relationships as *Talking to Women* by Nell Dunn [14] as an example. One tendency in much modern culture and comment shown here is to elevate infidelity and 'sexual freedom' – compensations for ego-weakness – to a high value. To believe that schizoid depersonalisation is a high form of life goes with a posture of 'amorality' which offers itself as enlightened, realistic, and 'advanced'. In an exchange from this work, between Nell Dunn and Edna O'Brien the conversation goes thus:

> NELL: Do you have any definite moral code, do you think you know the difference between right and wrong? You see I think this is one of the problems almost of our generation, that everything seems to have gone under our feet and why we're so insecure is that we –
> EDNA: – have no moral code.
> NELL: No moral code and we don't really know what we're meant to be doing.
> EDNA: I believe in only one or two sins, cruelty, killing, injustice. These are sins, everything else, lust, sex, adultery, covetousness are venial, you know, they're just little flaws. . . . (Dunn [14], p. 82.)

Making allowances for the sloppy expression of a tape-recorded interview we can yet see that Edna O'Brien wishes to believe that the destructiveness and hate in sexual behaviour is not 'there' – or, if it is, it is not as harmful as the hate in 'cruelty' or 'killing'. She goes on:

> But I apply that moral code only to myself because I imagine I have intelligence and discipline enough to get through life sensibly . . . I think that oddly enough with the fierce sort of so-called freedom, sexual freedom and Sunday orgies and smoking marijuana and all that, there is a much greater morality than there used to be. I really do think that. I think there's greater heartlessness and I think people at parties who say to each other, as I hear people saying at parties, 'Feel like a fuck' is a terribly joyless thing really. But I think that in itself it reflects a sort of aching morality. Because they're not enjoying it there's no abandon . . . when the people who pick up a boy or a girl in the tube and go home and make love even there's nothing immoral in their action because the whole thing is a nothing. It's as casual to them as going to Wandsworth Baths and having a swim. There's a fierce hollowness in relationships now. This creates a new morality. The morality of the lovely and the uncommitted. The uncertainty! The feeling that maybe it didn't happen – as in *Last Year at Marienbad*. I think morality is intrinsic to people's natures. It just takes on another complexion.

> (Dunn [14], p. 83.)

Edna O'Brien's point of view here may serve usefully as typical of what may be called the attitude of London 'enlightenment'. Her words are rambling. But in so far as they convey anything, it is that her attitudes to personal relationships are essentially based on the endorsement of false solutions and inverted values. They offer 'False Male Doing' as valid without any sense of how 'being' and the True Self may be violated. Her values (and her tone) endorse the schizoid attitude to experience despite some uncanny insights. Later in the same interview she says, typically:

I have never sort of examined my body, my entire body. Even if I look at it, I don't *examine* it
because of my squeamishness. The words vagina and womb, these words fill me with terror . . . the
bulk of my body is closed to my enjoyment of it . . . I think of my body as a sort of vehicle for sin. . . .
This preoccupation with sin makes for a greater excitement in the act of love. . . . (Dunn [14], p. 89.)

That a woman can talk in such a way shows that we have all been persuaded that
the schizoid attitudes prevalent in our culture are marks of 'realism' and 'frankness
There is no sense of any offence to the True Self or to 'being'. The prevalent ethos urges
an attention to sex which is depersonalised, and seeks to elevate to the highest values that
de-emotionalised sex from which dependence and emotional commitment with all their
dangers have been excluded. It is fashionable to deny the anguish of the problems of
identity and human need for confirmation involved in such a sphere. Our ethos cannot
find a high value in sex as the expression of the meeting of human beings who commit
themselves to each other as persons of human value, so we exaggerate the amount of
'hollow relationship' in the world, and try to believe that this is the (acceptable) norm.
Edna O'Brien has enough insight to see the joylessness and meaninglessness of casual
sex – but she seeks to elevate this 'reduction in quality of the relationship' desired into a
'new morality'.

It is true in a sense that it is a 'new' morality, in the sense that it substitutes hate for
love, as she herself does by finding a 'greater excitement' in using her own body, of which
she is so greatly afraid and which is 'closed to enjoyment' as a 'vehicle of sin'. This
impulse certainly has a heroic 'moral fierceness' because it manifests such a desperate
need to feel real by 'bad thinking' and 'bad activity' where other sources are not available.

The level of debate in Nell Dunn's book is, of course, banal ('And as marriage is still
very much with society, it really is, that this is the only way you can sort of say it and
even if it's going to break up a year later I don't think it matters all that much because
for a while you really said that thing, you know . . .'). But the effect is to communicate
a certain strength of inverted values which convey the impression that is it 'modern' and
'progressive' to deny one's humanity – and that a strength of identity can be built on
this denial. 'I am sort of horrified by the idea that one should marry and make love to
one man and that should be one's whole life. . . . There seem very few practical reasons
for sexual fidelity in marriage. . . .'

While we can condemn such misrepresentation as anti-human, we can understand
how today how easy it is for such writers to adopt schizoid attitudes (and how difficult
it is to resist them). The women expressing such rejections of life are often beautiful,
and the covers of their books are decorated with nudes, to arouse our sadistic
interest.

It is, however, important to invoke the truth as it seems to the student of human nature
who knows individuals in need, when all false solutions have broken down: 'The mani-
fold forms and manifestations of infidelity (being the outcome of most varied ways of
development and expressing in some people mainly love, in others mainly hatred, with
all degrees in between) have one phenomenon in common: the repeated turning away
from a [loved] person, which partly springs from *fear of dependence*.'

Melanie Klein sees the problem as one of weak identity and fear of loss: 'I have found
that the typical Don Juan in the depths of his mind is haunted by the dread of the death
of loved people, and that this fear would break through and express itself in feelings of
depression and in great mental sufferings if he had not developed this particular defence –
his infidelity – against them'. (Klein [39], p. 86.)

Guntrip reports in a private communication that a typical promiscuous patient said: 'I'm sick of sex: it's a much over-rated activity'. None of this man's women meant anything to him at all as persons. One of the most important things we learn from object-relations psychology is confirmation of the human fact that such 'sexual freedom' often means relational inadequacy, and is a False Male Doing activity to sustain a weak identity. For this reason the effect of the 'sexual revolution' has been, as Farber says, if anything, to tend to destroy the validity of sexual experience itself.

Edna O'Brien is correct in acclaiming the modern obsession with depersonalised sex as a fierce (inverted) morality, in a sense, because it is a defence against the fear of loving. It is a fierce schizoid morality of 'pure' inversion of hate for love. Their de-emotionalised sex ('Feel like a fuck') belongs to a desperate quest to feel alive – which they must, however, do by exerting the will over the realm of being in order to hold off its dangers. They cannot, and *must not*, love. The root of such aberrant conduct is in failures of earliest environment, and the consequent failure to become fully human. For, as Melanie Klein goes on: 'By means of this "infidelity" "the unfaithful man" is proving to himself over and over again that his one greatly loved object (originally his mother, whose death he dreaded because he felt his love for her to be greedy and destructive), is not after all indispensable since he can always find another woman to whom he has passionate but shallow feelings.'

To Melanie Klein a Don Juan, for instance, 'by turning to other women and giving them pleasure and love he is in his unconscious mind retaining the loved mother or recreating her. . . .'

There is a destructive element, since 'In reality he is driven from one person to another, since the other person soon comes to stand again for his mother'. But there is also a healing impulse: 'In unconscious phantasy he is recreating or healing his mother by means of sexual gratifications (which he actually gives to other women), for only in one aspect is his sexuality felt to be dangerous; in another aspect it is felt to be curative and to make her happy . . .' (Klein [39], p. 87).

From the point of view of object-relations psychology we can see that depersonalised promiscuity may be 'curative' in its intentions. But in the cultural exploitation of depersonalised sex we have thus the tendency to deprive individuals even of the recognition of this curative impulse. Where writers fall for schizoid inversion, they tend to encourage individuals to feel that the activity intended to be 'curative' is health itself: and that such bad thinking and 'doing' is enough to solve the problems of being. Attention is thus diverted from genuine problems and the paths by which real solutions could be sought by promulgating attitudes to the sexual life which involve a complete inversion of the human facts.

There is thus a complete divergence between the 'human truths' established by philosophical anthropology and those asserted by the fashionable literary world of novels and plays. So much in our present-day culture derives its appeal from the denial of dependence and the taboo on weakness that it must actually make the quest for fulfilment more difficult for millions.

The capacity to bear dependence, one's need for others, as we have seen, is a concept of great importance to social and political thought, since many human woes and horrors spring from our capacity to deny these in various forms, as we have seen. No society can look forward to true freedom in which individuals regard each other with respect as equals unless a majority can accept their humanness and seek meaning in mature love. Attitudes to the sexual life in a culture are therefore crucial to our political health: where we have degeneration of attitudes to identity and love we have the threat of nihilistic decadence – a lesson we should have learnt from the Germany of the 1930's, as Frankl points out, from his most terrible experience of the consequences.

Will the reader agree with me, after following through these examples, that something is disturbingly wrong with our cultural atmosphere and its standards? We can admit that something strange is happening without, I hope, flying into the arms of 'reaction'. There are no true solutions in hypoparanoia. But yet it remains true that hypomanic solutions are often nothing but delusions.

Yet I believe *more resistance* to hate in culture is necessary. It is necessary to insist, from Camus's recognition of the right of others to live, that there is a fundamental ethical principle, that we cannot be allowed to live at the expense of others. As cultural comment becomes increasingly involved in what I have called schizoid modes, it tends to vindicate hate as a solution to the problem of life. To escape these false modes of thinking, we must recover our confidence in being human. Loss of this confidence threatens us with dissociation at the roots of our psychic security. Where such a false manifestation occurs, as we know from history, there are likely to be outbreaks of another kind in reaction, themselves based on hate, in a desperate quest for a sense of significance – but through false solutions.

The problem is thus not merely one of 'public morals' or 'a tide of sexuality': it is a problem of sources of confirmation of identity and of finding significance in life itself. If we could be persuaded by schizoid modes of thought that to seek significance in life is futile, then a barbarism far worse than Nazism could eventually ensue, out of a desperate need to find some positive by which life could seem to have a meaning. Since normal paths to find our humanity would then be blocked, methods might be likely to be adopted which were anti-human – the pursuit of some new 'purity', or perhaps some ultimate schizoid depersonalisation (as in extremist sexuality).* There is no real strength in schizoid solutions – despite the braggadocio, the 'black' sex, and the aggressive 'frank' talk and cult of violence. The postures of our modish *avant-garde* culture are as empty and sentimental as those of commercial culture and journalism because they cannot accept human fact and arise from a flight from life. Genuine solutions can only come from recognition that we can be no more than human. Yet, obviously, this is what in the predominant ethos we can least bear to recognise. The truth of being human such as we know in ourselves because it is in each of us has virtually ceased to be a touchstone for any critic, and it is this that will not do, as it betrays us to the anti-human. In my invocation of the attitude to man inherent in object-relations psychology I am seeking to restore this preoccupation with true humanness.

* See the present author's *The Pseudo-revolution*, Tom Stacey, 1972.

PART III

Conclusions: The Need to be Human

CHAPTER 26

The Redemption of Creativity

ONE problem that can be tackled is the organisation of culture. The technology of culture itself seems to place a premium on false solutions to the problem of life and to foster the predominance of schizoid symbolism. The traditional attitudes of liberal tolerance will not serve to deal with this problem because they are not realistic enough. A recent debate on censorship in *The Author*, journal of the Society of Authors, was concluded by an editorial with a quotation from Chekov: 'You cannot find a better police for literature than the author's own conscience. People have been trying to discover such a police force since the creation of the world – but nothing better has been found.'

Alas, as we have seen, there are authors whose approach to human experience is based on something which is even worse than a lack of conscience, for their most energetic impulse is to reverse the processes of conscience altogether so that it becomes good and vital to seek to press harm into others and even to invert human values completely. Moreover, authors can be highly rewarded for doing so.

Here there are considerable philosophical problems involved. The problem of finding an adequate basis for cultural discrimination can be seen, I believe, in the work of Professor Jules Henry, whose *Culture Against Man* makes such very valuable criticisms of the trends of our social life towards the anti-human. While he makes trenchant criticisms and has many insights, Professor Henry seems unable to find fundamentally effective grounds for his protest. This is so because he remains a Freudian and believes that culture is a modified form of 'release of instinct'. Because of this he shares the same fundamental attitude to man of his opponents in advertising and commercial culture. Yet if we explore his work in the light of the schizoid diagnosis we can see that his objections to what is happening have ethical grounds enough if we see them in terms of how they affect identity.

It is no distortion of Winnicott's distinction between False Self activity and True Self 'being' to apply it to these social spheres at large and say that our society has come to attach the sense of being real and alive to False Self Doing at the expense of True Self 'being' and the discovery of the essentially human. Buber says something similar when he speaks of the 'bustle' that distracts us. Our acquisitive society has attached the sense of identity largely to 'pseudo-male' activity without sufficient roots in the female elements of intuition, creativity, and sympathy. Some of Professor Henry's strictures would seem to be compatible with this view.

For instance, Henry takes strong objection to the forms of present-day teenage dancing:

> In interpreting [teenage dancing] I used a very fierce expression, 'where there is no meat, hungry
> dogs will not salivate' because I wanted to make clear the degradation implied in our culture by such
> flamboyant provocation. . . . The degradation derives from the fact that the girls convert themselves
> into mere 'backsides'. Turning their buttocks to the boys, the girls are really saying, 'We know that
> there is nothing to *you* except the capacity to rut at the sight of our fannies.' (Henry [29], p. 271.)

He complains that these children 'degrade one another to their sexual components'·
But on what grounds, according to Freudian theory, could he object? It is, however,
possible to object, in terms of the depersonalisation of sex and the way such 'release'
activity leads to a situation in which their 'sexual components' or part-object qualities
are divided from persons while human value is depreciated ('There is nothing to you
except . . .').

Henry makes many comments on our cultural predicament not from the point of view
of Freudian theory but from intuitive common sense, and here it is significant that object-
relations theory confirms his insights. For instance, he says: 'In a competitive culture one
envies anything good that happens to anybody else: it is enough to know that
somebody – anybody – has something good, for one to become depressed or envious or
both. In a competitive culture, anybody's success at anything is one's own defeat, even
though one is completely uninvolved in the process' (Henry [29], p. 153).

This suggests that where identity is based on ingestion the problem arises of ingestion
at the expense of others: on envy. From our analysis of *Goldfinger* it will be obvious how
this envy goes with paranoia and other hate mechanisms. The promotion of envy
inevitably offends basic ethical principles.

The need to assert the identity at the expense of others, plays havoc, as Henry says,
with the American woman. Here, especially, we can see the relevance of Winnicott's
insights into the relationship between *being* and *doing*:

> The idea that a woman does not have to *do* anything to prove herself, that she need merely *be*, and
> that in the fullness of motherhood, as she produces one child after another her femininity will be
> obvious for all to see, does not fit contemporary America. It does not square with Madison Avenue,
> where a lot of money is spent for advertising that tells a woman how to prove to the world and to
> herself that she is every inch a female. . . . (Henry [29], p. 153.)

Again, according to Freudian tenets, there is no objection to persuading a woman thus
to base her sense of identity on incorporation and on her 'sexual components'. In the
light of schizoid diagnosis, however, there is a danger – which is hinted at by Henry
here – that the 'partial object' aspect, or the 'backside' aspect of woman, as an edible
'dish', may become over-emphasised at the expense of the person, and at the expense of
being, and of her wholeness as a human creature.

She can be deflected from True Self, Feminine Element, Being, into False Self,
Pseudo-male Element Doing. Yet her satisfactions are in being a woman and in seeking
the potentialities of the True Self as an individual. And, in so far as this happens to
woman, it happens to the female element in men too. A glance through *Seventeen* magazine, or at Henry's analysis of teenage life in America, will reveal in this light the essential
falsity of a culture which prompts individuals to base their sense of identity so exclusively
on 'doing' aspects of themselves, and on a 'taking' approach to relationship and experience.

American children have to exert frenetic pretend-sex, sustained by padded bras, on
the one hand, and 'steady' relationships at an over-early age, as a protection against
insecurity, on the other. This frenetic False Solution activity obviously undermines
genuine youthful relationships, and so the whole problem of identity. But at a deeper

level still this promotion of false solutions distracts from the necessary 'confrontation of the problem of existence' at the heart of being.

Underlying the hedonistic ethos of commerce and advertising there lies a 'philosophic system' which Henry analyses. From our point of view, where humanness is denied and the ways of hate are followed, we would expect to find an underlying essential contempt for humanity emerging from the fear of being human. This is exactly what Henry, from his very different point of view, finds in commerce and especially in advertising. Moreover, the fear of being human which promotes the contempt for people is also associated with the manic element, so evident in the American glossy magazine. Its 'part-object', 'stream of milk' symbolism asserts 'aliveness', but this must be split off from ambivalent, mortal, human reality: everything is surface-gleaming and happy. Public optimism must be sustained for the sake of the sales drive and commercial activity. But beneath this manic 'vitality' there is a fear of inanition itself – and of the *necessary* silence in which one can establish touch with oneself.

The public is being conditioned all the time to feel that the reality of existence would become unbearable unless the manic mood of the acquisitive ethos – in expansion and bustling 'doing' – were sustained. Without advertisements, without continual 'pop' music, without the preoccupation with such pseudo-events as the high-school girl's dream of a conventional wedding and other 'external' activities, how could the humdrum round of life be endured?* At the same time there seems to be a growing clash between the actuality of the life of the poor and 'disadvantaged' in America and the delusions and dreams of the affluent society displayed in the next street and on television. In the face of this, certain deprived social groups resort to the false solutions of rioting and looting. These seem 'meaningless' – unless we see them in the light of the schizoid diagnosis, when they may be seen as the expression of anguished concern to find a genuine sense of being real, diverted into envy. Yet the hedonism and the acquisitive ethos which prompt the rioter merely seem mocks and empty lies – which in the light of our deeper needs they indeed are.

Such outbursts of anti-social hate expose the essential falsity of a form of social organisation in which the sense of the meaning of life is attached to 'taking' and its concomitant envy. In such a society there is in all a widespread unconscious yearning for 'giving', 'meeting', and 'finding' and for genuine 'creative reparation'. But this commerce must divert into 'taking' and manic 'activity'. In this the industrial-commercial use of the powerful media at its disposal is manifestly cynical, and can be seen to be seeking to control human beings out of fear and contempt.

The essential fear and contempt for humanity in commerce is not hard to find. Henry points out that in advertising we sometimes find a horrifying indifference to human beings and their welfare:

> Perhaps the most terrifying revelation before the Senate Committee came in connection with the examinations of the advertising policies of the *Journal of the American Medical Association*, where it was brought out that an advertisement for a drug called *Norlutin* bore no warning that thirty-six pregnant women had given birth to sexually abnormal daughters after being given the drug. Meanwhile, according to the testimony, the very issue of the *Journal* carrying the article that made these disclosures had an advertisement for *Norlutin* also. The ads continued for three months thereafter. (Henry [29], p. 56.)

Such episodes reveal, as Henry says, that commerce regards individuals as 'expend-

---

* The bizarre nature of commercial culture in seeking to preserve the manic even in the face of death is evident in the American mortician business. Even the corpse, rouged and fitted with a 'breathing' device, is enlisted in 'manic denial' and 'false doing'.

able'. Certainly, advertising is indifferent to its effects on identity: 'some new cosmetic may make her imagine for a moment that she *is* something. But such "help", such *product therapy*, is merely palliative at best and lethal at worst; for products in fancy dress sustain and support underlying flaws, while assuring girls that they have nothing to offer a man but allure.'

Advertising, as Henry indicates, plays on women's fears of not being feminine and on men's fear of woman ('many men retain a lurking fear of woman'). Henry discusses this in Freudian terms: it offers an orgasm which 'does not unite one overwhelmingly to another human being': this we can see as a 'make belief' whose aim is not to find the person. It puts 'a rising living standard in the place of true self-realisation'. And it lowers the standard of human dignity. 'The modes of thought and the view of man entertained by pecuniary philosophy have been shown to derive in part from fear and contempt. Thus we have discovered that an industry now contributing nearly 12,000,000,000 dollars to the national product derives much of its dynamism from contempt and fear. It has also the most radical conception of *Homo sapiens* that has ever been proposed. . . .'

This conception of *Homo sapiens* may be radical, but it also tends to be schizoid and implies a reduction of human value. What is most schizoid about it is that it regards the 'system' of commerce as far more important than the human individual.

Henry, interestingly enough, even sees Madison Avenue as itself schizoid in its cultural amorality:

> . . . we are asked to believe that advertising brings us CULTURE.
> Being a separate society islanded in the winds of Madison Avenue, advertising cannot perceive how bizarre it is. Advertising is out of contact with us and so is unable to see that you do not address yourself in double-talk, in 'pecuniary-think' to adversaries who are criticizing you for it. Furthermore, to try to fob off on their critics the notion that the radio and TV catastrophes are CULTURE is beyond belief in people not harboured safely behind the protective screens of a psychiatric hospital. Let me put it this way: a fundamental index of schizophrenia is disconnectedness, so that one is unaware of how other people think and feel. When a person is crazy or merely pathogenic and functions in a schizoid way we say he is out of contact or disconnected. When a large group of people acts in this way towards us we say that they constitute a separate culture. . . . (Henry [29], p. 94.)

Henry says that advertising will not see its ethical position according to traditional orientations. This schizoid dissociation, as I have tried to suggest, is not confined to advertising, but is a feature of our whole commercial culture and journalism *which depend upon advertising economically*, and so become increasingly divided from traditional values which are based on a disinterested concern with humanness. Henry uses the term schizoid in a loose way: but he has, by intuition, put his finger on the essential problem.

He sees the social dangers of this schizoid element in commercial culture. Advertising, for instance, develops an arrogance which impels it to appeal to children over the heads of their parents, as a separate 'market' – and he finds parallels between this and Nazism: 'His arrogance is terrifyingly reminiscent of another appeal to children over the heads of their parents: that of the Nazi Youth movement, for it too usurped parental function. The way the Nazis did it was by making society state centred. What we have done is to combine product-centredness with child-centredness to produce a unique American amalgam.'

The sum of the huge cultural force which advertising exerts 'exercises great moral pressure on the morals of the country'. The trouble is that truth to the advertiser is 'what will sell the product' – so there is a dissociation at the heart of this morality which is disseminated by a power at least equal to the effort put into education.

In journalism today we have the promotion of 'amorality', based on no authentic philosophy. In advertising, as Henry points out, we have a new 'realism' which declares that it may as well admit that it is vulgar, and takes up a stance on a schizoid denial of the relevance of values:

> Aesthetes and apologists can rail at its vulgarity, its brashness, its aggressiveness, its insistence, its lack of cultural values, its crass commercialism, its loudness and its single-mindedness – but let them rail, he contended. (Mr William D. Tyler, executive president of Benton and Bowles, and co-chairman of the Committee for the Improvement of Advertising Content in America). These are the qualities 'that have built the nation,' Mr. Tyler said. 'They are qualities of virility.'
>
> The agency executive went on, 'This is not to say that advertising should glory in vulgarity. But let's face up to the fact that frank and honest materialism is not a weakness. It is a sign of strength. So if advertising reflects us as vulgarly virile, let's not blame advertising. Let's change it, but not blame it. Because the mirror does not lie. And let's accept it as a lusty fact of life, not necessarily admirable, but nothing to wring your hands about either.' (Henry [29], p. 99.)

The 12,000,000,000 dollars spent annually on advertising in America is hardly concerned to 'mirror' human nature. It is rather devoted, incidentally, to persuading us to develop a certain radical attitude to human nature and to think of ourselves in a certain way for purposes which are quite separate from any disinterested concern with the nature of man. Because it needs to persuade us to base identity on part-object and manic symbolism, it tends to be anti-human for reasons we have seen. From the point of view of Freudian psychology, which advertising tends to find congenial, it is true that it would be difficult to reject the argument that 'frank and honest materialism' is a 'sign of strength' or that 'vulgar virility' is 'lusty'. However, in the light of the schizoid diagnosis such an assertion would appear as an attempt to vindicate false solutions of a schizoid kind. It may be true that such false solutions of 'False Male Doing' have 'built the nation' – but this may also be what is wrong with the nation. For many problems in our world arise from the inability of a whole civilisation to find a true sense of being human and a true sense of the point of life.

Behind the calculated charm of the public relations façade lurks always the 'realism' of pragmatic utilitarianism by which individual human being is necessarily sacrificed to 'drives', the system, and to the debased attitudes to man inherent in it. Behind commerce and advertising there lurks a hominoid – a dehumanised product of ideation in the sphere of I–It, from which the I–Thou is rigorously excluded, a creature fit only to be exploited for the sake of keeping activity going. To this activity true individual needs may be sacrificed if this becomes necessary, and the advertising world is always ready to reveal that beneath its pretty surface lurks a ruthless pragmatic utilitarianism as indifferent to the humanness of others as James Bond. Indeed, this symbolic psychopath, as hero, has obviously been of great value to the advertiser in enlarging his scope (e.g. recent Cusenier advertisements on the London tube trains have implied that *Crème de menthe* will give one the sexual potency of a James Bond).

So, in recent years, a 'frankness' parallel to that of William D. Tyler has appeared in English advertisements, concerned to invert values in the sphere of cultural achievements itself. Here is an example – from a Vodka advertisement in a colour supplement:

CLIFF ADAMS   MUSIC TO BUY BY

> 'I ran a vocal group called the Stargazers. We were big stuff after the war, playing the BBC Show Band, the Forces Show, the Palladium. The Stargazers were around for years. Then one day I realised I'd grown out of it. I didn't want to be behind the footlights any more. So I took off the make-up, grew a beard and that was it.'
>
> Cliff Adams is like that. He faces a situation, makes a decision and sticks with it. Writing and arrang-

ing music for commercials. One of his first for Fry's Turkish Delight is still around. And he still likes it.
    This is the new type of Englishman. The professional. There's nothing of the dilettante about Cliff. Nothing of the frustrated musician who apologises for commercial work saying he'd really like to write a symphony. Cliff Adams works to order. He works for money. And what he does, he does very well indeed. He says this attitude is what the English revolution is all about. He talks about how people have changed. How they face things squarely. They want life to be straightforward, not full of unwritten rules. He says it shows in everything they do. The way they dress talk, write, think, even drink. He talks about what people drink nowadays. He says it's vodka. Cossack Vodka because it's a clean drink. Cossack Vodka because it's straightforward and makes no pretence. Cossack because it's a good clean drink that mixes well with everything. And tastes good on the rocks.
    Cliff Adams knows what he's talking about. Being successful is what counts in England now. He's proving it every day. So's Cossack Vodka.

The copywriter by his aggressive tone may reveal uncertainty of himself – perhaps discomfort at being a copywriter himself 'for money'.

The nervous arrogance of the advertisement surely goes beyond anything necessary or relevant to the business of selling vodka. It can be seen in one sense as an attempt by the copywriter to vindicate his own role. We should (he claims) relinquish discrimination against people who 'create' for commerce. But he goes beyond seeking to persuade us that Cliff Adams need feel no shame at being a hack ('He still likes it'). He wants to use the advertisement to invert values in the sphere of cultural activity, so that to make symbolism over to the utilitarian needs of the sales drive may be regarded as not only realistic, but admirable and accomplished. To invert values in this way, he claims, is part of a 'revolution' in the English cultural climate.

To write hack tunes for television advertisements is to be 'changed', to 'face things squarely', and 'to want life to be straightforward, not full of unwritten rules'. The 'unwritten rules' are conscience and those established values by which we tend to believe that it is of more human value, of more *distinction*, and much harder work, to write a symphony than to write a jingle for Fry's Turkish Delight. What is more important than such old-fashioned discriminations is for us to make it possible by a new realism to enable 'Cliff' not to feel 'frustrated' in working 'to order', when writing low-grade music for money. We should regard him as 'the new type of Englishman'. 'Being successful is what counts in England today'. To be unprincipled is to 'grow up' – to become sophisticated, to put away ideals and to accept the view of man which regards him as an 'animal' whose civilisation is a veneer and a delusion.

There is, however, another kind of 'realism', as we have seen, which makes it plain that the price of 'growing up' in any such way would be to suppress certain feelings and to deny certain fundamental human truths. That is, such a 'realistic' advertisement reveals a philosophy which is based on the endorsement of false solutions and the denial of primary human needs. There is an essential distinction to be made between that symbolism which is devoted to ego-maintenance as a genuine creative process and that which is devoted to the exploitation of appetite.

The cultural problem everywhere today may be associated with the failure to make this essential distinction. All nations today seem to need to maintain the sense of identity at large by various forms of symbolism based on false solutions. Identity is sustained by external activities, the manic, by acquisitiveness, and also by a complementary paranoia. In the present study we have seen how even in commercial entertainment and no less in *avant-garde* culture we find the same paranoid–schizoid solutions implicitly endorsed – as by prompting the delusion that in order to survive we need to divide the world into 'objects to be consumed and enemies to be attacked'. Success in sustaining an identity thus comes to be felt to be bound up with anti-human modes of behaviour and attitude, and these we feel we cannot relinquish without some peril to our collective sense of identity.

In the 'consumer field' people are reduced to objects for exploitation, sub-human entities which have only functions to be served, for which we need have only contempt. As Henry says:

> The truth in the advertisement is that men in our culture, often looking down on women as 'nervous' somewhat feeble-minded, and vapidly whimsical, tend to soothe them with false promises; but this is acceptable because it is a 'fact of life' ('The Facts of Life: Promise her anything but give her – ') 'Quiet her down; tell her anything; you don't have to make good' is the silent communication of this message.
> (Henry [29], p. 83.)

Meanwhile, in the field of external affairs, the identity requires a phantom of impending threat to sustain it.

> The concept of no ceiling on wealth has ripped the sky away, so that the idea of limitless space has come to play an enormous role in the twentieth century imagination. It is no accident, therefore, that Russia, the Great Nightmare of our time, should be imagined as vaulting in upon us from outer space to rob us. . . . (Henry [29], p. 10.)

As we have seen, from our analysis of *Goldfinger*, the paranoic fear is taken to be a reason why we are entitled to exploit others, control them, and treat them with contempt. Our own ego-centric hedonism has its roots in primitive envy and emptying: we fill ourselves at the expense of others, to offset the fear that some Great Nightmare shall empty us. Both impulses arise from the fact that we are, at the core of being, terrified of the emptiness within, where there should be a rich sense of being human. This diagnosis cannot be reached by Freudian thought. Henry is significantly restricted in his diagnosis by the way he divides human propensities: 'Ours is a driven culture. . . . Above all it is driven by expansiveness. . . . Drives like hunger, thirst, sex, and rest arise directly out of the chemistry of the body, whereas expansiveness, competitiveness, achievement, and so on are generated by the culture. . . .'

Here there is a dichotomy which arises from the Freudian picture itself. To Henry, the ('real') basic impulses are 'drives': they are only held in check by 'values' which belong to the Super-ego (which is not so real). It is as if 'values' were only *unwillingly* generated within human beings, and are neither real nor primary: 'Side by side with these drives is another groups of urges, such as gentleness, kindliness, and generosity, which I shall call values, and in our culture a central issue for the emotional life of everyone is the interplay between the two. Values and drives – other than physiological drives – are both creations of the culture. . . .'

Here, it will be seen, there is an implicit belief that altruistic 'values' have no primary origin in the human psyche and have no primary reality in human life. So 'love, kindness, quietness, contentment, fun, frankness, honesty, decency, relaxation, simplicity' are the mere products of coercion or of 'culture' and do not spring naturally from human being. Our 'real' self is the animal, which is what the ad-man, with Pinter, likes to believe.

We need to insist, from 'philosophical anthropology', that what is most real about man *are* these civilised values, and that he could not survive as a being unless each child 'creates civilisation within himself'. If this is so, where we find such essential needs to be civilised, thwarted, and reduced to secondary importance we must find that our essential humanity is being crushed. Many 'drives' of our culture from this point of view now appear as bustling forms of 'pseudo-male doing' by which individuals are seeking to hold a self together – with no real hope of doing so because there is no engagement with true needs and no path open to the True Self. Henry seems to find no place for the need to 'confront the problem of existence', for stillness, and contemplation, and, being a Freudian, he finds it difficult to find a true place for culture. It is this true central place for symbolism on which we must insist.

What hope is there, however, when so much cultural effort goes into the promotion of the symbolism of false solutions?* What hope is there of the primary function of symbolic creativity being redeemed, to be employed as it needs to be employed, solely in the realm of I–Thou, of meeting and confirmation of identity? For the legitimate pursuit and maintenance of humanness and the rejection of homunculism?

* No doubt there are those who feel I should have dealt with the work of Marshall McLuhan. I have never been able to take him seriously. The best comment I have seen was that made in a most thorough and considered account by Professor D. W. Harding in *The New York Review of Books*, 2 January 1969. Harding said: 'That such writing can be accepted raises discouraging questions about the reading capacity of the educated public. Tom Wolfe . . . suggested that people will begin to insist 'Start proving it.' That suggestion seems late in the day, but in fact a prior demand is necessary: 'Start saying it' – i.e., make a statement sufficiently unambiguous, with terms sufficiently defined, to be capable of proof or disproof. . . .' The cult of McLuhan seems to me a false solution in itself, and offers nothing with which one can engage profitably.

The Protection of Symbolism

OUR only hope of redeeming creativity is through the development of a realistic kind of humanist conscience such as I try to define in *Human Hope and the Death Instinct*. Even if we discover this kind of conscience in ourselves, we shall have a long struggle to establish grounds from which to challenge the prevalent exploitation of cultural trust.

Firstly, however, there must be no going back on the emphasis Raymond Williams makes when he insists that mass media for instance *are teaching*: 'here, centrally, is *teaching*, and teaching financed and distributed in a much larger way than in formal education'. (Williams [52], p. 15).

As I have emphasised, such 'teaching' radically affects our view of human personality – of how we conceive of ourselves. It therefore affects us at the root of being and in our pursuit of life-solutions. The view of human nature communicated in this 'education' is not at all the same as that conveyed by those who would seek to encourage us to develop potentialities through the humanities. On the contrary, it promotes subservience and the acceptance of a certain 'radical', but often cynical, view of human life. As Raymond Williams says: 'Organised economically, in its largest part, around advertising, it (the material discussed in his book) is increasingly organised culturally around the values and habits of the version of human personality . . . (which belongs to a capitalist society) which retains as its central principle . . . the idea of a few governing, communicating with, and teaching the many.' (Williams [52], p. 15).

That is, despite its claims to the contrary, mass communication is coercive. It claims to operate in the service of the 'freedom' of 'releasing' our acquisitive urges. But, as we have seen, it is entirely geared to the operations of an 'ingestion' economy, and so its concepts of 'freedom' and 'release' are falsified. It abuses the area of trust in culture by using symbolism for ends which dehumanise us. Its kind of 'teaching' is always subordinate to economic needs, and so its content is continually threatened by the need to deplete its human essence. Its main goal must remain the economic activity for its own sake. 'There is the widespread dependence on advertising money, which leads to a policy of getting a large audience as quickly as possible, to attract and hold advertisers. From this it becomes one of the major purposes of communication to sell a particular paper or programme. . .' (Williams [52], p. 33).

This affects our whole culture for, as Williams says, 'newspapers do not survive or fail according to how many people want them, but according to their suitability *as media for advertising*' (Williams [52], p. 29; my italics).

The consequence is that 'All basic purposes of communication – the sharing of human experience – can become subordinated to the *drive to sell*' (Williams [52], p. 33; my italics). At the deep level this means subordinated to a certain form of 'doing' in which activity is taken to be its own justification, while symbolism is limited to this purpose alone, and the underlying attitude to human nature must be so aligned as to permit this. The teaching of the mass media tends to endorse nihilistic homunculism.

One consequence which has become increasingly obvious in recent years is that human principles, ideas, values and opinions in our culture at many levels have become subordinate as never before to the assumed needs of economic activity and to 'economic survival'.

There was perhaps a time when these tendencies could be absorbed by traditional culture or contained, as by education. Today, however, the world of commerce seems disinclined to tolerate anything less than the complete subservience of culture to the 'needs of the economy'. At the same time the cultural minority largely become dependent upon commerce itself while even the 'protesting' minority becomes involved – as the case of Kaprow indicates – in a cultural homunculism essentially based on hate whose meaninglessness parallels the culture of the supermarket. In this situation, the journalist who serves the world of economic 'realism' can even treat the world of a disinterested concern with the humanities with disdain, and even see a pre-occupation with human values as 'suicidal'.

Thus in *The Times* of 19 February 1967 Clive Irving, writing on The Crisis in Communications, attacks 'introversion' in the media. In the background was the recent take-over of *The Times* by the Thomson organisation. However, 'in spite of such examples of union for commercial reasons, the day-to-day operations of the various media are conducted as though they remain in separate cells. Especially in the older industries, like newspapers, there is discernible in places a resentful introversion, a last-ditch suicide stand against a swiftly-changing environment.'

The tone and implications here are significant: everything must be subordinate to 'commercial reasons' and 'swift change'. To 'remain in separate cells' is not to fit in with the hard truth that, for the 'media', 'whatever market they are aiming for their commercial viability is decided by their effectiveness as a platform for selling'. To have any doubts about 'realism' and the need to subordinate everything in mass culture to it, is a 'suicidal' 'last ditch' stand: what matters alone is survival in a 'swiftly-changing environment'. That the environment is changing swiftly is itself nowadays accepted widely as a hallowed goal to which many human things must be subordinate. Because everything is changing, this must be for the better.

Here we must follow America in 'flexibility': 'By using "spot" editions . . . an American advertiser can buy space . . . in mass circulation magazines . . . in just one city . . . this . . . provides an excellent platform for test-marketing schemes. . . . In Britain, where commercial television offers many permutations of time and area, the printed media have lost a lot of potential advertising because of mechanical flexibility.'

The writer discusses other matters, of making the 'product' more attractive. This will involve the subjection of 'editorial instincts' to 'refined and accurate monitoring of reader behaviour'. Here the use of the word 'creative' means the use of imaginative and inventive capacities in the service of selling. It is significant that no concept is invoked of editorial independence nor any sense of cultural responsibility to public needs apart from the assumed public need to be exploited for *the drive to sell*. To this writer there are no human considerations in the needs of symbolism, meaning or 'being': there is only 'economic survival' at stake:

> All this brings great dangers of a split between the commercial and creative side in publishing;

between managers eager to introduce modern marketing techniques and editors who regard such devices as mumbo-jumbo . . . you cannot programme inspirational editorial talent into a computer. Nevertheless, an alliance between editorial instincts and really refined and accurate monitoring of reader behaviour could be opposed only by Luddites.

As Henry shows, 'refined' techniques here imply the use of psychoanalytical insights and those of other 'depth' psychology, to coerce individuals, exerting on them forms of coercion which express the contempt and fear of the ad. man and his willingness to exploit human needs, whatever the effect. To this, editorial 'inspiration' and 'creativity' must be subdued. There is no conception here that publishing has any service to perform or any cultural role except that of surviving in a situation dominated by economic demands and the need to keep the system going. There is no awareness of a human individuality in the realm of 'being' which might benefit by being defended at times against exploitation.

To resist the subjection of the editorial role to the dominance of the commercial 'market' is to be a machine-smasher – an opponent of the excellence of technological development. It no longer matters if that 'excellence' demands the falsification of the relationship between man and his creative symbolism and between man and himself.

There is a new Machiavellian tone of realism in this writer's advocacy: 'Those newspaper managements which have been caught napping . . . tended to complain that the advertising industry had been too harsh with them. . . . This is nonsense. No advertiser owes any publisher a living, and advertising will only go into those papers whose efficacy as a selling platform is proven. . . .'

The answer is 'increased efficiency all round': but efficiently measured solely in *selling power*. No standards of newspaper editorship or questions of freedom of democratic expression are invoked. Yet the advertisers who call this tune are to have no responsibility to any individual medium or newspaper. These, too, will be treated with contempt: a situation which perhaps suggests that even in order to survive at all newspapers had better begin to accept the need to begin to consider other forms of organisation than the present system of dependence on advertisers who 'owe no-one a living'. This is what the writer called the 'chain-reaction quality of the communications business': 'a crisis or an initiative in one sector very quickly leads to problems or opportunities in another'.

This is the ultimate philistine, pragmatic utilitarian, attitude to 'communications': yet it is no longer even a principle, but merely the ruthless opportunism and *laissez-faire* of a commercialism indifferent to human need. Even in some areas of education and in government there is no longer any sense that we are faced with an ever increasing cultural crisis as we continue to lose even those influential organs of opinion which may still be independent of the need to subject policy and 'creative' content to commercial needs to exploit the consumer. As Williams says:

> The pressure here is actually increasing. The old kind of newspaper proprietor, who wanted control so that he could propagate his opinions, is being replaced by a kind of proprietor who says he is not interested in opinions but simply in selling as many papers as he can. What was once a means to some larger policy has become in many cases the policy itself. The organisation of communications is not for use, but for profit, and *we seem to have passed the stage in which there has to be any pretence that things are otherwise*. (William [52], p. 33.)

Vindicated by this new Machiavellianism, 'This emphasis inevitably extends into the substance of communication . . . manufacturing and marketing of personalities . . . packaging of experience . . . making the gloss, the substitute for the experience.' And, as

I have tried to suggest, exploiting anxiety and hate, by contempt and fear: 'The human effects of such tendencies are bound to be serious, but attention to them can be discussed as "idealism" while the emphasis on selling is seen as normal and practical' (Williams [52], p. 33).

Concern with the quality and meaning of human life, in so far as it generates doubts about exploitation, is already regarded as 'Luddite' opposition to swift change to an efficient society. This change comes from those who lead assent to the trends of commercial culture, often because their livelihood is bound up with these. But this problem can be looked at in another way. The exponent of the needs of economic necessity often supposes he is concerned with 'efficiency'. But the 'Luddite' in this realm is concerned with a larger problem of efficiency – that is, the effectiveness of individuals in solving their whole problem of life, in the realm of being. He knows, for instance, that activity, expansion, and growth, which are believed to be necessary for economic viability, cannot be translated by analogy into the sphere of personal life and development: nor into symbolism and culture, which are concerned with the eternal and universal problems of love, hate and continuity of identity. Indeed, essentially what the 'Luddite' objects to is the *inefficiency* of a community which is increasingly depriving its individuals of a rich and genuine range of opportunities for symbolism, and of free communication, as means to share experiences, and to discover a sense of meaning in life. He knows that such inefficiency is likely to sap the community by deepening that existential frustration which lies at the root of so many ills. As Williams says: 'The irony is that the only *practical* use of communications is the sharing of real experience. To set anything above this is in fact quite unpractical. To set selling above it may seem normal, but it is really only a *perversion* to which some people have got used.' (Williams [52], p. 33).

As the new Machiavellian trend continues we lose our human cultural freedom. While editorial content becomes subordinate to the ruthless demands of advertising, ownership of the media becomes increasingly limited to a few monopolies. So, even though the extension of communications has been an extension of democracy, 'In the modern trend towards limited ownership, the cultural conditions of democracy are in fact being denied: sometimes, ironically, in the name of freedom' (Williams [52], p. 54).

Also, while the growth of communications has gone with a real process of human growth, 'the control of the new forms' may pass 'to men who are not interested in the growth of society, or in the human purposes the expansion is serving'. They are certainly not interested in being and meaning. It is this which lies behind the anti-human tendency in our culture and its increasing reliance on hate and fanatical moral inversion.

The essential falsity in the way a merely manic sense of identity is fostered by commercial–industrial society is surely what lies behind the criticisms made implicitly by such a writer as Williams when he uses such terms as 'synthetic culture' and 'bastard art'. Williams speaks of the 'vacancy' of commercial culture:

> . . . isn't the real threat of 'mass culture – of things like television rather than things like football or the circus – that it reduces us to an endlessly mixed, indiscriminating, fundamentally bored reaction? The spirit of everything, art and entertainment, can become so standardized that we have no absorbed interest in anything, but simply an indulged acceptance, bringing together what Coleridge called 'indulgence of Sloth and hatred of vacancy'. (Williams [52], p. 106.)

Williams properly sees this manic element of 'distraction from distraction by distraction' as inimical to true creativity. Every individual needs creative opportunities in his way, but all he gets is a minimal reassurance that he is still alive:

You're not exactly enjoying it, or paying any particular attention, but it's passing the time. And in so deadly an atmosphere the great tradition simply cannot live.

Most of us, I think, have experienced this atmosphere. At times, even, we take it as a kind of drug: in periods of tiredness or convalescence, or during tension or anxiety when we have to wait and when almost anything can help us to wait. Certainly as a normal habit of mind this would be ennervating and dangerous; there is a lot of reality that we cannot afford to be cut off from, however much we may want some temporary relief. (Williams [52], p. 106.)

Williams indicates that our commercial culture offers little more than a minimum of manic assurance in the realm of that symbolism which contributes to ego-maintenance. It conveys to us just that we are alive: just – but no more. ('You are never alone with a transistor.') The way I have put this is, however, obviously different from Williams's approach, for I do not believe the problem is being 'cut off from reality' but cut off from oneself (and so, too, from reality).

As soon as any manic phenomenon of commercial entertainment has been exhausted, little is left in terms of creative gains or enrichment of inner resources. Once the set is switched off, or the periodical put down, little or nothing has been essentially communicated to the dynamics of internal communication with oneself upon which the perception of the external world depends. There has been nothing taken into the personality in terms of content and structure, so that we can invest our world with meaning. The success of commercial media, as we have seen, indeed, depends upon there *not* being content and structure. They rather depend upon a residue of envy or anxiety left over until the next time, with the concomitant hunger. This hunger emerges from the exploitation of hate. After the sadistic episode in all-in wrestling matches comes the commercial in which mouths are being fed by sweets to soothing music: a manic image of the frustrating object being coerced by magic into the satisfying object.

Commercial culture is not interested in arousing true creativity. For, inevitably, since this involves engagement with the reality of ourselves and others, as we have seen, it is likely to provoke pain, meet resistance, and even encourage a thirst for genuine satisfactions. The satisfaction and strength we need through creativity are gained only at a cost – often the cost of depression, guilt and fear – because what is involved is awareness of the most disturbing realities of our inward life, ultimate problems of existence, even despair. Sometimes the artist, like the scientist, has to wait many years to be heard because he is concerned with truth. Commercial culture, because it depends on mass audiences and is subject to the sales drive, cannot be creative because it dare not arouse the reactions and resistances creativity inevitably evokes nor can it permit anything like the recognition of human ego-weakness to explode its manic façade. So it must continually reduce the value of humanness and trivialise experience.

Williams is referring to this tendency when he speaks of communication that 'moves us to respond'.

It can be the reporter breaking through our prejudice to the facts; the dramatist reaching so deeply into our experience that we find it difficult in the first shock . . . it is sometimes a disturbing challenge to what we have always believed and done, and sometimes a way to new experience, new ways of seeing and feeling. Or again, in unexpected ways, it can confirm and strengthen us, giving new energy to what we already know is important, or what we knew but couldn't express. (Williams [52], p. 106.)

Here Williams points to the effect of creative symbolism in strengthening the identity; and thus the reality sense. But from my point of view this critic still sees the problem too much in terms of whether or not culture *reflects* a reality that is 'there'. Is it true that he speaks of new ways of seeing, and reminds us of how the painter suddenly shows us 'the shape of a street so clearly that we ask how we could ever have walked down it differently'.

But object-relations psychology suggests an even deeper problem, which is that what we 'see' is in fact an imaginative interpretation of sense data which we project back over the world. Whatever affects our imaginative life affects our capacity to give our world meaning in this way.

Unless we explore this basis of perception by subjective disciplines we cannot find grounds to object to the exploration of hate in entertainment. Obviously the paranoid-schizoid elements in commercial culture affect our relationship with reality in a very deep way. Perhaps Williams does not penetrate into this problem sufficiently: he sticks at pondering whether such manifestations as violence on television prompt imitative acts. His most telling quotation here is from Dr. Hilde Himmelweit, who suggests that violence on television may suggest that 'violence is a rather ordinary thing', and that 'conflicts can be solved by physical violence'.

Williams indicates what a great deal of violence there is on television (7,065 acts of violence in one week's viewing in New York) but fails to decide whether or not this is disproportionate. It is, of course, true that violence is 'normal', since we have all experienced ruthlessness, cannibalism, and primitive savagery in infantile phantasy. But Williams does imply in a way which endorses my approach that violence as unmodified symbolism thrusts us back to primitive states (as he does by invoking Mark Abram's word 'noxious'). And he emphasises (properly) the fact of individual resistance: 'there will be wide difference of character and stability. . . . A psychopathic adult may be more easily affected, and may as a result do more damage, than a very young but secure child.' (Williams [52], p. 116).

But the concept here of medium and effect is too direct as the concept of 'reality' is too simple. The fact is, as I hope I have shown, that the symbolism and processes of hate, because they seek to involve us in false solutions at the deepest level of phantasy, tend to lessen the capacities' of *all of us* to make effective interpretations of reality, *especially human reality*. They dehumanise us and thrust us *all* back to savagery, whoever we are. The paranoid-schizoid and manic symbolism of commercial culture tends to divert our living energy and deplete our resources. Here it is true in a larger way that they restrict our resources and freedom: and, as Williams says 'Any restriction of the freedom of individual contribution is actually a restriction of the resources of the society' (Williams [52], p. 118).

What I hope I have shown above is how the effect of the symbolism of hate in our culture must undermine everyone's identity and potentialities by arousing unconscious anxiety to which energy has to be diverted. By stimulating envy and paranoia it prompts us towards false solutions whose essence is that they should tend to deny human qualities and avoid confrontation with the problem of existence. Of course, there can be no external evidence of this: but if we accept the validity of subjective disciplines, in exploring such problems, there seems plenty of evidence that false solutions can be encouraged and fostered (as they were so terrifyingly by the Nazis and are today by schizoid philosophies of violence). The exploitation of false solutions in our culture could be a deep threat to our human civilisation. At best, it diverts us from the quest for meaning in life, into pseudo-meanings.

But how are we to resist the schizoid trends in our culture while yet avoiding censorship and all its evils? Williams places an important emphasis on the artist's need to be allowed to develop his own voice (because he must develop his own way, in the first place, of communicating with himself). A problem arises, however, with which Williams does not satisfactorily engage, though he refers to it when he speaks of 'how in certain cases if can be deeply held that there are certain things which ought not to be offered, because they are likely, on the evidence available, to harm people' (Williams [52], p. 131).

Williams does say that he believes that 'with the pressure of profit lifted there would be less work of this difficult kind'. I share this belief, and also believe that the 'most open discussion', including the contributor's reasoning, is the way to deal with the problem. But it remains true that there will always be a schizoid minority who seek, through utterance, to thrust harm and hate into others. It is the existence of this anti-social and anti-human minority which presents the greatest problem. As we have seen, this schizoid minority has much to offer because of its need to ask the existential questions. To accept its gifts, while resisting its anti-human distortions, requires some deeper insight and deeper assurance on our part – a new kind of realistic humanist conscience, both in those individuals directly concerned and as the expression of the collective standards of a society.

When we find (for instance) groups of derelict old people left to rot or to become vegetable and non-human, we are horrified. But when this happens to a whole culture our conscience seems suspended. In modern communications and in our culture at popular and modish levels we have a parallel situation to that in the 'obsolescence' hospital of which Henry writes so horrifyingly. Here, too, 'nothing real is communicated, learned or felt' – and so 'there is nothing human either'. Communication with human inwardness has broken down in our society, and we cannot find the True Self. Because our inner needs are not satisfied and our inner life is not enriched by our culture, our capacities to deal effectively with the real world suffer.

Despite the huge expenditure of the advertising world and the clamour of the periodical press, despite the occasional good things and the 'extension of democracy' that the scale of the whole industry represents – because so little is actually communicated that is really human, that contributes by its symbolism, to the dynamics of identity, *'humanness is ebbing'* in the cultural area at large too. Meanwhile the 'insurrectionary' art of the schizoid *avant-garde* merely pursues the false solutions of hate and the anti-human, for the most part, into nihilism and irresponsibility to our gift of uniqueness of being.

The exponent of 'technological excellence' in the 'media' may seem a 'realist', but only in a limited and narrow, sectional sense. He does not see that it is utterly unrealistic to let a culture become inhuman. Because of its very nature the quality of human content in industrial–commercial entertainment and communication is bound to decline in value and quality for reasons which are often made evident by the most hard-headed realists in the business itself. As an American commentator said, while the problem is not yet solved in America of how 'commerce and culture can co-exist on an equal footing', television TAM ratings have 'become a tool in the finance market'. In consequence the viewer has no real choice: 'The choice for the viewer is illusory, being a choice between likes in programming not dislikes . . .' – while, in fact, the programmes are 'glutted with sameness'.

In fact the public has no choice as to whether to accept *Batman* or not. It can only decide whether or not to watch and, of course, *Batman* can be used to engage the attention of human beings – because it is a contrivance which exploits a form of primitive universal phantasy. It has been found by financiers that people's infantile phantasies of omnipotence can be exploited by such a phantasy, and by this ploy they can rivet the attention of millions so that TAM ratings can be high and Stock Exchange business good. All the public can do is to decide whether it will be exploited and hypnotised by one psychological trick or another, while the question of the influence of the phantasies on them is never seriously examined by any authority with power. Nor can the commercial mind ever recognise essential creativity, for creativity such as we find in the genuine artist inevitably provokes resistance, and also envy of creativity, which can be very disturbing. True creativity means pain as well as satisfaction, and so is of no value to commerce. How, then, can symbolism ever be controlled by public bodies? Williams suggests four systems of controlling communications. (Authoritarian, Paternal, Commercial, and Democratic). We may agree that the only possible solution is the latter, but there remain many problems merely skimmed over by Williams's remark: 'I do not believe that, when this is done (i.e. open discussion of work) people usually choose wrongly . . . (Williams [52], p. 131).

This leaves out of account the need for individuals to be *trained* to accept creativity. There is also the problem that any kind of control would require executives trained to hold the ring for creative expression which may be disturbing and revolutionary. There will inevitably have to be, in any democratic control, a body of individuals who take important decisions. Inevitably, control would require some form of organisation which was fraternal, if not paternal, and which would have problems which required considerable delicacy in handling – and sufficient public backing to give confidence to such control. But such control would be better than abandoning symbolism, as we have done, to those who exploit it.

In the development of the possibilities of such control, outside the commercial sphere, of communication and the arts, creativity in education is crucial. Here I find Williams's attitude disappointing because of his concepts of creativity as 'play' and 'therapy'. It is important to stress, as he does, that education should not set 'practical' work about imaginative work, and that it is important in school to 'show how important and satisfying the arts can be to almost everyone'. I might delete that 'almost'; but I would also wish to change the emphasis. I cannot see the problem being solved at all until we accept creativity in all its ranges not only as important and a source of satisfaction, but the very basis of human identity. If it is so, then creativity must be the central discipline in education – the positive effects of which would eventually be felt in our society at large.

This in itself would represent a greater recognition of the needs of 'being', and with it would come a recognition of the need to protect these. But hopes of such a change seem slight in the face of the prevalent onslaught of hate, impelling us to base identity on false solutions, in so many directions.

Here I can only gesture towards possibilities of overcoming the problem of the predominance in our culture of hate and its mechanisms. Eventually, surely, we shall be forced to become so convinced of the importance of culture that we are prepared to defend it against exploitation in any form at all levels. There seems to the present writer no doubt, for instance, that we must somehow remove symbolism from the hands of commerce altogether.

But any such change could only be justified and made effective by a body of authentic criticism based on subjective disciplines which established a significant relationship between culture and human make-up. For this, we certainly need a more relevant cultural criticism – certainly more substantial than the predominantly modish approaches to art which dominate comment in the commercial press of our society. This in its turn requires us to re-examine the nature of conscience and the way in which conscience can enable us to establish effective human values, and employ these to expose and resist any tendencies which seem likely to damage or inhibit our quest for existential meaning.

But how do we judge this?

CHAPTER 27

The Need for a Revival of Conscience

THE problem of hate in culture, in its relation to our inner dynamics and behaviour, is no simple one, even once we have diagnosed it. As Dr. Gregory Zilboorg says in his study of crime and punishment from a psychoanalytical point of view:

> Would it were . . . simple. What happens psychologically is this: before they are ready to come out in the form of real action – suicidal, or homicidal, or some equivalent of both or either – the aggressive drives within us live their own life as it were, a life of most elaborate unconscious presentations and imagery. There are fantasies of biting and tearing and cutting and tormenting, and fantasies of being bitten and torn and cut and tormented. These fantasies are not limited to neurotic and psychotic individuals: they become more manifest in neuroses and psychoses, but they are present in us all. They may reach a considerable richness of elaboration and emotional intensity. (Zilboorg [62], p. 54.)

What turns these phantasies in some into 'real action' we do not know:

> They may even enter consciousness and yet not lead to any action, nor even anxiety. They may go on for years and occupy a considerable part of a man's day-dreaming life, or fill his nightmares, and yet not make him break out into action – the technical term is 'acting out' one's forbidden fantasies.
>
> The mysterious thing about the whole matter is that there seems to be as yet no satisfactory explanation of why certain individuals start *acting out* their fantasy life either in the form of annoying neurotic social behaviour, or in the form of criminal acts. Psychoanalysis has discovered a wealth of clinical data enriching our understanding of the deeper psychology of the normal, the neurotic, and the psychotic, whether he be criminal or not. But it has no answer as to what it is that makes man succumb or give in to his fantasies so that they become criminal acts. (Zilboorg [62], p. 55.)

Obviously a great deal of research is needed here – of the kind which investigates 'from the inside' what happens when symbolism breaks down, and there is a reversion to 'acting out' by 'equation'.

From such research, implications for culture might follow so that cultural acts could be seen and judged as between true and false ways of feeling real, and as between human and anti-human. The crux of the cultural problem then becomes the ethical question, of how, and at what stage, does a 'false solution' pattern begin to bring about the reduction of the living capacity of another human being? It seems from psychoanalytical theory that this does actually happen. Where one person disturbs another by their hate it may be necessary for so much energy to be diverted to ego-maintenance in consequence that there is a 'disturbance of adaptation to reality and of . . . object-relationships'.

As we know, this does happen with children when actual circumstances are distressing.

> In those cases in which the significance of reality and real objects as reflections of the dreaded internal world and images has retained its preponderance, the stimuli from the external world may be felt to be nearly as alarming as the phantasied domination of the internalized objects, which have taken possession of all initiative and to whom the ego feels compulsively bound to surrender the execution of all activities and intellectual operations. (Klein [34], p. 263.)

254

Cannot something of the same happen to those who are exposed to *symbolic* phantasies which are calculated to *seem* real or emerge from a schizoid need to substitute hate for love, or to make 'equation attacks' upon the audience? Cannot such experiences be 'stimuli from the external world' which are felt to be 'nearly as alarming as the phantasied domination of the internalised objects'? And could they not contribute to a 'surrender of initiative and the execution of all activities and intellectual operations'? And cause actual feelings of disturbance of bodily viability? What is our reaction to a Pinter play, a Fleming novel, or a Buñuel film? Is it not one of being raped in the very core of the personality, arousing pain and shock, against which we now have to exert a remedial energy – to get back to the state of equilibrium of ego-maintenance from which we have been disturbed – at the expense of our living power?

While commercial culture needs to rape us more and more for its money, false philosophical vindications of this tendency, as we have seen are pre-eminent. The exploitation of hate, it is hoped, can now be indulged without a twinge of conscience alongside the manic hedonism and all the false solutions that an economy based on bustle and ingestion offers. They may be underlying reasons for the promotion of the ethos of demoralisation, but philosophical anthropology gives the ethos of 'amorality' no support.

The belief in 'demoralisation' as a solution to our problems was long ago exposed by Ian D. Suttie, from a point of view which object-relations psychology further endorses, as I indicate in *Human Hope and the Death Instinct*. The theory that 'contact with the broad-minded analyst' 'demoralised' the patient so that he could now feel, as about sex, that 'Now you are grown up you are permitted to wish these things', was discredited in 1935 – indeed, was never valid, 'though it was popular with rebel temperaments . . . who embraced analysis for anti-social reasons . . .'. Object-relations psychology confirms Suttie's view that 'demoralisation' merely leaves an individual more isolated than before. What we need is a more dynamic ethic, not 'amorality'.

From such a point of view as that of Winnicott it seems realistic to insist that the recognition of the existence of positive values is essential, for each individual to develop his 'healthy moral sense', so that 'civilisation can be created anew' in each. Whether or not we have religious faith, these values can be perfectly adequately established, as Professor Wisdom indicates, by naturalistic description. It is not true that 'if there is no God, then everything is possible'. Values are continually created and re-created: 'rightness is constructed from what really seems right to A., to B. etc. and really seems right to A. is constructed from seem right to A. at first blush, seems right to A. after review, compassion, etc. It is with the business of the transition from 'seems for the moment acceptable and right to A." to "seems really right and acceptable to A." that one is concerned.' (Wisdom [61], p. 106.)

Money-Kyrle implies that our civilised society can continue because most individuals achieve a 'common type of moral character' which he calls humanist. Meanwhile, he believes, psychoanalysis seems to be yielding a real common standard of ethical truth: 'the hunch about a common standard for all wise men, which so many philosophers have tried to prove by non-empirical arguments, seems probable in the light of recent empirical discoveries'. (Money-Kyrle [44], p. 112).

The study of human nature made by object-relations psychology establishes as human facts of the inward life (a) an innate impulse towards integration primary to consciousness, (b) a moral dynamic or healthy moral sense in most human beings, (c) the possibility of non-transcendental non-absolute, but by no means merely relative, humanist values, established by the collocation of concepts of considered 'rightness' between individuals, explored and expressed through culture, and (d) the need in each individual for continual engagement with hate and guilt, in the search to become integrated, and to establish relationships from an integrated self with a world recognised as real, towards living by the cycles of love rather than by those of hate. In every human being there is a True Self which yearns to 'be': and an energy of ego-maintenance, in which symbolism is a primary need. On these human facts a living ethic can certainly be based. I have tried to suggest the implications for culture.

The major implication here may be taken that, if symbolism is primary, and if it is bound up with our need for integration, and our need to overcome hate, as philosophical anthropology seems to tell us, then it is surely too dangerous to leave the use of symbolism in the hands of those who are indifferent to its consequences and who need to exploit it for other purposes.

Here, as yet, aesthetics and ethics seem to be in some confusion. The essay on 'The Relevance of Buber to Aesthetics', for instance, is by far the least satisfactory of the essays in the symposium *The Philosophy of Martin Buber* [8]. Louis Hammer says:

> What this view does attempt to do is to connect art with an account of what man is, an account which is in the nature of a personal testimony or witness. It suggests to me that the main thing in the encounter with works of art is not a judgement of good or bad, but the creation of a dialogical relationship. One who encounters works of art may meet a world in the richness of its presence. The fulfilment of this opportunity rather than the development of 'taste' would seem to be of first importance.
>
> (Buber [8], p. 626.)

This latter point may be agreed: a mere concern with 'taste' could be precious. But Hammer in discussing the 'beat' poets makes it plain that he feels considerations of 'good' and 'bad' are relevant: 'beat' poetry he says:

> ... often resembles a man agitating in public. Its content as well as its form feeds on rebellion, on angry and loud posturing before a society judged guilty and corrupt. The 'beat' poet sees himself as a victim and his poems become weapons of resistance. The poet tries to 'succeed' through the poem because society will allow him no other achievement. Unhappily, however, the 'beat' poet usually mistrusts genuine inwardness as much as he mistrusts 'square' society. His poems are loud but empty.

Here, surely, are invoked value judgements which are necessary in culture? In distrusting inwardness, the 'beat' poet implies an attitude to man which complements the philistinism of his society: in that he is loud and empty, he is a true child of a dehumanised society which neglects 'inner needs'. If the aim of art is to give an account of man, his view is a loud and false assertion of identity based on schizoid solutions in terms of the 'protest' of 'endless violence' – and so further flight from the human. The 'beat' type of cultural manifestation threatens the whole development of a 'dialogical relationship' – and so, inevitably, the critic must seek to defend this form of 'meeting' against those who would undermine it, destroy it, or exploit it. The basis of our criticism can therefore be in distinctions between what it is that makes for a genuine account of man and what is falsified.

Fortunately, it would seem that among those well qualified to judge, an intuitive sense of the reduction of symbolism and a recognition of the elements of hate in our culture are growing. For instance, in an article on *The Third Theatre Revisited*, Robert Brustein, Dean of the Yale School of Drama, said:

> What once seemed daring and original now often seems tiresome and familiar; stereotyped political assertions, encouraged by their easy acceptance, have replaced instinctive, individual dissent; and the complex moral and metaphysical issues of great art are being obliterated by a simple-minded nihilism.
>
> (Brustein [6]).

Brustein relates this development in the *avant-garde* theatre to the schizoid developments (as I would call them) in 'protest' politics:

> . . . the anti-war and black power movements as they have changed from noble acts of non-violent resistance by highly serious individuals to disruptive and histrionic acts by infantile 'revolutionaries'. For just as the frustrations over the endless conflict in Vietnam and the unresolved dilemmas of the black peoples have given a vaguely totalitarian coloration to certain cadres of the Left, so the success of the third theatre, which reflects these frustrations, has tended to sanctify its failings and conventionalised its virtues.

Brustein sees that the 'inversion of values' in art is itself a kind of sentimentality which merely complements the sentimentality and philistinism of conventional 'bourgeois' art:

> Its anti-intellectualism, its sensationalism, its sexual obsessiveness, its massacre of language, its noisy attention-getting mechanisms, its indifference to artistry, craft, or skill, its violence, and, above all, its mindless tributes to Love and Togetherness (now in the form of 'group gropes' and 'love zaps') are not adversary demands upon the American character but rather the very qualities that have continually degraded us, the very qualities that have kept us laggard and philistine in the theatre throughout the past three decades.

Brustein discusses the work of Julian and Judith Beck in the Living Theatre. Like the two sex emancipationists discussed in the Introduction, this pair seem impelled by a 'missionary programme':

> . . . no longer . . . interested in coherent theatrical productions. What obsessed them now was their missionary program; they were more eager to convert their audiences, *through whatever means*, to their special brand of revolutionary politics. In production after production, the company demonstrated its remarkable capacity to manipulate minds. Playing upon a general sense of emptiness in a world where even individual salvation seems far too complicated, the Living Theatre proselytised among the young. . . . (My italics.)

While the apparent campaign was in the name of 'love, freedom and anarchy', we can, I believe, see this manifestation from our point of view as being essentially schizoid. It begins with the 'sense of emptiness', and a world in which there are manifestations which seem to make it impossible to find 'salvation' – or a sense of human identity. So far, so good: here is the positive existential preoccupation of the schizoid individual. But, as we have found time and time again, the schizoid 'revolutionary' impulse fails to be informed by a sufficient sense of human ambivalence, complexity, and *value*, while essentially symbolic engagements with inner reality are abandoned, and there is a regression to 'equation' and acting out – 'by whatever means'.

So, the Living Theatre brought about a reduction of the 'artistry, craft and skill' of the theatre itself:

> . . . in the audience-participation epic, *Paradise Now*. . . . it . . . virtually abandoned its interest in creating serious drama. It was now clear the the Becks' previous efforts to examine the boundaries separating art from life . . . had been expanded into a fullscale assault upon any separation whatever between the spectator and the stage. Audiences were invited over the footlights to join some performers while other performers wandered through the house; actors whined plaintively about their inability to travel without a passport, live without money, smoke marijuana, or take their clothes off, after which they stripped down to loin cloths and bikinis; students peeled down, upon this encouragement, to jockey shorts; mass love-zaps and petting parties were organised on the stage among couples of various sexes and sexual dispositions; and after the endless, loveless, sexual groping was finally over, everyone was exhorted to leave the theatre and convert the police to anarchism, to storm the jails and free the prisoners, to stop the war and ban the bomb, to take over the streets in the name of the people – and, then, to disperse quietly lest any of this end (as it did one night in New Haven) with somebody in jail for disturbing the peace.

Inevitably, such a schizoid 'mission' ends in depersonalised sex, its vindication based on Freudian 'release' theory, and so in a 'reduction of the quality of the relationship desired' – with an implicit lowering of human value, conveying an attitude to human meeting and sharing which is by no means reconcilable with that freedom which is based on mutual respect. To 'grope' at a stranger sexually is to treat that person as a 'part-object' for one's own 'automatic satisfaction', and thus a stage 'petting session' of this kind merely complements the essential contempt for human beings of the world of advertising, commerce, and war. It is incompatible with true equality. Moreover, from such a fundamentally pessimistic view of man, how can attempts to 'convert the police' end in anything but a confrontation between 'beasts' and those who are necessary to coerce them?

As Brustein says, the position of the Living Theatre was essentially 'meretricious':

> The Living Theatre inevitably took refuge in its theatrical function whenever things threatened to get out of hand. For all its emphasis on reality, the company never quite managed to escape from its performance; for all its emphasis on spontaneity and accident, it still followed an almost fixed pattern which ended in the same way every evening. To extend a theatrical action into the audience is not to annihilate the performance, it is to annihilate the audience – everyone becomes a performer, the seats become part of the stage.

'Spontaneity', without genuine creativity, becomes an act of will: because of this the Living Theatre is 'still in the brothel' in more senses than one. The sexual activity on stage is itself a kind of masturbatory brothel sex. As Leslie H. Farber says: 'Before the age of sexology, objectifications of the sexual act were to be found in pornography and the brothel ... both suggesting the relatively limited manner in which will ... could be joined to sexual pleasure' (Farber [19], p. 68).

The sex of the *avant garde* is even more limited because it is so mental. The Becks also find themselves 'still in the brothel' in Genet's sense, for 'when the Becks appeared recently on the Merv Griffin show, outlining their political theories between a series of night club acts, they only dramatised further their imprisonment to show biz' (Brustein [6]).

Yet from this imprisonment, they obviously managed to do a great deal to influence those Brustein calls 'impressionable ... young audiences' – in the direction of schizoid hate, and towards the anti-human, in the name of 'freedom'.

Under this mask, hate pursues its own purity, and Brustein reveals the ruthless aggressiveness and inhumanity lurking beneath the surface. The schizoid individual fundamentally cannot allow human beings to be, outside his 'contempt' and the control it makes necessary.

> What was finally most disturbing about the Living Theatre was the content of the ideology it was marketing under the name of anarchism. In spite of all the invitations to participate in free theatre, it was constraint and control that remained most conspicuous. No spectator was ever allowed to violate the pattern of manipulated consent. At Yale, we saw a female student launch into a passionate denunciation of the Living Theatre, only to be hustled offstage by a group of performers who embraced her into silence – unbuttoning her blouse, feeling her legs, and shutting her mouth with kisses. ...

This stage rape could be taken to symbolise the underlying contempt for human individuality and for the realm of 'being'. In the Living Theatre, so much for 'spontaneity'. It also symbolises the impulse to rape others, inherent in such a schizoid manifestation: to thrust harm into them while they are disarmed. In this there is a highly moral (though inverted) motive. The purity of hate thus goes with a religions and intolerant solemnity:

> The company, particularly vulnerable to ridicule because of its lack of humour, allowed no alien laughter ever to penetrate its relentless solemnity, self-righteousness, and self-importance.

Love and brotherhood were continually on the lips of the actors, but no actors in my experience have bristled with so much aggression or more successfully galvanised the aggression of the spectator. As for love and brotherhood, all one saw or heard was herd love and brotherhood among the anonymous.

It is the schizoid dictator who cannot allow humour – for humour is deflating. Wit recognises that we can be no more than human, and it implicitly admits the infantile, the regressed libidinal ego, the ambivalent within us, as does the comedy of a Charles Chaplin, with his endlessly exploited 'little man'. Humourlessness belongs to the split-off idealism of the worship of an intellectual system endowed with all the mystical attractions of the Iron Virgin. The sex of the Living Theatre, like that of sexology, pursues this mythical goal: looked at in our way, it is the willed sex of aggressive schizoid hunger. The *avant-garde* theatre thus comes, in the end, to look like Nazism: 'It was, finally, not a vision of human freedom that one took away from *Paradise Now* but vague, disturbing memories of the youth rallies in Hitler's Nuremburg.'

Brustein himself seeks a theatre which will contain, in Synge's words 'reality and joy': 'which is to say it synthesises the principle of work and of pleasure, discipline and imagination, form and process, reflection and improvisation, age and youth.'

But this is, as he says, a theatre which is not found in the American 'way-out'. Moreover, involvement in the anti-human retreat from creative symbolism in this area has influenced many impressionable young people, so that they turn on civilisation itself:

> We honour the young because without them there is no future. But there will surely be no future either unless the more extreme of our young can cease from trying to annihilate the past. . . . The most radical inventions of the new generation are nothing if they proceed from the same violent and mindless sources that originally brought our civilisation to this terrifying juncture. . . . We fail the future when we surrender what we know and value for the sake of fashion and influence, and we fail the theatre when we countenance the rejection of language, form, and accomplishment in favour of an easy culture . . .

and, I would add, in favour of a schizoid retreat from creativity itself, towards ways of feeling real based on equation activity. It is merely to complement the philistinism of our world to believe, as the *avant-garde* seems to do, that 'outer' activities are 'more real' than our engagement with 'inner reality'. Yet that is surely implicit in what one of his students said to Brustein: 'I don't give a shit for art. I want to create events.'

By contrast, perhaps we can quote from Synge himself – a reference to the disciplines of imagination proper:

> The morning had been beautifully fine, but as they lowered the coffin into the grave, thunder rumbled overhead and hailstones hissed among the bracken.
> In Inishmaan one is forced to believe in a sympathy between man and nature, and at this moment when the thunder sounded a death-peal of extraordinary grandeur above the voices of the women, I could see the faces near me stiff and drawn with emotion.
> When the coffin was in the grave, and the thunder had rolled away across the hills of Clare, the keen broke out again more passionately than before.
> This grief of the keen is no personal complaint for the death of one woman over eighty years, but seems to contain the whole passionate rage that lurks somewhere in every nature of the island. In this cry of pain the inner consciousness of the people seems to lay itself bare for an instant, and to reveal the mood of beings who feel their isolation in the face of a universe that wars on them with winds and seas. They are usually silent, but in the presence of death all outward show of indifference or patience is forgotten, and they shriek with pitiable despair before the horror of the fate to which all are doomed.
> Before they covered the coffin an old man kneeled down by the grave and repeated a simple prayer for the dead. . . .
> A little beyond the grave I saw a line of old women who had recited in the keen sitting in the shadow of a wall beside the roofless shell of the church. They were still sobbing and shaken with grief, yet they

were beginning to talk again of the daily trifles that veil from them the terror of the world.
(Synge [50]).

'Human kind cannot bear very much reality': we need 'the daily trifles' that veil us from terrors. Yet, obviously, where there is such a real confrontation of the problem of existence as Synge found in Aran, there is a tremendous satisfaction rooted in true strength of identity. This strength is developed by the emotional wrestle with mortal actuality and by the exercise of the capacity to be ('usefully') depressed, in the discovery of humanness. There is also true communication at the level of 'being' by symbolism. The peasants were willing to suffer the utterance of their own keening protest, and so the manic 'trifles' at the end represent a genuine return to a sense of being alive. Real mourning has been achieved, by accepting and working through depression, and the result is a deeper sense of 'the point of life'. This is realism indeed.

Our hope must be in the natural urge, especially of young people, to pursue the question 'What is it to be human?' – a pursuit which leads them to seek the genuinely creative in art, despite the Kaprows and the Becks. In a letter to *The Times* Dr. Roger Polle made these comments on his experience of the Promenade Concerts in 1968:

> The players play, and the listeners listen, with what amounts to passion, to commitment. Even the applause, the cheers, the cries, are committed – the commitment of the young to the best there is, mediated to them by music and appreciated as a kind of final end, rather like the Church must have been in the brutality of the Middle Ages.
> . . . Here is the commitment that so many people accuse the young of lacking. . . . If the music at the Proms is the expression of the suffering and joy of all humanity, then the young participate in this with all the humanity and goodwill of which they are capable – and they are capable of vast amounts of it. In the face of a world which seems to be becoming more and more inhuman, the reaction of the young is to become more and more passionately human. (*The Times*, 17 September, 1968.)

As the world grows more inhuman, alas, education which could help restore the balance often remains too uncreative and too little preoccupied with the essentially human. But there is also hope in the truth that a foundation of 'ontological security' is established in most people through the contribution of family life and personal relationship, while many do break through to find a culture that satisfies their deeper longings for existential satisfaction.

It is worth pondering the possible causes of ontological insecurity in our society in the light of psychoanalytical theories. Can it be that where there is a lack of such security that good mothering and infant management are to some extent undermined as natural processes by the conditions of modern life themselves? Perhaps the very pattern we have created – of Megalopolis, commuting, cars, and machine-living itself inhibits intuition in the spheres of primary relationship, and reinforces inhibitions on the 'female elements' in human make-up? Perhaps our manic bustle is itself a manifestation of a flight from life, and a way of escaping 'the human problematic' and the needs of 'being'? Certainly adult life in our society grows increasingly deficient in provision for creative activities by which the identity is sustained and inner dynamics nourished. We can see this if we compare 'organic' communities and our own. Despite great material advances, there has been a loss of symbolic richness, and it is this difference which divides our modern world from many communities of the past despite our many gains over the material world.

A culture based on schizoid hate can do nothing to remedy this predicament. While art remains in a state of regression, to 'symbolic equation' activity, as in the work of the *avant-garde* theatre, for example, it may provide satisfactions to the artist and performer, but nothing but a reduction of the sense of being human for the audience at large.* Here, obviously, we are on the brink of a huge subject, where serious art is concerned, which can only be tackled once the problem is seen to exist.

Yet, despite the essential vacuity and dehumanising influence of solutions based on hate, it is these that seem predominant in the cultural ethos of today, while the ways of love and creativity tend to be devalued and made to seem weak and ineffectual. Perhaps the more human cultural modes have been rejected because they are painful and too real. Perhaps true creativity reminds us too much of our vulnerable 'female element', our weakness at the core of being, and our ambivalence and essential dependence. Yet it is only in these regions that we can find true satisfaction and really find a sense of the meaning of life.

Art is surely of value because it is a disciplined collaboration, in which we can participate, in the natural organising processes of man's symbolic capacities, such as all normal men are capable of. In this sense it is still necessary to insist as D. H. Lawrence did that 'the essential function of art is moral'.

Whenever one examines great art – whether one takes Shakespeare's tragedies or Mahler's symphonies or the painting of Bonnard or the painting and sculpture of Degas – one finds an impulse towards integration by the exertion of symbolism as a force of love and sympathy towards strength of identity. Such art is never 'amoral' but full of that creative moral energy which asks, What is it to be human? and What is the point of life? There is a concern in such creativity to celebrate human potentialities, and the capacity of man for goodness and beauty, despite his destructiveness, his mortality, and the treachery in his make-up. Even where the outcome is not explicit in moral terms one may have, as in Dostoevsky, the experience of having explored the worst that human destructiveness might do. Having survived such an imaginative exploration of the utmost potential meaninglessness of life, we feel we can overcome our worst fears of loss of identity. It is possible, through imagination, to triumph over our deepest existential despair – even without God, as Mahler did. It is dreadful to think that we have allowed such human powers to be trivialised, exploited, and abused.

We need to restore the critical concern with art as having to do with 'living ethics', perhaps in some such terms as those Gorki used in *My Childhood*:

> As I remember these oppressive horrors of our wild Russian life, I ask myself often whether it is worth while to speak of them. And then, with restored confidence, I answer myself – 'It is worth while because it is actual, vile fact, which has not died out, even in these days – a fact which must be traced to its origin, and pulled up by the root from memories, the souls of the people, and from our narrow, sordid lives.'
> And there is another and more important reason impelling me to describe these horrors. Although they are so disgusting, although they oppress us and crush many beautiful souls to death, yet the Russian is still so healthy and young in heart that he can and does rise above them. For in this amazing life of ours not only does the animal side of our nature flourish and grow fat, but with this animalism there has grown up, triumphant in spite of it, bright, healthful and creative – a type of humanity which inspires us to look forward to our regeneration, to the time when we shall live peacefully and humanely, to our regeneration, to the time when we shall all live peacefully and humanely.

---

* In a useful article 'Beyond the Plot Barrier' in *The Times Saturday Review*, 7 September 1968, John Russell Taylor suggests that the effect of television which has to compete with the distractions of life at home is to devise a kind of drama 'which will keep bringing back the wandering attention with a new tit-bit at regular intervals. How the transition from one tit-bit to another is achieved remains fairly immaterial.' He associates this with Artaud's desire for an audience 'ready conditioned', perfectly prepared to abandon ratiocination, and take drama straight on the solar plexus – i.e. as victims of equation attack. Both seem complementary – but neither offers enough creative sustenance.

Gorki conveys a great sense of what it is to be human, despite recognition of the sufferings and the savageries of which man is capable. Yet how distant now his view seems from that of the fashionable culture of today! While we need to make careful distinctions between the morality of art and the morality of life, there should surely not be such a dissociation in our culture from everyday morality and from what we know to be our own experience of human truth?

Bibliography

1. BALINT, M., *Primary Love and Psychoanalytical Technique*, Hogarth, 1952.
2. BANTOCK, G. H., *Culture, Education, and Industrialisation*, Routledge and Kegan Paul, 1968.
3. BANTOCK, G. H., *L. H. Myers, a Critical Study*, Cape, 1956.
4. BARRY, SIR JAMES, *Mary Rose*, Hodder & Stoughton, 1931.
5. BOWLBY, J., *Child Care and the Growth of Love*, Penguin, 1953.
6. BRUSTEIN, R., The Third Theatre Revisited, *New York Review of Books*, 13 February 1969.
7. BUBER, M., *I and Thou*, Clark, Edinburgh, 1937.
8. BUBER, M., *The Philosophy of Martin Buber* (ed. Schilpp and Friedman), published in England by Cambridge, 1968.
9. BURNHAM, D. L., Communication with Schizophrenics, *Journal American Psycho-analytical Association*, **3,** 67–68 (1955).
10. CAMUS, A., *The Rebel*,
11. CASSIRER, E., *An Essay on Man*, Yale University Press, 1944.
12. CHALONER, L., *Feeling and Perception in Young Children*, Tavistock, 1954.
13. CONRAN, M., *Schizophrenia and the Problem of Indifference*, unpublished communication, 1968.
14. DUNN, N., *Talking to Women*, Pan Books, 1967.
15. COOKE, D., *The Language of Music*, Oxford, 1959.
16. ERIKSON, E., *Insight and Responsibility*, Faber, 1966.
17. ERIKSON, E., *Childhood and Society*, Penguin, 1965.
18. FAIRBAIRN, W. R. D., *Psychoanalytical Studies of the Personality*, Tavistock, 1952.
19. FARBER, L. H., *The Ways of the Will*, Constable, 1966.
20. FERENCZI, S., *First Contributions to Psychoanalysis*, Hogarth, 1925.
21. FERENCZI, S., *Further Contributions*, Hogarth, 1926.
22. FERENCZI, S., *Final Contributions*, Hogarth, 1955.
23. FERENCZI, S., *Thalassa: Versuch Einer Genitaltheorie*, Psychoanalytical Quarterly Inc., U.S.A., 1938.
24. FLEMING, I., *Goldfinger*, Pan Books,
25. FROMM, E., *The Fear of Freedom*, Kegan Paul, 1942.
26. GUNTRIP, H., *Personality Structure/and Human Interaction*, Hogarth, 1961.
27. GUNTRIP, H., *Schizoid Phenomena, Object-relations and the Self*, Hogarth, 1968.
28. HAYMAN, R., *Harold Pinter*, Heinemann, 1968.
29. HENRY, J., *Culture Against Man*, Tavistock, 1966.
30. KAPROW, A., Interview with Richard Kostelanetz, *Twentieth Century*, vol. CLXXVII, 1968.
31. KAPROW, A., *Assemblage, Environments and Happenings*, Abrams, U.S.A., 1966.
32. KHAN, M. R., The Function of Intimacy and Acting Out in Perversions, in *Sexual Behaviour and the Law* (ed. Ralph Slovenko), Charles C. Thomas, U.S.A., 1968.
33. KLEIN, MELANIE, *The Psychoanalysis of Children*, Hogarth, 1932.
34. KLEIN, MELANIE, *Contributions to Psychoanalysis*, Hogarth, 1948.
35. KLEIN, MELANIE, *Developments in Psychoanalysis*, Hogarth, 1952.
36. KLEIN, MELANIE, *New Directions in Psychoanalysis*, Tavistock, 1955.
37. KLEIN, MELANIE, *Envy and Gratitude*, Tavistock, 1957.
38. KLEIN, MELANIE, *Our Adult Society and its Roots in Infancy*, Tavistock, 1963.
39. KLEIN, MELANIE (with JOAN RIVIÈRE), *Love, Hate, and Reparation*, Hogarth, 1938.
40. LAING, R. D., *The Divided Self*, Tavistock, 1960.
41. LANGER, SUZANNE, *Philosophy in a New Key*, Harvard, 1942.
42. LANGER, SUZANNE, *Feeling and Form*,
43. MENNINGER, K., *Man Against Himself*, Harvest Books, 1938.
44. MONEY-KYRLE, R. E., *Psychoanalysis and Philosophy in Psychoanalysis and Contemporary Thought* (ed. J. D. Sutherland), Hogarth, 1958.
45. MURDOCH, IRIS, *From the Enchanter Fleeing*, Penguin Books,

46. PEARSON, J., *Life of Ian Fleming*,
47. SEGAL, HANNAH, *Introduction to the work of Melanie Klein*, Tavistock, 1964.
48. SEGAL, HANNAH, Notes on Symbol Formation, *International Journal of Psychoanalysis* **38,** 383.
49. SUTHERLAND, J. D., *Psychoanalysis and Contemporary Thought*, Hogarth, 1958.
50. SYNGE, J. M., *The Aran Islands*,
51. TOWERS, B. and LEWIS, J., *Naked Ape—or Homo Sapiens?* Garnstone Press, 1969.
52. WILLIAMS, R., *Communications*, Chatto & Windus, 1950.
53. WINNICOTT, D. W., *Collected Papers, Through Pediatrics to Psychoanalysis*, Tavistock, 1958.
54. WINNICOTT, D. W., *The Child and the Outside World*, Tavistock, 1957.
55. WINNICOTT, D. W., *The Child and the Family*, Tavistock, 1957.
56. WINNICOTT, D. W., *The Family and Individual Developments*, Tavistock, 1965.
57. WINNICOTT, D. W., *The Maturational Processes and the Facilitating Environment*, Hogarth, 1966.
58. WINNICOTT, D. W., *The Child, The Family and the Outside World*, Penguin, 1964.
59. WINNICOTT, D. W., Mirror Role of the Mother in *The Predicament of the Family* (ed. P. Lomas),Hogarth, 1967.
60. WINNICOTT, D. W., The Location of Culture, *International Journal of Psychoanalysis*, **48,** 368 (1966).
61. WISDOM, J., *Philosophy and Psychoanalysis*, Oxford, 1957.
62. ZILBOORG, G., *The Psychology of the Criminal Act and Punishment*, Hogarth, 1957.
63. YEATS, W. B., Introductions to *Gitanjali*, by Rabindranath Tagore.
64. WINNICOTT, D. W., Male and Female Elements in the Personality, *Playing and Reality*, Tavistock, 1971.
65. HOFFMAN, F. J., *Samuel Beckett – The Language of Self*, University of Southern Illinois, 1966.
66. KHAN, M. R., Reparation to the Self as an Idolised Internal object. *Dynamische Psychiätrie*, 2 Nov., 1968. Berlin.
67. FRANKL, V. E., *From Death-camp to Existentialism*, Beacon Press, Boston, 1959.
68. POLANYI, MICHAEL, *Personal Knowledge*, Routledge, 1959.
69. MAY, ROLLO, *Love and Will*, W. W. Norton, 1969.
70. GRENE, MARJORIE, *The Knower and the Known*, Faber, 1961.

Index